The Rochester I Know

Books by Henry W. Clune

Seen and Heard (1933)
Seen and Heard (1935)
The Good Die Poor
Monkey on a Stick
Main Street Beat
By His Own Hand
The Big Fella
Six O'Clock Casual
The Genesee
The Best of Henry Clune (1966)
O'Shaughnessy's Cafe
The Rochester I Know

The Rochester I Know

HENRY W. CLUNE

1972

Doubleday & Company, Inc.

GARDEN CITY, NEW YORK

For Lawrence P. Ashmead

ISBN: 0-385-06950-2
Library of Congress Catalog Card Number 72–76140
Copyright © 1972 by Henry W. Clune
All Rights Reserved
Printed in the United States of America
First Edition

ACKNOWLEDGMENTS

Many kind persons have given assistance with this book. Some who have done so are mentioned in the body of the text and I shall not repeat their names in these paragraphs. My thanks to them is implied. I should like here particularly to express my appreciation for the unstinted efforts made in my interest by Miss Doris M. Savage, head of the Local History Division of the Rochester Public Library; by her assistant, Miss Shirley Iversen, and by Miss Catherine D. Hayes, Assistant Director of Libraries of the University of Rochester.

I am indebted also to Lloyd E. Klos, of the Gannett Newspapers Library, and to the following present and former members of the Gannett organization in Rochester: Miss Jean Walrath, Howard Hosmer, John W. Brown, Vincent S. Jones, William J. Butler, Francis Bonn, Vince Spezzano, Bill Beeney and Alfred Weber. I am beholden to Mrs. Ruth Papegaay, of the Rochester Board of Education; to William H. Morris, of the Nixon, Hargrave, Devans & Doyle law firm; to Edward P. Doyle, former executive editor for the *Chicago American;* to Dr. Thomas A. Bonfiglio, of the University of Rochester Medical Center; to John VanBuren, Health Information Officer for the Monroe County Health Department; to Frank L. Smith, former treasurer of the Eastman Theater; to John Merchant, Mrs. Harper Sibley and James V. Chiavaroli.

This book was written more or less at the suggestion of Mrs. Eleanor Johnson, head of the book department of the Scrantom's store, and the manuscript was prepared for the publishers by Mrs. Frank Kaiser, who has typed all of my books and short stories.

My recollections of Linden Street go back to a time in the 1890s when a stubby little trolley car turned from South Avenue into our street and rocked its way over an abominable roadbed to the Mt. Hope Avenue corner, when it turned south and continued to a terminus at the old, or first, gate of Mt. Hope Cemetery. The tracks were on both sides of a dirt road. My father and several of our neighbors agitated for the removal of the tracks. When they were finally torn up and Linden Street was paved with asphalt, its residents boasted that ours was the most attractive thoroughfare in the southern section of the city, and the boast was not unwarranted.

Henry W. Clune
Scottsville, New York

Introduction

Every noon, when I went out to lunch, it was my habit to stop first at Meyer and Lester Spector's big newsstand on the west side of Clinton Avenue South, and stop again to visit with Izzy Schwartz, a squat, stoop-shouldered little fellow who for thirty-five years hawked newspapers at a stand at the southeast corner of Main Street East and Clinton Avenue South. Both the Spector brothers and Izzy Schwartz were keen observers of the passing show. They gave me the downtown gossip. All were friends of long standing. One noon, in the very late days of World War II, I was in conversation with Izzy when I felt a gentle poke in the back and turned to confront a lovely blond vision.

"Hello," said Mrs. Stuart Symington.

Mrs. Symington, whose husband later became United States Senator from Missouri, is the granddaughter of the famous John Hay, daughter of the late United States Senator James W. Wadsworth, and first cousin of John Hay (Jock) Whitney.

I introduced her to Schwartzy, as we called Izzy, and after a moment we moved away from his stand.

Mrs. Symington, whose husband had some war post in Washington, explained that she had left him for a few days to visit her parents in Geneseo, said that she would be back in Rochester again in two days, and accepted an invitation to lunch in the Hotel Seneca upon her return. It was a pleasant lunch, and she gave me a story for my newspaper space.

Evelyn Wadsworth Symington is a daughter of the oldest family in the Genesee Valley, an aristocrat if such is authenticated in our American heritage. Izzy Schwartz had been peddling newspapers in Main Street since before he put on full-length pants. The pair were poles apart, I suppose. But I was delighted to bring them momentarily together and to feel that I could be as comfortable in the company of one as in the company of the other. I like people. To me they are the most fascinating of all the earth's phenomena, and during the years that I worked for Rochester newspapers I had access to various strata of the city's society and had good friends in all of them.

This book is not in a true sense an attempt at a history of Rochester, which has been written, rewritten, and written again, often by very competent historians. It is rather an account of some of the interesting inhabitants of my native city and an impressionistic report of a community that for many years was the object of my professional scrutiny.

In recent years great changes have taken place in Rochester and the city has lost much of its old order and tranquillity. Areas which in earlier years were places of great delight now have a spent quality; they seem defunctive and exhausted. We have ghettos which urban renewal has not yet eliminated. Formerly a sequestered precinct of careful manners and a quiet, reserved, and graceful style of life, the old Third Ward is a teeming black belt, and the effort to provide these people with decent housing and generally improved conditions has not yet succeeded. East Avenue, once our finest residential thoroughfare—once, indeed, one of the most handsome streets in the eastern section of the United States—like so many others districts in Rochester has lost its primal character. In all its length only three private dwellings are lived in by their original occupants. The large, imposing, thick-walled houses, set far back from the pavement, have been converted into apartments and high-rise apartments pop up whenever contractors manage to circumvent the legal obstacles thrown up by those who wistfully strive to preserve something of the Avenue's former status. There are depressed areas in other sections of the once fashionable East Side, a shabbiness in many once bright and cheerful residential sections all over town. And the exodus from the city to the suburbs has not been arrested by the building of apartment houses or, in two or three instances, by the ingenious grouping of individual town houses.

But Rochester is not a lost city, forlorn, beaten down, and discouraged. Its great industries give employment to scores of thousands, and one of these, the old-line Bausch & Lomb Company, is enjoying at the moment a very lively boom. Rochesterians (as all residents of the metropolitan area must now be considered) have, if they participate in civic enterprises, keen civic pride. They are often singularly loyal. They recognize that their city has, as have most other cities in the country, grave problems, but the more forward-looking of our citizens refuse to concede that these problems are insoluble.

We have a great and enormously wealthy university, the excellent and greatly expanded Rochester Institute of Technology, the Monroe Community College, two splendid Roman Catholic colleges, and two theological seminaries. We have a famous medical center, a fine music school, and one of the most beautiful theaters in the land, since the Eastman's recent face lifting. A great lake is at our northern boundary, and smaller lakes and wide open spaces and rolling hills may be reached in half an hour's drive from the city's southern border.

I always loved Rochester. I was born in the city and with the exception of a year's hitch in the AEF and a total of eight or nine months' employment by newspapers in New York and Detroit I have lived all my life in or within thirteen miles of my Rochester birthplace. I have had no desire to leave; abstracted from home I am never fully happy until I return. In my youth, in my early manhood and in middle age I thought Rochester the finest city in the land, and I am not convinced that this is not still so. For nearly sixty years I walked the city's streets as a newspaper writer and because I have outlived so many of my contemporaries it may be that I know as much about the city's people as any person alive.

HENRY W. CLUNE

1972

The Rochester I Know

BOOK I

Chapter 1

Jake Abeles had the grocery store at South Avenue and Gregory Street, and Will Glotzbach was his right-hand man. There were other grocery stores in the neighborhood: Fred Schultz's at the South Avenue corner and Pauckner's at the Mt. Hope Avenue corner of Cypress Street, but our little group in the middle of Linden Street (in those days the Street was limited to the half-mile stretch between Mt. Hope and South avenues) traded with Abeles.

Will Glotzbach was as comfortable and homey as an old porch rocking chair. He'd come around in the middle of the morning with Betsy, Abeles' sorrel mare hitched to a yellow delivery wagon, throw off the halter block, and amble around to our back door, and Eliza, the Canadian girl who cooked for us, would call upstairs, "Mrs. Clune, the groceryman's here."

His order book open, Will would be comfortably adjusted on one of the back vestibule steps, settled as if for a morning's stay, when my mother would bustle down from whatever she had been doing on the second floor.

"Will," she would say scoldingly, for he had perhaps interrupted some phase of her preparations for our family's celebration of a holiday, "you know very well I ordered everything we need for Thanksgiving when you were here yesterday. Now, when I have so much to do, why are you bothering me again?"

"No, no, not everything," Will would protest, with a gentle shake of his head, and he'd smile up at her from his seated position on the steps. "No punkin. You didn't order any punkin."

"Ah—ah, well, maybe we aren't going to have pumpkin pie Thanksgiving. Eliza might make a nice mince pie, mightn't you, Eliza?"

"If you want one," Eliza would say.

"With your family, you ought to have two pies," Will would

15

say. "Mince and punkin. I'll put you down for a nice punkin, got a fresh load in from the farmer today. Just dandy."

"We-e-ll, all right. Just one pumpkin. It doesn't need to be big, either."

"And what about onions?"

"We've got plenty of onions, haven't we, Eliza?"

"Well, we've got some."

"Don't want to run short—not on Thanksgiving. Turkey without boiled onions!" Will would wag his head reproachfully. "I'll put you down for a sack of onions. Cranberries?"

"You know I ordered cranberries yesterday."

"Yes. Yes, that's right." Will's was the soft sell. On a frosty fall or a blustering winter's morning he enjoyed sitting comfortably on the back vestibule stairs and despite the fuss she sometimes made about his badgering her, my mother liked having him there. His coming was an anticipated morning event, perhaps more exciting than the visit of the postman.

And Will Glotzbach was something of a quidnunc. He brought news of the neighborhood. It wasn't scandalous gossip, spoken behind the hand with innuendoes and intimations of evil. But Will might know that Willie Teifel, across the street, had the croup and that his parents were up all night giving him steam inhalations from a tea kettle; that a rat had killed a setting hen in the Kieses' chicken coop; that Mr. Thackeray, the eccentric carpenter, who stabled his little horse in a shed back of his house, had removed the shoes from the animal and put it up for the winter; that Mrs. Herbert Jones, the only member from Linden Street of what might sketchily be called the beau monde, would entertain her whist club the day after Thanksgiving with a lunch of oyster patties, artichoke salad, and candied sweet potatoes.

"And by the way," Will would say, pencil poised over his order book, "you got no sweet potatoes."

"We have white potatoes, Thanksgiving."

"And coffee? You sure you got enough coffee?"

This sort of thing might go on for ten or fifteen minutes, and Will, tactfully countering my mother's protests, often prevailed. He would leave with his order book half filled. With his departure, my mother would shake her head hopelessly. "That Will Glotzbach," she'd say to Eliza, "he's just a caution."

* * *

Holidays were not a communal festival in our part of Linden Street. We were neighborly, indeed quite closely bound together in spirit and sympathy, but not organized. On Fourth of July, there was mild competition among the Tiefels, the Maloys, and ourselves to be the first to creep through the diaphanous dawn and arouse the neighborhood with the explosion of a giant firecracker, and from then until the sport languished in late morning we all contributed to a fairly constant cannonading. It was all spontaneous and individual, and after dark there was no pyrotechnic display under community sponsorship, as in many other sections of the city, but only desultory shots from a Roman candle or now and then the corruscating twirl of a Catherine wheel.

If not unique among Rochester residential streets, Linden Street was at least atypical. There was nothing quite like it in the city in the closing years of the nineteenth and in the early days of the new century. At the time when I was first sufficiently sensible of my surroundings to fix their details in memory, there was a line of pleasant but undistinguished houses on the north side of the street, clapboard for the most part, with small pridefully kept front lawns and back yards that were often studded with fruit trees or geometrized into plots for flower or kitchen gardens.

In all of this, of course, there was nothing distinctive. There were innumerable residential streets in Rochester whose householders prided themselves on their homes and gave meticulous attention to their lawns and gardens. It was not the houses or yards, or the people in Linden Street who provided the singularity that the street enjoyed, but the prospect, as one looked south across the asphalt pavement of the finest display nursery on the American continent. It was like living on the edge of an elaborate private park that might have been designed for a potentate.

The nursery property was confined behind a high picket fence, weathered a pastel yellow, which had been constructed along its border the full length of Linden Street. There were no stern enjoinders, "Keep Out," "Private Property," "Trespassers Will Be Prosecuted," and little need of them. Although an agile boy might easily have scaled the picket fence, I never heard of vandalism being perpetrated in the nursery or of the theft of its stock or produce except as a passerby on the south sidewalk might reach up and snatch a ripe plum or an Anjou pear or a spy apple from a laden branch that depended on the street side of the fence.

Only one house backed up to the nursery property on the south side of the street until close to the turn of the century. This had been built by Ellwanger & Barry, the greatest nursery company in the land. It was occupied when I first knew it by Charles Maloy, who for more than sixty years served the nursery company successively as messenger, clerk and secretary and whose daily peregrinations between his home and the company office on Mt. Hope Avenue had the precise rhythm of a metronome.

Mr. Maloy was a fixture in our street. The neighbors said you could set your watch by his passing. He walked easily, unhurriedly, puffing his pipe. He was a kindly Christian man with a calm and easy temperament who knew that the sequoia, like Rome, had not been built in a day, and that even the cultivation of a pansy bed or the growing of a prize rutabaga needed patience and the benignity of nature, and that nature in its processes was not to be importuned or harried.

Although we in Linden Street were not particularly conscious of this, the nursery that perfumed the summer air we breathed and offered visual delights of green velvety walks, neatly hedged by arborvitae or California privet, of wide and brilliant floral displays, and exotic ornamental trees, symbolized the city in which we lived.

The Flour City, as Rochester had been known ever since it had metamorphosed from a tiny stick-in-the-mud settlement in a fetid swamp at the edge of the Genesee River to a booming mill town, had gained a new sobriquet. It was now the Flower City, largely because of the Ellwanger & Barry Company, and a gift by its proprietors of twenty acres of their property for a municipal park which today is internationally celebrated for the variety and beauty of its lilac bushes.

At one time the acreage upon which Linden Street was formed had been part of the growing lands of what originally had been known as the Mt. Hope Nurseries. The company had been founded in 1840 by Patrick Barry, an Irishman, and George Ellwanger, a German. At the height of its career, the Ellwanger & Barry Company cultivated six hundred acres, and Cypress Street, which immediately parallels Linden Street, made the northern boundary of this domain.

As the centrifugal pressures of population jumped land values in the outlying sections of the city, the nursery company now and then sheared off a slice of its herbaceous beds or its orchards to make a residential thoroughfare. Linden Street was the result of one of these sporadic ventures into the real estate business.

In this instance there was nothing like a land boom. Besides the nursery property that intervened between Linden Street and the not distant southern boundary of the city, there were several acres of rough and hilly pasture land, unsuited for street development, that adjoined a romantic pile traditionally known as Warner's Castle, and Rochester's largest cemetery, Mt. Hope. Opportunities for building were limited unless the nursery property was to be given over to this design, and despite its natural beauties this southern section of Rochester (happily for those of us who lived within its range) never achieved a vogue.

The house in which I was born stood directly across from the Ellwanger & Barry—or Maloy house—the only residence on the south side of the street, until my father, taking a deep breath and what for him must have been a considerable gamble, bought two lots next to Maloy's and built a square dwelling with an attic trap door which allowed access to the flat parapeted roof, two toilets outside of the one in the bathroom, a dumbwaiter, a speaking tube that connected the kitchen with the master bedroom, and a special apartment known as the "bicycle room."

Our new home was much the newest, and possibly the largest house on the street, and the "extras," the tricky appurtenances my father caused to be built into it, together with is marginal position on the nursery property, gave it singular distinction. We were rather fancy people for a time, except to the Kieses, the Owens, the Maloys, the Tiefels, the McGlennons, and the Joneses of our own mid-street group, who, if the truth were out, indulged a faintly snooty attitude toward other Linden Street residents.

The bicycle room was something of a novelty. It was fairly commodious, it had a closet at one end with a glittering array of tools, each tool always in its precise niche, and it was depressed two or three steps below the main floor level of the house. In it my father kept a tandem, on which on Sunday afternoon he sometimes rode with my mother, two bicycles for himself, and one for my oldest sister. He was an ardent cyclist, and the time he flung his Columbia racing bike on the grass of the front yard and left it there during a rainstorm became something of a Linden Street legend. Moreover, it gave proof that even the most carefully adjusted lives occasionally divert from their fixed patterns and that human behavior cannot be anticipated with anything like slide-rule exactness.

My father's profligate act had been observed by several neighbors, and talk of it was bruited up and down the street. When the talk presently reached his ears, he passed it off with the remark that a man could do strange things in an emergency. And this, decidedly, had been an emergency.

My father was a very meticulous man. He had been handicapped by lack of education and his boyhood on the plains of Dakota Territory, the only child of an impecunious widow, had been devoid of youthful recreations and pleasures. His formal schooling ended when he was nine years old, and from then on he was a full-time wage earner. Since nothing had come easily to him, he cherished and gave excessive care to all material possessions.

He abominated waste: waste of money, goods, time, and health.

He neither smoked nor drank intoxicants. And though he was indomitably not a churchgoer and, I am sure, skeptical of revelation, he never used vile language or gave way to profanity.

He broke this rule only once in my presence. One scorching Sunday afternoon, in the early days of motoring, two tires of his Packard 18 blew out, each of which he repaired uncomplainingly. When a third went flat with a sickening sss-swish, he cried out angrily, "Oh, hell!" and followed the imprecation with an apology, "Excuse me. I guess I lost my temper."

A slight, almost frail-looking man, my father had a good deal of fortitude and enormous determination. When he moved from the Midwest to Rochester to work first as a railroad telegrapher and then to serve a mining company as auditor and treasurer, he devoted the new leisure these occupations allowed him to activities he had been denied as a boy. He had not learned to read until his midteens, and now he read everything upon which he could lay his hands. He had had no previous opportunity to engage in sports and games, and he took to these with youthful zest. Although he had no marked athletic aptitude, through persistence he became a pretty fair athlete. When the bicycle craze was at its zenith during the last decade of the last century, he rigorously devoted himself to this sport.

At that time the baseball diamond at Culver Field, the home of the Rochester Baseball Club, was encircled by a board bicycle track which for a couple of seasons attracted many of the best riders in the country. On this banked oval, when he was in his thirty-seventh year, my father rode a mile back of triplet pace in one minute and fifty-one seconds, for an amateur city record. Major Taylor, the great Negro sprint rider, who came to town a few days later, told my father that if he had had the same kind of pace Taylor had been given when he set the professional record at Springfield, Massachusetts, he might have come close to the national amateur record. This of course was conjecture. Taylor may have been making polite talk.

My father had very set ideas about finance and economy. He abhorred debts of any kind and sternly refused to purchase anything for which he could not pay cash on the barrel top. He contended that a balanced budget was the only way an individual could live in peace with himself or a nation exist in prosperity. It is shuddering to contemplate the bleeding ruin the national economy would suffer if these quaint, anachronistic principles of my father were in force today.

In my youth the purchase of a piano was a vital issue in our household for some time. My mother very much wanted a piano. She said all of her relatives in Buffalo had pianos and she couldn't see why she couldn't have one, too. My father answered that it might be possible in time, but at the moment he could not afford a piano. When my mother remarked on his possession of two racing bicycles, he replied that he had acquired both at low cost, since it was the practice of dealers to sell their machines under the list price to riders of reputation.

The argument had not been resolved on Memorial Day when my father left the house shortly after lunch on one of his racers. For days he had been in earnest training for a road race, and that morning he had spent considerable time putting his Columbia bicycle in condition for the contest. When not in use, his bicycles were suspended on hooks attached to the bicycle room ceiling, and he bestowed upon them the loving care Heifetz might give to a priceless Stradivarius. They were rubbed and oiled and adjusted daily. They were never taken out in the rain and after months of use they still looked as new and shiny as bicycles in a show window.

My mother did not sympathize with my father's racing. For a man of his age, she thought it unsafe and imprudent, and not a little undignified. When he left that afternoon with his bicycle polished like a jewel and the narrow racing tires blown hard, she called nervously, "I wish you weren't going to that race. You're too old. It's not becoming. You might get killed."

We heard nothing of my father until late in the afternoon, when he rode up jubilantly. The day had grown cloudy, and rain was beginning to fall. My father called to me that he had won the big race. Then he noticed a team of dock-tailed horses, hitched to a victoria, a coachman on the box, standing at the curb.

"Oh," he cried, suddenly chastened, "is the doctor here?"

The doctor was the celebrated Dr. William A. Keegan, and I told him he had been in the house for some time. With that, my father flung his bicycle on the grass, even though the rain was now falling in earnest, and rushed into the house. The storm grew, the rain pelting down fiercely, and I was driven indoors by it. I was not, however, allowed to go upstairs, and I waited a long time, knowing something momentous was happening, but not knowing what it was.

Presently the doctor came downstairs with my father and I heard him say, "Well, you just made it in time, George. But your worries are over now. She's going to do fine."

My father seemed greatly relieved. When the doctor left he took me aside and explained that I had a baby sister. He talked to me for quite a time and I could see that he was proud and happy. The rain was still falling outside. Suddenly he leaped up with a cry of horror. "I've left my wheel out in the rain!"

He rushed out of the house, retrieved the bicycle, and he was a long time rubbing it with oily rags and oiling the sprocket and chain. Tenderly he replaced the machine on the hooks that depended from the bicycle room ceiling. Then he took me upstairs to see my mother. She was very weak and wan but she patted my head and allowed me to kiss her. My father looked down at her with a sheepish smile.

"Well, Hattie," he said, "we've got a new daughter. And you're going to have a piano."

"A piano?" There was a quickening interest in my mother's eyes.

"I won it in the race today."

It came the next week. And although my father could not play it, he was ever so careful of it. He was always fearful that its surface would be marred; he polished it himself, and he insisted that the cover be lowered over the keys when it was not in use.

He was not again going to be wantonly careless of his possessions, as he had been when he left his bicycle lying out in the rain.

*　　*　　*

At the time when I was growing up, there were various sections of the city that were villagelike in their singularity, that were neat and cozy, and often exceedingly clannish. Rochester was spoken of as "a city of homes," and this was not a misnomer; a city of homes and trees!

There was only an aspersion of apartment houses, and these for the most part were confined to the downtown sections. Substantial burghers wanted none of them, and the aspiration of the newly wedded was invariably to own a home on some tree-lined street, of which there were many in both the fashionable and middle-class sections of the city.

Before the motorcar and the movie theater began to lure householders from their homes, the residential districts of Rochester had innumerable neighborhood cliques similar to our little coterie in Linden Street. The city itself animated a spirit of neighborliness. To be sure, quarrels occasionally developed over the placing of a fence post, a marauding dog, or a boy who batted a baseball through a window pane. But Rochester generally was a genial little city. I know that people in our crowd, in revenge for some real or fancied wrong, never dumped garbage into a neighbor's yard. On the contrary, we were always running next door, or two doors away, or to the house across the street to borrow a rolling pin, or two lemons, or a pair of hedge clippers, or an onion for a stew.

On pleasant summer evenings the front porch was the gathering place for the entire family. We were habitual and contented porch sitters. Once the supper dishes were "done," the mother of the family and the daughters of her brood might gather at one end of the veranda, while the paterfamilias, ensconced in his favorite chair at the other end, scanned the evening paper against the failing light and blew smoke from his mellow pipe through the darkling fronds and creepers of the morning-glory vine. Below, on the steps, the small fry would squat, reviewing the day's events and planning for the morrow.

The front porch also had a function in the morning. It became a sort of forum when Mrs. So-and-So came out to shake the dust of a small rug against the railing and discuss with her next-door neighbor her husband's lumbago, the price of eggs, the summer sale of muslins at Sib's (the big Sibley department store downtown), little Cathy's poison ivy, and weren't those tough boys from down around Clinton Avenue who went hooting through the street at midnight just awful?

Today, the front porch is an architectural anachronism, and most modern dwellings lack these pleasant sheltered appendages. They have no purpose in the suburban home with its patio, its swimming pool, its air-conditioning unit; the urbanite would have no patience sitting on a front porch inhaling the noxious fumes of carbon monoxide with only the pricking glints of fireflies to divert him.

And city dwellers no longer have back yards where one might, if one wished, raise chickens, play croquet, sift ashes, paint a screen door, grow an eggplant, breed dogs, experiment in floriculture, dry curtains, or plant a quince tree: The space once available for these pursuits is now consumed by an asphalt drive and a two-car garage.

As a neighborhood group, our little clique in Linden Street was particularly cohesive. There were quarrels, and days when some of us passed without speaking, but these were exceptional occasions and confined to the younger members of the families. We were not snoopers and there was no commerce among us of neighborhood scandal. But we knew a good deal about the internal affairs of our neighbors and they knew a good deal about ours. Our sympathies were mutual; our services reciprocal. If someone was ill we were quick to offer comfort and, if need be, nursing aid; we were prodigal with jellies and wholesome homemade soups during the patient's convalescence. In the canning season, if the experiments of one housewife resulted in a particularly desirable mustard pickle or an improved peach preserve, the innovator flounced about the neighborhood proud to display her achievement and share its secret with her compeers.

As Linden Street matured, the Maloys and ourselves lost our sovereignty. We no longer were the only residents on the south side. One, then another, and soon several houses that abutted on the nursery property went up, and it wasn't long before "Sleepy Linden Street," as the newspapers defined it on rare occasions when anything happened there worthy of their mention, resembled,

24

with rows of opposing dwellings, many other pleasant but modest residential streets in Rochester. Except for this single point of difference: The nursery was still there to delight the eye with its horticultural beauties and refresh the nostrils with its summertime perfumes.

In 1918, the nursery company, assuming a new function, stopped selling the arboreal and floral products of its extensive lands and started selling the lands themselves under an altered company name, the Ellwanger & Barry Realty Company.

But that part of the company's property that adjoined Linden Street remained inviolate for more than thirty years, a long period of grace for old residents who were accustomed to awaken summer mornings to the chittering of blackbirds and the fragrance of roses. They still lived, they felt, on the edge of a pastoral retreat, and Linden Street still retained something of the character of a small village. Then Fred Barry, a gentleman, a Harvardian, a bachelor, and a beau of semielderly ladies, who lived alone in the graceful white house on Mt. Hope Avenue in which he had been raised, gently countering the petitions of those who wanted no apartment houses in the neighborhood, sold the nursery off to people who ultimately built a series of apartments from South Avenue almost to Mt. Hope. Fred Barry died shortly thereafter, the last of three grandsons of the cofounder of the Ellwanger & Barry Company. Now his house in Mt. Hope Avenue, and the splendid brick Victorian mansion directly to the north, "The Patrick Barry House" by the Landmark Society's listing, and the company's delightful, tree-shaded office building, with its gables, its turrets, its open hearths, and, in its small counting room, a breast-high, stand-up bookkeeper's desk, precisely out of Dickens, has with adjacent property been expropriated by the very rich University of Rochester, which for years has been bursting out of its golf-links campus to spread sporadically over the southern part of Rochester.

Chapter 2

My own early impressions of Rochester were colored by the parochialism of growing up in Linden Street. In public fancy, that thoroughfare was hardly so significant as the space devoted to it in the foregoing chapter might seem to indicate. Actually, it was a seldom-heard-of street, tucked away in the Fourteenth Ward, and the Fourteenth in those days was not particularly distinguished. It was sometimes referred to as the "graveyard ward," since a considerable portion of it was taken up by Mt. Hope Cemetery. Also included in its compass were such desolating institutions as the Monroe County Penitentiary, an expanding state hospital, and what was commonly spoken of as the Pest House.

The Pest House was officially Hope Hospital, the city's makeshift isolation center for epidemic diseases. It stood in sinister remove in a cut between two railroads, and on the spot now occupied by the summer theater of the University of Rochester. It was approached over a rutty wagon track, dignified on city maps as Wolcott Street, but better known as the Feeder Road. The title was appropriate. Wolcott Street ran along the edge of a narrow channel of malarious-looking water that replenished the Erie Canal at times when flatboats threatened to scuff the bottom of that statewide artery of travel. The Pest House was in close propinquity to the back hills of Mt. Hope Cemetery. During a fierce smallpox siege in 1902–3, ghoulish, half-believed tales were told of bodies being lugged like cordwood up the cemetery hills and dumped into a common grave.

Neither the graveyard nor the Pest House did much to enhance the reputation of the Fourteenth Ward which, nevertheless, had more natural beauties and more breathing space than most of the other wards. It had a number of new, pleasant tree-shaded streets in the developing Highland Park area. In general, the character of the ward was respectable bourgeoise. But far up Mt. Hope Avenue hill was an elaborate residence known as Warner's Castle and below this, in a brief stretch of the avenue, two rows of dwellings that offered more than a hint of affluence and lent a quiet note of fashion to what was predominately a middle-class section of the city.

These were the large handsome houses, ornamented by lovely gardens and set widely apart on scrumptious lawns, of the nursery people—the Barrys and the Ellwangers. The Barry houses faced west and across the cobblestone pavement of Mt. Hope Avenue were the more elegant and more withdrawn Ellwanger residences. There was strife among the last-named clan, and a bitter lawsuit, in which a will would be broken, was to ensue, but to the passerby all looked delightfully serene. Immediately to the north of the last Ellwanger house stood the bulky, red-brick domicile of Henry J. Moore, surely, with its family of twelve, its bounteous hospitality, and the myriad activities engaged in by its occupants, one of the most unusual domestic establishments in Rochester.

Distinguished (and the term may need exact definition) or not, the Fourteenth was a comfortable and roomy ward. Its topography has been altered in the past seventy years, but it still extends westward to the right bank of the Genesee River, and today the riparian border of its lower precinct opposes, diagonally across that stream, the southeastern extremity of the old Third, or, as it was traditionally known, the "Ruffled Shirt" ward.

And the old Third *was*, and is still, historically distinguished. It is the Genesis of the city of Rochester. In its primordial state, part of the area of which it is composed was a miasmic lowland, reputedly the source of an often fatal ague, a sort of backwoods Black Plague, and it was also notorious as a breeding ground for rattlesnakes. White men knew it scarcely at all, and the Indians avoided it except in transit. It was a forbidding homesite; an unlikely location for the founding of an industry: yet, during the decade that followed the close of the Revolutionary War and at a time when white speculators were cozening the Seneca Indians out of their Genesee Valley lands, a picaresque character, Ebenezer "Indian" Allen, came to this sullen forest morass to erect first a saw and then a grist mill next to one of the river's lesser cataracts.

Allen was not an Indian by blood. The epithet that prefixed his surname had come to him because of his aboriginal skills and habits, and because he had begot two half-breed daughters by an honestly espoused squaw. He was an entrepreneur of sorts, implicitly an opportunist, possibly a murderer, a polygamist, and a man

27

whose effect on women appeared to be electric, if not indeed atomic. He was an expert woodsman, and his knowledge of the lower Genesee country probably exceeded that of any other white man.

In 1789, Allen moved twelve miles down river from a partly cleared acreage upon which he had squatted in the present village of Scottsville to take up a catch-as-catch-can existence in the mill buildings at the river's edge, and to validate the claims of latter-day historians that he was the first white man to locate on territory that is now part of Rochester.

He had been granted one hundred acres, part of which was later to be included in the old Third Ward, by Oliver Phelps, a New England land promoter, who the year before had procured for himself and his partner, Nathanial Gorham, a huge parcel of the poor Indians' Happy Hunting Grounds.

The big land grab was consummated at a council at Buffalo Creek, sixty miles west of the Genesee River, at which Phelps, as the active head of the Phelps-Gorham combine, met with the Indians. The council lasted several days. Phelps coveted all of the Senecas' paradisiacal valley, which that virile and charismatic tribe had dominated for generations. He was disappointed when the chiefs, who had most likely come away from other councils with their holier-than-thou Christian brothers, depleted, disillusioned, and forlorn, agreed to sell 2,600,000 acres on the right side of the Genesee, but refused at first to part with any of their property west of the stream. Phelps persisted. The Senecas were an agrarian tribe, with a polity advanced beyond that of many of their red-skinned fellows. They often lived in log houses, they toilsomely ground their corn with a stump mortar, and laboriously cut their logs with an ax.

When Phelps suggested that he would build a set of mills on the lower Genesee, the Indians were interested. An accommodation of this sort would be a boon. Phelps, of course, would want some slight emolument for his services; what he got was a piece of west-of-the-river land, twelve by twenty-four miles in size—a pleasant little lagniappe! The property included what came to be known as the 100-Acre Tract. This Phelps gave to Allen with the stipulation that the latter erect mills on the site.

Phelps hadn't wangled from the original owners all of the land he desired. He still had a bargain. He paid $5,000 down, and agreed to pay $500 annually "forever" for something better than two and a half million acres, and only the oldest and most astute of the Seneca sachems probably knew how equivocal the white man's definition of that adjective could be.

The grist mill was completed late in the autumn of 1789, and its raising was appropriately celebrated. Only a few white men lived within a wide radius of Allen's 100-Acre Tract, but all came a-running. They brought rum that had come from a trading vessel that had recently put in at the mouth of the river. The guests to the number of an odd dozen frolicked. They wassailed, they sang, they kicked up their heels. Then the rum ran out, and the party was over. And Indian Allen was in business.

But neither Allen's mills nor the real estate projects of Phelps and Gorham were a howling success. With the war over, the promoters had envisaged migrants from the rock-studded farms of New England pouring into the immensely fertile lands of the Genesee Valley like Moslems hustling on to Kaaba. They came, instead, in dribbles. Phelps and Gorham discovered they were land poor.

Real estate transactions that involved the western New York wilderness were often complicated. Although the Senecas concededly owned the land, sovereignty over it had been ceded to New York and Massachusetts had the right of pre-emption of the soil, or first purchase from the Indians. This prerogative had an interesting history. It dated back to 1629, when Charles I of England had imperiously handed over to the Massachusetts Bay Colony a property that he had never seen and that he did not own, and that extended into the vast terra incognita of the American continent and included the Genesee Valley.

Before they dealt with the Indians, Phelps and Gorham had been obliged to acquire from Massachusetts the right of pre-emption. The cost was high: They were to pay something like a million dollars in three installments. The land promoters had sold dribs and drabs of their property to prospectors who occasionally struggled into the Genesee country over the difficult wilderness paths from the east, but the revenue from these sales was insufficient for their requirements. Pressed by Massachusetts for a first payment, Phelps and Gorham reneged. They turned back to that commonwealth two thirds of the land they still possessed and sold the remaining third to Robert Morris, who had been George Washington's friend and money man during the Revolutionary War.

Once reputedly the richest man in America, Morris suffered a druglike addiction to land speculation. His holdings were enormous; his desire for more land insatiable. He had greatly overextended himself in western New York, where he had never set foot, but where he had sent his bright young son, Tom, to represent him. The young man tried valiantly to avert the impending rout of his father's fortune. He failed. Ruin came to the elderly Morris, he was remanded to a debtors' jail in Philadelphia, and most of his Genesee Valley property was gobbled up by the Pulteney Association, an English syndicate.

The syndicate selected Charles Williamson, a flamboyant, highly personable, early Madison-Avenue type to supervise, advertise, and sell its western New York lands. Williamson did the job, bang up. He built roads, he founded villages, he promoted sporting events; he brought fancy food, and, some say, fancy women into the territory. He delighted in entertaining the trade—prospective land buyers. He did it with style and grace, and the figures on the swindle sheet meant no more to him than Assyrian cuneiform. In the end, Williamson was overslaughtered. The Pulteney people thought him too rich for their blood. They replaced him with Robert Troup, who watched the decimal points with a microscopic eye, and kept the company's books in balance.

Troup had all the promotional instincts of a gravedigger. Williamson, for his part, had brought hundreds of settlers into the area. He was partial to the gentry. He wanted to attract to the Pulteney lands men who would erect important houses on large estates, who would encourage the urbanites, cultivate the arts, participate in gentlemanly sports, and give grand balls.

In the autumn of 1800, three tourists who at least in the matter of wealth and breeding met Williamson's qualifications, rode into the upper Genesee River country to observe for themselves the property the land agent had alluringly told about in his advertisements. The trio had come from Maryland, a slave and pack horses following at a deferential distance. Its members were Major Charles Carroll and Major William Fitzhugh, Maryland natives, and Colonel Nathaniel Rochester, a Virginian by birth, who now resided in Hagerstown, Maryland.

Impressed by what they saw, the visitors did not return to

their homes until they had contracted with Williamson to purchase, for $2 an acre, twelve thousand acres of land on the east side of the Genesee River, thirty-odd miles upstream from Indian Allen's millsite.

Carroll, Fitzhugh, and Rochester did not return to the lands they had bought from the Pulteney Association for three years. By that time, Charles Williamson had been relieved of his post, and the Southerners were met by John Johnstone, a Pulteney representative. When the visitors expressed a desire to acquire a millsite Johnstone led them over the river trails to the lower Genesee, and the 100-Acre Tract upon which Allen had erected his mills.

The builder of the mills had departed, and the tract that had been given him by Oliver Phelps was now a Pulteney property. His restless nature inevitably beguiled by a golden mirage in the sky, Allen had left after only a two-year tenure. Several successors had operated his ponderous contraptions with indifferent success. The grist mill was now in execrable disrepair, and the saw mill was gone, swept off in some spring turbulence of the Genesee.

The odium attributed to the place only a few years before by a visitor who pronounced it a "tangled wilderness, a fever-infested swamp, the abode of wild beasts, savages, and rattlesnakes," was not entirely unwarranted in 1803. The millsite was still remote. Not a dozen families lived within a day's walk, and the family that actually resided in the rickety mill building existed in a sort of wilderness slum. The astute Southerners nevertheless saw promise in the location. Some clearing had been made in the ominous forest swamplands near the river's edge, a mill race dug by Allen still had functional capacity, and water ran swiftly over the fourteen-foot cataract. The trio from Maryland made a deal. They purchased the 100-Acre Tract for $1,700, turned south, and rode home.

Owning broad acres in the upper river country and a third interest in the 100-Acre Tract, the man whose name would grace the fledgling community that was to take form on Indian Allen's millsite did not settle in the Genesee Valley until seven years after his second visit to the territory, and did not take up residence at the Falls, as Rochester was first identified, until 1818, and by that time the village had several hundred inhabitants.

Nathaniel Rochester's roots were deep in Hagerstown. He was

a man of notable integrity, highly respected and honored by his fellow townsmen. He was president and one of the founders of the Hagerstown bank. For years he had engaged in various profitable enterprises. He had been married in Hagerstown, and all but one of his dozen children were born there. It must have taken great soul-searching, and required a momentous decision to wrench away from these close and solid moorings, and begin, in his fifty-ninth year, a journey to the northern wilderness with his wife, his nine living children, his chattels, and a covey of slaves, who shored up the Conestoga wagons when they sank into mires, minded the pack horses, and helped prepare the meals. The journey was undertaken in 1810; three weeks passed before the caravan came to a halt on lands that Rochester owned near the present village of Dansville.

Well into middle life at the time he left Hagerstown, Colonel Rochester was anything but a swashbuckling frontiersman, eager to savor raw adventures in a primitive land. His habits were fixed; generally they were sedentary. He was a conservative. He was a man who laid his plans carefully and methodically set about their execution. One of his motives in abandoning a community in which for a long time he had been admirably adjusted was his feeling that his numerous progeny would have greater opportunities to expand and express themselves in a new and untrammeled territory than they would have in what he termed the "old and settled country" of Maryland. Another reason for his northern migration was his abhorrence of the endemic evil of his native southland—slavery!

And at once, when his party reached its destination at Dansville, Colonel Rochester manumitted the Negroes who were part of it and relied upon their voluntary co-operation to help him initiate a new life in the slowly opening lands of the Genesee Valley.

Rochester remained five years in Dansville. He made expensive improvements to his property and farmed a considerable acreage. He sawed logs and ground corn for the frontier market, and manufactured paper. He prospered. Now and then he rode a horse forty miles northwest to the 100-Acre Tract to mark off town lots and offer them for sale. Buyers were woefully scarce. His reeking swamplands had little appeal to the occasional investigating prospector.

He became discouraged with the investment he shared with his southern friends. Carroll and Fitzhugh were still in Maryland. They did not follow Rochester into western New York for several years, and when they did move north their mode of life was unlike that of their energetic partner. They settled in large houses on ample estates in the upper river country and pursued the leisurely, graceful, country-gentleman existence they had known in their native Maryland. Presently Rochester, lamenting his inability to develop the 100-Acre Tract, expressed a desire to sell his share of the property. His partners protested.

"Hold on," Carroll told him earnestly, "and you'll have an estate for any man."

The prophecy was confirmed not many years later, when Rochester's portion of the 100-Acre Tract was appraised at $100,000, a not-to-be-sneezed-at fortune in the early years of the nineteenth century.

But before this, the colonel moved again. He and his family made their home for two years on a large farm in West Bloomfield, several miles southeast of the 100-Acre Tract, but considerably nearer to it than Dansville. Here he was in fairly easy access of the lower Genesee, and in that area there was now a bustle and stir of life. The War of 1812, with its threats of Indian raids and British incursions, had ended, and the new security the river country enjoyed had stimulated emigration. A crude bridge had been thrown across the Genesee a short distance south of the stream's spectacular ninety-two-foot cataract, and migrants from the east who walked, or rode horses, or guided creaking carts over its rough surface sometimes did not continue on the westward trail. They found promise in the settlement that was building on and around the 100-Acre Tract. The forest had receded under the ring of pioneer axes; the swamplands were drying up, and gaunt wolves no longer prowled the night, howling on kitchen midden heaps. Trade was beginning and the river's swift waters offered abundant hydraulic power.

Eight years after he had brought his family into western New York, Colonel Rochester made his final move. He left his West Bloomfield farm to establish a permanent residence for himself, his wife, and his children in the riverside settlement that had formerly been called the "Falls," and that now, largely because of his own petitions to the Legislature, was incorporated as Rochesterville.

In calendar years, Rochester was the oldest resident in the community, but far from doddering in body or mind or depressed in spirit. He was a tall, lean, slightly stooped, patricianlike figure at the age of sixty-seven, but eager, hopeful, forward-looking. He had the welfare of the village he had adopted, and that had taken his name, deeply at heart. He lived in a solid, well-designed brick house in the old Third Ward, and upon that precinct the traits of his character were etched like an intaglio. These were, conspicuously, his decency, his orderliness, his propriety, his conservatism. He was also, to a degree, provincial; a quality so implicit in the Ruffled Shirt Ward that in later years its residents opposed the intrusion of public carriers, proclaimed an ordinance that prohibited horses moving faster than a walk, and prided themselves on an insularity afforded by the moatlike channel of the Erie Canal which obstructed, except for a couple of lift bridges, vehicular and pedestrian penetration from the north.

* * *

Although Colonel Rochester is called the founder of Rochester, he did not live long enough to see the village in which his civic, business, and domestic interests were concentrated achieve the status of a city, and of course he was a long way from being the first resident. He was really a Johnny come lately, for Rochester was a fairly populous community when he settled there, and his residence continued only the last thirteen years of his long and useful life. The first permanent settler, in contradistinction to Indian Allen and the transitory occupants of the millsite who followed him, was Hamlet Scrantom.

A New Englander by birth, Scrantom had briefly tried living in the Black River country of northern New York. The climate was rigorous. Early in 1812, he wrote to his Connecticut-based father that he was leaving because it was "too cold and snowy." On May 1, Scrantom's ox-drawn wagon, with a linen canopy for the protection of his wife and several children, lumbered up to the east bank of the Genesee River in a snowstorm.

Scrantom had previously arranged to take over a cabin on the west side of the river that had been built by one of the two or three men who lived not distant from the stream's east bank. The trick now was to get his family across the river, for the wooden bridge that later in the year would span the Genesee was not yet completed. He finally found a flat-bottomed scow, which functioned as a ferry, and upon this and his wagon he and his family were transported across the water. There a new difficulty confronted the homeseeker from the north—the domicile that awaited him was roofless. Scrantom somehow made do overnight. In the morning he must have wondered if the long wagon trek over tortuous trails to escape the inclemencies of his former situation had been worth the effort. The countryside was covered with a foot of snow on this second day of May.

If not as gently bred and as gifted as Rochester's founding father, Rochester's Number One citizen had the recommendable qualities for frontier life of perseverance and fortitude; the frontiersman's knack for expediting necessities. Scrantom got a roof over his cabin, and made it snug and tight. It stood on a site now occupied by the Powers Block, which, for a decade or two after its erection, was the pride of downtown Rochester. The cabin was small for a bulging family of eight, and Scrantom soon moved to a larger and better house, for his estate was steadily improving.

Scrantom's career in Rochester, which continued uninterruptedly for nearly a quarter of a century, was concomitant to a progressive series of historical events. He saw the completion of the first bridge that crossed his part of the Genesee, and he greeted migrants from the east who passed over it to become his neighbors on the 100-Acre Tract and property that adjoined it.

The War of 1812 began not long after he had settled in his cabin, and although the area in which he lived was fairly remote from the war's battlegrounds, Scrantom suffered a moment of apprehension when a landing party from a British ship raided a warehouse at Charlotte, where the river enters Lake Ontario, seven miles north of his home.

Before hostilities ceased, a few families joined the lone pioneer on the west side of the river, and the inchoate settlement became known as the Falls. As I've mentioned, the name was later changed, first to Rochesterville and then to Rochester. The village grew steadily after the war. Wheat from the upper Genesee Valley, the fertility of which was often compared to the fertility of the Nile Valley, was begging to be ground into flour and sent on to market; and mills quickly sprang up along the cataracts of the lower river. Hamlet Scrantom for a time was engaged in the milling business. He was a respected burgher who was active in civic, religious, and educational affairs. He had great faith in the community that he had seen virtually rise out of a swamp. In less than a decade after the close of the war, he must have sensed the shape of things to come when Governor Clinton's Big Ditch was dug, clean up to the right bank of the Genesee, and soon after an engineering phenomenon—"a bridge that carried water"—was raised on Roman arches above the river, and Scrantom saw rectangular flatbottoms hauled by horses east and west through the channel of the Aqueduct of the Grand, or Erie Canal.

Scrantom left Rochester in the mid 1830s, lured westward by what he thought was the greater promise of Buffalo. His was not an irrevocable apostasy. He returned, and the village honored him as its first pioneer. Before his departure, he had witnessed not only the opening of the aqueduct and the western section of the canal, but the dedication of the entire stretch of an inland waterway that linked Lake Erie with the port of New York. The second event followed the first by two years. It was signalized in late October 1825 by a catenation of artillery explosions that reverberated across the state, and by the beginning of a Grand Canal Tour, west to east, of Governor Clinton and an impressive entourage in the swiftly drawn packet *Seneca Chief*. On the second day out, the *Seneca Chief* put up in Rochester, where the visit was marked by civil ceremonies.

Even before the opening of the canal, the village of Rochester was aware of the beginning of a boom that would be greatly accelerated once the canal was put into use, and that has never been repeated in spite of the development in later years of a number of industries that have given Rochester international fame and wealth that may surpass that of almost any other city of its size in the land.

The cataract-whitened waters of the Genesee, which powered the mills that stood along the river's banks, the torpid water of the Erie Canal, which facilitated the transportation of the mill's products, and Rochester's location on the main road to the western frontier were the factors responsible for the development of a village that bore some resemblance to a gold-rush town a dozen years after Hamlet Scrantom had settled in his lonely cabin on a site described by one of his progeny as a "wild and deserted place . . . cheerless in daytime, and doubly dark at night" where "wild beasts crouched and serpents innumerable crawled."

In 1820, Rochester was a hustling market town and the provisioning center for migrants who came plodding over the new road bound for Ohio and other lands opening up east of the Mississippi. A year later, the village had four flour mills and a greater number of saw mills. The flour was lugged in carts mostly to markets in the East, or shipped to Canada from the lake port of Charlotte; the saw mills made lumber for houses that were going up with something of the feverishness of split-level developments in modern suburbia. Shopkeepers were doing a land office business selling clothing, tools, hats, shoes, and food to transients who paused in their western hadji in Rochester for supplies, and sometimes prolonged their stay into permanent residenceship because they either took a fancy to the place or were too weary to press on.

The Erie Canal ran smack-dab through the heart of Rochester, and its opening was the greatest boon the village had yet known. Because it provided a means for the transportation of Rochester-made goods, the canal greatly stimulated commerce and industry. New businesses were continually springing up, and newcomers flocked into the bustling, busy river town, all eager, in the parlance of a later day, to "have a piece of the action."

Rochester had half a dozen hotels several years before it had a city charter, but the accommodations were inadequate for the teeming concourse of transients on the westward march, for the artisans seeking jobs, for the land agents, and for the wheelers and dealers who are always attracted to a place that is on the boom, and Rochester was the first boom town in America.

Scrantom saw the panorama of Rochester's early history unfold before his eyes: the building of the first school, the organization of the first church, the establishment of a daily newspaper, the erection of Reynolds Arcade, still a downtown landmark, in which the Western Union Telegraph Company was founded, the death of the venerable Colonel Rochester, and in 1834, the acquisition of a city charter by a community which had begun in a forest swamp only twenty-two years before.

Properly identified as Rochester's First Citizen, Scrantom survived an epidemic of cholera (commonly spoken of as Genesee fever) which took the lives of more than one hundred residents. It was a dreadful disaster for a community that had been, until this black pall spread over it, exuberantly on the boom. There were days when the death toll was so desperately high that carters who

37

gathered the corpses might have called out, as did the ghoulish collectors during the London plague, "Throw out your dead!" There was grim irony in this bad business: The death rolls might have been appreciably reduced had not several of the doctors who had come to town to practice medicine abandoned the Hippocratic oath to try to get rich quick selling real estate.

Hamlet Scrantom lived until 1850, which was the year the University of Rochester was founded in the old United States Hotel in what is now Main Street West. By mid-century, Rochester had a population of better than thirty-five thousand, a steam railroad, telegraph service, gas street lamps, and a new aqueduct over the river. Its industries were wholesomely diversified. It did a thriving business in the construction of canal boats, it was gaining recognition as a nursery center, it manufactured shoes and clothing, and had a number of profitable foundries.

Gradually Rochester's congenital business—the industry of its birthright, the milling of flour—would lose its paramount position as the great wheat fields opened in the West, and the milling industry moved west to settle upon their borders. This did not happen, however, until sometime after the Civil War; in fact, five years after the close of that struggle, Rochester's thirty-one mills achieved an all-time peak production of one million barrels of flour in twelve months.

Scrantom probably had no acquaintance with Sam Patch, but he very likely saw the man who may have done more to bring Rochester into general prominence than any other person until George Eastman put the word "Kodak" into the language and the instrument the word represents on the international market.

In the autumn of 1829, Sam Patch, a loose-gaited fellow who some said was addicted to brandy, and who surely was given to braggadocio, arrived in Rochester with the announcement that he proposed to leap over the ninety-two-foot falls of the Genesee River.

Patch was known as the Jersey Leaper. His specialty was dropping into water from high places, and shortly before his arrival in Rochester he had made a sensational jump over Niagara Falls. His reputation had preceded his coming to a town which, since the opening of the Erie Canal, had been so engrossed in self-aggrandizement, so preoccupied with the thrust of material expansion, that it had found little time for urban divertissements or professional entertainers.

Patch flaunted his daring in gaudy posters and handbills, and the local press aided his promotional efforts. The public's imagination was aroused. The exhibition was scheduled for November 13, and speculation was widespread as to whether Patch could make the leap and live. When the day came, scores of persons poured into Rochester from outside, coming afoot, on horseback, in wagons, and by canal packet to join most of the village residents at the brink of the falls.

The day was cold and autumnally bleak. Clouds lowered portentously over the largest gathering the village had yet known. The chill waters spilled noisily over the rocky ledge of the cataract, foamed and tossed in the pool below; then, smoothing out, slipped quietly as a shade through a channel that led to another cataract farther north and the ultimate destination of Lake Ontario.

There was no sound from the crowd as Patch took his stance, not at the brink of the falls but twenty-five feet above it, on a jerry-built platform he had erected to add fearsomeness to his stunt. A considerable delay ensued. It continued until it seemed as if the Jersey Leaper had lost faith in his infallibility and was disinclined to leave his awesome perch. He made a speech. He explained that while Napoleon and Wellington could win great battles, neither was capable of the feat he was about to perform. His talk was a little ragged, and some in the crowd who professed to know his habits believed that he had been trying to screw his courage to the sticking point by unscrewing the cap of a brandy bottle.

At a point when the crowd's quivering anticipation had become all but unbearable, Patch leaped into space, and his plummeting body quickly disappeared in the riotous pool below the falls.

A great chorus of cheers rose high above the noise of the falling waters, echoed and reverberated; rose again—and still again! Eagerly the multitude peered into the water at the foot of the cataract, spectators in the rear ranks huddling on the backs of those in front, all intent to shout out their discovery when the hero's head bobbed to the surface of the river.

But nothing extraneous appeared in the vortex ninety-two feet below; no body floated on the surface of the smoother water beyond. Soon a low, grave murmur was heard. Where was Patch?

What had happened? Minute after minute passed and the first fears congealed into a conviction of tragedy. The gallery that had gathered to enjoy a show had, it almost seemed, been an accessory to the death of the actor. Feet moved; the assemblage began to disintegrate; as its members shuffled away from the brink of the cataract, they had very much the demeanor of men and women who had attended, for the spectacle of the thing, the execution of a man who was now known to be innocent.

Patch never appeared to receive the reward that should have been his. As his gallery had surmised, he had leaped to his death, although absolute proof of this did not come until his body was recovered from the early spring ice floe in the lower Genesee.

But long before this, the witnesses of his performance had been castigated by local and foreign clergy as abettors of a homicide; threnodies had been sounded in the press of several cities, and a great deal of mawkish doggerel had been dedicated to the memory of the Jersey Leaper by poetasters in various parts of the country. The extravagance of some of this cast Patch in the heroic mold of the recently deceased Lord Byron.

In a long narrative verse, a New Jersey doctor (seemingly with a perfectly straight face), placed Patch among such immortals as Galileo, Columbus, Franklin, Lord Nelson, and Newton, and declared that he had died a "true martyr to science." Legend quickly formed around the Jersey Leaper; Patch became a figure in folklore, and posthumously Rochester's first press agent. The place became famous, not because its flour mills were making it the "breadbasket of America," but because of the stunt man who had jumped over its falls. Until deep into the nineteenth century the pinnacle of the ninety-two-foot cascade from which Patch had plunged was the first point of interest visitors to Rochester demanded to see. In time, trains on the New York Central Railroad, in their passage east or west across the river trestle, stopped directly south of the falls to allow passengers to observe from windows and vestibules the scene of the fatal leap.

Among the thousands attracted by this cynosure was the caustic, observant Mrs. Trollope, mother of the famous Anthony, who told in her controversial *Domestic Manners of the Americans* of a visit to the Upper Falls, "renowned as being the last fatal leap of the adventurous madman, Sam Patch."

Nathaniel Hawthorne also visited the scene.

"How stern a moral may be drawn from the story of poor Sam Patch," he later mused in print. "Why do we call him madman or a fool when he has left his memory around the falls of the Genesee more permanent than if the letter of his name had been hewn into the forehead of the precipice? Was the leaper of cataracts more mad or foolish than other men who throw away their life, or misspend it in pursuit of empty fame, and seldom so triumphantly as he?"

The city of Rochester has never done anything to commemorate the memory of a man whose name is inalienably related to its history, who gave it a bizarre celebrity that continued a great many years, and who provided it, as the Rochester Press Club once pointed out, with its first sensational news story.

A stone and marker placed in recent years at his grave in Charlotte Cemetery compose the only tangible memorial to the Jersey Leaper, and the fund for this was not raised by public subscription but by young Patch enthusiasts at Charlotte High School.

Chapter 3

The boom days had passed for Rochester by 1850, and the city had begun to take on a character that persisted well into another century, and that to a considerable degree reflected the decorum, the reserve, and the mild snootiness of the old Ruffled Shirt Ward.

Residents of the Ruffled Shirt—or Third Ward, to give it its proper numerical identification—were self-sufficient, kindly, withdrawn, quiet (except on occasions of gentle tribal ceremonies), and so opposed to ostentation and display that a true warder might feel as embarrassed at seeing his name in a newspaper headline as he would if discovered at one of the ward's proper soirees with the fly of his trousers unbuttoned.

The Third Ward was unique; according to its devoted residents there was nothing quite like it in the world. It came into the height of its glory before the Civil War, and persisted as the Mayfair of Rochester—the city's West End—until late in the century. It was still a district of dignity, and grace, and Brahmanic condescension in the early 1900s.

In their purest form, Third Warders were indigenous to the ward. Curious about the biographies of some of the ancient residents, a woman historian approached Miss Milly Alling, a lifelong resident of the Third. Miss Alling told of the careers of several of her feminine contemporaries. The historian persisted. "But what about Miss Baker?" she asked, referring to a nonagenarian she supposed was one of the ward's institutions.

"Oh, but my dear," Miss Alling protested. "You wouldn't call Miss Baker a Third Warder. She was fourteen when she moved here."

The ward's catechism read in part:

Q: What is the chief and highest aim of a Third Warder?
A: His chief and highest aim is to glorify the ward and fully to enjoy it forever.
Q: Are there no other wards in Rochester?

A: Politically, yes; socially, no.

Q: Can the ward be definitely bounded by a social sense?

A: It cannot.

Q: Why not?

A: Can the sunset be bounded?

Q: How does one account for Third Warders?

A: Heredity and environment.

Q: How may one become a Third Warder?

A: By birth or marriage or immemorial usage.

Q: Is there no other way?

A: None. . . .

Despite the rigid tenets of the catechism, the old Third was occasionally invaded by aliens who, because of their personal charms or notable merits, were able to flout the ward's orthodoxy and still make themselves acceptable to its hereditarily established residents. Two such aliens were the Jerome brothers, who came to the Third from the nearby village of Palmyra, built large square impressive houses next door to each other in South Fitzhugh Street, quickly ingratiated themselves into the favor of their neighbors, and took over the publication of the *Daily American*, which ultimately became one of the components in a journalistic merger which evolved into the *Democrat and Chronicle*, Rochester's flourishing morning newspaper.

After a few years in Rochester, Leonard and Lawrence Jerome removed to New York. There, and in London, Leonard was noted as a financier, sportsman, and social luminary; and, posthumously, as the father of the beautiful Jennie Jerome and grandfather of Winston Churchill.

During World War II, when the Allied world gloried in the eloquence, courage, and leadership of the British Prime Minister, Rochester boasted that the great man's mother had first seen the light of day in the Fitzhugh Street home of Leonard Jerome. I knew differently.

A few years before the beginning of the war, and at a time when Churchill was in some political disrepute, he came to Rochester to speak on the gold standard, and I was sent as a reporter for the *Democrat and Chronicle* to interview him in a suite in the Sagamore Hotel. I was ill-fitted for the assignment. For one thing, I knew nothing about the gold standard. At first flush, Churchill was unprepossessing. His feet were loosely held in scuffed carpet slippers, the dressing gown that encompassed the bulky, slope-shouldered figure was untidy, he was unshaved, for it was morning, and I was quite sure from his demeanor that it was the morning after a hard night. He was bored with this too-early visitor and glowered at me over spectacles that had slipped down his nose; he answered my questions with grunts and gutturals. Nothing that he said made much sense; yet I was curiously awed by the man. I felt indeed like a pygmy at the knees of a giant. I said, "Your mother was born here."

"No," he said flatly, "she was born in Brooklyn." He got a little clumsily to his feet, took the stopper off a port bottle, and opened the door. And I went out.

I said nothing in the newspaper about what Churchill had told me, and the myth that his mother was a native Rochesterian persisted in the early years of the war until indubitable proof to the contrary gave a sharp blow to local pride.

* * *

As a subteen-ager, I learned something about the old Ruffled Shirt Ward when I was enrolled in the ward's public elementary school, No. 3, in Tremont Street. My own school in Gregory Street, No. 13, was being replaced with a new building, and while I should have been transferred to some school on the east side of the river, I pleaded with my father to be allowed to attend No. 3 in order that I might walk to school with my neighbor and best friend, Charlie Maloy, who was a student at the Immaculate Conception in Plymouth Avenue South, a stone's throw from No. 3. My father arranged this through Henry J. Moore, a man he greatly admired, who lived with his wife and a brood of ten children in the large red brick house in Mt. Hope Avenue, directly across from Linden Street.

Mr. Moore was a native of the Third Ward. He had been born in lower Plymouth Avenue South near Spring Street, and had moved into the big house in the Fourteenth Ward to accommodate his expanding family. He himself had been a student at No. 3, and all of his children attended that school, although, as residents of the Fourteenth, they should have been enrolled in No. 13.

This irregularity in the matter of a school district was an unstartling anomaly for a family whose individualism often caused its members to do many things that were at variance with the customs of their peers. The Moores lived on their acre and a half fief in Mt. Hope Avenue, with a staff of servants who appeared to be held in benevolent bondage. They seemed completely independent, and this and the expansiveness of their way of life gave them a sort of sovereignty, of which those of us who had access to their grounds, their house, and their entertainments were extremely sensible. As remarked in an earlier paragraph, the Moores constituted one of the most unusual domestic establishments in Rochester, and at this point it may not be improper to divert momentarily from the Third Ward to tell about this family of a Third Ward expatriate.

On the mantel in the billiard room stood a large photograph of the offspring of Mr. and Mrs. Moore. They made a perfect flight of stairs, beginning with the youngest, Dan, and ending with Chadwick (commonly called Harry), the oldest. Between these extremes were four other boys and four girls.

Jean, the youngest daughter, was the member of the family I knew best. She was a pretty, spirited girl, with light hair, who wore no hair switch, lipstick, rouge, furbelows, corset, and who played on the finest private tennis court in Rochester, which was the one built in the Moore back yard. If the fancy struck her, she played in her bare feet—and this, mind you, in an era of incredible decorum in Rochester, when a girl bathing barelegged off a public beach exposed herself to arrest.

Jean rode polo ponies with a handsome, beautifully dressed young man named Seth Brady, who later in southern horsy resorts played on scratch tours with some of the internationalists, and had a two- or three-goal rating. She rode astride, following a precedent established years before by her mother, the first woman in Rochester—outside of circus riders—to assume that position on a horse.

Mrs. Moore was a Chadwick, from nearby Fairport. She was a gently bred, small, strong-willed woman, extraordinarily independent, whose outward attitude toward her children was more practical than sentimental. She was close in their supervision, but not demonstrably affectionate. It would be difficult to be precious or doting with all ten. She wanted each child to develop into a well-rounded citizen, and went to considerable pains to attempt to achieve this end.

In an era when Rochester had a tight little social hierarchy, and people with new wealth were striving mightily to "get up" with the Joneses, the Moores, who "were up" with any family in town, paid almost no attention to what was narrowly described as "society." If they chose, they might move about in it at will, but they were indifferent to its conventions and very little interested in its functions.

If some of us, who lived modestly on Linden Street, and other youth who lived even more modestly on nearby Cypress and Sanford streets, were friends of some member of the Moore family, that was all that was necessary to admit us and them to the bounteous hospitality of the large brick house and to the variety of entertainment that was offered there. Nathan (Jack), second youngest son, had as a boon companion a boy who later became a telephone linesman; Gaius's alter ego was a young man known as "Old Man" Loveny, a machinist in a shop; I think it was at the Moore house that Thomas J. Hargrave, not long out of Harvard Law, met his future wife. Hargrave in time became board chairman of the Eastman Kodak Company. Big Bob, the Moore's gardener, a broth of an English lad, boxed and wrestled with the older boys, and one winter slept with one of them in a back-yard tent, since both were devoted to the same health cult. And so it went. Class distinctions were unknown at the Moores'. Everywhere there was evidence of wealth; never any mention of it.

The brick house, which is now the property of the University of Rochester, has three stories. When the Moores occupied it, the girls and the older members of the family were housed on the second floor, the boys on the third, and there was very little invasion by one group of the quarters of the other. The formal front entrance to the house, which youth never used, was approached over a long walk that led from the Mt. Hope Avenue sidewalk; young people, who came to visit or play with the Moore progeny, followed a winding cobblestone drive that led to a porte-cochere and a side door, and continued to a large barn, constructed of red brick to match the house. As the zoological tastes of the Moore children changed, the barn successively served as a menagerie for a semitame raccoon, guinea pigs, white mice, and rabbits. It was used also as a chicken house, an aviary for homing pigeons, a kennel for dogs, and a stable for riding horses. Bicycles, toboggans, a pony cart, a motorcycle, and the largest bobsled and the largest teeterboard I have ever seen were stored in the barn. Sometimes a canoe or a light skiff, which was used on the river that flowed less than two hundred yards behind the property, was held on racks against the wall. When the Moores acquired their first automobile, the carriage space on the main floor of the building became a garage.

One section of the upper floor of the barn was partitioned off as an infirmary. This was a wise precaution in a family as numerous as the Moores, where even minor infections could become major medical problems. If a boy or girl was taken ill, he or she was removed to the barn, and a nurse was put in attendance. The other, and main part of the second story, was used in inclement weather as a playhouse. Here, on a memorable occasion, I represented the hero in *Over the Quarry Brink*, a melodrama that we had seen played by a professional cast at the Baker Theater. In the entr'acte, Jack Moore, who fancied himself a trapeze artist, suffered a slight concussion when the rigging gave way and precipitated him head foremost to the unmatted stage. We picked him up and lugged him to a cot in the infirmary, and holding to the trouper's traditional discipline that the "show must go on," continued our performance, although our lines at times were overtoned by the off-stage moans of the sufferer.

A considerable staff kept the Moore house in operation. At the time, there were a number of large houses in Rochester that employed numerous servants, and a few that had a first and second butler. This was swank. The Moores had one butler, and no swank at all: There the service was functional rather than ornamental. The butler opened the front door for adult guests, youthful callers themselves opened the side door and called through the back hall, "Jack!" or "Jean!" or "Dan!," their halloos sometimes relayed by one of the upstair maids. There was a male cook in the large kitchen who wore a high white toque like a hotel chef; there was Mrs. Filer, an old, old fixture in the Moore house, a kindly woman of great tolerance who had some indefinable occupation in the basement; there was Big Bob, the gardener; in time, Ernest, the chauffeur; and for many years, Miss Buck, who lived as a member of the family.

Miss Buck was a slim, angular, genteel, quiet-voiced English woman who had been brought to Rochester from her native land by the elder Moores in one of their frequent trips abroad. I suppose she functioned in the triplex capacity of housekeeper, secre-

47

tary for Mrs. Moore, and chaperone for the girls. As time went on she became perhaps the most leaned-upon member of the household. Her word was law, and a law that wasn't to be trifled with. She played a bang-up game of tennis wearing a wide-brimmed, floppy hat and ankle-length skirts, and employing the twisting underhand service that was uniform with English women players until after the first invasion of the British Isles by the famous May Sutton.

*   *   *

Henry Moore was a tall, lean, long-faced man with a mane of white hair. He bore some resemblance to the beardless Abraham Lincoln, who told good stories and laughed at his own jokes, rather than the sad-eyed, tragedy-burdened leader popular with Lincoln's portraitists. He was an amiable and kindly man, with a warm sense of humor, who seemed to delight more in the company of his younger children and their friends than in adult society.

In a white linen suit, his laughing eyes shaded from the sun by a broad-brimmed Panama, Mr. Moore would sit for hours on a summer afternoon in the back yard of his home, watching and participating in, to the extent of calling out good-natured advice, a baseball game, a tennis match, a croquet tournament, or a Wild West show. He encouraged his family to confine their entertainments to their home, and to include their young friends in their sports and festivities. He was not present, however, at the Wild West show during which an ambushed "Indian" armed with a BB gun shot out one of Gaius Moore's eyes. From then on, Mr. Moore sternly barred guns from the premises.

Gaius recovered quickly. He wore the artificial eye that replaced his natural one with a kind of bravura. He seemed to feel that it gave him a distinction. If he were to engage in any bodily contact sport, he would pop out the glass eye and hand it with a high theatrical gesture to a friend; once he whimsically lent it to a youth who placed it on taw, as an agate to be shot at with marbles.

My first ride in an automobile was the time Jean and Nancy Moore invited me to sit with them in the tonneau, entered by opening a curious little rear door, of the family Rambler, which Ernest drove to the South Avenue corner of Linden Street and back. The only ride I ever had on a motorcycle was when Gaius, after elaborate instructions, allowed me to test his Indian for half a mile over the Mt. Hope Avenue pavement.

Jean had skis long before most young people in Rochester ever heard of these long, slim, glazed boards upon which—she said—the Swedes and Norwegians zinged down snow-covered hills at express train speed. She first practiced on them over the undulating terrain of nearby Mt. Hope Cemetery, sometimes sportily leaping over a snow-mounded grave, and once came a cropper on a headstone.

We nicknamed Gaius Moore "Cap," and we were fond of him. He was a hulking, good-natured youth who, unlike most of his brothers and sisters, was acutely acquisitive. He was proud of his possessions. He wanted them to be the biggest and the best, and he flaunted them.

Each summer, until he tired of the sport, Gaius won the annual kite flying contest sponsored by the Park Department at Genesee Valley Park. His three box kites stood higher than a tall man's head. They were secured by thin wire, rather than twine. They were so powerful in flight, that a huge reel, with teeth and a pawl, which was encased in a heavy iron frame that stood on the ground, was needed to fetch them to earth.

Gaius had a twelve-passenger bobsled, with a steel steering wheel. It was a wonder in our part of town, and I doubt if there was anything quite like it anywhere else in Rochester. One night in mid November, after a snowstorm that made the streets as fit for sleighing as they would be in the dead of winter, he had the big bob dragged to the top of Mt. Hope Avenue, and with a load of younger boys, including Charlie Maloy and me, made a couple of trial runs to glaze the course down the curving hill. He then replaced the younger passengers with older and heavier boys and girls, got a hearty shove to start the big contraption, and the bob went careering all the way to the Cypress Street corner, slowed after that, and inched on to a point opposite Clarissa Street, for what still must stand as a world record.

Eric (Pete) Moore, a prominent shellback at the Rochester Yacht Club, once owned the *Wenow*, a schooner-rigged yacht, and later acquired the *Genesee*, one-time defender of the Canada Cup. Hugh, poor fellow, was killed in a cane rush at Boston Tech, and Chadwick—Harry—left Rochester in early manhood for London, where he engaged in business and served, during the 1920s, as drama critic for the *Sunday Dispatch*, one of London's great newspapers. He died shortly after World War II in the Turf Club, in Cairo, where he was recuperating from shell shock suffered during the London blitz.

His only son, Beecher, has lived in London ever since he was six months old, except for a short period in an American preparatory school and two or three years at Harvard. He was born in Linden Street, where his parents took a house at the time of their marriage. He is an urbane, erudite man, with cosmopolitan tastes, who has inherited to a marked degree the Moore family's intrinsic sense of individualism. He lives in the Middle Temple, though not a lawyer. His interests are multifarious. He is reputedly one of the great small-boat sailors of Europe, and once won the world's sailing championship. He has been a theatrical producer, joint proprietor of one of London's distinguished restaurants; he manages an offshoot of the Moore family's printing business; he has dealt in perfumes, women's clothes, and manufactured small sailing boats. Although he rarely visits America, Beecher Moore has retained his American citizenship.

The Moore house was often the hospitable rendezvous of eight or ten youthful Sunday supper guests. The enormous dining-room table would be extended to its full length, and card tables would be requisitioned for the overflow. The menus were simple but hearty, and "seconds" were no problem, with the cook, in his white toque at the kitchen range, and a maid to assist him.

Occasionally during the winter months Mr. Moore would give a coasting party for his younger children and their friends from the neighborhood at the Oak Hill Country Club. The clubhouse was a low, sprawling farmhouse that stood close to the site on the River Campus, now occupied by the Administration Building of the University of Rochester. The Oak Hill was very young in those days. Mr. Moore was a charter member and the club's first treasurer. Incredible as it may seem to contemporary members, an article of the by-laws read:

No wines or liquors shall be sold or given away on the premises of the club.

On hand sleds and toboggans, we coursed down a great hill, called Gibraltar by the golfers. Later, blustering into the clubhouse from the cold outdoors, our appetites sharpened by the vigorous exercise, we would find mounds of delicious sandwiches and pitchers of hot chocolate set out on a refectory table in front of an open fire. The Oak Hill in time replaced the comfortable old farm-house with a modern building; and eventually moved from its original location to a much more elaborate establishment in Pittsford, and the character of the club changed with its physical expansion. The great hill on which we coasted is scarcely discernible today. It was diminished by earth movers to an insipid knoll at the time the university took over the property.

The Moores' Oak Hill coasting parties were casual affairs; their swimming classes were ritualistic.

The latter were the province of Mrs. Moore, and she organized them with efficiency and managed them with command. There was very little nonsense about Mrs. Moore. She was not given to trivialities or small talk, and what softness there was in her character seemed reserved for her idol, her true love, her husband, Henry.

She was determined that her children and the friends of her children should learn to swim, and for two mornings a week for a couple of summers the downtown newsboys were chased out of Dockstader's baths, on the west side of North Water Street, not far from the Main Street corner, while the Moore party took over.

Dockstader's swimming pool, or plunge, as it was known, was a square basin filled with cocoa-colored water pumped up from the river. Each of its four sides was overhung by a wooden ledge, upon which the instructor Dockstader walked with a pole that resembled a rod a deep sea fisherman might use in taking a thousand-pound tiger shark from the South Atlantic. A stout rope, with a wide canvas band, which was fitted around the upper body of the student of natation, extended from the pole.

There were two rows of wooden lockers, with doors that would not lock. The roof leaked. The two or three windows were high, narrow, and unwashed. The place had a gloomy and sinister air, and was pervaded by a dreadful stench that emanated from a sulphur spring on the premises. The sulphur spring was the establishment's *raison d'être;* the plunge merely an adjunct. Sufferers from arthritis and similar disorders who were not sufficiently affluent to try the fashionable waters of such spas as Vichy or Saratoga or Carlsbad, tottered into North Water Street for treatments Dockstader administered in a recess of the resort we youngsters never saw.

The plunge was rarely used by adults. Its chief patrons were newsboys, whose number was substantial in an era when Rochester

51

had five competing newspapers. These youthful hawkers would pop in off the streets, shuck their tatterdemalion garments in one motion, and plunge in the altogether into the cooling waters. They had not been instructed on the end of Dockstader's rope; they were self-taught. And they were probably the most expert swimmers in town at a time when no one knew anything about the crawl or the butterfly, and the single overarm was considered the stroke of champions.

I attended the Moore swimming classes, as did Charlie Maloy. Charlie liked them fine; I hated the instruction. Dockstader was a stolid man, who moved slowly up and down one of the overhanging ledges of the swimming pool, a cold cigar in the corner of his mouth, a sputtering youth in the canvas harness at the end of his pole. "Stroke, stroke, stroke," he'd say. "Kick, kick, kick." He must have taught scores of boys to swim and the four or five girls in the Moore party, but those were the extent of his instructions. We did not know whether he himself could swim, and no one I knew had ever seen him in the water. I went to the classes reluctantly, and once only after my father had given me a paddling. I was healthy enough and physically active, but I had all sorts of phobias and a difficult temperament. In youth, I was virtually a vegetarian, and my father attributed what he said was my weakness of character to my dislike of meat.

After a time I learned to swim, and from then on the stench from the sulphur spring that had been poignantly related to my dislike and even dread of Dockstader's no longer seemed as offensive as before, and I delighted in paddling about the murky waters of the dreary little natatorium, in dropping from Roman rings that swung out over the pool, and in making crude dives from the overhanging ledges. At noon, when we left Dockstader's and news-boys started flocking into the pool, sometimes in their impatience stripping their clothing at the entrance, Mrs. Moore would take our party to Whittle's candy store at the corner of Main and North Water streets for ice cream sodas. Whittle's was the fashionable confectionary; it was the only store in town that charged ten cents for an ice cream soda. Its delicious candies and ice cream were made on the premises. It outclassed all local competition, and the attempts of such syndicates as Huyler's and Page & Shaw's to lure away its trade were abortive. After a long stand at Main and North Water, Thomas A. Whittle rented larger floor space in the building owned by Thomas W. Finucane, at Main Street East and East Avenue. In this new location, the fame of Whittle's as a confectionary continued and the establishment gained added celebrity as the place of employment of two lively and attractive young women widely known as the Candy Kids, one of whom later became the friend of a Vanderbilt.

As they grew older, the tastes in entertainment of the Moore children became more sophisticated. They gave box parties at the old Lyceum Theater. Their entrance always created a little flurry of which they may not have been entirely insensible. People in Rochester knew one another in those days, and the Lyceum patronage had rather a familial character. "There are the Moores," people would say, turning in orchestra chairs, or peering over the railing of the balcony as the small party, usually headed by the brilliantly attired Jean, who seemed to skip rather than walk, proceeded along a side aisle to the box.

From the Moores' box, I saw Miss Maude Adams, that lovely, haunting sprite of a woman, fragile as a Tanagra figurine, play *Peter Pan*, and I still recall the ineffable grace of her movements. I also saw two or three musical comedies. In one of these, featuring the comedian Richard Carle, the chorus line danced barelegged, and the shocked Mr. Moore expressed regret that he had exposed his daughters and their youthful friends to this unchaste spectacle.

Mr. Moore died before he reached the age of sixty, and the spirit of his wife appeared to die with him. Her eminent practicality was no defense against death, and her grief was cataclysmic. She lived several years after the passing of Henry Moore, but as a broken woman whose emotional suffering was aggravated by a slow physical deterioration. For several years she was conspicuous as a tiny, shrunken figure in black who rode through the streets of Rochester and the adjacent countryside in the rear seat of a chauffeur-driven limousine at all hours of the day and night seeking solace from her suffering in locomotion.

Several of the Moore children had left the large red brick house at 575 Mt. Hope Avenue before the death of the matriarch who had governed it, and others departed soon thereafter. They became widely dispersed: Chadwick, in London; Lois, in Paris; Jack, on the eastern shore of Maryland; Jean, to marry a Norwegian Quaker and live out the remainder of her life in Stavanger; Dan, in New Mexico; Nancy, wife of a Midwest college professor; Ruth, in

53

New Jersey, married to the president of the Vacuum Oil Company (now Mobil). Only Gaius and Eric remained in Rochester to manage the John C. Moore Corporation, manufacturers of Moore's Modern Methods. Now they are gone, and only two of the Moore children, Nancy and Ruth, survive.

Stark and empty, a mockery of the busy vital hive it once had been, the old house for a time flaunted a "For Sale" sign in its weedy front yard. In time a man down Linden Street picked it up for how much of a song I do not know, and converted it into a tourist home. It survived, if it did not flourish. The tourist host died, and the house was again for sale. Clean, neat, functional, its lawns well mowed, it is now the property of the University of Rochester and so devoid of its former character that it fails to excite even a twinge of nostalgia as I occasionally pass it on my way downtown.

The Landmark Society, dedicated to the preservation of noble and historical old residences, had no interest in the Moore house; it lacked architectural distinction and historical significance. It was merely the home of a large and extraordinary family, who lived bounteously, fully, deeply—clean up to the hilt; indeed, in a manner that probably has never been imitated in the city of Rochester.

Chapter 4

Perhaps because it is the only educational institution ever to reward me with a diploma, I retained for a long time after I left No. 3 in Tremont Street an odd sense of attachment for the school. I was there only two years, but during that time I had a feeling of affection for the teachers who instructed me in the two grades in which I was successively enrolled, the seventh and eighth.

No. 3 was considered one of the two or three top elementary schools in Rochester. It had the tradition, which it prized, of having taught the children and the grandchildren of the city's founding fathers; it was noted for its academic excellence, for the manners of its student body, and for its principal, James S. Cook. Mr. Cook was a rather historic figure. He had been appointed principal shortly before the close of the Civil War and he was still in that office when I left No. 3 in 1904.

I particularly enjoyed the seventh grade. This was taught by Miss Mary Blair, whose enthusiasm—or pedagogic genius—often made it possible for her to transfigure a classroom filled with a heterogenous company of youth into a place of exciting romance. Miss Blair had had a summer in Europe, where she had visited a number of the shrines of culture, including Stratford-on-Avon, and the date of the great bard's birth was as luminously fixed in her memory as the date of the signing of the Declaration of Independence.

Shakespeare was not part of the seventh-grade curriculum, but Miss Blair managed to interpolate into her classroom program not a study of Shakespeare, with tedious concern for the nuances of his meaning or the definition of his odd words, but a living representation of the plays themselves. We did bits from *A Midsummer Night's Dream*, from *The Merchant of Venice*, and on several historic occasions, readings from *Julius Caesar;* and once I was allowed to render, with what histrionic gestures I was able to evoke, Brutus' sonorous third act apologia: ". . . Romans, countrymen, and lovers!"—and briefly I betrayed my Promethean goal, and wondered if my role in life was not to be an actor on the stage.

Charlie Maloy alone knew of the shining grail to which I was sure my life was consecrated. Each school day we walked together from Linden Street to Mt. Hope Avenue, across Clarissa Street bridge, and along Greig Street to the circle at Plymouth Park. There Charlie entered the Immaculate Conception School and I continued half a block to No. 3.

Charlie knew of W. G. George. I had talked to him tiresomely about the great English professional foot racer ever since I had read in a book in my father's library a tribute to George's "marvelous mile time of 4:12¾ seconds [Lillie Bridge, London, August 23, 1886]—the finest performance witnessed in the authentic annals of athleticism, irrespective of distance or class of contest; in fact," the author continued with impressive rhetoric, "a performance besides which the picked feats of cycling, swimming, and all other sports pale their ineffectual fires."

It was a world record, of course; it stood for twenty-nine years, then to be beaten only three-twentieth of a second. My own total engrossment, which included daily petitions to God, was a mile one-tenth of a second under four-ten, a performance that actually was not achieved until forty-five years after George's great run at Lillie Bridge. Often, in extravagant fancy, it seemed to me that if the watches clicked in that time, and I expired a yard beyond the finish line, my life would have been fulfilled, and death unbitter.

I recall with the deepest longing afternoons when I ran long miles over the roads of the nearby countryside accompanied by Charlie on a bicycle. Those were the days of castles in the air, and the conviction, on my part, that the world—or the only part of it in which I was deeply interested—might be rolled up, like a short rug in the front hall of our home, and carried lightly off under my arm.

The autumn was the special time of these delights because Charlie could not continue to accompany me when the winter snows denied traction to the wheels of his bike, and I would struggle on alone, through slush, and winter rains, and blizzards, and footing that was sometimes knee-deep in snow, blindly obedient to the general notion that the mile record would come to an American only if he were able, as were English athletes, to run all the year round.

In the days before the motor car—the "horseless carriage," as I remember its first being called—the soft dirt roads on the country-side south of Rochester were sparsely traveled. We had various routes, Charlie and I, one of which took us through Genesee Valley Park, where I would leave the cyclist to course over the undulating meadowlands and rejoin him on the road at the north-ern entrance to the park. On Friday, we made a point to approach the city line over the West Henrietta Road, now a wide intensely busy highway, flanked on either side by car hops, tawdry night spots, gas stations, shops of brummagem display, used car lots; then it was a pleasant, quiet, tree-shaded artery leading into the city.

Charlie's loyalty was a deep and abiding thing, which continued unabatedly throughout his long life. It was this rather than any lively sympathy for or interest in my fetish that caused him to continue for several years to ride the bicycle at my side during our long silent peregrinations over the countryside.

I might say to him, as we walked to school after a particularly good spin the day before, "I'll get it! I'll get that old mile record if it takes ten years! Or fifteen! Or until I'm thirty! That's how old W. G. George was when he did four twelve and three quarters."

"Yeah, but what's it going to get you?" Charlie would say. "Just running four times around a track, in four minutes and nine seconds. Heck, what's that?"

It was a shockingly incredulous inquiry. A profanation!

"What'll it *get* me? *Why—*"

"What did W. G. George get? Maybe five hundred dollars? A thousand? You don't know."

It was difficult to make Charlie understand what imperishable renown would accrue to a four-nine miler, and it was only on Friday afternoons that he displayed more than an apathetic interest in all this running. On Friday we would almost certainly come upon a hunched old fellow in a light spring buggy, drawn by a lively bay mare, who would be returning to town on the West Henrietta Road after a week buying cattle in the country.

Out of the corner of his eye, he'd catch sight of Charlie on the bike and me on foot, his hunched shoulders would straighten, and he'd jerk the mare into action. "Huh! Huh! Huh!" he'd cry, and elbows flared out, driving like Pop Geers on the Grand Circuit, he'd hold the mare at a sharp trot, and we'd press on for a mile or so, the old fellow inching to a slight lead, to tease us, to pull us out, but deliberately never going clean away. We'd usually go on to the city line, where the cattle buyer turned east. He'd pull up at the corner and wave, and shout, "Keep it up, kid, and you'll be champeen of the world, sure!"

At that moment, inspirited by our little hippodrome, Charlie half believed what the old fellow said; to me his words merely confirmed a prefixed destiny.

* * *

I recall only one Negro pupil in No. 3 while I was there, although there were probably a handful in the lower grades. She was a forlorn little girl, in the eighth grade, which was taught by Miss Nellie Echtenacher, a fixture in the school for forty years, first as teacher, then succeeding Mr. Cook as principal. Today No. 3 is limited to a kindergarten, and a first, second, and third grade, and the youthful student body is 99 per cent black.

Miss Echtenacher was a grave, quiet, kindly woman, who was particularly solicitous of the Negro girl, whose name I believe was Minnie. She tried tactfully to bring Minnie into some sort of fellowship with the other students, but she well knew that the conventions were opposed to this and her efforts were hardly successful. It was accepted dogma that Minnie was not acceptable.

She was not treated badly by the other boys and girls; merely ignored. They spoke to her pleasantly enough, for they were generally well behaved, and I never heard her disparaged because of her color except by a tough little hombre named Frankie something or other. Minnie and I had been sent to the blackboard to work out an arithmetic problem, and at recess Frankie accosted me. "Hey, *you* and that *nigger* girl!" he snickered. "Niggers oughta go to a school they got for themselves, not go where we go."

I am sure that Frankie's segregationist attitude was shared by Minnie. She could not have been happy at No. 3, where she was as completely outside the spirit of our white microcosm as if she had been relegated to a room in the schoolhouse occupied by no one but herself. At that time, there was still a good deal of wealth in the Third Ward that had not been lured across the river, "out East Avenue way"; and Minnie was the issue of one of a few quiet, hat-tipping Negro families who lived in a small settlement on the western edge of the ward and maintained themselves by serving "the gentry" as housemaids, coachmen, butlers, and handymen.

The Ruffled Shirt Ward had been tick-tocking along for many years with the assurance that it was the most exclusive and inviolate precinct in the city of Rochester. It was keenly aware of its tradition and convinced that its prestige would be preserved untarnished for a remote posterity. Those who had lived there for a long time and were deeply informed with the spirit of the ward were made myopic by their loyalty. They failed to see the unmistakable signs of dry rot that were beginning to show not long after the opening of the new century. In their zealous faith in their beloved domain they could not conceive that in the not too remote future it would display the sad and dingy image of gentility in reduced circumstances, becoming long before the middle of the century a community of pinchbeck lodging and rooming houses, and presently, shockingly, metamorphosed into a Negro ghetto.

Snug, tidy, and clannish at its core, the Third Ward was so efficient at regulating its internal affairs that it was able to prevent the installation of trolley car service in Clarissa Street, the clangor of which might disturb occupants of the Kimball mansion at the Troup Street corner of that thoroughfare. The ward was theoretically protected from intrusion by the moatlike ditch of the Erie Canal and in times past had connived at, or chose to ignore, conditions on sections of its perimeter that were physically putrid and morally gangrenous.

Even at the period of its history when the ward was at the peak of its aristocratic glory, it tolerated scarcely a stone's throw from its sequestered, tree-shaded streets with their carefully kept houses and handsome gardens, a rank of foul doggeries on Exchange Street that was not inappropriately known as Murderers' Row.

This sinkhole of human depravity that trafficked in liquor, prostitution, dope, thievery, and occasionally murder continued as a malignant tumor on the eastern boundary of the Third Ward for years. The clergy inveighed against it from the pulpit. Societies for "sacred purity" passed resolutions demanding its abolishment. The police sporadically raided it, and the health department, oddly inept in the 1870s and '80s, complained about the deplorable condition of sewer traps and lateral drains, and appeared to do nothing about these, or the venereal disease that abounded among the habitués of Murderers' Row.

And it was not the Third Warders themselves who finally brought about the razing of these noisome and wicked resorts, but businessmen in lower Exchange Street, and their motive was one of dollars and cents rather than moral indignation. Their business places were being harmed by their proximity to Murderers' Row.

I learned about the Third Ward during my two years at No. 3 from the only male pupil in the school I am able to recall with the exception of Frankie, the youthful segregationist. The boy who instructed me in some of the ward's history, and inadvertently provoked me to make further inquiries on my own, was Louis Decker.

Louis was a native Third Warder, whose ancestry went straight back to the early Hudson River Dutch. His father was a prominent lawyer, and a member of a coterie of intellectual politicians who were known as Silk Stocking Democrats. Louis was an unusually articulate youth. To my adolescent fancy he seemed to have universal knowledge, his self-confidence was supreme, and for a long time—indeed, until our eighth-grade acquaintanceship blossomed into an adult friendship that continued until his death—I was not a little awed by him.

It was Louis who first informed me about the Fox Sisters, Lewis Henry Morgan, and Matilda Dean, all of whom had once resided in the Third Ward. Morgan and Madame Dean were hardly personages to stimulate inquiries by eighth graders, and I doubt if Louis had ever heard of them at the time we were pupils of Miss Echtenacher. It was later, when he was a student at Exeter Academy and I was enrolled in Phillips Andover that he enthusiastically pronounced Morgan the "greatest man Rochester had ever produced," which may have been a ratification of his father's judgment, and Matilda Dean a "magnificent whore—a virtual Madame Pompadour."

While we were at No. 3, Louis excited my youthful imagination with vivid descriptions of the spiritual manifestations of the Fox Sisters, and once took me to a house that he professed was the one they had occupied when they came to town from their Wayne County home to stay with their older sister and demonstrate the famed "Rochester Rappings" that gave impetus to modern spiritualism.

I doubt if his identification of the house was correct, since even local antiquarians were in dispute about its exact location. On this point, however, Louis was emphatic. Once he launched out on a subject, he gave the impression of having imperial command of it. He was a remarkable raconteur. If a story was good enough he told it with flourishes and drumbeats and all sorts of imagery, and he never cravenly submitted to the tyranny of facts.

The genius of the Fox Sisters has long been an issue of contention. Some have proclaimed it a divine afflatus; others have ascribed it to their ability to make sharp rataplans by manipulating the bones of their great toes. The sensation they caused in their first public appearance in Rochester rolled out like a ground swell far beyond the boundaries of the bustling little city that straddled the Genesee and brought to the two pretty half-ignorant country girls an international celebrity that continued for a surprisingly long period of time.

Shortly before the middle of the last century, John Fox, a blacksmith, who had come from his native Canada to the United States, moved his wife and two of his daughters, Margaret, an early teenager, and Catherine, twelve, into a small house in the hamlet of Hydesville, not far from Newark, New York.

The family's new abode had a local reputation of being haunted. John Fox, a solid, literal-minded man, devoted to the Methodist Church, gave no credit to this. He passed off the portentous tongue-wagging of his neighbors as a silly superstition, until one night in the early spring of 1848 the family was aroused by sharp raps that came from the walls and by odd scraping sounds behind them that were unlike the pattering feet or gnawing teeth of rodents.

The mysterious noises continued. If her parents were alarmed by them, Cathie, a lively, impish, unafraid child, found them entertaining. "Hey, Mr. Splitfoot," she called out challengingly, one night "do as I do," and when she snapped her fingers three times, the challenge was met by three decisive raps.

If the specter could count, Mrs. Fox seemed to feel that he might do well on the circuit. She had Cathie and Margaret (because the older of the pair quickly displayed a talent for spiritual communication similar to her sister's) hold a seance for rural neighbors during which questions that might be answered by a count of raps were submitted by the girls. What was the price of butter by the crock? Give the age of the oldest member of the audience. How much for a dozen eggs?

The spook was letter perfect. After this, Mrs. Fox sent Cathie and Margaret thirty miles to Rochester, where they were put in charge of Leah, their older, widowed, music-teaching sister. She learned quickly about promotion. After Margaret and Cathie had played to several overflow audiences in Leah's home, the manager moved them to the recently built Corinthian Hall where hundreds of persons turned out to be awed by the "fair young priestesses of mystery," or to sneer at and denigrate them as charlatans, or to prosecute serious scientific investigations into the causes for the rappings and other poltergeist manifestations which the girls were able to evoke.

Although reports of the "Rochester Rappings" were exciting curiosity in many parts of the country, Margaret and Cathie Fox continued for some time to confine their public performances to Rochester and its environs. Their audiences were usually divided into two factions, those who apotheosized them as spiritual mediums and those who assailed them as frauds. Once they were forced to flee the Corinthian stage when a group of front-row thugs attempted to mob them. Their repertoire expanded as they became more skilled in occult arts, and Cathie developed a knack for mirror writing, the corpus of which has been published as the *Fox-Taylor Record*. When they left Rochester to tour the land for gold and glory, they won the attention of many notable persons and for a time enjoyed the sponsorship of Horace Greeley, who, concerned about the sisters' lack of education, was responsible for Cathie's enrollment in a New York private school.

Governors, judges, and other men high in public life; the poet William Cullen Bryant, the novelist James Fenimore Cooper, the geologist Louis Agassiz, and Jenny Lind the Swedish Nightingale were included in audiences that turned out for the Fox Sisters. Margaret, still in her teens, was courted by Dr. Elisha K. Kane, the noted Arctic explorer. He professed his love, and pleaded that she withdraw from practices that he himself seemed to believe were humbug. After Kane died in Cuba from an illness contracted during one of his explorations, Margaret avowed that she had become his child bride in a common-law marriage. Her attempt to claim a widow's share of the Kane estate got her little more than heartache and calumny.

The sisters crossed the Atlantic to repeat in England the successes they had achieved in the United States. They played to packed auditoriums, and for a time were the pets of London drawing rooms. Cathie, who had a bent for high life, married an English barrister, and acquired—as did Margaret, to a lesser degree—an addiction to brandy. When they finally returned to the United States, the older of the two, in a rash of conscience (or for much needed gold) agreed to "tell all" in a large hall in New York. The curious filled the place on the night of the lecture. Margaret confessed that she and Cathie had made the mysterious rappings that had baffled two worlds by cracking the bones of their great toes. Cathie concurred. Later, both women appeared to realize their mistake, and they attempted to recant, but it was too late to have an effect one way or another. The original doubting Thomases had nothing to say but "I told you so"; the believers, fervid in their faith, had given little heed to the exposé. The latter now numbered thousands upon thousands in this country and in England. Margaret and Cathie, after probably the most sustained careers in the history of mediumship, faded from public view and died in relative obscurity. In the end, they were dealing more with spirits that came out of bottles than the communicable ones in the ambient air.

* * *

What Louis Decker told me about Matilda ("Till" or "Tilly") Dean, was more romance than biography. His exact information about the notorious woman, who was probably Rochester's best-known madam, was limited. Louis was a religious skeptic and something of an amoralist, and while his prurient itchings may have been no more irritating than those of other youths of his age, he was much more sophisticated than many of us, and some of us were shocked by his sexual unabashedness.

His talk was never the cloacal gabble of privies. Louis was the issue of cultivated parents, and he did not betray his heritage. He was extraordinarily gifted with words. He had an insatiable curiosity. He eked out his limited dossier on Madame Dean with the colorful embroideries of his fancy, and he spoke of her as a living, breathing personage, although she must have died approximately at the time he was born. Because he made her a romantic and seductive figure my imagination was stirred by his talk, and the name Tilly Dean became fixed in my memory. Years later, when I served the *Democrat and Chronicle* as a police reporter, I heard of her again from veteran members of the Detective Bureau, who spoke of her with respect and sometimes with affection, and I learned more about her from Ernest R. Willard.

Her last place of entertainment was on Exchange Street, but beyond the scurf and feculence of Murderers' Row. The police had shifted in and out of Tilly Dean's place like a reprise in a sonata, but their hearts apparently were never in their raids. They, and the city itself, seemed to concur with the apothegm of the brilliant Montesquieu, "Virtue has needs of limits." The hospitality of her domicile was noted from New York to Chicago, and the ladies under her roof had charms that sometimes brought admirers with trunks, who moved in for a week or two, using the Exchange Street House of Joy as their home away from home.

Once a jealous admirer of Madame Dean attempted to cut her with a razor. She notified the police. The would-be assailant was arrested and brought to trial. When Tilly appeared against him, the judge packed him off to Auburn Prison for five years. The court found no reason to remark the traffic in which the complaining witness was engaged: between the law and Madame Dean there seemed to be a tacit sympathy and understanding.

Another time, a handsome young man moved in with a Gladstone bag filled with fancy clothes, and after passing several nights in Miss Mollie Mansfield's company, departed with her jewels, valued at several hundred dollars. The chatelaine of the menage was outraged. She was as solicitous of the tender buds in her charge as the headmistress of a young ladies finishing school. She was determined to make an example of the caitiff who had violated the hospitality of her house and gulled one of its lovely inhabitants, and publicly announced a $100 reward for the arrest and conviction of the thief.

Matilda Dean was baptized Julie Mary Simpson. She was the daughter of a Presbyterian clergyman, who preached in Savona, in Steuben County. She professed to have become the mistress of a government official in Rochester after being deflowered and abandoned by a Rochester businessman. After the government official, she went out on her own. She had flourished in two or three other resorts before she quitted the house on upper Exchange Street with $50,000 "gained," as the newspapers later reported, "in her nefarious profession."

Much of this was told to me by Mr. Willard, who before my time on the newspaper, had been editor of the *Democrat and Chronicle*. He was a man of charm, erudition, and urbanity. Early in the century he had married the widow of Hobart Hubbell Perkins, granddaughter of Hiram Sibley, organizer of the Western Union Telegraph Company. Mrs. (Perkins) Willard, was one of the great ladies of the town, as Mr. Willard was one of the town's true gentlemen.

The Willards lived in the house at East Avenue and Sibley Place that had been the home of Mrs. Willard since childhood, and that had been willed to her at the death of her father, Hobart F. Atkinson. It was known then, and is still known—since, happily, it has been preserved as a museum by the Rochester Historical Society—as Woodside because of its settings in a stand of noble trees from the original forest.

During the full century that it served as a private dwelling, Woodside helped to ornament an avenue that was often spoken of as one of the most attractive residential streets east of the Atlantic seaboard. The house was built for Silas O. Smith, an early Rochester merchant and industrialist, in the late 1830s by a master builder whom Smith had imported from his native New England. It passed in time into the hands of the original Hiram Sibley, who gave it to his son-in-law, Hobart Atkinson.

Almost square in design, this distinguished block-mass Greek revival mansion represented, certainly under the ownership of Mr. Atkinson's daughter and her life there with her first and her second husband, the epitome of Rochester culture and good taste.

I knew Mr. and Mrs. Willard by reputation and by sight. They were the wealthy communicants of the back-street parish of St. Andrew's Protestant Episcopal Church, whose rector was the Reverend Algernon Sidney Crapsey. I was confirmed in St. Andrew's, and occasionally attended church services with my mother, who was sensible of social distinctions and once pointed out, with considerable deference, "The Willards—those rich people from over on East Avenue."

Later, I heard a good deal about Mr. Willard's devotion to the Rochester Chapter of the American Red Cross, of which he was chairman for many years, and about Mrs. Willard's quiet philanthropies; but I never met either husband or wife until one day, several months before her husband's death, Mrs. Willard telephoned me at the *Democrat and Chronicle.*

"My husband isn't well," she said. "He doesn't leave the house. You know he was a newspaperman?"

I told her that I knew that he had retired from active editorship of the *Democrat and Chronicle* shortly before I started to work there in 1910.

"He reads your column 'Seen and Heard,'" Mrs. Willard said. "He'd like to talk to you. Could you come here tonight?"

I agreed to do so. It was a February night, and Rochester was in the throes of a blizzard that had come in off of Lake Ontario. The hard-flung snow opaqued the street lamps and the great trees behind the East Avenue curb creaked like the masts of a schooner in a storm-tossed sea. The thermometer stood only a few degrees above zero. There was a bull-whip snap and crackle to the gale as I bent into it on my way to the Willard house. I mounted the stone steps to the Doric-columned front porch. A maid opened the door at my ring, and quickly closed it after I crossed the threshold. Mrs. Willard greeted me at once.

The contrast between the rigorous arctic night of the streets, and the warmth, the soft lights, the quiet elegance and the harmony of this delightful home excited an almost emotional reaction. It was a polar transmigration.

My central impression of the interior of the house, as I stood in the main hall, was the spiraling grace of the stairway which, I was told, ascended to the third floor and continued on to a cupola that rested on a balustraded deck above the roof. The stairway immediately gave the house a sense of amplitude. I had a feeling that it was designed in such a way that a guest in it might enjoy hospitality that would permit him, if he chose, to retire to some remote and quiet recess. That in this retreat he would not be enjoined to come and take a hand at bridge, or participate in twenty questions, or charades, or pin the tail on a donkey; that at Woodside a discriminatory host would consider that the tastes and inclinations of those under his roof were sovereign.

I was taken to a room where the sheer whiteness of the walls contrasted dramatically with the dark oil paintings, the dark wood of the furniture, and the black marble fireplace. Applewood logs burned merrily on brass andirons. Mr. Willard sat in a large chair a little to the side of the fire. He half rose to take my hand; then subsided into the chair. He looked wan and frail. Our conversation was tentative, as we groped for a subject of mutual interest. We found it quickly: the newspaper business.

We talked about modern techniques and the changes that had taken place since Mr. Willard's time. He seemed stimulated by the discussion. He had become alert, his eyes brightened, and his voice was firm and decisive. He launched off on a recital of newspaper experiences that dated back well into the last century, when he had first come to Rochester from his native Jamestown, New York, to work as a reporter for the *Democrat and Chronicle*. I was fascinated. At the time of my visit with Mr. Willard the Rochester police were prosecuting one of their periodic vice crusades and the newspapers were printing voluminous accounts of it. We mentioned this. Mr. Willard asked, "Ever hear of Matilda Dean?"

"Yes," I said. "A friend of mine, who lived in the Third Ward, often told me about her. He was my age. Of course, he never knew her. I knew old-time policemen who did know her. They seemed to like her."

"A great many people liked her," Mr. Willard said. "She was quite a—I shouldn't say lady. Quite a character."

He told me that she had left Rochester for Chicago after the police had made, instead of a token raid, a foray against her house that resulted in her being hauled into court and fined; and from old newspaper files I later learned that her departure had been some time in 1884.

In Chicago, Madame Dean opened an elaborate resort known as the Palace of Mirrors, which antedated by several years the dedication of the even more elaborate Everleigh Club of that city, which became, under the sponsorship of Eve and Minna Everleigh, "the most famous brothel in the world," according to one enthusiastic annalist.

When she left Rochester, Matilda took with her James Bliss, a retired army officer, and a woman named Cora who had been her housekeeper in Rochester and continued to function in that capacity in the Palace of Mirrors. After half a dozen years in Chicago, her popularity waned, her wealth vanished, and her health failed. She died in December 1892, and her body was returned to Rochester. In a lengthy obituary headed NOTORIOUS WOMAN DIES, the *Democrat and Chronicle* told of Matilda Dean's "flagrant and prosperous" career as mistress of several "houses of ill-repute," and reported that "her remains were accompanied by a woman in black whose name could not be learned and who left immediately after the ceremony at the (Mt. Hope) Cemetery."

Sitting this blizzardy February night at the side of his warm fire, in the handsomely appointed room in which I had joined him, Mr. Willard told of Matilda Dean's return to Rochester.

"It was Cora, her faithful housekeeper—faithful in life, faithful in death—who brought her body back," he said. "She was the only mourner. She sat alone in the single hack that followed the hearse to the cemetery. I was out of town, and wasn't aware of Matilda's death until I returned. But d'you know, Mr. Clune, if I had known what was to happen, I'd have climbed into that single hack beside Cora." He turned in his chair, and his eyes glinted angrily. He shook an emphatic forefinger. "That funeral was a disgrace. A shameful neglect on the part of Rochester men—an indictment of their manhood. Why, if the men who had delighted in Matilda's entertainment had followed the hearse, the cortege would have reached from the Four Corners to the first gate of Mt. Hope."

A few days after Matilda's burial, a woman named Angeline M. Sargent defended the "notorious woman" of the *Democrat and Chronicle*'s obituary in a letter to that newspaper that read, in part:

"Not many years ago, in a prominent church in this city, where noble and philanthropic women were gathered to discuss methods of reforming the 'fallen women' . . . a closely veiled woman arose after the discussion had continued for some time and said,

" 'Ladies, if you will devise some method for reforming the men, I will be with you. I am the daughter of a clergyman, and was led from the path of rectitude by one of the wealthy businessmen in this city.' That was Matilda Dean, who wouldn't allow an innocent girl to remain a single night under her roof," the letter writer concluded. "A notorious woman indeed!"

At the conclusion of our discussion of Matilda Dean, Mr. Willard reflectively quoted a line spoken by the title figure in Shaw's *Mrs. Warren's Profession*, " 'the only way for a woman to provide for herself decently is for her to be good to some man that can afford to be good to her.'

"I suppose Matilda acquired a good deal of Mrs. Warren's cynicism. And like Mrs. Warren," Mr. Willard continued with a wry smile, "she was good to a great many men—the concourse of hypocrites I mentioned, who should have been mourners at her funeral."

The morning after my visit at Woodside I had a telephone call from Mrs. Willard. "Until last night, Ernest hadn't been up after nine o'clock in months," she said. "Last night he was up until after midnight. He told me he had the best time he had had in a year. I thank you."

Mr. Willard died in 1937 and his wife's death occurred three years later. I never saw either of them after the evening I spent with Mr. Willard, but at the time of the birth of our youngest son, my wife received a beautiful and complete layette at the hospital, the gift of Mrs. Willard and her friend Mrs. Algernon Sidney Crapsey, widow of the rector of St. Andrew's Church, who had been defrocked as a heretic.

I do not recollect the message, if any, that was written on the card attached to the gift; I only remember a brief note Mrs. Willard wrote separately to me, "A slight remembrance in appreciation of your kindness to my husband."

The Willards had outlived the Edwardian age to which they rightfully belonged. Their gentility was almost an anachronism even in the third decade of the present century. They had no conscious sense of superiority or a feeling that because of inherited wealth or ancestral descent they enjoyed moral or social superiority. They were kindly people. They had a deep sense of humanity and justice, and they had gracious manners, which faciliate human relations despite the disesteem this rude and chaotic age displays toward the old-fashioned symbols of "lady and gentleman."

Chapter 5

"Lewis Henry Morgan," Louis Decker told me, chortling, his lips drawn away from his large and prominent teeth, "refused to kiss the hand of the Pope."

It was the first thing he told me about Morgan, and because Louis delighted in seeing authority flouted, he put undeserved emphasis on a trivial incident in the biography of a man who achieved international renown during his life in Rochester. Morgan may not have been, as Decker subsequently proclaimed, the "greatest man Rochester ever produced," but he definitely belongs in the city's parthenon of notables. A scholar of distinction, he was also a very practical businessman, and a politician who was not always above expediency. The paradoxes in his career make its study a lively pursuit.

Although Morgan seemed generally a gentle and tolerant man, he had inflexible prejudices. One of his biographers related that his temper could be aroused by a loss at backgammon or by mention of the Roman Catholic Church. He came to Rochester as a young lawyer in 1844, settled in the Third Ward, and continued to live there for the rest of his life. In mid-life, after his scientific writings had brought him fame, and fortune had rewarded his business acumen, he made the Grand European Tour. In England, he lunched at the home of Charles Darwin and visited other distinguished men with whom he had been in correspondence on the subjects of ethnology and anthropology. In Rome, he had an audience with Pope Pius IX.

When the Pope extended his hand to be kissed, Morgan rejected the traditional gesture. "Your honor," he explained, perhaps with a little swank, "in our country we do not kiss a distinguished man's hand, we shake it."

Pius graciously concurred. "We will follow the American custom," he said, and the two men shook hands.

As a youth in his native Aurora, New York, Morgan developed

a romantic interest in the American Indian. This interest continued during his undergraduate days at Union College, where he organized a secret society designed as a tribal cabal, and it expanded, when he moved to Rochester, into a profound scientific investigation of the New World aborigines.

His sentimental and romantic interest in the Indians continued even as he made them the object of scientific examination and analysis. He knew the chiefs, and he knew the Indians who were not chiefs. He was sympathetic toward them. He was outraged at the manner in which they had been exploited by predatory whites, and more than once he employed his legal skill in an attempt to redress the wrongs done them or to prevent further fraudulent expropriation of their lands.

Living, as a resident of Rochester, in the Genesee Valley, which for many years had been the homeland of the Senecas, the dominant tribe of the Iroquois confederacy, Morgan's studies of the history, the mores, the rituals, and the matriarchal social and political organization of the Five Tribes, led, ten years before the firing on Fort Sumter, to the publication of his *The League of the Iroquois*.

It was a *succès d'estime*, if not a work that the public made a best seller. In the dozen-odd years that he had lived in Rochester, Morgan had become a leading spirit in a select coterie of men of intellectual interests who met occasionally as a discussion group. Although his talks and the papers he read, which often had to do with his investigations of Indian life, were well regarded by his confreres, Morgan made no great stir outside of Rochester until *The League of the Iroquois* was read by men in this country and abroad who were devoted to ethnology or allied sciences, and who acclaimed it as an exhaustive study of a subject that had had in the past only fragmentary treatment.

To the surprise of many readers of *The League of the Iroquois*, who had previously considered Indians only a cut above the wild beasts who shared their forest habitat, Morgan showed that the Iroquois, at least, had developed a quite elaborate social system, that they had a government of laws, that they were given to philosophical speculation, and that they were not devoid of moral responsibility.

Morgan's fame grew as his work came to the attention of a widening circle of scholars. For a time he was accepted as the leading authority on Indian life, and *The League of the Iroquois* was looked upon as the definitive work on the Five Tribes which originally made up the League. Later, writers with fresh material disproved some of his theories. His history, however, is still, in many of its parts, the classical statement of the great confederacy of central and western New York Indians who Morgan and the historian Francis Parkman half believe would have controlled the continent if it had not been for European interference.

Morgan's continuing career as a scientist was concomitant with his success first as a corporation lawyer and then as an industrialist. While avidly persisting in his anthropological researches, he at the same time served as president of a company that operated a blast furnace and acted as legal counsel for and helped direct the operations of a railroad and iron mine in which he was financially interested.

His legal and business activities rewarded Morgan with a fortune (for those days) of $100,000, his scientific labors, which culminated with the publication of his magnum opus *Ancient Society*, greatly extended the reputation for scholarship he had previously gained from *The League of the Iroquois*.

In *Ancient Society*, Morgan traced social origins into the remote past, and showed in four epochs man's progress from savagery to civilization. This, and an earlier affiliated work, *Systems of Consanguinity of the Human Family*, published by the Smithsonian Institution, established their author as one of the founders of evolutionary anthropology, and brought him to the attention of many notable men.

Morgan, who enjoyed numerous kudos during his lifetime, became oddly celebrated after death when this rather bourgeois railroad and mining entrepreneur—this sound Republican, orthodox Presbyterian, petty politician, who was indifferent to the hard plight of the labor he employed and who was as relentlessly acquisitive as other money grubbers in the post-Civil War boom, became in spirit the pet of Karl Marx and Friedrich Engels, cofounders of Marxist communism.

Karl Marx died in London in 1883, two years after the death of Lewis Morgan in Rochester. The two men had had no contact; but shortly before his death, Marx read *Ancient Society* with avid interest, and remarked his astonishment that an American scholar had learned so much about the fundamentals of material history. Marx's enthusiasm for Morgan's masterpiece was conveyed to Engels, who was asked to bring *Ancient Society* to the attention of Social Democrats throughout Europe. Engels did the master's will to the full, with the ironic result that the work of a Rochester industrialist, who had no notion of the radical social doctrine his book had enunciated, became a Socialist classic.

Ancient Society went into dozens and dozens of editions and was translated into many languages, including Japanese. Three years after Morgan's death, Engels wrote *The Origin of the Family, Private Property and the State*, subtitled *In the Light of the Researches of Lewis Henry Morgan*; and the author, acclaiming Morgan's work one of the greatest books of its time, said at one point:

> For Morgan in his own way had discovered afresh in America the materialistic conception of history discovered by Marx forty years ago, and in his comparison of barbarism and civilization it had led him, in the main points, to the same conclusions as Marx.

Morgan was a Rochester phenomenon. He was a total abstainer, who lectured on temperance, and served his guests hard cider. He was an instinctive "joiner"—at heart, if not in fact, a brother Elk—who, had he lived in a later day, might have arrayed himself in red Zouave pantaloons, a fancy tunic, and a tasseled fez, and marched with a lodge drill team in street parades. He was successively an undistinguished member of the Assembly and the New York State Senate, under dubious sponsorship. He was sufficiently successful in business to bequeath the University of Rochester $80,000 for the establishment of an educational program for women, and he had nothing to do with Miss Susan B. Anthony, who had been campaigning for such a program for years, although the eminent feminist lived only a few minutes' walk from his Third Ward home. He hated slavery, and abominated abolitionists.

If not monolithic, Morgan's published and unpublished works have, nevertheless, a formidable bulk (*Ancient Society*, as one item in an extensive bibliography, runs six hundred pages). How he managed to prosecute his investigations into the complex subjects about which he wrote, and how he found time for the actual writing while at the same time engaged in the practice of law and concerned with the operation of a railroad, an iron mine and a blast furnace, makes interesting speculation. Even in his era when the coffee break was unknown, the four-Martini businessman's lunch was not in vogue, and a cathode ray tube was not producing such tangential enticements as "Captain Kangaroo" and the "Beverly Hillbillies," it is still apparent that Morgan's industry was prodigious.

Proud though Rochester is of its sons and daughters who have achieved notable successes at home and abroad, it is not likely that more than one out of a thousand of its citizens (and this may be far too large a percentage), if interrogated by an inquiring reporter, would be able to identify Lewis Henry Morgan.

The mention of his name, even in a company of reasonably prominent contemporary Rochesterians, will induce little more than a blank stare or a perplexed furrowing of brows; then, sudden enlightenment—"Oh, he's the man who had the Morgan Machine Works, who lived out East Avenue."

The late Henry W. Morgan did head the Morgan Machine Company, and he did live "out East Avenue," but he and the famed Third Ward anthropologist were not related.

My interest in Morgan, which may have been fostered and sustained by the notion that even a superficial acquaintance with the life and achievements of one of the city's great men gave me a patronizing advantage over my less informed fellow townsmen, was first aroused by Louis Decker, whose own curiosity had been piqued by his father's devotion to Morgan's Indian works.

George P. Decker was still in his nonage at the time of Morgan's death, but he had already read *The League of the Iroquois*. He had been impressed by Morgan's first major work, and was stimulated by it into making investigations on his own that pertained particularly to Indians indigenous to central and western New York and to tribes immediately across the Canadian border. He was outraged, as Morgan had been, by the manner in which these native Americans had been decultured and impoverished by the frauds and peculations of white men. After he was admitted to the bar, he appeared, often without fee, as counsel for Indians who sought in courts of law redress of the grievances they believed they had suffered from those who had taken over their lands. He established legal precedent in some of these cases; once he went before the League of Nations at Geneva to plead for recognition of the rights guaranteed by Great Britain to a tribe of Canadian Indians. He wrote long, authoritative papers about Indians for the publication of the New York State Archeological Association, and he was prominent in the Lewis H. Morgan Chapter of the Association.

As a Democratic politician, well favored by the party's hierarchy, George Decker was once appointed Collector of the Port of Rochester and another time made Deputy Attorney General of the state of New York, probably in recompense for his sacrificial gesture in accepting on two occasions the nomination for an elective office that he had no chance to win in a community that was under tight Republican control. He was also counsel to the state's Forest, Fish and Game Commission. He enjoyed the favor of Woodrow Wilson, Franklin D. Roosevelt, and New York's Democratic governors. Through Washington connections, he obtained for his only son the post of vice-consul at Nottingham, England, and Louis left the consulate, and England, after a fairly short tenure, a rank apostate. He declared himself disenchanted with the State Department and disgusted with the party that had sponsored his appointment, and avowed that henceforth he was a Republican by registration and voting practice.

It was Louis Decker's genius to do the unusual. He was often in snarling dissent. He had wolfish-looking teeth, in a head of noble cast and proportions. When he snarled, he bared his teeth quite fully. His vituperations were often classical. I thought him the most versatile young man I knew and, for a time, the most brilliant. Immediately after World War I, he was one of a small group of bright young downtown veterans who, until their individual aspirations brought dismemberment to their junto, had more or less planned to take over the town.

At Exeter Academy, Louis's attitude toward his fellow students was condescending, and he chose to associate with masters. He avoided all forms of athletic activity and was scornful of such juvenilities as football rousers and victory celebrations. He proclaimed contemptuously that a second-rate gorilla could outcharge the entire Exeter eleven, and that a gazelle could outleap the track team's jumpers or easily run away from its sprinters. So why put importance on activities at which mere beasts prevailed? He felt that no one who had not read Lord Chesterfield's *Letters to His Son* should be considered a gentleman; that no one who was unfamiliar with Boswell's *Life of Johnson* should be accepted as a scholar.

It seemed to me that Louis had read everything. For a time,

Montesquieu's *Persian Letters* was his bible. He was politically inclined, and he quoted extensively from Montesquieu's greater work, *The Spirit of the Laws* and from Blaine's *Commonwealth*. He was devoted to some of the curmudgeons, particularly Jonathan Swift; was scornful of Henry Thoreau "playing adventurer in a cabin in a little woods, a couple of miles walk from a square meal in a village. And no women! Hell, if he lived today, he'd have lace on his underpants."

He went from Exeter to Hamilton College, and there roomed briefly with John Weaver, the poet, whom he did not like. In time, he transferred to his father's alma mater, the University of Rochester, where, probably having no more than a superficial acquaintance with the revered Dr. Rush Rhees, president, he pronounced him a "gargantuan stuffed shirt." Among Decker's numerous gifts was a talent for mimicry. After persuading me to move from Rochester to Scottsville, he built a small house next door, where he lived for eleven months. While the house was being built under his close supervision, I occasionally drove him the thirteen miles from the village to downtown Rochester, following a convenient course that took us past Mt. Hope Cemetery. Invariably, as we approached the broad acreage of this wooded and rolling burying ground which, devoid of its marble and granite grotesqueries, would have offered a delightful prospect, Decker would be inspired to delivery in mockery of Dr. Rhees a panegyric over the bier of the university's greatest benefactor, George Eastman, who was still very much alive.

It was a precise performance. Decker had mastered the formal diction of Dr. Rhees, and he delivered his impromptu with attention to the rounded, sonorous periods of the good doctor's best platform style. If I closed my eyes, and was unaware of Louis's presence, I might have thought that the president of the university was in the seat next to me, and that he was rehearsing an oration.

I admired Louis Decker's facility, and often felt that I was pedestrian and inept by comparison. He was not an idol of mine, but there was a time when he arrogated to himself the role of mentor, and I neither resented his presumption nor disregarded his counsel. He seemed to me encyclopedic. He knew about the stars, about Napoleon's campaigns, about Freud, before most of us had ever heard of Freud, or psychoanalysis, or the Oedipus complex; he spoke knowingly about the raising of sheep, about transcendentalism, the trial of Warren Hastings, Darwin's theory of evolution, and the breeding habits of the ruffed grouse. Questioned on almost any subject, he would answer discursively, and he spoke so well that his words had the cachet of authority.

Although he could not read a musical note, if he were in the mood, Louis, to the delight of all who were within hearing, would sing lively French canzonets and accompany himself on the piano. He was a good bird shot, until he lost the inclination to trudge through fields and woods seeking partridge cover; a skillful fly fisherman, who cultivated a small bed of herbs—sweet marjoram, thyme, rosemary, savory—which, as recommended by Izaak Walton, he used as he tenderly prepared trout for table. He painted, with more than a Sunday painter's competence. He made palatable bathtub gin during Prohibition.

When it was first founded, the loosely organized junto of downtown veterans—of whom Decker was one—came immediately under the inquisitive eye of George Washington Aldridge, who for many years had looked upon Rochester as his feudal estate. He was the Republican boss, and Rochester was the "blackest Republican city in the state." Aldridge was reputed to have great benignity; he did have enormous magnetism. At his death, his body lay a day in the rotunda of the Courthouse, under view of an endless stream of weeping sentimentalists. He lived excellently, for the greater part of his career, without visible means of support, and his wife had a pleasant little token of $350,000, which her husband now and then had given her, she once said, "for jewelry."

Aldridge was in the tradition of such political dictators as Richard Croker, Charles F. Murphy, Boss Tweed, and his downstate Republican rival, Tom Platt. He was a Protestant, but faith and race meant nothing to him when he was putting together political combinations. He wanted only the winning ticket. He had patience, sagacity, and a capacity for compromise. He wheedled Democrats into the Republican fold, and they voted his way for the city and county ticket; after that they were on their own. These renegades were, of course, rewarded. They were known as "Aldridge Democrats." They helped appreciably in the wards, and sometimes were a vital force in keeping the city solidly Republican, and securing the seat of power for the boss.

Always on the watch for new and fresh material, Aldridge respected the ambitions of the bright young downtown veterans to take over the town, and after looking them over carefully, he called in two or three or four, including Louis Decker. There was a distinction to being summoned to 96 Plymouth Avenue South, where Aldridge lived and practiced his political incantations in a richly furnished front room, in juxtaposition to a Tiffany-mounted bust of Napoleon, which, patently, symbolized his own monarchial rule. It was a Third Ward house that was passed by some on tiptoe, reverently, with obeisance, as though it were a sacred temple or a cathedral of more than ordinary sanctity.

Each of the bright young veterans was interviewed separately by the Big Fellow. Aldridge could alter his manner to suit the occasion. He was remote and untouchable with some of his idolaters, as an idol should be. He could be a hail fellow well met. Or an intransigent martinet. With Decker and the other veterans who had received the royal summons, he listened and nodded. He sympathized with the aspirations of the heroic men who had returned from the wars. They indeed were entitled to leadership, and of course they would not want to lose momentum by opposing the natural current of affairs, or dissipate their strength by going off in splinter groups. It was planning that counted. Organization! There was plenty of room at the top, and he, George Aldridge, would be happy to help such men as Louis Decker, and T. Carl Nixon, and Ray Fowler to get there.

After his first meeting with the Big Fellow, Decker left the house at 96 Plymouth Avenue South, completely under the spell of a personality that had exerted its charm and wizardry upon innumerable office holders, who, if they continued in office, wore the Aldridge insignia as indelibly as a thumb print on a Neolithic potsherd.

Decker's father had been defeated as a candidate for a seat in the Lower House. He had sillily adhered to the wrong party, which Louis himself had forsaken. He would show his father what a man could do under powerful Republican auspices, and his suddenly formed political aspirations winged off into fantasies of extravagant triumph. He himself would not concern himself with the Lower House. He would point for the Senate, or to the governorship. Or even to a cabinet post, once Woodrow Wilson's bungling pomposities were quieted and he was out of Washington. He felt that he was hand in glove with a kingmaker.

Louis later told half sheepishly an amusing incident of his thralldom, which did not wear off until he began to rationalize his meeting with the Big Fellow and the conviction bore in upon him that he had not actually been in the presence of a deity.

He had left the Aldridge house in the afternoon of a pleasant summer day, and still tingling with what he felt had been the touch of the accolade and desiring to prolong his recent experience, in peripatetic reflection, he took a circuitous course to his own Third Ward home. Although the ward had suffered erosions in this immediate postwar period that in time would completely destroy its character and pitifully disfigure its countenance, the old Third still displayed in some areas more than vestigial traces of the quiet charm and Ruffled Shirt dignity it had known at the summit of its social eminence in the 1800s.

Decker passed carefully kept lawns, some of which were studded with fruit trees. There was a tradition about the fruit trees. From the early days of the ward, its housekeepers had boasted quietly that the jellies and jams and compotes made with fruit from their own trees were of unsurpassed excellence. Here and there was a gazebo in the surround of an old-fashioned garden of pinks and sweet william and mignonette, as in the days when Colonel Rochester resided in the ward, with ladies in bright summer apparel taking their ease in its shade, and to several of these ladies Decker tipped his hat.

He was still a block or two from his own home, when a woman who was very old family in the ward, and a friend of his mother, rose up from behind a begonia plant on her front porch, and called, "Oh, Louis, will you tell your mother . . ." Curtly he turned away, and went on without answering.

"It was a stupid thing to have done," he explained, years later. "But the spell of Uncle George (Aldridge) was still on me. I remembered suddenly that Mrs. F——'s husband had turned on Aldridge when he ran for Congress. I had heard my father tell that he was one of the crowd who had brought out the fact that Aldridge had taken a $1,000 check from the insurance people after a bill favorable to their interests had been passed in the State Legislature. My father thought Aldridge had been bribed. He was a Democrat, and that was natural. Mr. F—— was an old-line Republican. At the moment, I was so entranced by Aldridge, that I thought Mr. F—— a goddamn turncoat, and traitor. I could have seen him hanged."

79

"It was only when I got home that I began to see things in normal perspective. Aldridge was a big man and a powerful leader. I was not forgetting that. But I decided then and there, that if I was ever called in again, I wouldn't grovel at his feet on the rich oriental rug in the front room like some craven petitioner for the job of foreman of the garbage collecting gang. And, of course, I no longer had any silly notions that he was going to put me into the Congress, or make me governor of the state. That kind of nonsense had blown clean out of mind. Hell, he couldn't get himself nominated for governor, or elected to Congress."

At the time of Louis Decker's death, at the too early age of fifty, a newspaper editorial spoke of him in these words, "Brilliant, capable, he commanded attention for his unusual talents and made definite contributions to Republican County morale." Some of the qualities attributed to him by the newspaper may have been discerned by Aldridge, an intensely perceptive man, in his first meeting with Decker, for he soon had him back at 96 Plymouth Avenue South, and it was not long before Louis was initiated into a small group of intimates the Big Fellow had drawn around him who were entrusted with classified missions, who were privy to his political secrets, and with whom he occasionally consulted as to the feasibility of this or that political proposition.

Decker at the time was having a fling at the newspaper business, which he had tried briefly before enlisting in a Rochester Medical unit that served eleven months with the AEF. Before the war, he had worked as a reporter for the *Evening Times;* the *Times* had now been merged with the *Union and Advertiser* by the rising newspaper entrepreneur Frank E. Gannett, and Louis was covering the court beat and doing general assignments for Gannett's new combination, the *Times-Union.* He was a swift and gifted writer, but not the best reporter on the staff, for his eagerness to make news stories picturesque disposed him to make fact subordinate to fancy. His compositions were sometimes loose gaited. "Perry," he wrote, reporting the murder trial of Joe Perry, a one-armed telegrapher for the Postal Company, who shot his wife, "threw both hands into the air in protest." He was devoted to H. L. Mencken, who was gaining great vogue, and he was as scornful as Mencken of bourgeois values.

Under the urge of the hustling, questing, enormously ambitious Gannett, the *Times-Union* overwhelmed its afternoon rival, the punily circulated, play-toy newspaper of its owner and editor, Francis B. Mitchell, and offered more than a token challenge to the prestige of the deeply entrenched *Democrat and Chronicle*, and the excellently edited, but financially infirm, *Herald*.

Gannett kept everyone in his Rochester organization on his toes. He himself had an unquenchable air of purpose. He was alert and in action at all times. He was the sort of go-getter who, had he put his mind to it, would have made a stunning success of a cheese factory, a chain of one-arm lunchrooms, or a gambling syndicate, for, despite a marked puritanical cast in his character, he had something of the plunging instincts of Nick the Greek, the celebrated dice shooter, or Pittsburgh Phil, who reputedly made two million dollars betting on race horses.

Dice and horses, however, were not Gannett's game. He gambled on newspapers. Like a theatrical trouper on one-night stands, he rode sleeping cars night after night after night, flushing up money to finance the new links that were being forged to his continually lengthening chain (he preferred the collective noun group) of newspapers.

The masthead of the *Times-Union* listed Frank E. Gannett as both publisher and editor, and although he was often physically remote from his Rochester property, his deputies were daily advised by telephone of his publishing and editorial decisions, and no one presumed to take advantage of an absentee boss who was capable of anatomizing every department of the newspaper; who was a trained bookkeeper, a crack salesman, and a clever promoter, as well as a talented editor.

Gannett was never out of touch; those responsible for keeping the pressure on his employees, and pressures were exerted particularly in the editorial, advertising, and circulation departments, were well aware of this. Slogans exhorting everyone to get in there and fight for the dear old *Times-Union* were heard in the city room, and editors and newsmen were summoned to an inspirational rally. It was horative, and at times dithyrambic. It resembled not a little the half-time gatherings of college football players in an era when locker-room evangelism was probably more effective than it is with today's sophisticated youth. There were rah-rah-rahs and zip-boom-bahs! One of the speakers even wept, as he pleaded.

The day after the rally was pay day. Louis Decker took his check from the cashier, walked out of the newspaper plant, and never returned as a Gannett employee. It was several days before a company emissary met up with him.

"Why did you leave like that, without giving a word of notice?" he was asked.

Louis bared his large, wolflike teeth. "Good God," he cried, in quintessential disdain, "they were holding pep meetings in the place. I never thought anything like that happened outside of Sinclair Lewis' novels!"

Decker left Rochester. He moved into the Avon Inn, in the pleasant village of Avon, twenty miles upriver from the city. He was done with the pomps of the world, and he laughed at his puerile fancies of political renown. He sought pastoral ease, a chance at good partridge cover, and the tranquillity of a trout stream, slightly north and west. He took a job as secretary to Mrs. Herbert W. Wadsworth, a formidable lady from St. Louis, who had married into the great clan of Wadsworth, whose earlier members had settled on Genesee Valley lands in the first year of the last decade of the eighteenth century.

Mrs. Wadsworth was a horsewoman who had slight tolerance for horse shows, with dinner-jacketed judges scrutinizing the mincing and finicky prancing of saddle horses and hackneys; she felt that horses had a more serious purpose than social ostentation. She herself was a famous equestrienne, who once rode from Washington, D.C., to her elaborate country place, Ashantee, just south of Avon; and another time made numerous circuits of nearby Conesus Lake with an escort of extremely weary United States Cavalry officers.

Horses were her paramount interest. With the assistance of a retired West Pointer, Lieutenant Nathan C. Shiverick, she organized the Genesee Valley Breeders Association; she built what was then the largest private riding hall in the country on her Ashantee estate; she rode with the Genesee Valley hounds, the third oldest hunt club in America; she produced good hunters by crossing thoroughbreds, sent to her by the Jockey Club, with farm mares and established a half-bred stud book that is now in wide circulation. She was a perfectionist; a lady of indefeasible command. Louis Decker started nobly in her employ.

Omniverous reader though he was, and the possessor of a patchy encyclopedic knowledge of a large array of subjects, Louis oddly knew very little about horses until he moved to Avon. There he was caught with Mrs. Wadsworth's enthusiasm. As with every new subject that briefly arrested his interest, he whacked away at this one with zeal. He talked horses with his employer and her horsy friends, and penetrated her specialized library. In his apt way, he quickly acquired the gloss of authority. The thoroughbred had become to him one of God's noblest creatures. Eloquently, with the cadence of expertness, he would trace its lineage back to the foundation strains of Eclipse, and Herod, and Matchem. Nothing however would induce him to throw a leg over a horse and he did not like to be close to horses in stables or in the open, for their scent made him sneeze. He was merely the greatest academic horseman in the Valley.

Decker left his Wadsworth secretaryship after a few months. He had never been conspicuous for submission to authority, and Mrs. Wadsworth was an authoritarian of the first rank. The collision that severed their relations was inevitable. Louis returned to Rochester, and was again in the councils of Uncle George (the Big Fellow) Aldridge, who had had vague hints that his one-man rule of Rochester might be challenged by another George, and one with a powerful purse.

*   *   *

George Eastman was the George with the powerful purse, but there was never a confrontation between him and the Big Fellow on the issue as to how the city of Rochester should be administered. It might have happened; it didn't largely because the Kodak magnate, who wanted the city taken out of the spoils system, did not institute a campaign for a city manager form of government until after Aldridge had died of a heart attack on the golf course of the Westchester Biltmore Country Club.

The two men had known one another since youth, and their careers, paralleling each other, had certain similarities. In their separate specialties, politics and industry, they had risen to Gargantuan stature. Neither was a native Rochesterian. Aldridge had been born and had lived for a short time in Michigan City, Indiana. In his seventh year, Eastman had been removed by his parents from his native Waterville, New York, to the city that his company spectacularly enriched and that his vast beneficence made notable in the fields of medicine, music, and higher education.

At the time of Aldridge's death, in June 1922, local newspapers carried columns of tributes to the political boss from prominent Rochesterians. Some were mawkish, but honestly compassionate; others were rhetorical, the effusions of men who may not have liked or respected Aldridge, but who felt that they must say the proper thing. George Eastman, who was not given to hyperbole, and whose emotions were always controlled, expressed himself simply and with obvious sincerity in these words:

> I have known George Aldridge ever since we went to school together way back in the early '60's under Mrs. Lang, in a little frame house that stood on what is now the northwest corner of West Main and North Washington Street.
>
> As we grew up, we lost contact with each other for a time and it was not until I became interested in the Bureau of Municipal Research about seven years ago that I came to really know him and to appreciate his many good qualities as leader of city affairs. The preliminary survey of the city made for the Bureau by the best outside experts that could be found showed that it was one of the best if not the best governed city in the United States under the spoils systems of government then universally in use. This in itself was a tribute to the man who had for so long a period directed and shaped its policies and accomplishments.
>
> Mr. Aldridge loved his city and had a great interest in its welfare . . .

George Aldridge doubtless did love the city that he was allowed to control for many years as autocratically as if it were his inherited demense, but his canonization by its citizens was more than a little ridiculous, and his contributions were negligible compared to the great wealth brought to Rochester by Eastman and the benefits the community derived from his endowment of its medical, welfare, and cultural institutions.

Chapter 6

George Eastman's career is the city's great saga, as he is Rochester's Great Man; historically, its Number One citizen.

His parents were old and good American stock, and his father was an educator, the proprietor, for a short time, of a business college. His death occurred not long after he had brought his wife and son to Rochester. At the age of thirteen young Eastman ended his formal education and left school to help support his widowed mother whose main subsistence for a time was taking boarders into her home.

A youth with a mechanical turn, a good deal of native intelligence, and, owing to his father's impecunity, an almost pathological fear of debt, Eastman mastered the trick of saving money at the time he received his first pay envelope from an insurance agency where he served as office boy. From then on he was never insolvent. From the insurance office, he moved to a bookkeeper's desk in the Rochester Savings Bank, and while there, as a pastime to relieve the tedium of an eleven-hour stint over ledgers, made his first experiments in the art and science of photography.

At that time, Rochester was approaching the penultimate decade of the nineteenth century and the commemoration in 1884 of its fiftieth anniversary as a municipality. In the post-Civil War period, the city had acquired an aspect of maturity and the rough edges of the former frontier settlement had been rubbed to urban smoothness, but its boom-town surge was a thing of the distant past, and in recent years population gains had been steady rather than torrential.

Rochester was a pleasant city, a "city of homes," as it boasted. It was reasonably small, tidy, and rather self-complacent. To help sustain its economy, it had the well known nursery and seed companies which accounted for its designation as the Flower City, and a variety of light industries that included carriages and wagons, shoes, men's clothing, optical supplies, coffins, and cigarettes, called "coffin nails," which were abundantly produced by the Kimball Tobacco Company. It was bumbling along quite contentedly, with no ardent megalopolitan aspirations or hope of a great industrial concentration, when young Eastman discovered a commercial potential in his hobby. Soon after this, he quit his bank ledgers—first to produce photographic plates, then a photograph film, and presently a small picture-taking box, with a happily chosen trade name, that was destined to make millionaires out of office stenographers, buggy whip manufacturers, schoolteachers, shoe clerks, and numerous other Rochesterians who had the temerity to buy early into the Eastman Kodak Company and the tenacity to hold on until the stock proliferated like amoeba in a petri dish.

Eastman's habits were orderly and his life was unsullied by personal scandal. He did not race horses or keep a mistress in a flat. He did not carouse, or back musical comedies, or gaudily display his wealth. He was a bachelor, devoted during her lifetime to his mother, whom he adored to the exclusion of all other women. Under a cold and quiet demeanor, Eastman nurtured an inexorable determination to give to his company, as he himself once put it, "control of the world," or that part of it that had to do with the production of photographic supplies and equipment, and for practical purposes this goal was achieved in his lifetime.

He died, with the image his admirers hoped might be perpetuated for youth—the poor, fatherless boy who by perseverance and the exercise of native talents had climbed to the heights—somewhat disfigured by the manner of his death. At the age of seventy-eight he shot himself through the heart, and left a note of explanation on the bedroom floor beside his body: "My work is done. Why wait?"

But long before this tragic act had removed the aging industrialist from a life that appeared to have become unbearably lonely, he began to plan for the disposal of his wealth, not only after death but during his lifetime. Bequests to individuals were mostly ruled out, for he had neither wife nor child. His scheme of giving was carefully devised. He had become interested in the care of children's teeth, and after establishing a dental dispensary in Rochester at a cost of $1,000,000, he endowed similar clinics in half a dozen European capitals.

In an era when civil rights were hardly considered the prerogative of the black man, and their education was being scandalously neglected in many parts of the country, Eastman handsomely enriched two Negro institutions of learning because he believed that the race problem, "America's most perplexing domestic question," might be resolved only by education.

He gave $20,000,000 to the Massachusetts Institute of Technology, and remained silent while newspapers attributed the gift to a "mysterious Mr. Smith." His outside munificences were many, but in the end it was the city in which his wealth had been acquired that benefited from the greater share of his fortune.

He built a handsome home for the Rochester Chamber of Commerce, dedicated the finest motion picture theater, then standing in America, to the citizens of Rochester, and with many, many millions initiated a program that resulted in the transfiguration of the small, proud, academically sound, but lightly endowed University of Rochester into a "greater university," with a new campus, innumerable new buildings, an internationally renowned medical school, an excellent music school, and an investment portfolio that may hold more blue chip securities than the portfolios of all but fifteen or sixteen universities in the land.

Eastman's interest in Rochester extended to many phases of the city. He was proud of the community which, as it advanced into the twentieth century, discarded its former title of Flower City for one that identified it with a product of the Eastman Company. It was now the Kodak City. His industry employed thousands of its citizens, and Eastman was the largest paymaster in town. In 1912, he introduced a program of employee benefits, conspicuously marked by the declaration of an employees' wage dividend, that in time put the Eastman Company far beyond most large corporations in the matter of management-employee relations.

Wise, humanistic, and, to a degree, methodic in the manner of the young bank clerk of his earlier years, Eastman began carefully to plan to make Rochester a better city for the residence of his own employees, who were so vital a part of the local economy, and other fellow townsmen.

He was not naturally politically minded. He had no intention of effecting a *coup d'état*. Eastman knew that George Aldridge was no Galahad. The Big Fellow was a periodic drunkard, and when drunk, a wencher, who sometimes careered in a horse-drawn hack "down the line"—Rochester's short, intense, segregated district in Hill Street—to roister in a fancy house, to break mirrors and gilded chandeliers, and slap the madam about. In his early career, he had been elected mayor, which office he left (after raising his own salary $1,000) for the appointive one of State Commissioner of Public Works. He made an unholy botch of that job, grossly mismanaged something like $9,000,000 of the state's funds, escaped prosecution by a thin hair, and resigned under pressure.

Although Aldridge's toga had been besmirched by outside accusation and calumny, he seemed in Rochester as free of criticism as an Oriental despot whose very name it is a crime to pronounce lightly, and he was warmly greeted upon his return from Albany by a compliant constituency, who seemed to feel that they needed his leadership. They believed, boss though he was, that he had given Rochester a far better government than the governments of other boss-ridden cities, which abounded in graft and corruption. This also was the opinion of George Eastman. "Limited by the political situation from which he [Aldridge] could never escape," Eastman once said, "he always gave it [Rochester] the best in his power."

Nevertheless, Eastman was not satisfied to have Rochester perpetually consigned to the hands of a boss who manipulated the mayor, the aldermen, the police and firemen, and almost all other persons on the city payroll, as adroitly as a master puppeteer would dance little dummies on a wire.

In his own plant, he had introduced, with the idea of bringing refinement to the products that went out from it, elaborate systems of scientific research; now (in 1915) he organized and financed a Bureau of Municipal Research which he hoped would discover ways to refine the government of the city of Rochester.

On trial for a period of five years, the Bureau's performance during that period pleased its sponsor, and Eastman continued to maintain it, at a total cost of nearly $700,000, until his death. Since then it has been supported by subscriptions from Rochester banks, industries, stores, and utilities.

From the beginning, Eastman's secret purpose was to have the Bureau reorganize the city government along the then new lines of the council-manager plan, and a hint of this in time was whispered in Aldridge's ear. If the plan worked, the Big Fellow knew that its sponsors would strive to keep it free of partisan politics. In theory, this would derive him of patronage, without which a political boss is as impotent as a four-star general without an army. There was a threat in this, but hardly one to provoke an old and seasoned war horse to panic.

With advancing years, Aldridge's native perspicacity had increased, and he was willing to concede that his political mystique was less than universal. He was not unlike a successful stage director, who could school other people in theatrical roles, without being able to play a part himself. He had discovered his limitations by painful experience. Once, aspiring to the gubernatorial nomination, he had been rejected by the state Republican Committee. Another time, he nominated himself as a candidate for the thirty-second Congressional District, and suffered a humiliating defeat when stanch Republicans, who docilely submitted to his local leadership, turned from the Republican standard in disgust at Aldridge's effrontery, to vote for his Democratic opponent.

The rejection of Aldridge's bid for the gubernatorial nomination, and his defeat at the polls had not in any way weakened his hold on the Republican constituency of Rochester and Monroe County. He was still indefeasibly the boss in the early 1920s, when President Warren G. Harding, as recompense for the Big Fellow's steadfast support of Harding's candidacy at the Republican National Convention, appointed him to the lucrative post of Collector of the Port of New York.

His week was now divided between New York, where he spent five days in the Collector's office, and Rochester, to which he returned weekends to give personal attention to the political organization that his skill and unending persistence had created and that he still profoundly controlled.

During one of his Rochester visits, he summoned Louis Decker to the political citadel at 96 Plymouth Avenue South. The secret was out about George Eastman's desire to replace the charter under which Rochester was administered with one that would give the city a council-manager form of government, and Aldridge had been tentatively questioned about his reaction to the proposal. He had been tactfully noncommittal. He wanted to know more about this form of government, and sent Decker to Dayton, Ohio, the first city with a population of more than ten thousand to adopt a manager form of government. The emissary returned with a decidedly negative report. Decker may not have been an entirely impartial investigator. He bared his wolfish teeth, and said that Dayton "stank."

"Well," Aldridge said, after half a minute of reflection, "I'll go along, if Mr. Eastman wants it. You can't fight thirty million dollars. Besides," he added, "the councilmen—if a council is to replace the Board of Aldermen—will have to be elected by the voters. The voters will be partisan. Maybe we can manage the manager."

Eastman always believed that Aldridge would have gone along with him, and with secret reservations he would have done so. He died before the new charter was adopted on a referendum by the voters, after a bitter political campaign. That was in 1928, and the first city manager—Mr. Eastman's choice—was Stephen B. Story, director of the Bureau of Municipal Research. Young, personable, and capable, Story suffered a tumescent sense of affluence once his modest salary as Bureau director was upped to a handsome $20,000. He became the owner of a yacht, and indulged in other extravagances. When the Democrats wrested control of the City Council, he left the city managership and went on to another well-paying job. He served gallantly in Europe during World War II, won the Bronze Star, and was made a full colonel. After the war, he became comptroller of New Hampshire. His tastes were still fancy. He apparently found that he could not afford to live as well as he wanted on his income, and after irregularities were discovered in his accounts, he was tried, convicted, and sent to prison. Upon his release, he returned to Rochester to work behind the counter of a candy store operated by a former court and City Hall reporter for the *Democrat and Chronicle*, and Story's loyal friend Hiram Marks.

As a reward for his services to George Aldridge, Louis Decker was made County Purchasing Agent. When he left that office, he edited, caustically, skillfully and well, the Republican Party's house organ, the *Monroe Republican*. But the force and spirit of the Republican Party in Rochester, adroitly fashioned over the years by Aldridge and animated by his charisma, had been lowered and dulled. Men of smaller stature who had attempted to assume the purple of the fallen leader were stark and grotesque in its ample folds. They were men of good political intent, but of no great political aptitude. Devoted to the party though he was, Decker, who had never been known for his forwardness in the face of adversity ("Oh," he'd say, "what's the use? Life's too short.") voluntarily left his post as editor of the *Monroe Republican,* and retired to the Churchville birthplace of Frances Elizabeth Willard, founder of the Women's Christian Temperance Union. There he filled a deep pit out back with empty gin bottles, and idled—and drank—away the remarkable gifts of his endowment.

At No. 13 School, I wore a blue sailor blouse with a wide yoke trimmed with white piping. Attached to the breast pocket was a celluloid button marked in bold black letters with the universal slogan "Remember the Maine." The button may have been worn perfunctorily, for I have no recollection of the excitement inflamed by the sinking of the American battleship in Havana Harbor in February 1898. I do, however, recall—and the incident is the earliest historical reference my memory is able to evoke—standing on the veranda of a house on Alexander Street, a few weeks after war had been declared, as a contingent of National Guardsmen marched by, presumably on their way to fight the hated Spaniards.

This was Sunday, the first of May, and thousands of frenetic stay-at-home patriots turned out to wave farewell to the citizen-soldiers as they paraded round Robin Hood's barn to give the town a show on their march from the Armory in Clinton Avenue South to the troop train at the New York Central station.

It seemed to my youthful fancy a glorious spectacle, and I was proud to think that the daughter of the leader of the 54th Regiment Band, which provided the most stirring music in the line of march, was a member of my grade in school. Although the 54th was very military in aspect, and its drums and brasses made heroic reverberations, it was not going to lead the guardsmen into battle. It was a parade band, famous in political torchlight processions and other street pageants, and it played inspirational music on the opening day of the baseball season and Strauss waltzes at skating carnivals.

Excited by the ranks of uniformed men, gleaming rifles at their shoulders, clicking smartly over the pavement to the strains of martial music, I applauded and cheered; then saw Mrs. Merchant in tears.

Mrs. Merchant was the wife of George F. Merchant, president of the Buffalo, Rochester & Pittsburgh Railroad, and I had been taken by my parents to the Merchants' home to watch a parade that included, besides the activated guardsmen bound for Camp

Black on Long Island, a contingent of naval militia and groups of G.A.R. veterans.

I turned to my mother. She was the daughter of a Civil War soldier, who had served a postwar enlistment with the regular army, and part of her girlhood had been passed at a military post in Nebraska.

"What's the matter with Mrs. Merchant?" I whispered. "Look. She's crying."

"Sssh," my mother cautioned. She touched my lips with her fingers. "Don't you understand?" she whispered, almost irritably. "It's sad. Those brave young soldiers may never come back. They —they're going to war!"

It is a singular characteristic of Rochester that it rallies to "causes" that it considers worthy. The war with Spain—needless, unholy, and in many ways opera bouffe—was, at the time that it incited the nation to fierce sword rattling, considered a very worthy cause indeed.

During the months that the Rochester militiamen spent in camps on Long Island and in the South, they continually enjoyed the bounty of their fellow townsmen. Business houses, social organizations, and citizens' committees vied with one another in dispatching boxes and barrels of food and other supplies to the servicemen, and the Home Front also took over the partial care of families whose breadwinners were in uniform. This back-of-the-line effort in the Spanish-American War, which caused the New York *Tribune* to remark that no other city of its size had done so much in the way of soldier relief as Rochester, was repeated with magnificent amplifications in World Wars I and II.

On the April day that the four months' war with Spain was declared, patriotism in Rochester reached a higher pitch than any other time since the surrender at Appomattox. American flags seemed as numerous as the lilacs that soon would blossom in Highland Park. Reporting this demonstration in detail, the newspapers discovered that the largest flag, a cloth of almost playing-field dimensions, waved from the ultrafashionable residence of Mr. and Mrs. Warham Whitney in South Goodman Street, and recalled that a much smaller flag had been stolen from the front of a business establishment. This heinous act, at once presumed to be the work of an enemy alien, was not to go unchallenged. John C. Hayden was acting chief of police. His patriotism was aroused and his fancies were inflamed. He may have pictured dark-visaged spies couched under the beds of Rochester's important citizens and Conquistadors with daggers and bombs lurking in the shadows of the Armory. He thundered an order. He wanted all Spaniards and persons of Spanish extraction rounded up and brought before him. His florid gesture was warmly applauded; happily, it was not categorically executed.

Approximately five hundred Rochester men served with various naval and military units during the brief war, and many of them were mustered out not long after the August armistice. The first large contingent of volunteers returned home, amply fed en route by Isaac Teal, Rochester's best-known caterer, who had been commissioned by a welcoming committee to meet the troop train at Watkins Glen and lay one of his famous spreads before its passengers. At the New York Central Station, the detraining soldiers were greeted by a clamorous throng. The 54th Regiment Band, whose booming marching airs had been a greater stimulus to recruiting than flag waving and patriotic proclamations, now played the old stereotypes, "Johnny Comes Marching Home" and "Home Sweet Home." There were *vivas* and strewn flowers; there were hugs and kisses.

From a coign of vantage at some remove from the rude and teeming multitude, the Daughters of the American Revolution and the Colonial Dames, whose petitions to politicians had in part been responsible for the speedy return of the Rochester servicemen, smilingly observed the happy results of their exertions.

Acclaimed by a grateful citizenry as crested heroes, none of the volunteer companies or the units of the National Guard had been bloodied or maimed in battle. Their suffering had been the hardships and privations of camps and training centers. Rochester lost only a dozen men in the Spanish-American War: three sailors died in the bowels of the exploded *Maine*, a regular infantryman was killed in a Cuban battle, and a soldier lost his life in a railroad accident; the others succumbed to diseases induced by lack of sanitation, impure drinking water, and bad food.

A war that hardly cast the United States in heroic mold and that might have been avoided except for the jingoistic press, Theodore Roosevelt's stinging taunt that President McKinley "had no more backbone than a chocolate eclair," and the impassioned but unproved suspicion that the *Maine* had been blown up at the orders of the Spanish Government, left few imperishable marks on Rochester.

Four years after the signing of the peace treaty, a trophy cannon was mounted in Highland Park, and in 1941, when war fever was again high, Carl Jennewein, the New York architectural sculptor, designed a four-ton bronze eagle, which now stands on the Court Street site of the war memorial, in commemoration of the Spanish-American War.

After the time I had been taken there to watch the parade of Spanish-American War soldiers through Alexander Street, I returned to the Merchant house on several occasions, always in the company of my father. Our visits were usually made on Sunday morning, after Sunday school, and during the hour that my mother was attending the eleven o'clock service at St. Andrew's Episcopal Church where Dr. Algernon Sidney Crapsey was the rector.

My father was an admirer of Dr. Crapsey, who in time was to become internationally celebrated as a heretic. He delighted in talking with him. But he did not subscribe to Revelation, and his churchgoing was restricted to a visit at St. Andrew's, under my mother's enforcement, every other Easter Sunday morning.

I enjoyed our Sunday calls at the Merchant residence, which stood on the east side of Alexander Street, not far from the East Avenue corner. The Merchants lived in a style befitting the family of a railroad president, in an era when railroads were the life line of industry and commerce, and the men who directed them had sovereign control of intracontinental transportation. Mrs. Merchant was a gracious lady. When I was in her presence she always pressed a silver dish of bonbons upon me. She seemed fond of small boys. I remember hearing her say to my father, in a surprised voice, "Why, George, I hadn't noticed before. Little Henry looks just like you."

My father laid a paternal hand on my head. "Well, don't you mind, son," he said consolingly, "so long as you've got your health."

In time I learned a good deal about the Merchant family, and came to realize that my father's attitude toward Mr. Merchant was not unlike the devotion of a loving son.

My father had not known his own father, an expatriate Vermonter, who had enlisted as a private in a regiment of Iowa volunteers at the beginning of the Civil War, and died in Texas shortly after being mustered out of the army with the rank of lieutenant colonel.

An impoverished widow with a small child, my paternal grandmother had a difficult time in Iowa and in the southern part of Dakota Territory, until, at the age of seventeen, my father obtained a job as telegrapher in the Vermillion, South Dakota, station of the Dakota Southern Railroad. There he enjoyed the kindly attentions of Mr. Merchant, general freight and passenger agent for the road, who moved him first to the station at Yankton, South Dakota, and then to the Dakota Southern's offices in Sioux City, Iowa.

George E. Merchant was a native New Englander, who had gone west as a youth and had grown up with pioneering railroads in the middle of the continent. He had served other roads before joining the Dakota Southern, which he left in the early 1880s to become general superintendent of a small financially troubled railroad operating in a southwesterly course from Rochester to the Pennsylvania state line. The company prospered under his skillful direction; it extended its trackage and became the Buffalo, Rochester & Pittsburgh, with headquarters in Rochester.

Busy executive though he was, Mr. Merchant had not forgotten the youthful telegrapher he had placed in two positions on the Dakota Southern, and in time he sent for my father, and installed him as a dispatcher in the Lincoln Park yards of the B.R.&P.

In Rochester, my father's fortunes appreciably improved. He advanced first in the railroad organization. Later he became advantageously associated with operating companies in the bituminous coal fields of western Pennsylvania, which supplied the tonnage that made the Buffalo, Rochester & Pittsburgh Railroad a profitable enterprise. He believed that what success he achieved was largely owing to Mr. Merchant's good offices; he often said Mr. Merchant was the only father he had ever known.

There were three children in the Merchant family. In my Sunday visits, I met Eleanor, the younger daughter, and once was given a condescending handclasp by a slim, handsome young man, who was not yet out of his nonage. He was Gerald Merchant, or "Gene," as his friends knew him. It was not until several years later that I met the older daughter, Maud, and was tremblingly aware of being in the presence of a woman of unusual loveliness. She was then Mrs. Albert H. Ely, of New York, and New York's "400."

To my knowledge only two or three Rochester women have become celebrated for their beauty outside the confines of their home town. The former Maud Merchant must be included among them. Her marriage in the autumn of 1891 to Dr. Ely, physician and obstetrician for many of New York's wealthiest and most socially prominent families, was the prime event of the local social season, as indicated by the opening line of a column-and-a-half account of the nuptials in the Rochester *Morning Herald:*

> The doors of old St. Paul's were thrown open to the elite of the city yesterday afternoon and for nearly two hours fashionable Rochester poured into the church its fairest flowers of wealth, fashion and position, filling the church from chancel to vestibule with the most stylish and brilliant assemblage ever gathered at a wedding in Rochester.

Maud Merchant Ely had entered what Ward McAllister had arbitrarily designated the "true society" at the time of her marriage, and she firmly held to its tenets and its proprieties. Her entertainments were not the tumultous routs of what later became café society, with night club mimes and mummers from Hollywood and minstrels just off the borscht circuit comingling with bearers of names that had once been included in McAllister's sanctified listing. Her parties were small, quiet, and discriminate. Her youthful beauty, with advancing years, metamorphosed into a regal handsomeness; in mid-life she was still an arresting figure.

Dr. Ely enjoyed the questionable distinction of being a close friend of Warren G. Harding, whose noble bearing, handsome features, and friendly manner effectively cloaked his inherent ordinariness. Harding was occasionally a house guest of the Elys, and once remained so long at their summer place, Fort Hill, in Southampton, Long Island, that the press referred to Fort Hill as the summer White House.

The younger Merchant daughter, Eleanor, married Francis J. French, and remained in Rochester. When her husband died, she moved into a suite in the lofty reaches of the Hotel Sheraton, the "golden aviary," so-called because of the prevalence on the hotel's upper floors of widows with millions.

Eleanor's husband had been co-owner with his brother, George French, of the R. T. French Company, producers of spices and mustards, on Mustard Street, which was sold in 1926 to Reckett & Colman, an English syndicate. Since the old firm had an enviable reputation in the food trade, the new owners wisely did not change the name of the plant, which still operates as R. T. French Company. The physical property has been greatly enlarged, the inventory expanded to include a wide variety of prepared foods, and what was once a $6,000,000 local business now does $100,000,000 a year.

English executives were sent over to manage the French Company. For the most part they have been men of charm, urbanity, and enlightenment—one was an Oxford don—who have fitted gracefully into the social life of the city, joined the proper clubs, cultivated Rochester tastes, cheered the local baseball team. They conduct a highly competitive business without seeming to suffer the pressures that bring lesions to the duodena of American business executives. Traditionally, in late afternoon they relax over tea and crumpets served, without the supplement of a shaker of dry Martinis, in their offices in the plant.

*　　*　　*

My father's unfaltering devotion to George E. Merchant made it impossible for him to be critical of the behavior or habits of any member of the Merchant family, but at times he lamented that "poor Gene hadn't had much luck."

During my youth, my only meeting with Gerald Merchant was on the occasion of the condescending handshake. His attitude was understandable: I was a boy in knee breeches; he was a gay and very precocious young man. I came to know him later on, when he was engaged, in a modest way, in the real estate business. He was then a personable and popular youngish middle-aged man with wide social connections; but he had not put to use the technical training he had received at Rensselaer Polytechnic Institute, and he had failed to fulfill the bright promises of his youth, not, as my father sadly reflected, because he "hadn't had much luck," but possibly because, as a very young man, he had had too much.

He seemed to live, to a degree, in glories of the past; his life had a fixed point of reference: *The time I went to Europe with Diamond Jim.*

Diamond Jim was James Buchanan Brady, a poor Irish lad from New York's Lower West Side, who started life smashing baggage in a station on the New York Central & Hudson River Railroad, and made millions as a railroad supply salesman, before he ate himself to death. His feats as a trencherman, his fame as a beau of great stage beauties, the Lucullian elaborateness of his entertainments, and the spectacular manner in which he encrusted his person with gem stones, have made him an authentic figure in American folklore.

Brady had already made a conspicuous success as a salesman for the railroad supply house of Manning, Maxwell and Moore, when he took up what seemed the forlorn cause of Sampson Fox, English inventor of a pressed steel undertruck for railroad cars.

At that time, American railroad cars were equipped with undertrucks (the carriages upon which railroad cars rest) made of wooden beams that were held together by iron bolts; and the consensus of railroad men in this country was that Fox's steel equipment was too rigid for use on cars that were hauled at high speed over roadbeds of innumerable curves. Discouraged at his failure to interest American railroad men in his invention, Fox was preparing to return to England when chance brought him into contact with Brady, who agreed to take on the Fox truck as a side line.

Parker Morell, Diamond Jim's most detailed biographer, has averred that Brady boomed the fortunes of himself and those of Sampson Fox by first selling the English equipment to the New York Central Railroad. Gerald Merchant believed that his father, George E. Merchant, gave Brady the first substantial order for the steel undertrucks, and that the deal was closed in Powers Hotel, the scene, in the latter days of the last century, of many big business transactions.

While the question of precedence may be difficult to resolve, the fact is that the elder Merchant, in conference with Brady in Powers Hotel, placed such a formidable order for Fox trucks, for installation on the Buffalo, Rochester & Pittsburgh Railroad, that the grateful salesman made young Gerald Merchant a member of the select retinue that accompanied him on his first visit to Europe.

Ensconced in the captain's suite on the S.S. *Normandie*, the Brady party left New York in midsummer 1898 on what Parker Morell said was the "grandest of the Grand Tours Europe had seen up to that time."

At this stage of his career, Brady had attained international fame as a party giver, and the fancy Dans of Paris, who, during visits to the States, had enjoyed his lavish soirees (at which, on occasions, comely naked girls were drawn on silken cords from pigeon potpies), outdid themselves to show the town to him and Miss Edna McCauley, and Diamond Jim's young Rochester friend.

In the company of his voluptuous patron and his patron's paramour, Merchant was royally feted. The experience of all this was a heady one for a tender college undergraduate, and it made an indelible impression upon the young recipient of Brady's bounty. After the fantasies of the Arabian Nights, he found his native city commonplace and jejune, and the exigencies of domestic economy seemed rather a bore.

In later years, Gerald Merchant composed a memoir of the Grand Tour, which, until a fatal illness forced him to abandon the project, was expanding into a full account of a friendship with Brady that continued several years. An intelligent and articulate man, Merchant corrected what he protested were the errors of his hero's biographers and the vengeful untruths of his detractors. He also provided interesting reflections on the spirit and mores of an era when profligacy in certain areas of American life was probably wilder than at any other time in the country's history.

It was a period when thim that has 'em (diamonds) wears 'em, when the new rich thought garish ostentation the cachet of social distinction, and the big quick-moneyed men built huge houses on the elegant avenues of New York, Rochester, and other cities, and often died from over indulgence and high pressures before they learned their way about the multiroomed labyrinth of their spang-new mansions.

Merchant professed that he was Diamond Jim's closest friend, and for a time this may have been true. He wrote cavalierly of riding on a gold-plated triplet (bicycle) with America's most extravagant sybarite and Lillian Russell, in a day when the fame of the blond hour-glass lovely was at perihelion; of momentous goings-on at Saratoga Springs when the fine stake horses Gold Heels and Major Daingerfield raced under the Brady silks; of Broadway first nights, when Brady, exquisitely in full fig, and aglitter with jewels, bought the first three rows of orchestra seats for friends, and after the show entertained them and the actors in the play at Bustanoby's, or some other gilded lobster palace.

Merchant's career as Brady's favorite courtier foundered in the end, and ended completely before the latter's death. Brady knew one true love in his life, Edna McCauley, the daughter of a

Brooklyn policeman. Lillian Russell, the Dolly Sisters, and various other theatrical beauties, who were often in his company, were mostly expensive showpieces. Nowhere in the tattered typescript pages of the Merchant memoir does the annalist explain why Brady, who left bequests in his will to many of his friends, failed to will Gerald Merchant so much as a diamond shirt stud. The most prominent theory about this is that Brady developed a suspicion that the slim, bright, and attractive young Rochesterian had become too attractive to his adored Edna.

Chapter 7

At the beginning of the twentieth century, Rochester boasted that its population exceeded 150,000, and the Chamber of Commerce, exultant, as if with the flush of revelation, declared that the city "may be said to have an ideal climate."

"It had become a matter of national comment that Rochester is the healthiest city of its size in the United States, and has the lowest mortuary record," read a pamphlet issued by the Chamber in 1901.

"This is largely due to climatic conditions. . . ."

Some support was given these affirmations by Professor Herman LeRoy Fairchild, geologist at the University of Rochester, who explained that "The exemption of Rochester from sudden changes in temperature (an exemption, it might be noted, of which many Rochesterians, who have known the temperature to vary as much as 40 degrees Fahrenheit in less than twenty-four hours, are hardly sensible) is due to the presence of Lake Ontario. The lake lies directly in the path of all cold cyclonic waves. They cannot cross it without being warmed by the water. . . . The effect of these waves may be felt on the high land south of Rochester, but it does not come here. Most of the cold weather which comes to Rochester is caused by storms which go to the eastward. . . . There is probably no other city in the world so well protected."

Rochester is notoriously non-sunny, particularly during the winter months, but Professor Fairchild found this fact no cause for lament. He said, as quoted in the Chamber of Commerce pamphlet, "On the whole, cloudy days are better than too many sunny ones. Clouds temper the heat and act as a blanket in the winter to keep the cold out (or, perhaps more properly expressed, to keep the heat in). The main objections to them are sentimental."

The Chamber's disquisition on the weather was printed a long time ago, and although the climatic pattern of Rochester has changed very little over the years, the attitude of Rochesterians toward the climate has changed appreciably.

Old, old-timers, long inured to Rochester winters, accept them philosophically, and stand them without complaint. God may not be in his heaven during much of the autumnal equinox, but land sakes alive, the old-timers say, you gotta have winter if you're going to have spring and summer. They live on, frequently in prosperous health, often stubborn in their disregard of the cardiac specialists' remonstrances about the use of snow shovels, to great age.

Younger residents, who are not young enough to risk their bones on nearby ski slopes, and find no joy in ice fishing, look upon Rochester winters as the *bête noire* of their existence. The complaints of the men are more bitter than those of the women. Many of the men live hopefully for the day when either a portfolio of blue chip securities or a sound pension from the Eastman Company will enable them to "get away from it all," and wear walking shorts and play shuffleboard all winter long in Florida.

Residents of Rochester who profess not to like the city because of its weather, cynically concede that our summers are pleasant —that there is no sleighing on the Fourth of July. The implication that summer is confined to that single holiday is unfair. June, July, August, and September are often delightful, and October has its peculiar charm, although by the time of its advent, summer is definitely past. But the October skies are sometimes less beclouded than those of midsummer. The air has an autumnal piquancy. It is bracing. There are frosts. Halcyon days, of course, are not guaranteed throughout the four weeks. Now and then, in the late days of the month, a snowstorm may blow in from the Canadian steppes to catch the Department of Public Works, not with its plows *down*, but with all of its snow-clearing equipment in estival retreat.

The Chamber of Commerce pamphlet, while admitting that Rochester does have its "quantum of disagreeable periods and degrees of cold that nip the ears and fingers," attested that these conditions "are of a health-giving nature and such as conduce to the well-being of a hardy, hustling people"; and added, that the "snow flurries hinder no one's business or pleasure . . ."

In 1901, the Chamber was a fairly young agency and probably

rather ingenuous. If the term "snow flurries" was intended to describe the extent of the fall of white crystalline flakes on Rochester during an ordinary winter, it was more than a euphemism; it was a vast understatement. To be sure, snow does not fall as quantitively on Rochester as it does, say, on the Stampede Pass in the Rocky Mountain area of the state of Washington, where it is measured in feet rather than inches; but there are no cities of comparable size in the United States, with the exception of the flanking communities of Buffalo and Syracuse, that match our snow precipitation.

"Rochester is in the snow belt," said John Williams, federal meteorologist, who is stationed at the Monroe County Airport. "We have to figure winter from November through April. It snows in all of these months."

"But surely, the snowfall here is nothing compared with that in such places as New Hampshire or Vermont," Mr. Williams was asked by this loyal Rochesterian.

"Rather, let us say, the snow here doesn't last as long or lie as deep on the ground," Mr. Williams corrected. He reached for his charts.

The charts showed that in 1968 the mean total snowfall in Rochester was 82.3 inches or approximately a foot more than the mean total of 70.6 inches in Burlington, Vermont.

"Vermont holds on to its snow longer, because the winter days and nights are colder than they are here," said Mr. Williams, continuing his exposition. "Burlington has considerably more sunshine than Rochester, but not as many thaws. In 1968, its mean temperature was 43.2 degrees. Here it was 48 degrees Fahrenheit."

Many who complain of the unpalatableness of Rochester weather fail to consider that the city is pretty well outside the disaster zone. We are rarely exposed to the whirling terror of a tornado, and earthquakes do not rock us from our beds. Floods we once knew. They came usually in the spring, when the swollen and rampageous Genesee swilled over its banks to inundate a small area of downtown Rochester. These were expensive disasters because of property loss, and grievously inconvenient; they were not attended by loss of human life, and they did not cause city dwellers to flee their homes. The threat of flood has now been lessened, but not entirely obviated, by the construction of a huge dam, forty miles upstream, which controls the flow of the lower river, and by retaining walls that confine the river within its proper channel.

The nearness of Lake Ontario to Rochester has a pronounced effect on Rochester weather. Winter storms howl across its watery expanse to fill our streets with snow or ice our pavements with frozen sleet. They wreak their devastation and move on, usually to the east, following what is known as the St. Lawrence storm track, on which the city is not an inconspicuous station. The lake is also responsible for Rochester's dubious distinction of being one of the cloudiest cities in the United States.

But Ontario is not a benighted body of water, cruel and uncompromising, devoid of grace and felicity. The advantages extended by it to the city of Rochester and the nearby countryside outbalance the inconveniences of lake-blown storms and the murky, unclear days of our winter season. Our climate is "moderated by the lake effect. . . . Rochester's summer temperature very rarely reaches 100° and the winter minimum falls to zero or below, on an average of only about 5 days per year," according to the Environmental Data Service of the United States Department of Commerce, and the observations of old-time residents of the city.

In summer months, the lake waters store up heat, which, slowly released in the autumn, prolongs the growing and harvest seasons, and aids the cultivation of apples, peaches, and cherries, long celebrated for their excellence, which thrive in the loamy soil of Ontario's littoral, immediately east and west of the city's northern reaches.

Ontario is a deep lake, and because of its depth, not given to capricious fits of temper. It provides fine sport for fresh-water shellbacks whose yachts of many designs sail out from their river moorings through the flat, cocoa-colored flow of the Genesee into the undulating, breeze-swept expanse of the smallest of the Great Lakes.

The lake is favored in the Rochester area by a shore line of white sand, but now the sparkling greenish-blue waters that lap at this periphery are said by health authorities to be polluted, and bathing from beaches that are controlled by the city has been prohibited for several seasons. Sun bathers in large numbers still gather on the warm sands during the summer months, and young muscle monuments display their naked torsos in competitions in bodily symmetry; there are volley ball courts, gymnastic apparatus,

and provisions for other athletic activities; but to the disgruntlement of great numbers of Rochester youth, the stern adjuration
of the health authorities continues: Hang your clothes on the locker
room hooks, but don't go near the water.

* * *

Rochester more or less grew up and lost its provincial character
shortly after World War I, and during the corybantic stock market
frenzy of the mid and late 1920s. Those were the years when
streetcar motormen were talking of their Big Board transactions,
and hallroom boys were bouncing in and out of their warrens
with hands full of Cities Service, and many of us believed the
end of the rainbow was no more than a flight-shot away.

The dreadfulness of Chateau Thierry and the Argonne Forest
was of the past, and tales of war horrors had begun to stale and
lose their pertinency. The idea in those early postwar years was to
get rich quick and concurrently cultivate the tastes and habits,
of those who had long been habituated to wealth, who knew about
fish forks, who crossed the Atlantic in A-Deck suites on the great
liners, and rode the Blue trains to what someone called the "pink
sewer" of the French Riviera.

In the days before the war, Rochester had had a tight little
social hierarchy. It was prideful. It was marked by distinct lines.
It was self-confident to the point of smugness; and it was coalesced
by two or three arbiters, and given further adhesion by Miss Emily
Munn, a gracious, genteel, old-family lady, whose Saturday column
in the *Post-Express* mentioned the names only of persons who had
proper certificates of pedigree and who were affiliated with what
Miss Munn considered the right clubs.

The social hierarchy continued after the war, and its arbiters
were still active and alert. And Miss Munn continued to write
her laconic, undecorated paragraphs about the goings and comings
of *her* people in a column that was tantamount to a Social Register.
But soon there were signs of erosion at the outer edges of the
hierarchy and porous spots were faintly discernible in its center.
The war had had a leavening effect on the organic life of Rochester. The masses had not actually fused with the classes, but
the common suffering, and the common effort exerted to advance
the prosecution of the war, had brought about a confluence of

people from various strata of society and quickened a sympathetic understanding among them.

Prohibition was also a factor in bringing about a change in the social posture of Rochester. Prohibition, and the permissiveness engendered by it. Persons of all classes were breaking the law. It was a smart thing to do, a mischief to boast about. Tender buds, from East Side homes of ultraconservatism, who had been reared in the swankiest finishing schools and who had "come out," were now so far "out" that they were drinking bootleg hooch in downtown speakeasies, and comingling with some of the "strangest people." It was exciting. It was adventurous. The tender buds bobbed their hair, rolled their stockings, and left their corsets at home. They avidly read F. Scott Fitzgerald, and had a warm sense of association with his characters.

Staid old Tories, who at the shank of the afternoon had always been served a scotch and soda by a uniformed attendant at a club or by a maid or a butler in their own home, were outraged at the law's attempt to prohibit this amenity; and they too flouted the law: the law and Andrew J. Volstead, whom they envisioned as a blue-nosed, pinch-mouthed reformer, with dandruff on his coat collar and bad breath. They were patriotic, law-abiding American citizens; but, by God, this infamous law they would not abide; and soon they were dealing with sinister-looking fellows, who might have been members of the Purple Gang, who crept around to the back door in the dead of night to deliver bottled goods which they whisperingly avowed had come "straight off the boat."

When people of acknowledged position, who had previously respected all the formulas and conformities began to break the law, this act of defiance was accompanied by a slow crumbling of old barriers.

In the middle years of Prohibition, when money from stock-market speculations was as loose as ashes, and new wealth was widely on display in Rochester, now and then one of the possessors of this new wealth, who prior to the war couldn't have gotten into the Valley (*Genesee* Valley) Club or the Country Club of Rochester without the use of a burglar's jimmy, was found acceptable, possibly because a broker or a banker on the membership committee had done a handsome stroke of business with the aspirant.

Such instances, however, were not common. At least they were infrequent during the decade between the Versailles Peace Conference and that obscene Thursday in October 1929, when market players who were unable to protect their margins began leaping from high buildings or were found dead under the exhaust pipes of their automobiles.

After that, all clubs began to feel the pinch. And now and then, when some hard-pressed old member of the Valley or Country Club was constrained to resign, rather than allow his name to be posted for non-payment of dues, his place was taken by an outlander of authoritative solvency—provided, of course, the candidate could be relied upon not to commit the gaucheries that perhaps were common to his place of origin on the other side of the tracks.

The Valley and the Country Club, the last two bastions of the city's social hierarchy, never broke down completely; they never went anything like public. But the membership of each expanded and became less parochial in character. These clubs needed added revenue; and presently their economy, and the economy of such organizations as the Elks, the Moose, and the Portuguese Social and Athletic Club was aided by the installation of batteries of slot machines. The slots—the one-armed bandits—were not hidden in corners, behind locked doors. They were as accessible to members and their guests as a pinball machine in a corner saloon. They continued in profitable operation for a considerable time, with no molestation from a police force that seemed universally afflicted with myopia.

The period of laissez faire was ended by a stern edict from the police, whose impaired vision was suddenly restored. The slot machines were to go, at once. The order brought moans of despair from house committees. It also restored something like sanity to women addicts, who were hooked worse than the men, and who would stand hours on end at one or two machines, and not leave when they should have left—to go to the bathroom —fearful that even a temporary absence would jinx their luck.

Most of the clubs had profited handsomely. So also had the popular manager of the Rochester Club, who resigned to open a restaurant of his own and to pursue the avocation of gentleman farmer. In time he married a second or third wife, and removed to Nevada. There he fathered twins, adopted a lion cub, and established a restaurant-gambling place high above Reno, which became a favored resort of the New York and Virginia City exquisite, the late Lucius Beebe.

Chapter 8

For many of us who lived in the modest circumstances of a middle-class family, Rochester was a particularly pleasant place until the Kaiser's gray-mantled hordes pushed into Flanders and the thunder of the guns of August resounded round the world. The dreadful phenomenon of World War I destroyed our fond illusion of intramural tranquillity, and the changes that came to Rochester following the war extinguished a form of life that will never be duplicated in our society.

Until the war, we had been a tight, unflappable, quite self-contained little community. We enjoyed a rosy glow of confidence in our well-being, and we believed that the world outside was congenial to our own happy state. It seemed bright and safe and readily manageable. At home we had our Main Street, where Rochester life came sharply into focus; our five theaters, our band concerts in the parks, our water carnivals on the upper Genesee, and, for several years, the finest outdoor "equine exhibition in the land"—the Rochester Horse Show—which provided a week-long gala that was unlike any other pageant the town has ever known.

Perhaps the war, which became real to us the day the United States joined the Allies, had a more traumatic effect on Rochester than on many other cities that lacked our rather provincial self-contentedness. For years we had boasted that ours was "the best governed city." We believed in this maxim. We felt fortunate in our condition and had no desire to disturb the status quo. But now the vaunting of our virtues had a hollow mocking sound; and we knew, and were deeply distressed by the conviction, that we could not exist as an enclave of peace, serenity, and orderliness with the world gone mad around us.

Shaken out of our traditional complacency, Rochester quickly adjusted to the emergency and wholeheartedly responded to the demands the emergency exacted. Under the leadership of George

Eastman, who had become by then the city's first citizen, 103,000 residents subscribed more than four and a half million dollars to what was called the Patriotic and Community Fund. Red Cross motor corps were organized, canteens for servicemen were established, city firemen went to knitting socks for "the boys over there," and hundreds of volunteers were used by a dozen agencies devoted to the Allied effort to win the war to end war, and bring extinction to the hated Hun.

The war took our youth, grown suddenly to soldierly manhood, and dispersed them widely over two continents; it sent civilians, who had previously not been much farther away than Niagara Falls, scurrying about the country on war missions; it put our population in flux. And when the war was over, and we advanced into the mad twenties—the era of Wonderful Nonsense—and the high flights of the stock market gave many of us an illusionary sense of wealth, many ordinarily stay-at-home Rochesterians became afflicted with the wanderlust. They had heard tales of faraway places from returned servicemen; their feet itched. Suddenly, they wanted to go places and see things.

And Europe was the first allurement. They went in small contingents composed of fellow townsmen, for Rochesterians, as Miss Edith Wharton might have observed, pursued "culture in bands, as though it were dangerous to meet it alone." They crossed on the big liners, and put up at the grand hotels. With Baedekers in hand, they pilgrimaged to the great cathedrals, and blistered their feet on the marble floors of innumerable museums. From the giddy peaks of the Alps they followed the tortuous roads conquerors had traversed; from delightful little chocolate shops they observed the sloping idyll of the Swiss countryside. They saw in Paris mementos of Big Bertha, and in London small craters made by Zeppelin raids. They sent back scenic postcards, "Wonderful time. Wish you were here," and returned to regale their friends with embellished reports of their adventures; and home-bound friends who heard them, quickly reckoning their stock-market winnings, often went directly to a travel agency to initiate the organization of a new tourist group; for European travel, with Rochesterians, had become very definitely the thing to do.

All who went abroad from Rochester (and for a time the movement eastward was like an exodus, so eager were our townsfolk to cultivate cosmopolitan tastes and assume cosmopolitan attitudes) did not go in pursuit of culture. Some who had heard of the heady goings-on "up the hill to Montmartre," went frankly in quest of Saturnalian experiences. They got drunk in Zeli's on something better than the chancy bottled goods represented by back-home bootleggers as imported whiskey. They hired pimps to guide them into the raunchier mantraps. They raucously acclaimed the *dusky* arabesques of Miss Josephine Baker.

In Harry's Bar they met apple knockers like themselves, ex-patriates from Boise, Idaho, and Rockland, Maine, and Kokomo, Indiana, all whooping it up on profits from Union Carbide, or A.T.&T. or Electric Bond & Share; they came home, sodden, beat out, but exulting in their high jinks, and boasting of their fellowship with the barmen at the Ritz.

It was during the booming, pre-depression days that Rochesterians, who seemed of different character from the solid, down-to-earth, rather pedestrian burghers of an earlier day, began to display an acute sensitiveness about Rochester winters.

All travelers from Rochester, even when there was a surplus of money to travel, did not make the Grand Tour of Europe. I think it was Bernard De Voto who asked, "Why go to Paris, France, if you haven't seen Paris, Illinois?" and De Voto's sentiments were similar to those of numerous patriotic Rochester natives. They wanted to explore their own land before going abroad, and they did so extensively, by motorcar over swiftly improving roads; by train, and in some instances by steamship. And they went to Florida.

In my youth, our knowledge of Florida was limited. We had learned from the history course in school that Ponce de Leon had found it while searching for the Fountain of Youth, and suffered a mortal wound when he attempted to expropriate it from the hostile Indians. We knew that oranges came from there; we had read in Mr. Hearst's lurid newspaper, which came into town on Sunday, that Palm Beach was the rendezvous of the very affluent, and sometimes scandalous gadabouts of high society. That was about all.

Now, in the period of Hoover prosperity, with a chicken in every pot and the promise of two cars in every garage, dozens of Rochesterians were speculating in Florida real estate, and going there to see what they had bought. What they had bought might have been a mangrove-cluttered swamp or a strip of land shored up by riprap at the edge of a tidal backwater. No matter. According to the affirmations of the promoters, every square foot of Florida soil had parity with solid gold, and the promoters were believed.

The land buyers came home to report extravagantly on the Golconda in which they had invested, to rhapsodize about the Florida climate, and to declare, ugh!—never again would they subject themselves to the brutality of a Rochester winter.

But all of this, of course, was during the period of suppositive wealth, when license and luxury were rampant, and the never-never land of the New America was thought to be oncoming apace. Before Wold War I, we had not considered our winters particularly brutal, and if the climate was actually ungenial during the most definitive months of winter (and, actually, it often was!), it was at that time of year that Rochester and its inhabitants seemed most highly energized. What many people considered the "season" opened the last week of August or the first week of September, when Lew Dockstader's gaudily attired Minstrels, the first road show booked into town, swaggered through Main Street behind a phalanx of hard-tooting brasses. The noontime parade preceded the evening performance in the Lyceum Theater, and when the curtain rose and the interlocutor pronounced his crisp command, "Gentlemen, be seated!" the transition from the vernal to the autumnal equinox, by the reckoning of many city dwellers, if not by astronomical calculation, was achieved.

From then on, almost continually until mid or late April, the ample stage of the Lyceum would display many of the choicest offerings of the theatrical "road"; across the street the Temple Theater, home of big-time vaudeville, would present its first bill on Labor Day, and farther west, in the vicinity of the Four Corners, three other playhouses would open their doors to the public. Seafood restaurants put oysters back on their bill of fares, bowlers returned to their alleys, and billiardists and pool hustlers to the green baize of their tables. Dancing clubs resumed their schedules. On Saturday night, Main Street was a teeming concourse, and the owl cars ran with straphangers. "Autumn is the spring of the city's life," said the famed Dr. Johnson; and at that season, bestirred out of its summer languor, Rochester came vitally alive.

Snow in the winter was the expected thing, a natural condition, and no one that I knew seemed to resent it very much. Provident householders, as we all were in our part of Linden Street, began to prepare for winter in late August when coal wagons trundled into the street and bulky, grimy-faced men dumped large sacks of coal into galvanized iron chutes that reached into cellars. The noise of coal rattling down the chutes was an emblematic late summer sound.

We often had snow—snow enough for sleighing—on Thanksgiving, and if we didn't have it at Christmas, quantitatively and virginal white, from a recent fall, we felt that we had been gulled; besides, there was an old wives' saying, nervously laughed at but half believed, that a green Christmas portended fat graveyards.

Kids, of course, reveled in the first snow, and when snow began to fall early in the morning of a Thanksgiving I particularly remember, very early in the century, Charlie Maloy and I, who lived next door to one another in the only houses on the south side of Linden Street, were soon in communication.

I was the proud possessor of an outsized Flexible Flyer, and we had another lower, longer sled, and these we decided would be our double hitch when, overlarded with food after our Thanksgiving dinners, we started in midafternoon for the steep, curving sidewalk that skirted the Mt. Hope Avenue wall of Mt. Hope Cemetery.

There we found competition. Boys who had been less ceremonial at their holiday dinners than we had been at ours already had made the Mt. Hope Avenue sidewalk a fast, glistening ribbon of ice, and one group, with *three* sleds hitched together, boasted that they had made a record by coursing well past the cemetery office and half a block past the cemetery gate.

"Let's see you beat that," they challenged.

Charlie and I tried, but we never quite reached the standard claimed by the three-sled combination. It was glorious coasting, though. As the afternoon waned, more boys came, some from quite distant parts of town, and of course the more traffic on the slide, the faster it became. The sport was at its zenith, and we had never known it to be so good, when two men, one with a bristling beard who was superintendent of the cemetery and lived on the property, started throwing buckets of ashes from the cemetery office on the glazed hill, and ordered us home.

I guess Charlie Maloy and I went docilely on our way. But among those on the hill were boys who had come from a section east of South Avenue known as Swillburg, and they didn't take it lying down. They taunted the superintendent as an old whiskered so-and-so of a goat, and it was only when he shook his fist at them and threatened to call the cops (and cops, in those days, suffered impertinencies from neither adolescent nor grown-up toughies) that they dispersed.

* * *

Rochester was one of the first of fifteen cities in the United States to be favored with a weather station under federal sponsorship. That was in 1870, and the station was established and manned by the Army Signal Corps. But long before this, amateur meteorologists had been putting down quite exact observations of climatic variances, and the most comprehensive of these early records were compiled by Dr. Chester Dewey, a Massachusetts native who became, in 1837, principal of Rochester's first high school.

A graduate of Williams College, class of 1806, Dr. Dewey was a teacher, a scientist, and a preacher with a formidable lifetime pulpit average of more than three thousand sermons. His talents were varied; his interests were wide. He was a popular platform speaker, and his non-religious lectures outnumbered by several hundred the number of his sermons.

The high school expanded and twice changed its name. It was known successively as the Rochester Seminary and the Collegiate Institute, and Dr. Dewey continued under both titles to serve it as principal. He was Rochester's earliest distinguished educator. Under his inspirited leadership, the Collegiate Institute became not only an admirable place of learning for the young but the center of intellectual life in the nascent and thriving little city of the Genesee. In 1850, Dr. Dewey left the Collegiate Institute to join the faculty of the newly formed University of Rochester. He was made professor of natural sciences. He was revered by his students for his wisdom and beneficence, and beloved by adult audiences for whom he often repeated in public halls, his stimulating classroom lectures and scientific demonstrations. At the time of Dewey's death, Dr. Martin B. Anderson, first president of the university, said of him, "To the whole population of Rochester his presence was a benediction."

The Dewey weather readings began about the time the good

doctor took over the high school principalship, and continued almost until the time of his death, two years after the close of the Civil War.

Drawn from file boxes in the library of the University of Rochester, the repository of all of Dr. Dewey's papers, the sere and yellow pages of the weather record books offer quite convincing testimony that the "brutal" Rochester winters, which now put so many Rochesterians to southern flight, were equally "brutal" in the good old (winter) days so charmingly depicted on Currier & Ives calendars.

On the margins of his statistical charts, which registered temperatures, winds, precipitation, cloudy and clear days, Dewey made annotations that told of the flight of geese, ducks, and pigeons. He commented on the return of the robin, of the flitting of the first bluebirds of spring. He wrote briefly of floral growth and other mutations of nature. He was exuberant about a beautiful winter's morning. He seemed constantly alert and observant. In substance, his marginal minutiae were not unlike the journals of Thoreau or those of the gentle and perspicacious Rev. Gilbert White, of Shelborne. He advanced the theory that the flattening of forest areas adjacent to the city would increase the severity of Rochester winters.

"This may not, indeed, be every winter," he hastened to add, "but we shall not be able to maintain that our temperature does not descend below zero."

In this he was prophetic. For on what he designated as the "cold Tuesday" of February 1855 (February 6, to be exact), the thermometer fell to 14, then to 16 Fahrenheit degrees below zero during the daylight hours, and plummeted to 25 below when the polar night closed in on Rochester.

Dr. Dewey did not resign from the faculty of the University of Rochester until he had attained an age much more advanced than the age at which university professors are nowadays arbitrarily relieved of their posts. He lived busily, usefully, and contentedly in Rochester for more than three decades. Nowhere in the comments that accompanied his voluminous weather reports did he complain about the severity of Rochester winters: he merely observed them as natural phenomena.

At a time when the control of infectious disease was largely given to chance and superstition, and the medical profession had no more than an inkling of knowledge of antisepsis, Dr. Dewey gave some support to the latter-day affirmation of the Rochester Chamber of Commerce that the "health-giving nature" of Rochester's climate is conducive to "the well-being of a hardy, hustling people." He lived to the handsome age of eighty-two, sentient and active up until the beginning of his brief terminal illness.

Today it is fashionable among great numbers of Rochesterians who do not ski, fish through the ice, or practice figure skating, to believe that to endure a Rochester winter, uninterrupted by a few weeks in Florida or on the Arizona desert, is to suffer the tortures of Tantalus.

They denigrate our weather as *vile, odious, beastly, hideous, terrible*—or just plain *lousy*. They would respond, not with scornful laughter, but with bitter invective to anyone who suggested that the Rochester climate which, perforce, must include the harsh inclemencies of the winter months, was beneficial to anyone except an Eskimo. And, of course, the long-ago allegation of the Chamber of Commerce concerning the city's admirable mortuary record was absurd—to the point of fantasy! Alice in Wonderland stuff!

But it wasn't all fantasy; the Chamber had the support of statistics. And even today, an inferential tribute may be due the Rochester climate, since many who are exposed to it appear possessed of unusual staying powers.

According to Dr. Wendell R. Ames, director of the Monroe County Department of Health, Rochester has a higher percentage of elderly persons—persons over sixty-five—than any other city in the country with the exception of St. Petersburg, Florida.

Asked if he attributed this remarkable record of longevity to the Rochester climate, Dr. Ames gently evaded a categorical reply.

"We are pretty well fixed here," he said. "We have less humidity than New York City, and less snow than our neighbor, Buffalo. We could do with more sunshine, and not quite so much snow. But this isn't an unhealthy climate."

Since Rochester has no soft winter climate to attract the elderly, the suggestion was made to Dr. Ames that many ancient residents, contrary to the migrants who invade St. Petersburg, must be natives.

"It isn't very likely that elderly people would choose Rochester as a winter resort," said Dr. Ames. "But some, who weren't born here, may have come early, attracted by the paternalism of

Rochester industry. And they continue to live here in retirement, enjoying the benefits of that paternalism."

* * *

When I was young, Rochester winters did have their terrors, but they were not excited by heavy snows, or by high winds that whipped the snow into morainelike obstructions on sidewalks and city pavements, or by near-zero temperatures. These disadvantages were countervailed by snow shovels and horse-drawn plows, by heavy ankle-length underwear and high boots, and a full bin of coal in the cellar.

The frightening thing about the return of winter was the reappearance on the front of dwelling houses, usually in ominous proximity to the place where a wreath or a crepe would hang if there was death in the family, of various cloth signs: red for scarlet fever, blue for diptheria, pink for measles. The first two were reputedly deadly diseases, and the stern adjuration on the diptheria sign, NO VISITORS ALLOWED BY ORDER OF THE HEALTH BUREAU, and the warning that anyone removing the scarlet fever plaque would be fined $25 were not commands to be flouted. On their way to and from school, boys and girls would often cross the street and proceed on the opposite sidewalk rather than pass close to a house officially identified as being infected.

There were other killers even more desperate. The Great White Plague of tuberculosis, which we called consumption, was considered mankind's greatest enemy; and lobar pneumonia, which the patient could not throw off, as today, by submitting to a penicillin injection in the buttocks, or by swallowing an antibiotic pill, big as a horse doctor's bolus, each winter exacted an unholy toll of deaths from its victims.

And there was smallpox!

Rochester had a Pest House at the turn of the century. It was a converted farmhouse which stood, as mentioned earlier in this book, in a railroad cut on the east bank of the Genesee River, close to the stagnant waters of the Erie Canal Feeder. It backed up to Mt. Hope Cemetery. It was called Hope Hospital.

Hope Hospital was as barbaric in its physical aspects as a lazar house, and antediluvian in its services. It would have done well in Defoe's *The Journal of the [London] Plague Year*. Dr. George W. Goler, the city's first full-time Health Officer, whom the politicians tried, and tried again, to make a sitting duck, protested that the building was utterly inadequate for the reception and treatment of patients suffering from contagious diseases. His protests were shrugged off.

In later years, Dr. Goler described the place in these words. "Hope Hospital was a two-ward and one-room, sixteen-bed hospital with one water tap in the kitchen, without a sewer, an old, partitioned privy in back labeled 'Ladies,' and 'Gents,' a two-room battered, unpainted shack for isolating suspects and an old grocery wagon for an ambulance—the horse had to be rented."

The "best governed city," whose moralities on occasions have been protean, to say the least, stood for this; and the politicians, and many other Rochesterians put Goler down as a quirky fellow, a crank who had better learn to march to the regular tunes if he was going to keep on marching in the parade. The Health Officer, who did not suffer politicians gladly, never learned to goose-step.

Protesting the inadequacies of Hope Hospital, Dr. Goler warned also of a possible smallpox epidemic, and urged general vaccination for the public. The public was apathetic. It had been some time since the city had experienced a smallpox "scare," and more than thirty years since a serious occurrence of the disease had taken the lives of thirty-eight persons. Wars, and Black Plague, and many other bad things, it was popularly believed, were discards of the past century, gone with it into limbo; this—the twentieth—was the age of enlightenment and promise.

This sense of community euphoria was somewhat lessened in February 1902 when four persons were diagnosed as smallpox sufferers and bestowed among the deplorable appurtenances of Hope Hospital. After that there was a brief pause in the incidence of the disease, but in late winter, all through the spring, and during the first weeks of summer, a great many cases were added to the original four, and macabre tales were circulated that Pest House inmates were "dying like flies."

And more than a hundred out of a thousand persons who contracted the disease did die in Rochester's most serious epidemic since the town had suffered the horrible scourge of cholera fifty years before. Dr. Goler attempted to command, then implored the public to be vaccinated against smallpox. His petitions were resisted. There was still a superstitious aversion to a technique of immunization that had been in use nearly a century.

During the first spring of the epidemic, patients arrived at the Pest House in such numbers that tents—to give the place, from afar, the gay and airy aspect of a summer camp—were raised around the main hospital building. The tents were used mostly for convalescents, who sat forlornly on their cots and picked their scabs. The following winter, when the epidemic became more virulent than it had been even during earlier stages, portable election booths were trundled on flat wagons to the Pest House site, and in these flimsy structures, identified by grim humorists as "Idle Rest," "Hogan's Alley," and "Waldorf-Astoria," smallpox patients lived or died, as fortune—and the sturdiness of their constitutions—decreed.

The epidemic was a civic disgrace. Before it ran its course, a year and a half after the first smallpox cases were isolated and the slatternly old hospital building was put to the torch by an authoritative hand, a catch line, supposedly called to a complaining patient by either Dr. Goler or one of his aides, "Cheer up, cherries will soon be ripe!" got into the Main Street idiom.

Because of the original parsimony of politicians who controlled the public monies, Goler and his staff were woefully ill-equipped to grapple with a deadly and widespread epidemic. They were a little like soldiers with halberds assaulting a machine-gun nest. They strove valiantly against discouraging odds; eventually, they won out. For their pains, the conquerors of the epidemic got little more than calumny and accusation. The Health Officer himself was made the whipping boy for neglect and derelictions he had warned would result in disaster. He was brought into Star Chamber proceedings, and an attempt was made to ride him (some suggested, on a rail) out of office. Happily for the city of Rochester, the impeachment attempt was aborted, and Dr. Goler's tenure continued for more than three decades. In the end, he gained both the reluctant esteem of the local public and outside recognition as one of the most independent, enlightened, and advanced public health officers in the nation.

* * *

Although I had no idea that Rochester was distinguished in the matter of geriatrics until Dr. Ames informed me that only one other city in the country had a greater percentage of senior citizens, I had a vague notion that residents of rural communities adjacent to the city often managed to stay alive to a great age.

After I had lived nearly forty years on or within a two minutes' walk of my native Linden Street, we moved thirteen miles south of the city to Scottsville. It was a quaint village, a pretty, drowsy little rural community, whose somnolence, one might happily believe, would never be disturbed by the goading of that invidious thing called "progress."

And there was no progress for a long time. There were privies out back of several Scottsville homes. It was not suburbia. It was an independent community, agrarian in character, and only a handful of commuters went each day to town, and most of us made the short journey by train.

We got to our place, which was on a rise and remote by a quarter of a mile from the nearest neighbor, over a wagon track that serpentined through a wood. From our hill, the Genesee Valley lay in broad prospect to the east, and it seemed to me that the visual delight offered by this varied and lovely countryside compensated for the formidable inconveniences we soon discovered were the attendants of country living. We were both city bred, my wife a native of Manhattan. We had moved into our new home in a February blizzard, and that night she protested that she had never liked the country, that she would never *learn* to like the country, that now she hated it, isolated on the Siberian steppe; and two weeks later, the place was up for sale.

We had decided on the country in the first place because I thought it would provide a healthy way of living for our three small sons, and allow them to roam about, unmenaced by the ever increasing traffic of city streets. But we had not bargained on a septic tank that backed up the first week it was in use; on a power line that snapped under the stress of high wind and the burden of frozen sleet to shut off our lights at night, deaden our electric range, and require that we cook for two days over an open fire in the hearth. We had not calculated that our tinny little automobile would be immobilized thirty-six hours in a snow bank that blocked the wagon track leading out through the woods to something that resembled civilization.

And the water!

A salesman for a water-softening apparatus, who analyzed the water we drank, used in the laundry tub, and bathed in, pronounced it the hardest water between Scottsville and the Colorado Rockies.

This may have been apocryphal; the salesman could have been exercising his prerogative to exaggerate in the interest of American industry and the preservation of the national economy. Nevertheless, the water was so chuck-full of lime that it plugged the perforations of the shower-bath nozzle. When we placed a basin of water on a furnace register to serve as a humidifier, we would find, when the water evaporated, a gravelly deposit half an inch thick on the bottom of the basin. Neither soap nor prayer, neither muscle nor the strongest detergent would bring a speck of suds to that dreadfully calcified water. My wife and a young woman who assisted with the domestic chores were fit to be tied, in a state verging on neurosis. At night, when I returned from the city, my small sons would greet me, looking for all the world as if they were equipped with fright wigs, because their hair, which the women had attempted to wash, stood straight up, and was as rigid as hog's bristles.

I had advertised the property for sale, but when a man came to say that he was interested and to ask the price, my wife gave him short shrift: The place was NOT for sale!

Somehow we muddled through the winter. We found we were resilient; we could bounce back. The spring refreshed our souls, even as it brightened the little yellow bells of the forsythia bushes, and made the dogwood bloom, and laid a rich carpet of myrtle over the floor of the woods, which we had once thought eternally shrouded in polar snows. A pair of cardinals flounced out of the copse, appeared to like what they saw, and stayed around. The air across the valley was sweet and warm and blue. We seeded a lawn and planted fruit trees. We got around to see the folks, at chicken-pie and pot-roast suppers at the churches, and at strawberry festivals. Many seemed very old; it was as if the young had deserted the village, and left it to their ancestors. The villagers were ancient, but often ruddy and spry. They made garden, bred coon dogs, painted houses, kept bees, and tied trout flies that they used in the fine stream that crossed the southern boundary of Scottsville on the last leg of its run to the Genesee River.

We lived more than twenty years in Scottsville before contractors from the city came to blight our village with rows of tossed-up little houses that resembled nothing so much as grids on a waffle iron. It was inevitable, I suppose, that in time we were to be drawn into the city's orbit, and made more or less a Rochester bedchamber; but the transition from a rural community to a suburban unit might have been accomplished with more grace and less disfigurement had avarice been restrained and some scheme of civic planning enforced.

After the city contractors had committed their first desecration, and the rows of flimsy little dwellings had been occupied, Scottsville enjoyed—or suffered—something rather like a vogue. In the past, the approximate ratio of home building had been one new house every other decade. Now they went up a dozen at a time. We got dial telephones when previously we had had to hand crank the instrument to get Central; a sewer was installed for favored residents. Today, we have a shopping plaza, a new central school, a bowling alley, three saloons, and our little library is served by the large public library in Rochester. We have a new firehouse, a new post office, a bank, and a new school. Yellow school buses carry kids to school who live no more than a five- or ten-minute walk from the schoolhouse. Our taxes have risen astronomically.

We still have lovely old houses on two or three of our streets, and great widespread trees, and here and there the ambiance of tradition. But we are definitely suburbia. I confess I liked it better when some of our neighbors had privies out back, and one might walk to the post office and know everyone along the way. Now I know almost no one. And the ancients have disappeared. I am sure several of them will never die, unless shot with a gun. But they are undercover and overwhelmed. The suburbanites have taken over. They are young, or youngish middle-aged. They play golf on nearby suburban courses. They wear walking shorts when they garden, and brilliant blazers, with crests at the breast pockets, at summer cocktail parties. They ride saddle horses. In the winter, they have ski racks on their station wagons. They are a new breed, and I have scarcely a nodding acquaintance with any of them. Before they came, our side—the west side of the Genesee River, previously not considered the fashionable side—was favored by the arrival of a very wealthy Rochester brewer. His mailing address was Scottsville, but the thousand-acre tract, with buildings, that he took over, was four miles nearer the city.

Louis A. Wehle was a man whose self-indulgences were legendary. He had enormous capacities for material success. When Prohibition became law, he turned to the bakery business and made a fortune; with repeal, he returned to his brewery and made millions. He was lush, gregarious, lusty. He was a guest at White House dinners, and played host to White House aspirants. He wanted what he wanted at once, and got a great deal of what he set about to obtain. Highly acquisitive himself, he greatly admired Napoleon, and started a Bonaparte museum on property he acquired on the St. Lawrence River that had once been designed as a place of refuge for the harried little Corsican.

His estate on the Scottsville Road, six miles south of the Rochester city line, is a show place on that highway. When Wehle first arrived, he enlarged the commodious dwelling house that stood already on the property to dimensions that would accommodate his elaborate entertainments. He built a decorative brick barn, facing the road, for the stabling of his handsome twelve-horse brewery hitch. He fenced his meadow lands with white paling, and raised blooded cattle, and bred and raced trotting horses. He built homes for his two sons on the property. He had a swimming pool, a tennis court, a range for trap shooting, greenhouses, and a pheasant preserve.

He proclaimed himself a conservationist, and once briefly held the post of state Conservation Commissioner. He also sponsored fishing contests to promote Genesee beer. He went on safaris to Africa, and struggled through the bush as the headman of a caravan of motor lorries bearing refrigerated food, an armory of modern weapons, native *valets de chambre*, beaters, cooks, outrunners, white hunters, and such, and returned with heads of many of the most notable animals of the jungle.

A large man, with a commanding presence, who gave the appearance of robust health, our prodigal neighbor down the road had a phobia about various diseases, and always had on call what was tantamount to a personal physician. The doctor needed scarcely any other patient. In time, Wehle acquired large cattle lands in Florida, and made his winter home in Palm Beach.

Each year, he extended his southern stay, and he descanted on this one day in early autumn as he was leaving the Scottsville drugstore with a packet of expensive prescriptions his physician had recommended.

"When you get fairly well along, you simply have to get out of this hellish winter climate, if you want to stay alive," he said. "I'm staying in the South eight months, this time."

I mentioned that there were a number of septuagenarians, and even octogenarians, who wintered in our village, and all seemed to be doing quite well.

"I don't know 'em," Mr. Wehle said, bristling. "I don't see 'em."

"But they're here," I insisted. "Why, there's Mr.——, for example. He's eighty-four. In August he was shingling his roof, and fell off the ladder."

"Well, *he's* gone!" Mr. Wehle said, almost triumphantly.

"Oh, no. No, he isn't."

"What happened to him?"

"He was laid up for a month. But he was back on the roof, yesterday. I saw him. Finishing the shingling job."

*　　*　　*

It would be tedious to particularize about residents of Rochester and Monroe County who live on, defying the harsh elements of our climate, well beyond the three score and ten years of the biblical actuaries, but any discussion of the geriatric phenomenon of the region must include mention of our most notable centenarian, James A. Hard.

A Monroe County native who fought as an infantryman in some of the bloodiest battles in the Civil War, Hard's life span of 111 years was longer than that of any other member of the force of more than two million and a half that served under President Lincoln and when he died, March 12, 1953, only one Union veteran of America's great fratricide survived him.

One day each year, during the closing period of his long life, Hard was a conspicuous personage. With the passing of his local comrades in arms, he alone represented the Grand Army of the Republic in the Memorial Day parade. It was his moment of pomp and circumstance. A frail figure in the blue regimentals of the Union forces, he sat erect in the first car in the procession and responded with trembling salutes to the applause of the curbstone watchers, who accepted him as a legend and cherished him as a Rochester institution that linked them with the historic past. For years, up until the last year before his death, he was honored as the parade's Grand Marshal.

James Hard, who survived in our climate well beyond the century mark, was not, I suppose, atypical. In Rochester, as in most other places, women generally outlive the men, and widows of great age, who go on and on, many of them ever so affluent, are too common to excite notice. It isn't, however, difficult to call to mind the names of a number of widowers of notable durability. Offhand, I can think of a couple of dozen who are still hale, although into their eighties. I speak of only one.

Ray A Miller, a red-faced, twinkling little man, with a quiet, kindly manner, and a briar pipe that is almost as natural an appendage of his visage as his nose, continued as an engineer for the Eastman Kodak Company five or six years beyond the ordinary retirement age of sixty-five. He still lives in the house he occupied with his late wife in the Monroe County town of Hilton, a short distance northwest of the city, and twenty-five miles from Scottsville. If you telephone and ask, "Ray, will you come over for dinner tonight?" he'll say, "Wait a minute," and there'll be a pause while he dials down to piano softness the gabble of the television performers. "Yes—yes," he'll say, returning to the phone. "What time?"

By his own admission, he was eighty-eight (one of his sons has implied that that figure may be a little like the age a not-too-young actress of dwindling fame might give the editor of an almanac, or a baseball player half a yard short of his former speed might give a manager) at the time this was written, and a month before it was written, Ray drove over to Scottsville for dinner. We had a pleasant meal. Later we sat with our knees drawn close to the fire, refurbishing old memories. We both know a good deal about the mores, the practices, and the people of Rochester during a much earlier period in the century, for I, too, am an octogenarian.

At ten-thirty, Mr. Miller took a small swallow of whiskey and got up to go. We went with him to the door. The weather had worsened. The wind howled angrily, and the air was thick with whirling snow. We petitioned him to remain overnight.

"Oh no, thanks," Mr. Miller said cheerfully, tightening the muffler at his throat. "Nothing to this."

And there wasn't, apparently. He made it home handsomely through the storm, as we learned when we telephoned later that night to be certain of his safe arrival.

Chapter 9

Until the grotesqueries brought to light by the mini-skirt vogue destroyed the illusion that women's legs, categorically, were alluring and exciting appendages, the common saying was that the girls in Syracuse, our neighbor to the east, wore shorter skirts than our girls, and had more zing; that Buffalo, immediately to the west, had more life, and big city sin.

Because of its traditional conservatism, and its aspect of high respectability, Rochester is often put down as a lumpish place by transients whose acquaintance with the city is superficial rather than intimate. They seem to feel that the town is inherently provincial. Their feeling about this, however, is possibly less intense than the judgment of "Captain" George D. Ball, a fellow of lithographic smoothness, and charm—charm so compelling that the wealthy Mrs. Harriet J. Brewster, a lady of solid East Avenue standing, was constrained to entrust him with $140,000; after which, the Captain and Mrs. Brewster's money seemed to blow away, like thistledown in a wind.

After a long, tortuous pursuit, Captain Ball was apprehended in Paris, and returned to the scene of his alleged peculation. He was in irons. As he descended under police escort from the train that had brought him from the seaboard, he fixed his gaze for a moment on the dingy prospect of that part of Rochester which may be seen from the platform of the New York Central Station, and a shudder of revulsion passed over his stylish figure. "I hate," said the Captain bitterly, "to get knocked off in an apple orchard."

Over the years, an array of critics have disparaged Rochester as dull, Pecksniffian, mediocre, and outrageously self-complacent. The critics have sometimes been persons who were more or less passing through, such as Philip Hamburger, of *The New Yorker*, and Stanley Levy, of the now defunct *Saturday Evening Post*.

Mr. Hamburger appeared to fulfill his assignment in the Rio Bamba, a small, ornamental, and expensive restaurant in a converted house on Alexander Street. There, each night of his brief visit, he made penetrating observations of Rochester life at a tucked-away piano bar, where Sara, a pretty black girl, entertained with low-throated melodies and tinkling little arabesques.

When he presently got around to put his lucubrations into print, Mr. Hamburger spoke pleasantly of Sara, told that our town had no reputation for razzle-dazzle, and that traveling men in quest of after-dark gaiety left us quickly and pressed on to Buffalo. He avowed that George Eastman was a bachelor. Persisting in his researches, he discovered that at the dinner party given by Mr. Eastman to celebrate the opening of his great new house on East Avenue (now a national landmark), October 7, 1905, the eighth course was pumpkin pie and cheese, the ninth, Nesselrode pudding.

In Rochester, Mr. Hamburger found, the touch of the accolade was reserved almost exclusively for those members of the male population who were known as Kodak men. They were the favored sons. They wore clean shirts, kept their suits pressed, raised their children assiduously, and returned directly from work each day to putter in their gardens. He reported that Rochester was proud of its innovations: that here were made the first street car transfer, the first gold tooth, and the first fountain pen. We numbered (at the time of his investigations) 322,488 inhabitants; lived at an altitude 543 feet above the level of the sea.

Mr. Levy's discussion of Rochester, in the *Saturday Evening Post*, a much more in-depth performance than *The New Yorker*'s slight essay, expressed conclusions that were merely hinted at by Mr. Hamburger. He too asserted that traveling men dreaded to remain long among us, presumably because, as he put it, Rochester "doesn't have much fun." He called attention to our cleanliness, our prosperity; remarked that we were comfortable, well adjusted, home loving, acutely conscientious about civic matters, and dull. And he wondered if perhaps our triumph wasn't, as other critics had suggested, the triumph of mediocrity.

One would think, from the manner in which we have been anatomized by those who have come to observe our institutions and our form of life, that we have no more sensibility than a lung fish, or the shrimp of the Great Salt Lake; that ours is a Boeotian community, uninspired, without aspiration, the habitat of dolts and clodpoles whose only concern is to remain sleek and fat, and keep on breathing.

Even Carl Carmer, who once lived briefly among us and taught at the University of Rochester, and whose historical works and enchanting tales of New York folklore have endeared him to a great many Rochester readers, examining the city in *Listen for a Lonesome Drum*, concludes that we are anesthetized by "conservative mediocrity"; that the only rousing elements in town are the press and the university.

"What is the city but people?" the immortal bard has asked; and if our critics from outside believe that Rochester is dull, spiritless, and mediocre because its people are dull, spiritless, and mediocre, they ought to stay around a little longer, and make their investigations more profound.

It is true that we have never sent a President to the White House or produced a heavyweight champion of the world; but two Nobel laureates have lived contemporaneously in our midst, and one, Dr. George H. Whipple, is still a resident of the city. Rochester is the home of the world's best pocket billiard player, men who have won Pulitzer prizes for music and poetry, and the president of the Associated Press. Until his recent death, the Zen Buddhist who invented the device that has made billions for Xerox lived quietly on the edge of town.

The above is the merest sampling of a roster which, if complete, would identify thousands of persons living here whose talents and achievements roundly discredit the fusty judgment of critics that Rochesterians are unaccomplished.

For years, while we sustained not with dishonor our position as third largest city in the great rich state of New York, our detractors continually harped upon what they described as our provincialism, until one would almost believe that our milieu was as pastoral as Vergil's *Eclogues*. I suspect that this attitude derived from the reputation we had of being a one-street city, and that visitors who glanced merely at our superficies had a notion that once they left Main Street and its environs they would need a tent for shelter, an ax to hew firewood, and a fowling piece to bring down edible game. We were hay kickers, apple knockers. Travelers knew that the New York Central's famous Twentieth Century Limited, approaching Rochester, lessened its speed to forty miles an hour, but did not stop; passengers saw only the glinting lights of the station platform.

Years ago, Robert J. Berentsen, organist at the Eastman Theater, on a motor trip to New York, slipped unconsciously through a Fifth Avenue traffic light, and was hailed to the curb by one of New York's finest.

"What's the matter with you?" growled the officer. "You've gone through a red light."

"I am sorry," replied the organist. "I really didn't see it."

"If you can't see, what you driving a car for?"

"I'm very sorry, indeed," Mr. Berentsen persisted penitently.

The copper closely scrutinized the man behind the wheel. Then asked, "Where you from?"

"Rochester, New York."

"Oh, my God!" the officer exclaimed. "Well, go ahead, and do the best you can!"

The Eastman Company, Bausch & Lomb, Taylor Instrument, Hickey-Freeman, Xerox and a score of other industries, the University of Rochester and Medical School and Midtown Plaza have brought national and international attention to Rochester, which once was known to many people only as a place where *some* east-west trains stopped to take on or discharge passengers. Now our sprawling and thickly populated metropolitan area and the vast millions spent on midtown high rises have given Rochester a definitely big city character, and we are not likely to be slighted by inadvertence, or in the manner reported by a Mrs. Walton, who worked for a local society weekly which this writer edited during its mayfly existence.

Mrs. Walton was a former society reporter for the New York *Herald Tribune*, and while she may not have found her new job of scribbling notes on Rochester society actually demeaning, there was something in her attitude of *noblesse oblige*. She had many tales to tell of what Victorian novelists called the Great World, and the bigwigs she had known in New York and at fashionable eastern resorts, and one of these concerned Warham Whitney, husband of the biggest bigwig in Rochester society.

Although at the time of Mrs. Walton's appearance in Rochester, the social hierarchy had been slightly bloodied and somewhat mangled by the intrusion of a small company of outlanders whose open sesame! had been the democratizing influence of the war, the hierarchy still retained some of its former protocol, a modicum of its earlier aloftness, and—more important for its existence—the leadership of a lady whose charisma had held it solidly together for many years before the war.

Mrs. Warham Whitney seemed, on the surface, indifferent to the leadership that had been conceded her. She made no fuss about it, wore no plumes to identify her dictature, yet all under her sway knew that it was as tangible and unequivocal as the muzzle of a pistol pressed against the heart. No one trifled with her, and at her slightest word her peers and the eager, hopeful sycophants in the offing gathered their skirts about them and leaped through hoops. Her cards were engraved in shaded Roman, merely, *Mrs. Whitney*.

She was not a native; she had come from the southern tier of the state. Her husband was old Rochester family, a big-game hunter, a world traveler, a man of grace and sophistication who was well acquainted in the upper echelons of eastern society.

With malicious glee, Mrs. Walton told that once when Rochester was casually mentioned at a small gathering of social *flâneur's* in the Casino at Newport, one of the company was vague about the city's identity. "Rochester—Rochester, New York," he said reflectively, twisting the tip of his waxen mustache. Then, with sudden revelation, "Ah, yes. Isn't it that odd place, Warham Whitney comes from?"

"That odd place" from which Warham Whitney came, a city that has often been represented as dull, prosaic, and smug, was deliberately chosen as a place of residence by one of the most colorful Americans of his time.

For more than two years, William F. (Buffalo Bill) Cody, famous scout, Indian fighter, and showman, made his home in Rochester. He had his first look at Rochester in 1872 when he stopped here briefly on his way to New York at the invitation of Professor Henry A. Ward. Ward was a native Rochesterian with excellent connections, and Bill saw the city under highly favorable auspices. He must have liked what he saw. Two years later he moved his family here and settled them in a house on upper Exchange Street. Buffalo Bill, at that time was twenty-eight years old. He was an arresting and picturesque figure: straight up, with a flowing mustache, an imposing goatee, and hair curling down to his shoulders, à la the hippie of today.

In New York, he met Ned Buntline, a gifted hack who had given vogue to the dime novel by writing a series of highly colored fictions about Buffalo Bill. Now he had turned playwright and wanted Bill to represent himself in a melodrama Buntline called *The Scouts of the Prairie*, and Bill consented, although not confident of his histrionic talents. The show was a three-act gallimaufry of shooting, knifing, shouting, scalping, and more shooting; so bad, according to one critic, it was almost good.

Buffalo Bill toured with *The Scouts of the Prairie* for a couple of seasons, with time off during the summer months to return to the West for refresher courses in frontier heroics. The show played Rochester, and Cody was again impressed with the city. When he finally settled here, he made the most gallant effort of his life to adjust to domesticity, and lived all one summer—his all-time record of marital and parental devotion—in the bosom of his family.

Now and then ladies were inducted into the cast. One of these was a stunner, Mlle. Giuseppina Morlacchi, a "beautiful Indian girl with an Italian accent." Before dedicating her talents to Bill's show, then called *The Scouts of the Plains*, she had been a danseuse in Naples, London, and Lisbon. She had also introduced the cancan in America, and had her legs insured for $100,000 as, at a later date did Miss Ann Pennington of the *Ziegfeld Follies*.

When the show played the Opera House, a reporter for the *Union and Advertiser* wrote that the "entertainment was no doubt satisfying to those who witnessed it." He explained, however, that he would have to omit any precise critique, since the crowd was so dense he could not squirm through it to get a glimpse of the actors on the stage; and he predicted, "It is not probable that even an ordinary earthquake could keep away the crowd that will assemble tonight."

While still a resident of Rochester, Cody left his home to become a scout for the Fifth U. S. Cavalry and shot and scalped an Indian known as Yellow Hand during a punitive expedition against the rampaging Cheyennes. This lethal achievement enormously enhanced his reputation as a Western hero and provided lurid advertising copy for his theatrical enterprises.

Cody sent the Indian's war bonnet, shield and weapon to his friend Moses Kerngood, as a window display for Kerngood's Main Street tobacco store. When he himself returned to Rochester, Bill promptly launched a new production, with the assistance of J. Clinton Hall, manager of the Rochester Opera House (later

131

Cook's Opera House, still later, the Embassy Burlesque Theater,) on South Avenue, entitled *The Red Right Hand; or Buffalo Bill's First Scalp for Custer*. It was a "noisy, rattling, gunpowder entertainment," by Cody's own description, which had an extensive run and played to large audiences.

During his residence here, Buffalo Bill's family consisted of his wife, Louisa Frederici, called Lulu by her husband, two daughters, Arta and Orra, and a son, Kit Carson Cody. When Kit was five years old he was stricken with scarlet fever, and Bill, summoned from a theater in Springfield, Massachusetts, reached home only to see the lad die. He was the heir apparent of all that his father considered his domain, and the boy's loss was Buffalo Bill's great tragedy. Later he buried two more of his natural children and his adopted son Johnny Baker, the great trick shot with his Wild West Show, who was known as "The Cowboy Kid."

Cody's life in Rochester was much less tumultuous than it became once he achieved world celebrity. It was years after he left here that he became romantically involved with an English actress, exchanged bitter maledictions with Lulu during a messy divorce action, met kings and queens and Russian nobles, and lost great sums of money backing the English actress and in various other show business ventures. His defections in Rochester were not egregious: He was sometimes more extensive in his cups than made for domestic tranquility, he played poker, and avowed that his winnings went to a Chicago charity—a home for "deflowered frails"; he sported mildly with the girls of his troupe.

After Cody quit the stage to play the title role in Buffalo Bill's Wild West Show, Rochester was always included in the show's American tour, and here his off-the-lot routine was inflexible. He first rode in an open victoria to the graves of his children, invariably passing through Linden Street, thrilling its youthful residents, on his way to the first gate of Mt. Hope Cemetry; then made the second station, Leif Heidell's Cafe in South Water Street.

If a saloon may be invested with glamour, Heidell's had that quality. It was ornate, with a great deal of white marble, and a veritable picture gallery of Who's Who in the Theater. Heidell had once been a vaudeville monologist, and at heart was still a trouper. At the drop of a hat, he would recite, with Delsartian accompaniments, substantial sides from the works of Eugene Field and James Whitcomb Riley, or do effective bits from Goldsmith's *The Deserted Village.*

Riley, who was one of Heidell's particular favorites, had been honored at a dinner in the café, and the proprietor outdid himself in the matter of table decorations. A stream of running water wound around a scene represented as an autumn cornfield, with pumpkins tinted with paint. . . .

. . . a pictur' that no painter has the colorin' to mock—
When the frost is on the punkin and the fodder's in the shock.

Players at the Lyceum Theater—DeWolf Hopper, Nat Goodwin, Chauncey Olcott, Raymond Hitchcock, and others of that standing —once the final curtain fell and they rubbed away the grease paint, would surge through Main Street in a sea-going hack and turn into Water Street to bib, swig, and commune with Heidell.

Jack Foran, a later-day downtown character, one-time light heavyweight boxer and proprietor of the well-known House of Foran, which served hard liquor, and, on Sundays, hard-playing jazz, perhaps epitomized Leif's place.

"The man had a hell of a store," Foran said. "My old man used to take broads there, when he drove hack."

It was indeed "a hell of a store," and it was there, nights after his vigorous performance in the Wild West Show, that Buffalo Bill met his old friend Leif, and other Rochester cronies, and wassailed, and reminisced about the old days when he and Lulu and the children lived on upper Exchange Street somewhat in the manner of the comfortable bourgeois neighbors to the right and left of them, and across the street.

Chapter 10

In recent years, Rochester has been torn by racial strife. Murderers and muggers have made its streets unsafe at night, and at times its crime rate has advanced more swiftly than the crime rate in most other cities in the land. It has its youthful junkies; vandalism is often rampant. Its high schools have been closed because of violent internal disorders, and rape has been practiced in their lower corridors. The city has befouled and rat-infested areas that urban renewal has not yet reclaimed. All of this is incredibly out of character for a city that during much the greater part of its career as a municipality has been conspicious for orderliness and conservatism.

Rochester's conservatism goes back to its beginnings, when staid and solid members of the Establishment settled around Colonel Rochester in the old Third Ward and set a tone for the city that continued well over a century. It was also, since this condition was induced by conservatism, an orderly city; and at one point, following a series of revivals conducted by the Reverend Charles G. Finney, it imposed upon itself such rigorous forbiddances that it was orderly to the point of pain.

Finney came here periodically until shortly before the Civil War to call out the devil in our midst, and grapple with him, no holds barred. He caused his audiences to suffer, and they flocked to him with masochistic intent. His lurid rhetoric made it appear that man's career from birth onward was no more than a balancing act on a thin cord suspended over a flaming pit: One misstep and all was over—all, that is, except the tortures of Dante's circles. He put snakes into the boots of his listeners, made their scalps "grow tight with fear." He was the terrible bogey man for children who, after being dragged by their parents to his meetings, lay awake in their beds awaiting the terrors of the damned.

When Finney came to town, church discipline became as tight as a pipe wrench. He got things done, but he spoiled the fun. He promulgated the "doctrine of endless punishment" for those who played cards, took a swallow of grog, danced, smoked tobacco, violated the Sabbath, or went to a show. During one of his visits, the only theater in town was converted into a livery stable; an indoor carnival became a tallow and candle factory. "Hallelujah," cried his disciples, exulting in these achievements. "Hallelujah, glory be to God!"

According to one commentator, his exhortations brought about "a wonderful falling off of crime. The court had little to do, and the jail was empty . . . in stores and public houses, in the streets and in public conveyances, and everywhere, the work of salvation that was going on was the absorbing topic." It was further stated that Finney changed the character of the city, and that Rochester "has been famous ever since [his last visit] for its moral tone."

The celebrated evangelist put a great many perhaps wavering Rochesterians on the anxious seat, but one who did not join the trembling penitents on the bench below his lectern was the previously mentioned Henry A. Ward.

Ward was a creature of heterodoxy in a community that by the time he attained the reason of manhood had lost its brief boomtown rattle and was compassed by the proprieties of conservatism. His mother must have warmly approved the intransigent pietism of Charles G. Finney. She was a religious fanatic, so zealous in the name of all that was holy that she drove her husband, not only out of the house, but out of the state. Her determination was to have Henry enter the ministry: It was the predestined calling for her only son. The lad, who was later to declare himself a "Christian agnostic," had no bent that way. When little more than a toddler, he picked up a rare stone—a piece of gneiss, with unusual markings —on the Ward farm, which was centered approximately at what is now the corner of Gibbs Street and Grove Place. The discovery of the stone, which the child preserved as carefully as most youngsters would cherish a novel toy, was the first indication of Henry's abiding interest in geology.

Ward was one of a number of men and women who made their home in Rochester during the mid and latter years of the nineteenth century who were no more formed in the pattern of the city's rigid conservatism than a cloud shape. He was possibly the most traveled American of his time. Moving from one remote area of the world to another in the tinker-toy steamships of the immediate post-Civil War era, in outrigger canoes, in leaky luggers, in Chinese sampans, on railroads, on horseback, and on foot, he was more ubiquitous than today's most enterprising jet setter. He got to places where few white men had ever been before.

The collection of zoological and geological specimens was the passion of Ward's life. Family, friends, financial obligations, the Civil War (although during its tragic course he was at the prime age for soldiering) appeared to mean nothing to him as he ranged the world in search of fossils, the bones and fossilized remains of prehistoric animals, and meteorites. He became known as the "great museum builder," for much that he collected he sold to museums in this country and abroad.

Dr. Augustus H. Strong, a leading ecclesiastic and president of the Rochester Theological Seminary, identified Ward—who, perhaps, unlike Disraeli, was "not on the side of the angels" in the steaming controversy between the old-line theologians and the obtruding Darwinians—as one of two men of genius (the other, Strong mentioned, was Louis Henry Morgan) who had done much to make Rochester famous.

Ward doubtless did have a glitter of genius, and the institution he founded—Ward's Natural Science Establishment, which flourishes today as one of the city's less conventional industries—did bring recognition to Rochester, for its trade in objects of natural history was ecumenical.

The desertion of Henry Ward's father left his family in an impecunious state, and although Henry had rich relatives around him, he made it at first on his own. He went from school to school, eschewing Herodotus and Aristophanes, and other conventional sources of classical learning, to search out botanical and zoological oddities in fields and woods, and examine fucoids and wave marks and other fossil relics in the rock formations of rivers.

He tried Williams College, then Temple Hill Academy, in Geneseo. While a student at Temple Hill, he formed a friendship with Charles Wadsworth, a youthful member of the wealthy Wadsworth clan of that village, and also established an acquaintance with Louis Agassiz, the Swiss naturalist. Ward was a pragmatist. He never failed to heed the knock of opportunity; if the knock was long delayed, he often made the opportunity himself. When he learned that Agassiz was to lecture in Rochester, he walked—since he was short of funds—thirty miles to town to hear him, and later presented himself to the lecturer. Impressed by the ardency and geological knowledge of the young man, the famous scientist persuaded Ward to leave Temple Hill and enroll in Harvard, where Agassiz was professor of zoology and geology.

Ward's tenure there was not extensive. Immobilization was always repugnant to him; he had the kinetic energy of a mountain goat and a curiosity that was never sated. When chance came to go abroad, all expenses paid, to act as a sort of courier and student companion to Charles Wadsworth, whose father, James S. Wadsworth, had placed him in the Paris School of Mines, Henry Ward quitted Agassiz's lecture hall and the great university on the Charles to make the first of half a hundred crossings of the Atlantic Ocean.

In Paris, Ward's formal studies were patchy and intermittent. And it was not long after his matriculation in the School of Mines that he and young Wadsworth contrived a holiday that took them more than a thousand miles up the Nile and then across the desert from Cairo to Jerusalem. For Henry Ward, this was the beginning of a career of world-girdling exploration in the interest of museum collections that was to continue, with occasional stay-at-home interludes, until his long and adventurous life ended on a note of tragic irony. He was struck and mortally hurt by a motorcar as he was crossing Delaware Avenue in Buffalo.

Owing to a crop failure on his vast Genesee Valley lands, James Wadsworth in time was constrained to bring his son back to the States and withdraw the subsidy that had handsomely provided for penniless Henry Ward. Undaunted by the loss of this patronage, Ward stayed on in Europe. Everywhere he went—and he seemed to go everywhere—he added to his collection of fossils, which he packed and shipped home, or sold in Europe. He was developing a lively trade in extinct life. But the only meaning money seemed to have for him was to provide him with means to expand the range of his explorations and allow him to persist farther in the Grail-like pursuit of paleontological specimens.

In the first stage of his scientific odyssey, which comprised his first five years abroad, Ward glided in a balloon a mile and a half above the city of Paris in order to observe the geological basin in which the French capital was situated; visited Moscow and St. Petersburg, which were hardly tourist enticements in the 1850s; was menaced on the desert by hostile Bedouins with spears and razor-sharp scimitars; was abandoned on the African Gold Coast by an English ship captain, who was sure Ward was dying from a disease that he felt would infect himself and his crew. Too weak even to raise to his lips the water jug that had been left him, Ward lay in a semicoma in the blazing sun until a native woman, whom missionaries had made a Christian, discovered him, lugged him to her crude hut, and administered empiric treatments that restored him to health.

In time, Ward married a young woman whom he had left dangling when he left Harvard to go abroad. He took a professorship at the University of Rochester, started a museum on the campus, and made a gesture at "settling down." It was a good try, if unsuccessful. The groves of academe were too restrictive for his restless nature. After a few years, he left his professorial chair, and his subsequent world roamings took him across the South American continent from Valparaiso to Rio de Janeiro before rail travel was established, below the rim of Vesuvius, over wide areas of Australasia.

A bristling, bustling, bearded little man, with the nerve of a cat burglar, enduring, and rawhide tough, Ward penetrated Siberia. He visited the diamond mines of Kimberley, and tried gold mining in Montana. In Persia, he attempted to wangle a famous siderolite from the shah, and did manage to saw off a sizable chunk of the metallic mass. He would go anywhere for the specimens that were filling his Rochester museum, now moved off campus and converted into a commercial institution, with the jaws of a whale agape over its entrance. He got interesting eels at the Fulton Fish Market in New York; an unusual stuffed monkey from a hairdresser in Paris.

When Jumbo, P. T. Barnum's outsize elephant, was killed in an encounter with a speeding locomotive in Canada, the showman sent for Ward, who had taxidermists from his Rochester museum skin out the carcass of the huge beast and mount its hide and head, and Jumbo continued, posthumously, as a circus attraction.

Ward sold more than a million dollars' worth of museum specimens to American universities at a time when the natural science departments of many of these institutions were in a very formative state; he prepared large displays for expositions in this country and in Europe; he trained and sent out from Ward's Natural Science Establishment several men who later distinguished themselves as museum curators, taxidermists, and researchers in fields of science in which Ward himself excelled. With the financial assistance of a wealthy Chicago widow, whom he married after the death of his first wife, he put together probably the largest collection of meteorites in the world.

* * *

While Henry Ward was flouncing around Europe and the Middle East collecting museum specimens, his fellow townsman, Hiram Sibley, was collecting telegraph companies and, concomitantly, one of the important American fortunes of his time; Frederick Douglass, the Negro editor, orator, and abolitionist, was helping collect escaped slaves, who were forwarded to Canada through the city's lively Underground Railroad, and Miss Susan B. Anthony was agitating reforms that were to bring her international renown as a liberator of women.

All of these exciting personages, whose careers ringingly refute the syllogism often applied by implication to our town: A city is composed of people, Rochester is a dull city, therefore its people must be dull, are commemorated by tangible memorials. The commercial museum Ward founded is identified by his name; there is a Hiram Sibley Building, designed in the manner of Christopher Wren, at the East Avenue corner of Alexander Street; a statue of Frederick Douglass stands in a city park and a building at the University of Rochester has been named in his honor; the Madison Street home of Miss Anthony is one of the city's two national historical sites.

It would be impractical, of course, to attempt to mount tablatures or pin up plaques to all Rochesterians whose careers and achievements warrant the notice of posterity. But Rochester does seem remiss in not showing somewhere within its boundaries a memorial to George Baldwin Selden, whose invention of a "safe, simple and cheap road locomotive" was the primordial ancestor of the modern American automobile.

In the late 1870s, when George Selden dreamed up a contraption which for more than seven years was an object of contention in the federal courts, automotive nomenclature had not been developed. Selden didn't call his little wheeled oddity an automobile but a road engine. It was his fetish; his life hope. He wore in the knot of his necktie a diamond and sapphire representation of the vehicle depicted in his patent drawings. His dying words confirmed an undying faith in his road engine; his tombstone in Mt. Hope Cemetery bears a graven image of the much disputed machine.

The inventor was the scion of an old-line Monroe County family and the son of Judge Henry R. Selden, of the New York State Court of Appeals. The elder Selden was a friend of Abraham Lincoln, and the story is that Lincoln wanted him to accept the Republican nomination to the vice-presidency in 1864. When Selden refused (assuming the offer was actually made), Andrew Johnson became Lincoln's running mate, and subsequently the seventeenth President of the United States.

George Selden had served, as a teen-ager, with the Union forces in the Civil War. In early manhood he entered Yale University, but left when his father desired him to read law in the Selden office in Reynolds Arcade. His bent was patent law. On the side, he experimented with various inventions of his own. One of these was a barrel-hoop-making machine, which he patented and demonstrated at the Centennial Exposition in Philadelphia.

As a youth, Selden had seen the parasitical disease of epizoonosis, which attacks animals, kill or disable a great many horses in the city and adjacent countryside, and his lively fancy envisaged a means of road locomotion that would supersede horse-drawn vehicles. He had studied the experiments made in England of steam-operated road carriages. They were slow, their progress was continually interrupted by the need to stop and take in water, and they were so monstrously awkward that England, as a safety precaution, enacted laws that forced them off the roads.

Wondering what would take the place of steam, Selden found the answer when he saw several stationary Brayton gas engines at the Centennial Exposition, and in 1877, unceasingly dedicated to a self-imposed task, he created an internal combustion engine which, propelled by hydrocarbon fuel, was nearly eight hundred pounds lighter than the lightest stationary engine he had seen, and suitable because of this to be mounted on a road vehicle. Two years after he had perfected his road engine, which included an enclosed crank shaft, a foot brake, a clutch to allow the driver to vary the speed of the vehicle, a steering wheel, and various other elements of which the modern automobile is comprised, Selden filed an application for a patent. The drawings that accompanied the application were witnessed by two friends of the inventor, one a meticulous little bank clerk, with a great hidden urge, and a progenitive glint in his eye. His signature read *George Eastman*.

Sixteen years after the patent had been applied for, it was granted. There had been a good deal of correspondence and numerous emendations, and, seemingly, no great urgency on the part of the inventor. The specific date was November 5, 1895. On Christmas Eve of that year, Henry Ford, who was to become a deadly antagonist of George Selden in one of the most celebrated litigations in the history of America patent law, walked the streets with his wife seeking someone who would trust him for the price of a chicken for their holiday dinner.

Ford was then at the nadir of his fortunes. Eight years later, he was busy manufacturing automobiles, and Selden had not yet put a car on the market. Selden needed money, and it was not forthcoming from his friends or from his family. Years before, when Hiram Sibley was effecting the coalescence of independent telegraph lines, Judge Selden joined him in the enterprise, and the judge served on the directorate of the Western Union Telegraph Company. As mechanical improvements for the transmission of messages were devised, Western Union stock soared. Sibley was making millions, and lesser fortunes were being made by smaller investors. When the stock reached 225, the younger Selden pleaded with his father to sell.

The old man demurred. He was a Republican, a conservative, part of the Establishment.

"It wouldn't look well for a director of the company to sell," he told his son.

"By God, Father," George Selden cried angrily, "at 225, I'd sell the kingdom of Heaven!"

In the closing years of the last century, the Selden patent was virtually in limbo. It had not enriched the inventor, and little was heard of it. Progress was being made in the automotive art, but Selden, the man who had managed to combine the various mechanical features that made an automobile run, was left on the sidelines, out of countenance, and depressed by his inability to put the machine into production. His younger son, George B. Selden, Jr., has told of standing with his father at a window in the latter's office in Reynolds Arcade as the P. T. Barnum Circus parade passed through Main Street. Its vanguard was a crude little vehicle put out by Charles Duryea, which crawled sputteringly over the pavement without the aid of horses, while clowns capered in and about it. The crowd screamed with delight at the antics of the clowns, "oh-o-oed" and "ah-a-aed" in wonder at the novelty of a horseless carriage. Young Selden took a sidelong glance at his father.

"Tears were rolling down his cheeks, and he was talking very softly, almost as if he were talking to himself," the son related. "'By God,' he said, 'By God, George, there's my road engine!'"

* * *

Although the Selden patent seemed almost to die aborning, it became, shortly after the turn of the century, a conspicuous and viable instrument, and a threat to all makers of gasoline engines who were not paying royalties to the Pope Manufacturing Company of Hartford, Connecticut, to W. C. Whitney, the great Wall Street nabob, who backed the Pope Company, and to Selden himself.

This turn of events came about when the Pope Company which specialized in electric automobiles, started experimenting with gas-driven cars, and was told by a patent specialist that it was infringing on the Selden patent. At first, there was scoffing. Whitney was outraged. Who was George Baldwin Selden? And did anyone seriously believe that Rochester, New York, was the natal place of the automobile, and this obscure tinkerer the stand-by obstetrician who had brought it into the world? Absurd!

The patent specialist was a member of the Pope organization. He persisted in his argument; in the end prevailed. Whitney and the Pope people quickly and cannily arranged with Selden to have exclusive rights to the patent and share the royalties with the inventor.

The numerous producers of gas-operated cars were advised that they were infringing on the Selden patent and were requested to make compensation. Most of them ran scared. First one, then a second, and presently as many as twenty-seven manufacturers agreed to pay the royalty. They formed an organization known as the Association of Licensed Automobile Manufacturers (A.L.A.M.). Each car sold by a member of the Association bore a brass plate which certified that the vehicle was a licensed automobile. The A.L.A.M. warned prospective customers of unlicensed firms, *Don't Buy a Lawsuit with Your Car.*

Henry Ford was a conspicuous holdout. He contended that the Ford Motor Company, then in the incipient stage of the development that would make its founder a billionaire, was not infringing: He would not pay. He challenged Pope, Whitney, Selden, and the forces of the A.L.A.M., which represented something like $70,000,-000 to sue. They picked up the gage.

Other defendants were later named, among them the John Wanamaker store, which acted as Ford's New York distributor. The trial was drawn out to unconscionable lengths; the testimony grew to monolithic dimensions. Indeed, it was once remarked that two freight cars would be needed to contain the evidence and exhibits. Selden sometimes attempted to assuage his impatience with the bottle, which did not increase his effectiveness in court. He was not becoming extravagantly rich, since his codefendants shared more liberally than he in the royalty payments. But, finally, nearly six years after the opening of the trial, the court sustained the claims of the complainant and virtually pronounced Selden the inventor of the automobile.

It was a triumph, but not yet an occasion for dancing in the streets. The thin stubborn man from Detroit would not cry, "Uncle!" He registered an appeal which consumed another year and a quarter, during which time Ford—unrestrained by an injunction—continued to make unlicensed automobiles. Then the Court of Appeals decided that the Selden patent was valid, but that it applied only to the particular sort of vehicle described in his drawings, and Ford was in the clear.

It was the first great breakthrough for a man who had an intuitive sense about headlines. Ford's cars needed promotion, and they got it—free—through newspaper reports of the trial. And Ford made the most of the image fashioned for him by the public: A white knight on a charger scouring the wicked trust. He also discomfited an inventor who may have been the first person to envisage the social needs and the industrial potential of the automobile and who, at a time when Henry Ford was scarcely out of knee breeches, devised a road engine that some people of considered judgment still believe was the progenitor of the modern motorcar.

Had the fates been more kind (or had Selden brought better

order to his affairs), his inventive talents might have made him a very fine fortune. As it was, he took a few hundred thousand in royalties which, according to his son, George, Jr., were a bagatelle compared with the millions gained from his patent by the powerful interests to which he had assigned it. In the end his mismanagement, his extravagances, and his sometimes quixotic attitude toward money brought him close to bankruptcy.

A brilliant patent lawyer, Selden imperiously rejected a handsome offer brought to him in a gilded New York café by his younger son. Glenn Curtiss, the Hammondsport aviation pioneer, wanted him as a one-day consultant in an aviation patent litigation for a fee of $10,000.

"Those goddamn airplanes," Selden said angrily. "Man was not meant to fly through the air. Tell him, *no!*"

He raised his glass and went on drinking.

He was obsessed with the Ford case to the day of his death. "Morally," he mumbled with an expiring breath, "the victory was mine."

Henry Ford said, "Probably nothing so well advertised the Ford car and the Ford Motor Company as this (the Selden patent) suit."

Chapter 11

It was an axiom of my father's that one could not love an inanimate object, so it would be incorrect, I presume, to say that he loved Rochester. But the city delighted him from the moment he arrived here from the harsh, hard-bitten life he had known in the Midwest prairie lands and his devotion to it was abiding and unqualified. He had no desire to live anywhere outside its boundaries. During his married life, which continued more than half a century, he owned and lived in three houses. Two of these were on Linden Street. Late in life he built a third house, which is now the property of the University of Rochester, on an imposing piece of nursery land at the Linden Street corner of Mt. Hope Avenue.

Greatly enjoying life in an eastern city, my father was at pains to learn about the people and institutions of the city of his adoption. Some of the information he acquired he deliberately passed on to me, and I also learned about Rochester from occasionally attending to conversations my father had with visitors in our house.

For a time, while I was growing up, the H. F. Atwoods lived diagonally across the street from us. Mrs. Atwood was a good friend of my mother. She was a delightful, bubbly little Welsh woman whom everyone called Taffy. Atwood, who in time became a member of the Rochester Park Board, was, I believe, of English extraction. He was a bumptious but not an unkind man. His voice had a slight crusty inflection, and he expected his pronouncements to be accepted as dogma. He was considered a great wit—a joker. He once put my mother in tears by having me announce to her that I wanted to trade my newborn sister for a flying squirrel in a cage.

Atwood was growing affluent through close association with Frederick Cook, a former Secretary of the state of New York, who was president of both the German-American Bank and the German-American Insurance Company. When he became sufficiently affluent to warrant the move, he left Linden Street and he and Taffy settled in a large, handsomely appointed house on Seneca Parkway. That was often the pattern in those days. If one acquired wealth while living in a modest neighborhood, one might move first to one of the two or three fashionable streets in the Tenth Ward, and from there, if one's sense of status was acute—and fortune continued to smile—to the "East Avenue Section."

One summer evening, Atwood and my father were sitting back of the morning-glory vines on our front porch when I heard the former mention Susan B. Anthony, whose name, for what reason I do not recall, had been in the headlines of the morning newspaper.

"Blamed she rabble rouser in pants," Atwood said witheringly. "A harridan!"

I was appalled. Unchurchly though my father was, he never used bad language, and people did not ordinarily use bad language in his presence. I was sure "harridan" was synonymous with "whore," one of the several four- and five-letter words I had learned in the schoolyard, which surely were not to be used on our front porch, with the windows open and my sisters and mother within range of Mr. Atwood's voice.

My father demurred, but he was not angry. He seemed not offended by "harridan."

"Oh, I wouldn't say that," he said. "And she doesn't wear pants any more. That was a long time ago. Bloomers! I have a lot of respect for Susan Anthony."

"Well, you can have it," Atwood said irritably, and I heard his foot stomp on the porch floor. "I say she's a rabble rouser. A damn anarchist, pants or no pants. Been a good thing, if they'd put her in jail that time they arrested her."

"But H.F.," my father started in protest. Then he apparently thought better of pursuing an argument with a guest, and he turned the conversation to another topic. The word "harridan" stuck in my mind. When the guest left, I asked my father, "Why was that lady you and Mr. Atwood were talking about put in jail?"

"Oh, you were listening," my father said. "Well, she wasn't put in jail. They did arrest her."

"Because she was a ha—harridan?"

My father laughed. "So you've learned a new word. I am not sure myself what harridan means. I think it's a woman who blabs too much. We'll look it up in the dictionary. But she wasn't arrested for that. It was because she voted."

"Oh, a woman voting?"

"I think she had a right to vote, even if they did arrest her. She is a great woman. She is very old now. I knew her when I first came to Rochester."

Militant, dedicated, courageous, uncompromising, and immensely endurable, Susan B. Anthony for years was Rochester's stormiest petrel. A Quaker schoolmarm who had come here with her family from Massachusetts fifteen years before the outbreak of the Civil War, the slim, shy, not too articulate spinster by rights should have settled into the anonymity of a pedagogic routine. Instead, she blazed forth like a nova. She was a born crusader, though many used the term in a pejorative sense, and "causes" became the watchword and the passion of her life.

She crusaded for temperance, wanting hard liquor ("that destroyer of all true delicacy and refinement") completely abolished. She opposed capital punishment. She furiously agitated for the freedom of the slaves, and castigated the Great Emancipator, Abraham Lincoln, feeling that on the burning issue of slavery he was delinquent and dishonest. She was up to her armpits in the labor movement that began to acquire vitality and momentum shortly after the Civil War. She was pugnacious and unrelenting in her lifelong struggle to obtain property rights, civil rights, and the ballot for members of her sex.

Although Miss Anthony's biographers say that she was occasionally courted by male admirers, romance was not allowed to weaken her stern resolves. Unlike many of the less consecrated sisters in the suffragist ranks, she would not be "wholly dominated by *men* spirits—I spurn the whole lot of them." The rejected suitors should have hugged themselves for luck. Being married to the prickly Susan would have been like living in a briar patch. Except for such rarefied spirits as Wendell Phillips, William Lloyd Garrison, Parker Pillsbury, and three or four other male collaborators in her causes, Miss Anthony's attitude toward the common run of men seemed not dissimilar to the scorn and disgust Swift's horse creatures, the Houyhnhnms, reserved for the evil-smelling, viperish bipeds the Houyhnhnms called Yahoos.

She once cut her hair short and affected a bloomer costume, following the mode of Amelia Bloomer, who edited a temperance paper in nearby Seneca Falls, New York, and Susan's brilliant coadjutor, Mrs. Elizabeth Cady Stanton, also of that village. The new costume was worn as an insignia of independence. It allowed greater freedom of movement, it made a field day for newspaper cartoonists, and it gave to each of the bloomer wearers all the allure of a half-filled bag of loose cement.

But it was not the bizarre incidents of her career, or the eccentricities of her behavior, or her sometimes overdramatic sense of martyrdom (" . . . I have struggled as never mortal woman or mortal man struggled for any cause") that made Susan B. Anthony not only one of the most conspicuous but one of the most distinguished American women of her time. Her great and paramount purpose was to achieve for the women of the country the manumission that in time was to come to the Negro, for she passionately believed women were held in servile bondage by men.

For years Miss Anthony stumped the country, not obsequiously pleading but demanding that women be allowed, by the use of the ballot, to help shape the laws that were now man made and that grievously destroyed the political equipoise she believed should be maintained between the sexes. She was viciously reviled. She was mercilessly caricatured as a meddlesome old maid. There were occasions when bullies charged her platform, menaced her person, and savaged her reasoned discourse with hoodlum shouts. She was defiant, indomitable, and unafraid.

She was canonized by her ardent followers: the prefix "saint"— "St." Susan—was in their minds neither caricature nor a misnomer. "Oh, Susan, you are very dear to me. I should miss you more than any other living being on earth," wrote Mrs. Stanton, a seemingly devoted mother, and wife of the talented Henry B. Stanton.

Those who have written sympathetically about Miss Anthony have attempted to invest her with the soft graces of a gentlewoman, but one still has the impression that her stern, gray, unyielding manner was formed in a barracks square. There seemed to be little give to her; no lilts in her life, and very little laughter.

Yet my father, a young train dispatcher, and John F. Dinkey, later a high official of the Buffalo, Rochester & Pittsburgh Railroad, and John D. Lynn, a brilliant young lawyer, who sat with her at a table in a West Avenue boarding house for several months, all attested that she was charming.

They attempted to tease this experienced crusader, then in her mid-sixties, about her advocacy, in her defunct paper, *The Revolution*, of law-breaking and revolutionary tactics. They twitted her gently about the time she suffered arrest and conviction, and was fined $100 (which she did not pay) for voting in a presidential election. They took amusement in chiding her for suggesting that women, in competing in manual trades with men, need not be afraid of dirtying and hardening their hands. They found her amiable and good natured; they discovered that she was brilliant in repartee and that their wit was no match for hers.

The three young men developed a respect for Susan B. Anthony, and a sympathy for what at that time were considered her radical aims, which continued even after my father and Mr. Dinkey became deep-dyed conservatives (Judge Lynn, the consistent liberal of the trio, would naturally support women's suffrage).

My father always felt that it was a crying shame that the objective for which Miss Anthony had striven throughout her long life was not achieved until fourteen years after her death, when on August 26, 1920, the ratification of the Nineteenth Amendment gave women throughout the United States the right to vote.

She had, however, the satisfaction of seeing rescinded such stone-age laws as the one that required an employer to pay a working wife's wages to her husband, and the other equally Neolithic ordinance that allowed some "dolt" (Miss Anthony's designation) of a husband to expropriate a wife's inheritance on the day the conjugal vows were exchanged.

Susan helped change the policy of the University of Rochester, and women were admitted as full-time students. And this too happened during her lifetime, to illuminate with victory a campaign for equal rights for women that in its full course was often marked by frustration and defeat.

A few years before her death in her eighty-fifth year, a huge birthday party was given Miss Anthony by her fellow townsmen, many of whom may not have agreed with her opinions, but respected her courage, her inexorable pursuit of her goals, and her intellectual integrity. She was at last recognized as the great woman of Rochester. She was the city's most notable reformer, and perhaps —at that time—its most distinguished citizen. Posthumously, her fame has increased. Her home in Madison Street is the shrine of her followers; her grave in Mt. Hope Cemetery attracts worshipful pilgrims with floral tokens.

Where the action was, to employ an idiom of the 1960s, in the 1860s was the venue of Susan B. Anthony, Frederick Douglass, and

Hiram Sibley. All seemed to prosper in an atmosphere of tumult and strife. They were here, there, and everywhere in the pursuit of their respective interests. And while the public career of each of these Rochester luminaries began well before the Civil War, it was during and following that internecine struggle that Miss Anthony and Douglass, whirling in the vortex of controversy into which their chauvinism had plunged them, began to attain historic stature. It was also during this period that Sibley saw the struggling, suspect little communication industry his unflagging zeal had put together develop into the first great industrial monopoly in the nation.

Sibley was the oldest of the trio. In 1823, at the age of sixteen, he migrated from his native Massachusetts to western New York, where he soon displayed the genius for worldly success that was to mark his long and rewarding career as a financial manipulator and industrial entrepreneur. A youth of engaging personality, who was competent in several trades, Sibley prospered modestly in upper Genesee Valley villages before moving north to Mendon, in Monroe County.

In Mendon, he met Don Alonzo Watson, a young artisan who, like himself, had come from New England to try his luck in the promising Genesee country, and the pair became partners in the operation of a machine shop. It was a propitious arrangement. Watson was expert at applied mechanics; Sibley had implicit talents as a promoter. Soon the machine shop was a booming success, and Sibley, retaining his half interest, resigned its management to Watson. Always the tantalizing mirage of new wealth beckoned to him. He launched a new enterprise, a flour mill. This also succeeded. He bought land from a Mendon landowner and married the landowner's daughter in the Congregational Church of the township. The celebration that followed the wedding ceremony was a wingding. Many of the guests got so outrageously drunk that the disgusted bridegroom forthrightly took the pledge. He also forswore Christian liturgy and churchgoing.

Sibley knew well the bustling city near the mouth of the Genesee to which on past occasions he had proceeded on foot, carrying his shoes, until he crossed the Rochester line. It was a place where a shrewd, hustling operator should do very well, and in 1844—after he had been elected Monroe County Sheriff on the Democratic ticket—he and Don Watson sold their machine shop for $80,000, and moved into town.

His residence for a time was in Clinton Avenue North. Then he and Watson purchased thirty acres of land in what today is East Avenue and its purlieu, built large important houses, one of which still stands, and Sibley—who had resigned from his political office—was soon, skillfully and unceasingly engaged in the business of bringing a tangle of independent telegraph lines into a federation. First cumbersomely known as the New York & Mississippi Valley Printing Telegraph Company, the combination was later reincorporated as the Western Union Telegraph Company.

Organized in Reynolds Arcade in Rochester, where its headquarters continued until Sibley resigned its presidency in 1865, and the chief offices were removed to New York, the Western Union grew under his inspired leadership from a rather tentative, not-too-hopeful little company with a capitalization of less than $300,000 to a colossus of $42,000,000.

During the company's founding period, Sibley coaxed, cajoled, and importuned his Rochester friends to invest in his enterprise. He traveled the country, gripsack in hand, a Pan-like gleam in his eye, lusting for new lines to bring into his merger. Rival companies were enemies, to be expropriated as affiliates or scuttled as a buccaneer would scuttle a plundered galleon. In Hiram Sibley's day, as, indeed, today, promoters of monopolies were hardly governed by the playing field ethics of Eton and Rugby. To obtain what he wanted from a telegraph combination headed by Ezra Cornell, Sibley first bribed Cornell's partners (". . . the foulest piece of treachery . . . I have ever known . . ."), and later further discomfited the founder of Cornell University by preying upon his interests when Cornell was incapacitated by illness. It was all part of the game. In the end, the two men were reconciled, and Sibley donated a splendid building to the engineering school of Cornell's fledgling university, "high above Cayuga's waters."

The president of Western Union made millions for himself and fine fortunes for his Rochester friends who had the temerity to invest in what at first was inherently a Rochester company, and he importantly contributed to the development of his country. It was he who proposed and, over a good deal of opposition, executed the project of spanning the continent by telegraph wires. It was a magnificent achievement, brought off in the jig time of a few months, when skeptics had expected the task to take years. It brought instant communication between the eastern and western extremes of the nation at a juncture in the Civil War when this sort of communication was critically needed, and antedated by more than half a dozen years the historic moment when Leland Stanford drove into place the golden spike that connected the Atlantic and Pacific coasts by rail.

Sibley's audacity was not regulated by measure. Success pyramided on success. Once, however, he overreached himself; the fates turned against him, and an attempt he made to run a telegraph line through Alaska, across Bering Strait, and through Siberia to the European capitals failed. The failure was no hole-and-corner matter. It was on the grand scale, as were Sibley's triumphs. The thumping rout cost better than $3,000,000!

In the early 1860s the Atlantic cable had not yet been laid, and Sibley was convinced that an underwater telegraph line between Europe and the North American continent was impracticable. He and a fellow promoter named Perry McDonough Collins believed that the way to effect this junction was to string wires overland, with Bering Strait the only water crossing, and the pair went abroad to petition the Russians for a right of way across Alaska.

His wealth, his position as head of Western Union, his charm, and his charisma gave Hiram Sibley standing at the Russian court, and the novelty of his scheme to transmit wire-carried messages, say, from Rochester to Moscow, beguiled the fancy of Prince Gorchakov, the powerful Russian chancellor, who was curious as to the cost of the proposed undertaking.

When he was told that the job could probably be completed for $5,000,000, Gorchakov suggested that for that sum Russia would be willing to sell all of its American-held territory. Sibley pricked up his ears. Was Gorchakov serious? The chancellor assured him that he was.

The Rochester magnate promptly advised Washington of Gorchakov's informal offer, and a couple of years later Russia formally put Alaska on the block, and Secretary of State William H. Seward consummated the purchase on March 30, 1867, not at the bargain-basement figure Gorchakov had named, but for $7,200,000, still a very good price, for this vast continental land without people.

But before all this happened, Sibley's bold project of a Russian-American telegraph line was fully launched, and the promoter envisaged Western Union extending its American monopoly to a world-wide domination of the telegraphic industry. Gangs of men had erected thousands of poles in the Alaskan soil, and coils of hundreds of miles of wire had been rolled out to them, when announcement was made that Cyrus W. Fields's Atlantic cable had been hauled ashore at Heart's Content, Newfoundland. In a twinkling, the overland route between the hemispheres was as obsolete as the Ptolemaic system.

Sibley resigned as president of Western Union when the wheelers and dealers of Wall Street began to juggle and manipulate the stock. He no longer wanted anything to do with the company that his enterprise and promotional genius had founded. He sold his interest and put his wealth to new purposes. He bought railroads, he went into mining and lumbering; he owned a huge tract of forty thousand acres in the Middle West, an enormous farm in New York State, land in Canada. At one time, he had more farm property under cultivation than any other person in America. He bought a large Rochester seed company. The Midas touch was his; he was many times a millionaire.

The alliance formed in Mendon between Hiram Sibley and Don Watson continued as the pair grew into middle life. Sibley's daughter, Emily, married James Sibley Watson after she had been freed by divorce from Isaac Averill, a Rochester banker. The divorce was a very muted matter. In Rochester, in those days, it was axiomatic that a woman of the first order stayed with a man for life, let the devil have the hindmost. But Ike Averill was supposed to be a bad boy.

The marriage of a Sibley and a Watson further strengthened the union between the two families; there were mutual property interests and a tight social accord. And presently out of this combination emerged a little hierarchy—a microcosm of gentility, of culture, and of wealth, of which it has often been said, perhaps by the envious and sometimes in jest, the Watsons speak only to the Sibleys, and the Sibleys speak to God, all in a very broad "a" accent.

*　　*　　*

Hiram Sibley's achievement in effecting a system for transmitting messages across the vast western lands of the continent in a matter of seconds, when previously messages to and from California had been conveyed by such primitive carriers as wagon trains and the

Pony Express, contributed to the unification of the nation. For this, and perhaps for other accomplishments, the founder of Western Union should be put down as a public benefactor; but the Rochester public, when it remembers him at all, regards him mostly as the creator of a handsome fortune which, despite being liberally dipped into by earlier generations of his family, still allows present-day descendants to live in the style to which Sibleys have long been accustomed.

Contemporary though this notable Rochesterian was with two celebrated townsmen, Sibley apparently had no communication with either Susan B. Anthony or Frederick Douglass. They were do-gooders, dedicated to causes which they hoped would promote the felicity of mankind; Sibley was a go-getter, devoted to self-aggrandizement, and the advantages the public derived from his efforts were oblique rather than direct results of his purposes. His career was brilliant, constructive, and sometimes even romantic, but Sibley, unlike Miss Anthony and Douglass, is not enshrined in the parthenon of Rochester heroes, an honor that Douglass himself might have missed had a flintlock musket aimed at his head by a member of a prominent Rochester family not misfired.

An unlearned "chattel waif," who ran away from a Maryland slaveholder, and rose in mid-life to such eminence that President Lincoln pronounced him "one of the most meritorious men, if not the most meritorious man in the United States . . . ," Frederick Douglass, flush with triumphs as a platform speaker, arrived in Rochester in the autumn of 1847, and continued to make his home here for the next quarter of a century.

Douglass and his family moved several times during their residence in Rochester, and their last abode was far up South Avenue on property upon which later stood the greenhouses of John B. Keller, the well-known florist. Less than a quarter of a mile away, the family of Judge Henry R. Selden was sheltered in a house that fronted on what is now Rockingham Street. The Seldens had moved to Rochester from the judge's native village of Clarkson two years before the outbreak of the Civil War. Here they settled in a large dwelling that in time became the foundation building of the Hahnemann (today's Highland) Hospital.

The judge had several sons, the oldest of whom, George B. Selden, was to become a litigant in the famous automobile patent suit. Arthur, one of the younger boys, one autumn afternoon, oiled and polished an old flintlock musket that hung on a rack in the Selden barn, and with a couple of youthful companions went scouring the adjacent farm lands for game.

Suddenly, in their quest, the boys saw what they believed was a raccoon moving nimbly along the top of a high hedge. The musket was charged. Young Arthur took dead aim, and pulled the trigger. Flint clattered against steel, but there was no explosion; only a sputter of burning powder.

Arthur grunted an expletive, then saw, looming up over the hedge, the black bewhiskered face of his neighbor, Frederick Douglass. What the boy had mistaken for a living raccoon, was the dead pelt of one, which served as a cold-weather headpiece for the great Negro leader. Douglass wagged an admonitory forefinger, and passed on. The youthful hunter lowered his gun and shakingly made his way back home, anguished by the thought of the dreadful punishment visited upon those who take the lives of their fellow men.

Douglass never told this story. And he failed to mention in his autobiography the time Arthur Selden's father saved him from arrest by a United States marshal, and the fate of being hanged, which very likely would have been his had he been taken into custody.

Long before the fanatical abolitionist John Brown perpetrated the sensational raid on the federal arsenal at Harpers Ferry, he had confided his intentions to Douglass in visits to the latter's Rochester home. The intimacy of the two men was known. When the raid was actually made, October 16, 1859, there was a general belief in the South and considerable feeling in the North that Douglass was a conspirator in the misbegotten adventure.

By his own earnest asserveration, he was not involved. Douglass was a close friend of John Brown, the "white gentleman," who "is in sympathy a black man, and as deeply interested in our cause, as though his own soul had been pierced with the iron of slavery," and it was Brown who in part was responsible for the Rochester Negro's apostasy from the non-resistant abolition policy of William Lloyd Garrison, to which he had long been committed and which he had publicly espoused. In Rochester, after numerous conferences with Brown, he had changed; he had become a militant abolitionist, who looked upon slave owners as pirates, and who believed they merited the capital punishment meted out to those who pillaged under the ensign of the skull and crossbones.

He had listened, during Brown's numerous visits to his home, to the ole cap'n's detailed exposition of his first scheme to excite an insurrection among Virginia slaves who would be spirited through the labyrinthine passes of the Alleghenies to northern havens, from whence they would be processed to Canada. Violence, of course, would attend this enterprise; slave masters would be shot and stabbed to death by a protecting force which Brown intended to organize. Douglass had no compunction about this circumstance. But he doubted the practicality of the plan, which for various reasons was not attempted; and when, at a later date, Brown proposed an assault on Harpers Ferry, Douglass rejected the idea. He was sure it would not succeed, and he believed it morally wrong, even in the interest of the shackled and imbruted members of his race, to attack government property.

Brown's fanaticism was not to be quenched; nothing could turn him from his passionate purpose. And when his expedition was routed by Colonel Robert E. Lee and a detachment of Marines, and its leader captured, a United States marshal was sent to Rochester to arrest Frederick Douglass as a conspirator in the Harpers Ferry plot.

On the Rochester-bound train, the officer fell in with Judge Selden, to whom he confided his mission. The judge was a man of prominence in Rochester, where he had practiced law for many years even before he became a resident of the city. He was a man of liberal views. In later years, he ably but unsuccessfully defended Susan B. Anthony when the zealous suffragist was tried for voting in a presidential election. If not an active abolitionist, he was strongly opposed to slavery. He was a friend and neighbor of Douglass.

Judge Selden left the train with the marshal in hand; left him, several hours later, stony drunk in the taproom of the Eagle Hotel, and got word to Douglass that a warrant had been issued for his arrest. Acting upon this intelligence, Douglass hurriedly departed for Canada. From there he went to England, while John Brown's collaborators in the Harpers Ferry fiasco vituperated him for failing to support an incursion which he had never countenanced. Besides, he had philosophical reasons for opposing the raid and a personal reason. He admitted that "tried by the Harpers Ferry insurrection" he was "deficient in courage."

In the *Life and Times of Frederick Douglass*, an extremely readable autobiography and a social document that might profitably be perused in this period of racial tensions in America, the author attests that his father was a white man, but makes no further effort to identify him. In youth, Douglass was separated from his enslaved mother and put in service as a houseboy in an opulent Baltimore home. His mistress took a fancy to the small slave. She attempted to instruct him in the alphabet. Her husband's stern proscription ended the lessons.

"Learning," he said angrily, "would spoil the best damn nigger in the world."

The cabalistic characters—the ABC's—had come to have meaning for the boy before the lessons ended. Undaunted by the withdrawal of his teacher, he struggled to instruct himself and laboriously learned to read. And learning, as his master had foreseen, spoiled him as a slave. His perspective broadened. He realized that there were areas of the world where black men were not the driven brutes of white masters. He hungered for the freedom of the North. He attained it by stratagem, by guile, and by daring. His first haven in free territory was New England. There he became the pet of the Garrisonian abolitionists and a speaker in their lyceum series.

A man of innate intelligence, Douglass improved his natural talents by assiduous study. As his confidence in himself increased, he aspired to propagate his anti-slavery views by the written as well as the spoken word. He was familiar with the city of Rochester, where he had occasionally lectured. It was a city where good works were encouraged, and reformers were active. It was the home of Susan B. Anthony and William Clough Bloss, both ardent abolitionists. Bloss was a good man, who felt that he had started wrong. He had been the keeper of a tavern in Brighton which was patronized by canalers. Canalers were notoriously two-fisted drinkers. When Bloss realized the deleterious effects his spirits had upon his patrons, he sprung the bungs of his cask, dumped the contents into the waters of the Erie Canal, and took up the flaming white cross of temperance. He was also busy in prison reform, and intensely active in the anti-slavery movement.

Bloss and Miss Anthony were two of a stanch group of abolitionists, which included the members of the Rochester Ladies' Anti-Slavery Sewing Circle, an order whose contributions to the local traffic in runaway slaves was more impressive than its name implies. These and other Rochester women, in collaboration with male conspirators, continued even after the passage of the Fugitive Slave Act of 1850 to give succor and provide transportation for black men and women who were fleeing to the freedom of Canada.

Although warmly embraced by Rochester abolitionists, Frederick Douglass suffered from the city itself the indignities commonly experienced by members of his race. Hopefully, he enrolled his daughter in a private school, and discovered that she was not allowed to associate with her fellow students, even during periods of instruction; when he attempted to transfer her to a public school in the neighborhood in which the Douglass family resided, the girl was told to go across town to the little "nigger school" in a shabby section of the Third Ward. Douglass' name was listed only in the brief "Colored" section in the back of the city directory. Restaurants served him with overt reluctance. He was denied a bed in a prominent local hotel.

Douglass struggled manfully and with some success to overcome these discriminations. He was not only a prominent figure among local abolitionists but a personage in the city. He was in the prime of early manhood when he arrived in Rochester, and the years that he passed here were probably the most active and fruitful years of his life. He was a man of commanding presence, one of the great American orators of his time, and it was evident, once he launched his weekly anti-slavery paper, *The North Star* (later, *Frederick Douglass' Paper*), an able and forceful journalist.

While the great impulse of his life was to free the slaves and achieve full racial equality for the Negro, he was not insensible of other social problems. He opposed capital punishment, advocated temperance, and was active with Miss Anthony in the suffragist movement. It was natural that two such combative persons should quarrel: Eventually they did. They shouted at one another in public meeting. It was Susan B.'s implacable conviction that "intelligent and cultured women" should have the vote before the "ignorant black man"; it was Douglass' inflexible belief that the black man needed the vote more than the white female. He triumphed. He saw the passage of the Fifteenth Amendment. Miss Anthony, who outlived him, died several years before the Nineteenth Amendment was ratified.

Douglass published his newspapers in Rochester for sixteen years. They were effective media for the propagation of his views, but it was his talent as a speaker, his quality of leadership, his personality, and his personal petitions to men in high places (including at least two Presidents of the United States) that mostly accounted for the successes he achieved in the interest of members of his race. He was embroiled continually in controversy. His enemies were bitter and vindictive. The Garrisonians, who had started him as a speaker, cast him off when he failed to conform with their views. Their leader viciously denounced him. He was in the opinion of William Lloyd Garrison ". . . as artful and unscrupulous a schismatic as has yet appeared in the abolition ranks." Scandalous rumors were circulated about his relations with a white Englishwoman whom he took into his Rochester home, who worked with him in the newspaper office, and who aided his efforts to deport runaway slaves to Canada. He was vilified late in life when, after the death of the black Mrs. Douglass, he married a white woman.

Douglass seemed to thrive on all of this. He was strong and proud. He was supremely self-confident. He stalked imperiously through the sniping lines of vituperative gantlets and appeared to emerge unscathed. He left here for Washington, D.C., in the early 1870s, but still considered Rochester as "home." In the capital, new honors came to him, including an appointment as United States Minister to Haiti. Rochester exulted in his increased fame; the city more or less considered him a native son. When he died in the capital in 1895, his body was brought here to lie in state in City Hall before being interred in Mt. Hope Cemetery. During his lifetime, a bust of the black leader, sculpted—ironically—in white marble, was presented to the University of Rochester, and now reposes in the Frederick Douglass Building on the River Campus.

He wrote voluminously about his own life, and other writers have amplified the fascinating story of his career. He was prophetic. Ninety-nine years before rioting, which caused the death of four persons, did incalculable property damage, and resulted in the arrest of nearly a thousand rioters, erupted in the city's black ghettos, Douglass, speaking in the City Hall, had said:

"Let us not forget that justice to the Negro is safety to the nation."

How true, how prescient his words seemed, those hot and sticky nights of violence in the summer of 1964!

Chapter 12

One shouldn't allow tender recollections of a distant past to discredit the merits and advantages of the present, but at a time when dope was not an anodyne to the distressing malady of being fifteen years old, and youth at the cry "Cheezit, the cop!" didn't spit in a policeman's eye, but took it on the run; in an age when pretty girls were prouder of their dimples than their navels, and students revered rather than ravaged the ivy-mantled halls of their college campuses, it struck me that Rochester, New York, was the finest place to live in in the world.

I was very young then, and ingenuous. I had seen very little of the world outside. I lived in modest but comfortable circumstances, and I was fortunate in the choice of parents. Not that the rapport between my parents and myself was total, by any means. There were occasions when I lay awake half the night plotting to run away from a vicious old man who made me go to Dockstader's baths for swimming lessons and insisted that I wear to Sunday school a detestable brown derby which had come with my first suit of long trousers. I would run away, and when it was learned that I had suffered a horrible death riding the brakebeam of a freight car, the guilt would lie eternally on my father's soul.

Actually, my parents were wonderfully decent people. They tried earnestly to do what they thought was best for a rather weak and often stupid only son who at times was as contrary as a riptide. The slogan "Make a pal of your son" had not yet been put in circulation, but the idea that the slogan was to express was fixed in my father's mind and he attempted to put it in train. He failed. He discovered, as I later learned as the father of four sons, that the generation gap is unbridgeable: that it is not credible that a man in his forties should find delight in hamsters, a sailboat that floats in bathwater, or hopscotch. Nor would he be impressed by a stubby, redheaded, befreckled, snub-nosed little girl in the fifth grade, with a neck not too carefully scrubbed, such as the fifth-grade Circe who for a time brought one of our issue into trembling subjugation every time she condescended to speak to him.

There were differences between my parents and myself, and sometimes there were sharp differences between myself and my oldest sister, but our home was not a hustings of bitter dispute or an arena of continuous contention. We had quite close-knit relations. Like the homes of many other Rochester families of similar circumstances, our living room was graced by a center table lamp, whose benign rays, on a winter's evening, fell like a nimbus upon our several heads and gave to all a sense of security and familial union.

The center lamp, with its Welsbach burner, rested on a standard on a large living-room table in the middle of the room. Upon the ample surface of the table were arranged such current periodicals as *Harper's Weekly*, *Scribner's*, *McClure's*, the *Ladies' Home Journal*, for my parents; *St. Nicholas* and *The Youth's Companion* for my sisters and myself. And there was always the evening paper of my father's choice, *The Post Express*. It was not in my mind a very lively journal, but it was solidly Republican, quite proper, and it derived distinction from the literary style of its highly respected editorial writer, Joseph P. O'Connor.

There was no reading room mandate of silence when we gathered around the center lamp after supper, but during the early period of our assembly talk was subordinate to our ocular pursuits. Before taking up a magazine or a book, my father would rustle through *The Post Express*, while my mother might search the back pages of the *Ladies' Home Journal* for a novel dessert for her whist-club luncheon. In the light of the center lamp my oldest sister construed Cicero's prosecution of Cataline for her high school Latin class. It was there that I abandoned the Horatio Alger series to trudge with Kim and his patient lama up the valleys of the Bushahr in search of the River of the Arrow; that I overheard from the apple barrel on the schooner *Hispaniole* the fiendish scheme of Long John Silver to arouse mutiny among the crew and appropriate for himself and his desperate followers the gold of *Treasure Island;* that I discovered Sherlock Holmes, *The Three Musketeers*, and cruised down the Mississippi on a raft with Huck and Jim. There was so much to read and be thrilled by those long-ago winter nights at the center table!

Although Rochesterians are often cliquy people, with a profound predilection for forming coteries, serving on committees, joining clubs, and devoting themselves to the rites and rituals of fraternal orders, we were for many years a very homey people. In the other century, and for a considerable number of years in this one, the solid citizenry of the town prided itself on home ownership; our shibboleth was a City of Homes. One got a little place, planted a couple of fruit trees and a currant bush out back, made garden, seeded a lawn, and put a standing lamp on a center table in the living room. After that, a crewel-work legend, "Home Sweet Home," in a frame, was hardly needed as a wall decoration.

Rochester seemed a very manageable community early in the century. It was a hundred and sixty-two thousand in 1900. Once one left the bustle of downtown for the centrifugal expanse of the residential areas, with their quiet, tree-shaded streets and houses that were maintained with instinctive pride, one discovered the peculiar charm of the city. Some of the residential sections had a villagelike character. The proper and proud Third Ward, which set customs that were sometimes mimicked in other parts of town, had more than the aspect of a village. It was virtually autonomous; it made its own rules. There was pollution in Rochester, of course. Back of the houses of the wealthy were alleys upon which abutted stables and carriage houses. The alleys, like privies, were unmentionables. All was spit and polish out front; midden heaps and rats and bottle flies out back.

Third Warders stabled cows a couple of blocks off Main Street, and one resident of this privileged precinct had the cows boldly herded through the streets to outlying pasture, regardless of what the city fathers might think of the practice. He was Clinton Rogers, a partner of the Howe & Rogers Company, largest dealers in carpets in town. Mr. Rogers had married a granddaughter of Colonel Nathaniel Rochester. His own daughter, Mrs. Joseph Roby, told me about her father's cows. They were blooded Jerseys and very special to their owner. They were stabled in a barn back of the family home at the corner of Spring and Washington streets, and driven by a youthful cowherd every pleasant morning through Plymouth Avenue, to Greig Street, across Clarissa Street bridge, and up Mt. Hope Avenue, where they grazed all day on the lush grass lands of Warner's Hills.

This was shortly before my time. At least, I have no recollection of seeing the cows pass the Linden Street corner on their way up Mt. Hope Avenue. There would have been very little to impede their progress in the last stage of their passage. In those days, and through most of my youth, Mt. Hope Avenue bore no resemblance to the hub-to-hub motor speedway it has now become. There was a time when trolley cars, small, shabby, virtually of the Triassic era of the city's transportation system, bounced and swayed over a deplorable roadbed to a Mt. Hope Avenue terminus near the first gate of Mt. Hope Cemetery. There the motorman reversed the trolley for the return journey.

The cars that ended their southern run at the cemetery gate operated at such widely dispersed intervals that I once heard an impatient prospective passenger at the Linden Street stop complain that the schedule was fixed for every other Thursday. Funeral processions proceeded through the upper end of Mt. Hope Avenue, and farm horses, returning to their rural habitats in West Brighton and Henrietta with wagons that had discharged their contents at the city market, lumbered up the hill. The big carts of the Ellwanger & Barry Nursery Company were occasionally in evidence, and Pauckner's grocery rig would make deliveries in the avenue sometime each day. There was never a clutter of traffic during the daylight hours, and a flock of sheep, as well as Rogers' cows, might have been herded over the Medina block pavement without gravely discommoding other users of the thoroughfare.

After dark, upper Mt. Hope Avenue was as noiseless and sepulchral as the burying grounds from which it derived its name. The silence and solitude were so intense that one midnight, Steve O'Hara, a young policeman on the beat, who was overwhelmed by a sense of loneliness and desertion, fired his revolver into the cemetery wall. The two or three possessors of telephones in the neighborhood called frantically into Police Headquarters that murder had been done. Detectives hurried up Mt. Hope Avenue hill, where they met the copper on the beat, and O'Hara was in a brinky situation. In the end, he convinced the detectives and his superiors at Headquarters that he had fired in the air to try to halt an apparitionlike figure he suspected was a housebreaker. He was in the clear, officially; but he wanted no more of the witching-hour silence of Mt. Hope Avenue. He soon resigned from the force, and ultimately became proprietor of a popular saloon called Brighton Gardens at East Avenue and Winton Road.

"I couldn't take that Mt. Hope Avenue beat," he said. "Nothing there, except all those graves. It was like being in a tomb. And it was spooky, too, walking around that big castle, like I had to do every night."

The "big castle" which came under the nightly surveillance of Officer O'Hara has stood for more than a hundred years in a landscaped enclosure a few hundred feet east of the summit of the Mt. Hope Avenue pavement. Built in 1854 by Horatio Gates Warner, its towered and castellated formidability, its massive, fortresslike stone walls, and the elaborate arrangements of its interior quite accurately follow the over-all design of a castle that captivated the fancy of Mr. Warner during a visit in Scotland.

Horatio Warner was a man of parts. He had served as a judge in his native Madison County before moving to Rochester. Here he practiced law, engaged in banking and business, served as a regent of the University of the State of New York, and published the *Daily Advertiser*. The wealth he had accumulated by his own efforts was substantially added to by a legacy from his younger brother, Captain William H. Warner, who, after acquiring a large tract of land in California, was killed in 1849 by an Indian ambush as he was leading a small army detail through a defile in the northern Sierras. Horatio Warner crossed the continent to liquidate the holdings which, with the gold rush, had multiplied many times in value.

The older Warner brother was a cultivated man; he had a sense of the magnificent. He had extensive properties—besides Warner's Castle and its lands, he owned a large plantation near Atlanta, Georgia. There he settled his son, John B. Y. Warner, the only child of an issue of several to survive a familial epidemic of tuberculosis, immediately upon the young man's being graduated from Union College.

Although the elder Warner did not acquire the plantation until shortly after the close of the Civil War, he had developed before the outbreak of that struggle an admiration for the style and manners of the southern aristocracy, and his sympathies during the war were believed by many to be with the South. Apocryphal though it may be, a story persists that he once defied an armed posse of superpatriots by flaunting a Confederate flag from a turret of the castle. He was remote from Rochester's ardent group of abolitionists. Frederick Douglass despised him. It was Warner who implacably resisted the integration of Douglass' daughter with the white pupils of the private school in which her father had enrolled her. Warner's prejudices did not lessen the esteem in which he was held in Rochester. When he died in 1876, a local newspaper opened an extensive panegyric on the owner of Warner's Castle with this line: "Rarely has it been the case that the death of any citizen of Rochester produced such a general state of sadness as that we record this morning."

Warner predeceased his wife. At the widow's death, the Rochester property reverted to John Warner. Although he delighted in plantation life and shared his late father's admiration for the "beauty and chivalry" of the South, he reluctantly quitted the plantation and moved to Rochester. If he lacked his father's bustling enterprise, he had inherited his cultivated tastes. He established his family, which included three Georgian-born daughters, in Warner's Castle, and continued to live there for several years in a manner that complemented the baronial character of the imposing edifice and the lovely private park that composed its immediate setting.

There were many acres in the Warner property, including Warner's Hills (now part of Highland Park), where Clinton Rogers' cows were put to pasture. The farm lands were inside the city. Prohibitive assessments for city improvements were made against them. Warner found the burden of maintaining a large property within the corporation financially backbreaking. He first sold off parcels of land; then the castle itself which, during its years of occupancy by the Warner family, had been perhaps the most unusual private dwelling in Rochester. Since then, Warner's Castle has had several private owners. The last was a naturopath, who converted the building into a sanitarium and imposed upon his boarding patients, whatever their disorders, a regimen of orange juice and distilled water.

Inevitably, the naturopath became involved with the law, which charged him with practicing medicine without a license. He was a gentle and personable man. Many of his patients had implicit faith in his "cure." They were outraged when the sanitarium was closed, and they pledged support to their medical preceptor in his hour of trial. Among his loyal votaries was Fred Allen, popular stage and radio comedian, whose hypochondriac tendencies occasionally caused him to try various advertised health regimens and to trust to unlicensed "healers."

Today, Warner's Castle and the ornamental pleasance which its builder designed for its setting, is owned by the city of Rochester,

166

which uses it in part as a garden center. The austerity of the gray pile, which needed only a portcullis and a moat to evoke the days of chain armor and the crossbow, is relieved by a thick entwining of vines over the hand-hewn stones of its two-foot walls.

Its gate house, square, stern, with stone balustrades at the edge of its roof, and gray stone walls as thick as those of the castle itself, which stands at the Mt. Hope Avenue entrance to what is now called Castle Park, has lost its former forbidding aspect. Although built as a home for the Warners' coachman, the gatehouse, when I was young, so much resembled the outworks of a fortress that only an intrepid youth would dare dart past the portal it guarded to explore the exclusive precinct beyond. There was a half fear that such an action would be challenged by a sentry with an harquebus. The gatehouse is not a tumbling ruin; it is too solidly built for that. But it is years since it has been occupied, and its emptiness and desuetude are emphasized by windows boarded against the stones of vandals. It is an anachronism fronting an avenue through which the swish and snort of motorcars is continual, night and day; it stands as a mute reminder of an era when the three younger Warner ladies, gently bred in all the graces of the South in which they had passed their youth, were driven from their castle home in an open victoria or a shining brougham by a coachman in livery.

* * *

Mrs. Joseph Roby, who told me about her father's cows, also told me about her father's friendship with Leonard Jerome whom Clinton Rogers considered—according to his daughter's report— the most fascinating man he had ever known.

Rogers was not a native Rochesterian. He had come here from Worchester, Massachusetts, in 1854, and very quickly met the *right* people. Many of them were concentrated in the old Third Ward, and Rogers gravitated to that area. He was a personable and capable young man who fitted readily into the social and business life of the busy little community that had had a city charter only twenty years. One of the great beaux of the town was Leonard Jerome who lived with his brother Lawrence in South Fitzhugh Street. Rogers and Leonard were soon friends. They had mutual interests in music and blooded horses; each had a sense of the grand style, and both had a capacity to make money.

Jerome left Rochester ten years before the outbreak of the Civil War; Rogers stayed on. The carpet business he and his partner, John Howe, who had come with him from Massachusetts, had started, was prospering. He married the daughter of Henry, youngest son of Colonel Nathaniel Rochester, and settled in a large house at Spring and South Washington streets, which was the aorta of the city's historical life and the provenance of its aristocratic tradition. The Rogers' house was catercorner from the historical dwelling in which Colonel Rochester had formerly lived with his wife and his numerous progeny.

Rogers' tastes were expansive. He had more than a smitch of the flamboyance of his good friend Jerome. Once, learning that a French count desired a pair of black carriage horses, he crossed the Atlantic with a matching pair of his own, sold them to the count, and was royally entertained in Paris by the grateful purchaser. He took his wife and four children to Europe for a year, enrolled the youngest of the brood in schools in London and Vevy, and made the Grand Tour with his wife, his oldest child, and a French governess. It was a full-blown, first-cabin expedition. At home, Rogers lived in a manner consonant with a man who had married into the Rochester family, and who was growing wealthy not only from his carpet business but as the result of a $7,000 flyer he had taken in George Eastman's inchoate little enterprise.

Mrs. Roby outlived her lawyer brother, Rochester Hart Rogers, an older sister, who married a brother of her husband, and a spinster sister, Helen Rochester Rogers. Miss Rogers had artistic leanings and a considerable acquaintance among artists, musicians, and writers. One of her particular friends was John Masefield, England's poet laureate, who was an occasional guest at her summer home on Lake Ontario, and for whom she once helped arrange an American lecture tour. When Miss Rogers died, she left an estate of more than $3,000,000. Among her personal effects were sixty-six letters written to her by Masefield which, together with letters from artists, musicians, and such novelists as Hugh Walpole and Paul Horgan, were donated by Mrs. Roby, who had custody of the collection after her sister's death, to the University of Rochester library.

Proud though she was of her ancestry, Mrs. Roby did not wear it as a social decoration. A Third Warder would not be ostentatious about such a matter, and Mrs. Roby was a Third Warder by birth, by tradition, and by impregnation. The Third was the place of her impressionable youth and young womanhood; it was not the district in which she lived after her marriage. The greater part of her life was spent in a large house on the East Side, a block off East Avenue. There she lived with her physician husband, who served the city of Rochester with distinction as the collaborator and deputy of Health Officer George H. Goler; and there she died, more than a dozen years after her husband, at the age of ninety-one.

Until shortly before her death, which occurred a few months before this was written, Mrs. Roby was a vibrant—a very alive—nonagenarian. She delighted in talk, and she talked well. She knew a good deal about the lore of the city that was named after her distinguished ancestor, and the people who lived here contemporaneously with her parents and herself. She did not know Leonard Jerome, who was to become celebrated after he left Rochester as a financier, an assiduous lover, a sportsman, and the father of Winston Churchill's beautiful mother.

"Mr. Jerome was gone from Rochester long before I was born," she said. "I was a child when he died. I sometimes felt I knew him, my father talked so vividly about him. I did know, slightly, another of my father's distinguished friends. Hiram Everest. He moved from Rochester to California, but he came back now and then. My father called Mr. Everest 'the most successful failure in America.'"

Hiram Bond Everest, a farm boy out of Pike, a hamlet forty-odd miles southwest of Rochester, left home in 1849 with $250 in pocket, to teach school in a small town in Wisconsin. His diary of that year told of his homely ambitions.

"I wish to be an honest, industrious farmer," he wrote, "study and improve my mind, get me a permanent home and beautify it, live in close communication with God and let those chase after the gaudy baubles of life who will."

Teaching seemed not Everest's forte. He gave it a fair trial, then gave it up, successively to farm, to grow ornamental and fruit trees for the market, and to operate a sawmill.

The farm did poorly; the trees suffered winter kill; the sawmill twice burned to the ground.

A triple failure, Everest returned east and settled in Rochester. In failing, he displayed a unique talent: He made money at it. He had increased his original capital of $250 to $9,000, and he and a Rochester carpenter named Matthew Ewing went into the oil business.

Ewing had developed a process for distilling crude oil under vacuum. Everest backed him with the money he had accumulated from his successful failures, and in 1866 the two men incorporated what was known as the Vacuum Oil Company. The partners separated after a few years owing to a conflict of interests. Ewing wanted to concentrate on the sale of kerosene. Everest's idea was to develop "a new and improved product from petroleum for lubricating and other purposes."

To a degree, Hiram Everest held to the tenets of the life credo he expressed in his youthful diary. He let others "chase after the gaudy baubles of life"; he went after customers and the almighty dollar. A rich man in 1879, he materially increased his wealth by selling 75 per cent of his Vacuum holdings to the Rockefeller interests. His wife was ill. He wanted her in a more gentle climate. He left Rochester for the far West, and left his older son, Charles Marvin Everest, to manage the Vacuum holdings. The younger Everest managed well. When he died in 1917 (on his private yacht on Long Island Sound), the Vacuum assets in the merger effected by his father and John D. Rockefeller were valued at $76,000,000.

This was not bad for a little company that had virtually started in Matthew Ewing's back yard on Monroe Avenue, and moved to a plant on upper Exchange Street. It was picayune compared with the later development of the industry Ewing and Everest had founded. Rockefeller had the Standard Oil Company of New York, SOCONY for an acronymic trade name. There was swift wheeling and fancy dealing during the time that his company and Vacuum were known successively as Socony-Vacuum Corporation and Socony-Vacuum Oil Company, Inc. The combination was selling in a world market, and acquiring crude oil not only in this country but in Arabia, in Iran, and in Kuwait. As the business expanded, the name Vacuum was dropped, and the company operated under a variety of titles. It is now the Mobil Oil Corporation.

In the fall of 1966, Hiram Everest Clements of Rochester, was the honored guest at a dinner of the American Newcomen Society in the Hotel Pierre in New York that commemorated the founding by his grandfather one hundred years before of Mobil's earliest predecessor, the Vacuum Oil Company.

President Rawleigh Warner, Jr., of Mobil, the only speaker at the dinner, in outlining the history of the Vacuum Company and discussing the career of Hiram Bond Everest, explained that Everest's invention of Vacuum's 600-W cylinder oil assured the success of the internal combustion engine that powers the millions of automobiles that clutter the nation's highways and city streets.

While many people in Rochester have a vague notion that one of the very first automobiles was made in our city by George B. Selden, very few know that if it had not been for Everest's early development of an oil that would withstand high heat and intense pressure, Selden would never have attempted the construction of what he called a "road engine." The two men were friends, and Everest was a client of Selden, a patent lawyer.

"Hiram Everest was the city's greatest inventor," said George B. Selden, Jr., son of the automobile inventor. "He made the automobile possible."

In his speech before the Newcomen Society, Mr. Warner said:

"Mobil has never lost the pre-eminence that Everest established for the Vacuum Oil in the field of lubrication.

"We lubricated one of the earliest internal combustion engines in this country—the one patented by George B. Selden in the 1870s—and made it work; and we lubricated the winner of this year's Indianapolis '500' . . ."

Even before the great mushrooming expansion of the Eastman Company, and long before the advent of Xerox, the quiet, conservative, dull (by the judgment of critics who had known only superficially our character and history), little city of Rochester was alive with people who had scintillating ideas and talents to put their ideas to practical uses. The Vacuum Oil Company was hardly blown through Hiram Everest's nose. It was not a shilly-shallying sort of thing. It couldn't be and grow, as it has under the new name of Mobil, into one of the ten largest private enterprises in the world, with assets and annual revenues each in excess of $5 billion!

Sometimes our detractors make me laugh.

Chapter 13

In the very early days of the century we occasionally had at our house weekend guests who were distantly related to my mother. We called them Aunt Marcia and Uncle Billy. Uncle Billy, I believe, was superintendent of the Buffalo street-cleaning department. He was a pleasant little man, with gentle eyes and a little pudding belly, whom my father, after Sunday breakfast, would outfit in a black turtle-neck sweater and mount on the front seat of his Rambler tandem bicycle.

"You've got your Delaware Avenue, Billy," my father would say. "I want to show you our *East* Avenue."

In those days, East Avenue was the section of Rochester that residents of the city first displayed to aunts, uncles, and cousins from out of town, and visiting firemen. The word "tycoon" had not yet been given currency by the Luce publications, but East Avenue was the thoroughfare of our local nabobs. Because so many heads of business and industry were arrayed along its handsome length, it was sometimes called the Avenue of Presidents. It was not with envy but with pride that those of us in less favored circumstances identified for visitors the occupants of the large, important houses set far back on immaculate lawns or embosomed in ornamental gardens. We were boastful about East Avenue. It gave substance and prestige to our city.

When my father brought Uncle Billy back for Sunday dinner, after pedaling him not only over the macadam pavement of East Avenue, but also taking him for a spin through one of our parks, he supplemented with an oral resumé the wonders to which the vision of our guest had been exposed.

Uncle Billy heard him out politely. He conceded that Rochester was a nice *little* city, but he reminded us that Buffalo had sent two of its residents, Millard Fillmore and Grover Cleveland, to the White House; that the city had produced Frank Erne, the world's lightweight boxing champion; that it had staged the Pan-American

Exposition, one of the world's great fairs; and that President McKinley, mortally wounded by an assassin's bullet, had died in the great Delaware Avenue mansion of John Milburn.

"There's always a lot going on in Buffalo," Uncle Billy said. "Things happen over there."

My father couldn't match Uncle Billy's citations, but he went on doggedly about the delights and expansiveness of our city parks, which at that time were widely acclaimed throughout the nation; and about the prestige and beauty of East Avenue. There was nothing quite like East Avenue, *anywhere*. And had Billy Barnard noticed how the upper branches of the curbside elms entwined to form a green and living canopy over the pavement?

Uncle Billy agreed, from what he had seen of them, that our parks lived up to their billing. But he countered my father's professions of the unparagoned excellence of East Avenue by pronouncing the names of some of the residents of Delaware Avenue, most of whom, he blithely proclaimed, "had more money than Carter had pills."

Buffalo was considerably larger than Rochester, and at that time it probably was a more active and lively city. But all Buffalonians were not as impressed as was Uncle Billy by its liveliness. Mabel Dodge Luhin, the caustic, brilliant, much-married chronicler of Buffalo life as she had known it as a youthful member of the exclusive Delaware Avenue set, remarked at one point in her revealing book *Intimate Memories:*

"Life [in Buffalo] flowed on in an apparently commonplace way until, once in a while, something happened. Donald White would be found hanging to the gas fixtures in his bedroom, naked except for a pair of white gloves."

In Rochester, we had no annalist of Mabel Dodge Luhin's daring and irrepressibility. Those who wrote about our mores and our customs wrote gently about them. In the established East Avenue section and in the old Third Ward, a person who behaved in the outré manner of Donald White, stringing himself stark naked to a gas fixture, or who became involved in scandal, would thenceforth be spoken of only in guarded whispers; he would have become a pariah who had violated the code, and the quicker he was forgotten the better.

The Third Ward, of course, was singularly proper. Scandal there would be ignored. Third Warders appeared to have a faculty that allowed them to eliminate from their consciousness anything that might offend their finicky sensibilities. For years they had connived at the wretchedness, the filth, and the wickedness of the cloaca maxima in their midst that persons on the outside knew as Murderers' Row. In winter they walked high-headedly past the waterless basin of the Erie Canal, which made the moat of their exclusiveness, heedless of its litter of dead cats, tin cans, broken furniture, garbage, discarded screen doors, bones from butcher shops—all the scurf and sordes of a dump heap ". . . as unsavory a mess as one could imagine," wrote Miss Virginia Jeffrey Smith, in her delightful little book *Reminiscences of the Third Ward.* "We never thought to apologize for it—it was part of the ward and therefore all right."

The ultimate in manners and propriety gave a *sui generis* character to the Third. In another part of her essay Miss Smith tells how Mr. Charles Pound, one of the most deeply ingrained Third Warders, struck and felled to the pavement by an electric brougham driven by a feminine neighbor, arose, flecked the street dirt from his clothing, and profusely apologized to the motorist for being in her way.

But neither the Third Ward nor the rest of the corporate body of Rochester could ignore a scandalous catastrophe that occurred in the upper reaches of the Ward early in the morning of January 8, 1901, when a fire Moloch-like in its sacrifice of youth broke out in the main building of the Rochester Orphan Asylum.

The building, with its connecting wings and auxiliary structures, stood in Hubbell Park, a short passageway between Exchange and Greig streets. It was of brick construction, four stories high. It housed more than one hundred children. Twenty-nine of the youthful residents, most of them under ten years of age, and two adults died in the flames or shortly after the victims were removed from the blazing building by the heroic endeavors of firemen and institutional attendants.

This was the second great holocaust Rochester had suffered in a period of less than thirteen years, but the city authorities, learning little from the first, had taken no proper precautions to prevent the second.

In the earlier disaster, employees who were hoping to eke out their meager daytime wage by working on the night of November 9, 1888, in the plant of the Rochester Steam Gauge and Lantern Works were trapped when an explosion in the lower part of the factory belched flames through an elevator shaft and spread swiftly over the upper part of the building. The Lantern Works stood above the Upper Falls of the Genesee, at the foot of what is now Commercial Street. In desperate attempts to escape the flames, men leaped to their death on the jagged rocks of the cataract. Others were asphyxiated. Many were burned to death. The awful toll was thirty-eight dead.

A great hue and cry arose when discovery was made that safety provisions were tragically inadequate. The city was lax in matters of this sort; state laws were so ineffectual that doors were slammed in the face of a state agent assigned to examine factory buildings for fire hazards. When the Lantern Works dead were buried, and the laments and unofficial accusations quieted, the city's laissez-faire attitude toward the enforcement of fire-preventive regulations continued as before.

Two or three days before the Orphan Asylum fire, an explosion in the naphtha building of the Kodak Park plant of the Eastman Kodak Company caused the death of three city firemen, and a few days after the first-named disaster Coroner Henry Kleindienst, a solid Republican officeholder in the most solidly Republican city in the state, held an inquest to determine the causes of the tragedy.

The coroner called as witnesses several members of the Board of Trustees of the Orphan Asylum. They were men high placed in the community, and men high placed in Rochester at that time were invariably Republicans. Mayor George A. Carnahan was a trustee; Walter S. Hubbell, Mr. Eastman's lawyer, and the head of one of the largest men's bible classes in western New York, was another. Trustees Howard A. Smith, president of a Rochester business and a resident of the Avenue of Presidents, and Andrew J. Townson, secretary-treasurer of the Sibley store, who was noted for his civic activities, took the stand.

They and other trustees, gently questioned by the coroner, appeared ignorant of the seemingly criminal lack of safety devices in a four-story building that had dozens of small children sleeping in its upper reaches. One of the two fire escapes (Kleindienst believed there should have been one at every window) descended into the flames and was useless as a means of evacuation. The coroner had been told that a woman attendant made nightly rounds of the dormitories with a lighted candle in hand. The institution had no night watchman. Kleindienst asked Townson about this.

"Nothing was ever said to me about a watchman," the witness answered. "The running of the asylum is in the hands of the lady managers."

"Is it not the duty of the trustees to inspect the building now and then?"

"I did not understand it so. . . ."

Trustee Smith was asked, "Are not most of the trustees, trustees in name only?"

"No, sir."

"But I called several witnesses of the board and they say they know nothing about the workings of the institution," said the coroner.

The inquest lasted two days, and Mr. Smith, who sat through every minute of it, told the press that he couldn't see how it could have been more thorough.

The *Democrat and Chronicle* made this pertinent comment: ". . . Another direct result of the fire, with its long death toll, has been to call attention to conditions in other public institutions in the city. This, of course, is not unusual. Calamities like this always lead to apprehension, which is usually quieted without practical results, as the first sentiment of horror gradually passes away."

One of Rochester's prime characteristics is its spirit of good will. It is a well-meaning city. It has tolerated with seeming equanimity numerous abuses and wrongs; this has not been entirely from lack of a desire to correct the abuses and wrongs, but rather from a lack of knowledge as to how to enforce effective reforms. The city has always had a conscience. This was pricked by the Orphan Asylum fire. The dreadful vision of small children, beyond the reach of rescuers, pleading with childish wails and panicky gesticulations at the apertures of the inferno their foster home had become was deeply impressed upon the city's consciousness. There were resolves that no such fiendish disaster should again occur; how effectively these resolves were translated into action is a question.

The children who lost their lives on this infanticidal pyre were of obscure lineage. No one knew them on the outside. Their names were not names to be engraved on the city's immemorial tablets. Time relieved the public's imagination of the fantasy of horrors the fire had evoked. Rochester was consoled by the knowledge that the Orphan Asylum trustees discarded their original plan to rebuild on the grim Hubbell Park site in favor of a modern cottage complex in the wide open spaces of the Pinnacle Hills. The phoenixlike rebirth of the institution was celebrated with pleasant ceremonies. The group of buildings was not spoken of as an orphanage, but as the Hillside Home for Children.

Rochester's second worst holocaust presently passed out of mind, and the city has suffered no similar tragedy since. The Orphan Asylum fire is not a historic date. Rochester for many years remembered only one great fire. It was not life-consuming; no one was killed in the two days that passed before it was quenched. It was extensive enough to be defined as a conflagration, and its date was fixed in the public's mind for more than half a century. It was discovered early in the morning of the very cold day of February 26, 1904. It was known as the Sibley Fire.

*　　*　　*

The fire that destroyed the Sibley, Lindsay & Curr Company's store was perhaps the most exciting spectacle Rochester youth had ever witnessed, and the roll call in city schools on the February Friday that the flames began their devastating siege along a considerable stretch of Main Street East must have been widely punctuated by the non-response of absentees.

I was a high school freshman in the old South Fitzhugh Street building that had formerly been known as the Rochester Free Academy. Starting tractably enough for school on the morning of the Great Fire, I soon succumbed to wild rumors that all downtown Rochester was in flames, and diverted from my dutiful course to run through South Avenue in the direction of Main Street.

In my onward rush, I could see from as far away as Alexander Street a great cumulus of gray-black smoke riven at its lower formation by broad jagged red flames. By the time I reached Court Street there was an acrid taste in my mouth and a burnt-cork stuffiness in my nostrils. I could hear the pumpers even before I saw them. They didn't seem to throb and pulsate. From a distance, they sounded like dwarfed artillery. When I achieved the fire lines, the awesome prospect of Main Street appeared to validate the rumors that downtown Rochester was doomed.

The scene had the flux and confusion of battle. Chockablock at some points like cannon ranked on a redoubt, the pumpers threw tons of water into and against the burning buildings from whose windows great oriflammes of fire waved defiantly. Men with axes and hose lines and extension ladders were in constant movement. Commands shrilled above the groundly beat of pumpers. The morning temperature was close to zero and the fire fighters, their boots, their helmets, their rubber coats frozen stiff by spray from their lines, resembled strange carapaced bipeds as they slithered about on the icy Main Street pavement or stumbled over hose that lay in reptilian coils across it.

Masses of ice, sculpted in surrealistic character, that had formed on outside areas of the buildings, and huge stalactites that descended from ledges gave a weird, unearthly aspect to a scene which was unlike anything that Rochester had ever seen before. To the youth who, heedless of the bitter cold, pressed tight against the fire lines for hours, this was the grandest show on earth. We envied the brave men in the ice-stiffened boots and rubber coats upon whom the eyes of the entire city were fixed. They were the saviors of the town—if, indeed, the town was to be saved; and we followed them with admiring eyes as they advanced upon or retreated from some salient point of attack or paused to gulp hot coffee at one of the improvised field kitchens in the fire zone.

Known always as the Sibley Fire, the multimillion-dollar catastrophe did not originate in the Sibley store, which at that time occupied the lower floors of the handsome eleven-year-old Granite Building at the northeast corner of Main and St. Paul streets. Its beginnings were in the Rochester Dry Goods Company, a minor competitor of Sibley's, farther east in Main Street; but so quickly did the flames spread in the frigid gusty air that they soon engulfed adjoining and adjacent buildings and even leaped north across Division Street to menace the Sibley stables, from which, happily, the trembling, snorting, terrified delivery horses were led to safety.

Discovered in the fifth hour of the morning, by late afternoon the fire had transformed most of Main Street between St. Paul Street and Clinton Avenue North into the condition of an invested town. It now seemed as if all the buildings on the north side of that bustling commercial block would wither away in mathematical progression. And fears were expressed that if the wind quickened, the conflagration could not be confined within a single block, and that Rochester, often disparaged as a one-street city, might lose the only artery of trade that gave it metropolitan status. It was as if we were fighting on the barricades.

Help was offered from Elmira, Ithaca, Geneva, and Lyons. It was accepted from Buffalo and Syracuse. When the apparatus from these cities was removed from flat cars in the railroad yards, welcoming crowds lustily acclaimed the accompanying firemen as heroic reinforcements come to save the day.

But the day was not to be saved in the allotted span of twenty-four hours, and the struggle to quench the insatiable lust of the flames continued nearly two days.

The Sibley store—Sib's, as it was known in the parlance of the street—almost from the start of the fire had been of central interest to the gallery at the fire ropes and to the city at large. It was an institution with a proud history and a reputation of being one of the finest stores between New York and Chicago. It was Rochester's most notable emporium.

Rufus A. Sibley, one of the founders of the store and its president, was not in town when the fire was discovered. Other members of the firm were also away. Andrew J. Townson, secretary and treasurer, learned of the fire at his home in Oxford Street. Of English birth and American upbringing, Townson was one of Rochester's prized Minutemen. Despite his rather limp trusteeship of the Orphan Asylum, he had enormous capacities for getting things done. With his two older sons, he reached the blazing Granite Building in time to save a small quantity of silks and other stuffs and, more importantly, $40,000 in cash, which was rescued from the office safe.

The salvaged goods were first removed to the large bindery and print shop of the John C. Moore Corporation in Stone Street, which was headed by Townson's close friend, Henry J. Moore.

"We are absolutely out of business," Townson said, when interviewed in the Moore office.

It was true. The store's loss was something like three million dollars. For years, the Sibley, Lindsay & Curr Company had been a highly profitable operation. It would have been an easy thing for the partners to take the insurance and retire to luxurious indolence. But none had the predilections of a social *flâneur*. They were hustlers. Townson, who at that point was probably the sparkiest spark plug in the company, had started as a check boy at the age of twelve. The bundle boy was getting 50 cents a week more. "I

179

can carry as big a bundle as any boy," the youth boasted, and he became bundle boy! At the age of twenty, he started investing in the company; at the age of thirty, he was a member of the firm.

Plans for a new store on a site a block east on Main Street, at the northeast corner of Clinton Avenue North, had already been drawn by J. Foster Warner, an architect whose offices high up in the Granite Building had been destroyed by fire. Part of the corner block was then occupied by the Empire Theater, a show house for burlesque entertainers and an arena for professional wrestling matches.

Townson, who had a great deal to do with the selection of the new site for the store, later greatly influenced the New York Central Railroad in its choice of a block on Central Avenue between Joseph Avenue and Clinton Avenue North for its new station. The old station was a few hundred yards west. Townson wanted the new depot in the Joseph-Clinton block. This would send passengers leaving the trains for downtown Rochester directly through Clinton Avenue to the Main and Clinton Avenue location of the Sibley store. To facilitate this design, Townson purchased in the name of friends and relatives dozens of parcels of land in the Joseph, Clinton and Central Avenue area, which in time were reconsigned to the New York Central. At one point during these real estate transactions, Mrs. John Harvard Castle, Mr. Townson's very proper, old-family mother-in-law was the owner of the toughest saloon on Central Avenue.

Thirty days after the great Main Street, or Sibley, fire was pronounced "out," Sibley, Lindsay & Curr Company was again selling dry goods, clothing, and accessories. Townson had acted with his usual promptitude and efficacy. Under jury-rigged conditions, business was being carried on in the renovated Empire Theater, and in other buildings that stood on the site selected for the new store.

The company continued in makeshift quarters while the new building was being erected in sections on part of the block in which the Empire Theater was located. Early in 1905, the theater was abandoned, and Sibley's transferred its business to the apartments of the new structure that were ready for occupancy. The entire store was completed late that year. Faced with narrow, orange-colored brick, the building was utilitarian and plain, but not draggy in its exterior aspect. Its ornaments were its broad plateglass show windows with displays of merchandise that often showed a

Rue de la Paix glitter, and its graceful tower, in which was encased the Sibley clock, which has long been a cynosure for downtown Rochesterians. Inside, the conveniences and accommodations for customers were as modern as the next minute. Sibley's had been a fine store before; now it was one of the greatest, outside of the leading stores in the largest cities in the country. Its high quality was complemented by high revenues. In time, what is known as the Mercantile Building was attached to the east side of the main building, and the store now has more than a dozen acres of floor space. An abrasive quarrel developed between two of the firm's founding fathers. Both were men whose sights were unremittingly fixed on the main chance. They may have hated each other, but the luxury of personal enmity was not allowed to divert either from the primordial and perennial purpose of selling goods at a profit. The first Sibley and the first Lindsay ceased to speak to one another, and their mutual taciturnity continued until death. One by one, chief executives and the original partners died off, and Sibley's for a time was left to the tentative charge of descendants. Today, with its rich Rochester heritage, it is without Rochester management. Since 1957, it has been a unit in the Associated Dry Goods Corporation.

Chapter 14

A peculiar attribute of Rochester is the devotion it inspires in many persons who come here from other places and who, not unlike religious converts, sometimes display more enthusiasm for the city than those born in the faith. If an outsider is properly introduced, if he survives a winter or two, if he is caught up in one of the little cliques that in total compose the social fabric of the town, he is frequently a committed Rochesterian.

If he leaves, in retirement, to seek a softer climate in the South or in the West that he believes will relieve his high blood pressure, or his asthma, or his arthritis, he often leaves with reluctance, and sneaks back again and again to mingle with the old crowd, to lunch at the old club, to play a game of rotation pool, or sit in with the fellows at the bridge table after lunch, and to know, deep inside him, that it is here that his roots are really fixed. There is something contagious about Rochester.

Newcomers sometimes hate it. They revile it as a place that is cold, smug, self-centered, and antipathetic to strangers. If they stay on and become assimilated, they frequently come to love it. I, personally, have known men who left to pursue interests in other cities after a residence here of only a few years and who have voluntarily returned, perhaps at an economic disadvantage, to confess, half sheepishly, "Well, there's something about Rochester. . . . And the kids love it. And my wife, she missed it. I guess I did, too."

Of course, the city has changed greatly over the years. The changes are both physical and ethical. Rochester has lost something. Oldsters, who have known the city for many years, feel sadly about some of the changes. While I subscribe with reservations to Lord Macaulay's suggestion that no man who is correctly informed about the past will be disposed to take a morose or despondent view of the present, I also agree with Andrew Lang that "The little present must not be allowed to elbow the great past out of view." My recollections of my own past become more vivid and commemorative as the interim between youth and old age widens. As a lifetime resident of Rochester and its environs, I recall with nostalgic tenderness the delights and contentments of a city that was small, friendly, and neighborly, that had not yet suffered the abrasions of racial dissension, that was free of street violence, that knew nothing of the clutter and hurly-burly of our present metropolitan community. It had hypocrisies and nice Nellieisms that would be mocked at and ridiculed by the modern generation, and it had corruptions, some rather flagrant. But the Rochester of sixty-odd years ago, it seems to me, had a great deal to recommend it as a place for youth to experience the teen-age ordeal of growing up.

Native Rochesterians who leave town as young adults and remain away a long time often become reflective about the city.

"Unlike some who have undertaken to write about their boyhood, mine was not a misery," writes the Reverend William A. Buell, in a pleasant memoir of his youthful career. "I did not loathe school nor did I hate my parents. On the contrary, had I been given the choice, I could scarcely have chosen better."

Reading on in Mr. Buell's essay, one concludes that he also believes he could scarcely have chosen a better place than Rochester to spend his youth.

The Buells were old family. They were cultivated people. They lived in a large house at the Berkeley Street corner of East Avenue, in the heart of the city's most exclusive precinct. Very early in the Automobile Age they owned a Stevens-Duryea touring car. Young William Buell selected his toys from the F. A. O. Schwartz catalogue. His first schooling was at Miss Hakes' School for Girls, which accepted a few small boys in the lower elementary grades.

"Caroline Werner sat behind me," Mr. Buell writes. "She sometimes pulled my hair, and she chewed gum. She was destined to become the wife of Frank Gannett of the newspaper syndicate which he controlled."

William Buell attended a series of local private schools, and had a brief fling in Public School 23, which his parents thought would be a leavening influence. "In my seventh grade classroom I knew that Elizabeth Davey was beautiful," he reports. [Buell's discovery was hardly original. Numerous other admirers supported the youth's judgment, including Walter J. Salmon, multimillionaire real estate speculator and horseman, who ultimately married Miss Davey.] Leaving the Kalbfus School, the last Rochester private school in which he was enrolled, Buell matriculated at the fashionable St. George's School in Newport, Rhode Island, to which he subsequently returned as headmaster.

His boyhood life in Rochester, which continued until he left for St. George's at the end of the first decade of the century, was considerably different from that of most Rochester youth of his time. In the era before World War I, class distinctions here were more sharply defined than they are today. High school boys did not freely comingle with boys from the Kalbfus and Bradstreet schools. This was not owing to any particular snootiness on the part of the latter, but more because the friendships of the private school boys were quite naturally intramural. And their outside activities were largely shared with their school fellows and with the subdebutantes who were pupils in two or three of the city's private schools for girls.

No friends of mine, for example, attended the dancing classes "under the gracious direction," as Mr. Buell writes, "of Miss Ruth Quimby." These were held in the Genesee Valley Club, when the club was in its downtown quarters. There was a social imperativeness about the Quimby dancing school. Little girls who were later expected to "come out" were invariably enrolled.

"A white-haired gentleman, whose name I do not recall," Mr. Buell relates, "played the piano. We were taught the waltz, the two-step, the polka (slide, slide, and one-two-three) and for fun the Virginia Reel. We dressed up and wore patent-leather pumps. Some of the boys were naughty; girls hardly ever. Popularity played its part. The hands of a certain lady did not charm. As Othello says of Desdemona, 'This hand is moist.'"

Fortunate, or innocent, or intrinsically benevolent, Mr. Buell avers that during his Rochester boyhood, "I scarcely knew what a bad person was."

Mr. Buell was disassociated from the rag, tag, and bobtail of his native city. Even the public school he attended was in the East Avenue section. Riffraff kids were there in very limited numbers. He tells about the choosiness of his bringing up naturally and ingenuously.

"Our parents had many great and wonderful friends, of whom

we saw a good deal. They went on camping and fishing trips in Quebec with William and Alice Lee. Mr. Lee had been Woodrow Wilson's classmate at Princeton. Mrs. Lee was a lovely person, who at one time superintended the Sunday school. Once a question confused me, 'What famous person has just been a guest at your house?' For some reason I was tongue-tied. 'Why, President Eliot of Harvard, of course!' We memorized passages from the Scriptures, including all of the fourteen chapters of John.

"Games were not a part of Sunday, though for some reason we could play 'Store.' Father frequently read to us, sometimes from the Bible or a book entitled *Paul of Tarsus*. He was not averse to Hawthorn's *Wonder Book* or the poetry of Oliver Wendell Holmes, who had been a professor during his Harvard days. In warm weather there was frequently a carriage ride to the country in a two-seater hired from the livery stable of George Leader. At supper, Father presided over a chafing dish to produce his own recipe of matchless Welsh rabbit—seasoned cheese blended with Bass's ale. I did not dislike Sunday."

The great days in Mr. Buell's youth, in descending order, were Christmas, Fourth of July, and the day the circus came to town and paraded through Main Street two or three hours before the matinee. Boys in other sections of the city might slightly alter this order, and put the Fourth of July ahead of Christmas. And we gloried in the opening of the baseball season.

When I first knew professional baseball, the Rochester nine played at Culver Field, which was located approximately on the site in University Avenue now occupied by the Gleason Works. The weekday and Saturday games were played there; Sunday the city's Pecksniffian moral code made it necessary to transfer the contests to Charlotte. There had been a good deal of agitation about Sunday baseball. When an earlier team had scheduled a game in Irondequoit, the players had been arrested, tried, and convicted, but released on their promise not to repeat their heinous crime.

In the very early 1900s, the Culver Field diamond was encircled by a third of a mile wooden bicycle track. This had been erected by outside promoters, including William A. Brady, Broadway theatrical producer, one-time manager of the ex-heavyweight boxing champion, James J. Corbett, and father of the lovely and talented actress Alice Brady.

The track had a brief vogue. For a year or two it attracted some of the country's great professional riders. When local interest in professional racing waned, the promoters tried the novelty of a "ladies' six day race." They put up a wooden saucer track, perhaps fourteen laps to the mile, in front of the grandstand, and brought in six or eight women cyclists, who were first exhibited to the town in open carriages on Main Street with trumpets and fanfare.

The feminine stars rode an hour a night. I was taken to the contest. The winner was Tilly Anderson, a fine strapping blond girl in sheer white tights. She was quite a figure, hunched over the ramshorn handlebars of her racing bike, like Eddie (Cannon) Bald, the famous Buffalo speedster. The band played "Hello, My Baby."

I knew by sight some of the crack local cyclists, because my father was the anachronism—the old man—among them. Two of them sat directly in front of me, A. M. (Al) Zimbrich, a tall, handsome semipro, greatly beloved by the ladies, and Otto Kallusch, who lived on Cypress Street, a block north of our street.

"Jesus, what a leg that Tilly's got!" Zimbrich exclaimed, covetously. I shared his admiration. But I was a boy in knee pants. My feeling was aesthetic, rather than prurient.

The large bicycle track soon fell into disuse and was dismantled section by section over a period of years, and baseball became the paramount attraction at Culver Field. It became the absorbing topic of the town in 1901 when Al Buckenberger's Bronchos won fourteen road games in a row in the closing month of the season and the Eastern League pennant to boot. The club had speed and power. It played, as Bill McCarthy, Rochester's excellent baseball historian put it, a game that was "rude and leathery."

Opening Day was always a gala. The town did obeisance to baseball.

It was the Twenty-Third of April,
And the day was very fine;
The sun was shining brightly,
And the fans were all in line.

Rochester loved a parade, and in a day when vehicular traffic could be waved off Main Street for the better part of an hour without someone screaming that the city's commerce was being paralyzed, it had numerous parades. The ones on Decoration Day (as it was once called) and Labor Day were the longest; third in length was the Opening Day parade. The Opening Day parade was hardly military in character except for an assumption of orderliness in the front ranks and in the interstices of the long wheeled procession where bandmen in brilliant uniforms played lively marching airs. In full scope it was a rather tatterdemalion display, but gay and immensely good humored.

His Honor the Mayor would be well up in the van of the procession, in a shiny carriage, smiling upon his curbside constituents. It was his traditional function to throw out the first baseball from a box back of home plate. Behind his carriage would be a long concatenation of horse-drawn vehicles of various sizes and designs carrying men who represented labor unions, meat markets, bowling halls, clothing factories, hardware stores, saloons, and fraternal orders. And of course such organizations as the Hard-a-Lee Social and Athletic Club, whose members would go to the ball park in a large van with numerous kegs of beer and return only after they had transferred the contents of the kegs to their own corporealities.

Central in the line of march would be the Twentieth Century Tallyho of E. M. Higgins (Higgins, call 49!) the big downtown livery man. It was a six-horse hitch, and its upper deck, which was suitable for passengers, seemed as high up as a second-story window. It was the most spectacular vehicle in town. On Opening Day it was cluttered with visiting ballplayers, who dressed in the Livingston House on Exchange Street and rode to the fray suited up.

Professional ballplayers in those days did not try very hard to personify the clean-cut American boy. They had about their persons the "rude and leathery aspect" Bill McCarthy ascribed to their style of play. They canted their baseball caps far to the side of their heads, and their cheeks, filled with chewing tobacco, bulged out like a pocket gopher's. They rode atop the Twentieth Century with spiked shoes in hand and their feet, encased in Romeo slippers, sometimes dangling from the roof of the vehicle. They had a brave and cavalier bearing. The practice of collecting signatures of the famous had not yet become popular, and no one sought their autographs. Indeed, some of the players may have had no more chirographic talent than the great Joe Jackson, of the Chicago White Sox, who on payday made an X on the line of signature. But a small boy might run along the side of the tallyho half hoping that one of the Olympians on the wheeled pantheon would spit a small blob of tobacco juice on his blouse. It would be a memento to preserve, not wash away.

The roster of the early teams that I knew included a burly boy at third base, Ed Greminger, who, when the club played Sundays at Charlotte, cracked long balls clean over the lower river boathouses; Deerfoot Barclay, so swift afoot that he often imperiously made known his intention to bunt and not infrequently beat the throw; stylish Harry O'Hagan, a plumber in the off-season, who moved about first base with the grace of a dancing master and achieved the first unassisted triple play on record; the picturesque and talented Billy Lush, later Yale's baseball coach; and Reddy, brother of the famous Zane Grey, author of *Riders of the Purple Sage*.

One hot Saturday afternoon the icemen in their bright red shirts were out in Culver Field in force. The icemen were the club's most raucous cheering section. This day they had the support of several hundred other bleacher fans. The game had progressed to a late inning and the Bronchos were at bat. They were twitching for a hit. Baseball in those days was not a casual summer pastime. It was an article of faith that aroused passionate partisanship. The icemen "got on" the opposing pitcher. They taunted him with invective, then tried to rattle him out of control by sharply stomping their feet in unison on the wooden floor. The crescendo quickened as other bleacherites took up the beat. It was like a regiment crossing a bridge in parade-ground step.

Suddenly there was a seismic growl, followed by a sharp cracking sound of breaking timbers. The stomping ceased. The bleachers settled, then caved slowly inward. My seat on a bench in the second row from the top of the structure lurched forward and for a moment I peered into what seemed a bottomless abyss. I felt myself falling, and there was nothing to grasp. My descent was slow at first, for all of the uprights that supported the bleachers did not yield at once; it grew swifter as I approached the ground, which I hit at a fairly smart clip. Terrorized, but with no sensation of hurt, I scrambled out of the debris, stumbling over fallen bodies in my flight, and ran all the way to Linden Street. Along the way, the one-horse Hahnemann Hospital ambulance passed me, going in the opposite direction, its gong clanging portents of disaster. At home, I gave a breathless, panicky report of my escape from a calamity in which hundreds—*thousands!*—of persons had been killed.

Actually, no one was killed. I myself suffered a slight Charley horse and the loss of a new cap. The baseball management suffered a mess of lawsuits and went into receivership. When the season opened the next spring, the franchise was under the control of Adelbert P. Little, and a fiery little redheaded industrialist, politician, and sportsman, Charles T. Chapin.

Chapin soon moved the club from Culver Field to a new ball park in Bay Street, renamed the team the Hustlers, and imported John H. Ganzel to manage it. Chapin encouraged his manager to spend money for spirited ballplayers. His liberality was well rewarded. The team played to large crowds, including a king-sized gallery of more than eighteen thousand at a Saturday double-header, and gave the town the greatest thrill it had ever known from a sporting event by winning three consecutive pennants.

While this feat was being accomplished the baseball writers chronicled the day-to-day vicissitudes of the Hustlers as Plutarch relates the glorious deeds of antiquity. And Rochesterians who previously had not known the difference between an earned run average and a batting average, and had give no more than casual attention to the game, now snatched eagerly at the baseball extras to learn how the team had "come out." There was something liturgical about the city's obsession with the pennant race. When the team was on the road, fans crowded into the Genesee Amusement Hall in South Avenue to follow the play on an automatic scoreboard. As Bill McCarthy put it, Rochester was "baseball loco."

After the victorious Chapin-Ganzel regimen, seventeen years passed before Rochester won another pennant. In the meantime, the club moved again, this time to its present stadium at 500 Norton Street, and became the farm property of the St. Louis Cardinals. Under this ownership, the team—now called the Red Wings—zoomed into the empyreal blue. It won four pennants in a row, the last two in the very depths of the Depression and drew, during the 1931 season, more than half a million people into the stands.

If Rochester is not, in a general sense, a great sporting town, we may well be the most notable and enduring supporter of minor league baseball in the country. Rochester looks upon its professional ball club as one of its civic institutions. Its maintenance and perpetuity are a matter of general pride. In the late 1950s, the St. Louis Cardinals disjoined the Rochester team from its farm system. It was a cruel rejection after we had developed some of the greatest players on the Cardinals' championship teams. Rochester was shocked and disconsolate. Was the city to be without professional ball which had enlivened the dull droning dog days of summer since time immemorial?

There was a cry of distress. There was a need for action. In Rochester, a cry of distress is invariably heard; if action is wanted, men of action respond.

Carl S. Hallauer, head of Bausch & Lomb Inc., whose extra-curricular activities were of astonishing variety and amazing multiplicity; T. Carl Nixon, head of the city's largest law firm; John P. Boylan, president of the Rochester Telephone Company; Warren W. Allen, vice-president of the Lincoln-Rochester Trust Company; Frank Horton, who was later to go to Congress, and a remarkable little man named Morrie Silver, who had made a modest fortune selling phonograph records, leaped—as it were—into the breach.

To these men, the idea of Rochester without a baseball club was unthinkable.

They gathered other leading business and civic leaders around them in a loose organization that soon evolved into Rochester Community Baseball, Inc. They issued stock, and men from all walks of Rochester life—more than eight thousand of them!—bought up the shares, quite aware that their chance of financial return was thin as paper. They wanted baseball; they had it next year, without interruption. The Red Wings' general manager George H. Sisler, Jr., whose father many years before had closed one of the greatest careers in baseball playing for the Rochester team, was retained as general manager of the Community Baseball organization.

Under this ownership, first with Silver and then Horton serving as president, the club, which now had a working agreement with the Baltimore Orioles, did well for a time. Then lean days came. There was a brief succession of bench managers, none of whom produced the spirited, heads-up play that aroused enthusiasm. The gate slumped. Seeking a remedy for a situation that soon might become critical, the board of directors petitioned Morrie Silver to return as president. He succumbed to their pleas. He took off his coat and resettled himself in the Red Wings' office.

His health was poor, his spirit superb, his effort transcendent. He worked ten and twelve hours a day for a fee of $1 a year to restore the prestige of the slipping Red Wings. He and Sisler contrived various promotional gimmicks to help bring crowds back to the ball park. They were aided in this purpose by the press and by various keenly interested citizens. In 1966, Rochester Community Baseball showed a net profit of $113,000, and its team won the league championship under a bench manager named Earl Weaver, brought up from Elmira, New York. The following year, Weaver took the club to a tie for the pennant, but lost in a one-game playoff. More than 300,000 fans passed through the turnstiles.

Weaver went to the big league to guide the Baltimore Orioles to three league pennants and one World's Championship. Sisler resigned as general manager to become president of the International League. Morrie Silver moved to Florida to ease his ailing heart. His splendid citizenship is commemorated by more than a plaque. The Red Wings' ball park was renamed in his honor: it is now Silver Stadium.

* * *

Rochester, of course, enjoyed other sporting activities besides baseball. But not since John Ganzel's Hustlers won three and the Red Wings four Triple A baseball pennants had the community evinced the general interest in a local sporting event it displayed the first time the Oak Hill Country Club dedicated its testing and ornamental greens and fairways to the most important golf tournament in the world.

The club first temporarily disbarred domestic hackers from its beautiful rolling course to entertain the world's best professionals and the top amateur golfers in 1956. The United States Open of that year was such a thumping success that soon the heads of the club were negotiating for a second tournament. It followed twelve years later, and the Open of 1968 was a greater success even than the earlier tournament.

Golf is a participant sport, and Rochester has thousands of participants. Here the history of the game is memorable. Seven years after golf was introduced into this country, it was being played on the links of the recently organized Country Club of Rochester. That was in 1895. The Oak Hill was founded in 1901, on what is now the River Campus of the University of Rochester, and two or three years before that a nine-hole course (later expanded to eighteen holes) was laid out on what was commonly known as South, now Genesee Valley, Park. The Country Club of Rochester was one of the earliest country clubs in America, west of the seaboard; the public course in Genesee Valley Park was the fourth in the country to be maintained by public funds.

In the environs of Rochester there are now half a dozen country clubs whose membership is elective and a dozen golf courses that are operated as private enterprises for patrons who pay greens' fees or that are part of the recreational facilities of the Monroe County Park system. Rural villages in the adjacent countryside often have one or two of these semipublic courses, usually with a farmhouse reconstructed to provide a golf shop, locker rooms, a dining room, and occasionally a bar. The management of these establishments fill with water a basin about the size of a sitz bath, put a springboard at one end of it, and have, to enhance the country club status of the place, a swimming pool.

Meadowlands that are ideal for the grazing of cattle and fields with the rich growing soil of the Genesee Valley now display well-manicured putting greens and fairly well-kept fairways. Neighboring farmers are often patrons of these courses. Dismounting from their tractors, they replace their Sears Roebuck farm jeans with sports clothes that may have been selected from an Abercrombie & Fitch catalogue and flail their way over nine, twelve, or eighteen holes, depending upon the extent of the course and the period of remaining daylight.

The sporting interests of the predecessors of these rustic linksmen were limited to horseshoe pitching and harness racing. This last-named sport, now the promotion of city slickers, who have jazzed it up with night racing, pari-mutuels, and the movable barrier, in a more primitive form was once Rochester's most popular spectator sport.

In August 1874, five years after the formation of the National Trotting Association, which brought dignity and order to a sport that had previously been shabby, desultory, and lacking in social status, the Rochester Driving Park opened with a four-day meeting that introduced, among other notable racers, Goldsmith Maid, whose money winnings were not to be equaled by any other animal racing on the turf—irrespective of gait or breed—until well into this century.

In a free-for-all for the sizable purse (for those days) of $5,000, the great bay Maid outstripped the field and hauled a high-wheeled, hard-tired racing cart a single lap of the mile racing strip in the world record time of 2:14¾.

The first race meeting at Driving Park made a tremendous novelty for Rochester, which during sporadic periods of evangelical fervor and blue-nosed meddlesomeness had been a place of not much fun. Thousands were attracted to the race course, which lay north of Driving Park Avenue. The spectators came not only from Rochester and the surrounding countryside but by trainload from Syracuse, Buffalo, and Niagara Falls. The grandstand was ample and the surface of the mile oval was exceptionally fast. "It's like Indian rubber," one driver said. "My horse no sooner takes a jump, than he's half a mile ahead."

Mambrino Gift, the champion stallion; Jay-Eye-See, one-time record holder; the crack pacers Search Light and Star Pointer, and William H. Vanderbilt's celebrated Maud S were among the notable performers that raced at one time or another at Driving Park. Maud S twice trotted record miles on the course, the second time in the presence of her owner and a party of New York toffs who, the race writers said, attracted as much attention as the handsome little mare whose 2:10¼ mile (August 11, 1881) was thought to be the limit of trotting speed. The Grand Circuit held forth at Driving Park for several years, and the track continued to attract great trotters and pacers up to and briefly into the period of the pneumatic-tired sulky, which brought standardbreds closer to the mythical mark of two minutes, which was achieved in 1903 by Lou Dillon, but not at Driving Park.

Big-time harness racing slumped in Rochester in the middle of the Mauve Decade. For twenty years, Driving Park had provided the best the sport had to offer. Now bicycle races were tried on the dirt horse track, with no great success. Once it was the scene of a large bicycle carnival, a sort of gymkhana on wheels. The lightning-fast oval became weed-cluttered and unkempt, and the area it enclosed was used for fairs, circuses, and other outdoor attractions.

There was amateur horse racing in town. On fine winter afternoons, matinee drivers took their mettlesome steeds to East Avenue and raced them, hitched to spidery little cutters over the snow-covered pavement from Alexander Street to Culver Road. During these contests, traffic was shunted off the Avenue. I myself have seen galleries of a couple of hundred persons lining the curbs. It was a Currier & Ives spectacle, the drivers muffled to the ears in furs, the crowd shouting encouragement to its favorites, the horses throwing up divots of frozen snow. There was spirited competition. But the drivers were racing for fun, and horse racing is the least amateur of sports. To attract crowds and good horses, money is needed; and pari-mutuels or a betting ring.

After Driving Park was abandoned as a race course and divided into city lots, professional horse racing was resumed on a half-mile ring at Crittenden Park, now the site of the Strong Memorial Hospital and the boulevard called Crittenden by which the hospital is approached. Each year the Central Trotting Association sponsored a week's meeting at the track, and while the horses were not Grand Circuit caliber, they excited a good deal of enthusiasm in Rochester and brought numerous outside racegoers into town.

The southern boundary of the city was then at Elmwood Avenue; Crittenden Park was several hundred yards south of the line, and because it was outside of their province it escaped the persecutions of Rochester's professional spoilsports and do-gooders of whom in an earlier day there was a considerable and irritating contingent.

I was a daily habitué of the race track during the week of the trotting meeting. There was always a loose slat in the not-too-solid board fence that could be pulled aside to allow a boy, slim as a garfish, to slip through. Once inside, the place was a veritable wonderland of novelties.

There were no pari-mutuels at the track, gambling was illegal, but the county authorities beneficently kept their eyes averted from the broad, marquee-covered area just beyond the grandstand in which race pools were auctioned. I was not allowed to encroach upon this privileged domain. If I came too close, I'd be shouted at, "Hey, kid, gitoutahere! Beat it—you!" But I could stand at a discreet distance and hear the abracadabra of the bookmakers on their little stools, wondering what in the world they were gabbling about, and observe the cryptic notations on their blackboards.

Before each heat there was a great stir and bustle as men frantically scurried from one combination of bookmakers to another seeking the best odds in the betting ring. Although I had only a vague notion of the cause of this frenzy, the shouts, the bustle, the display of large wads of bills made it an enthralling spectacle. And in the midst of the turmoil, there was my mother's distant cousin, Fred Stryker from Detroit, who was one of the ring's leading bookmakers.

Cousin Fred to me was a heroic figure. He was a short, stout man, shaved to the blood and very carefully manicured, who stood in the betting ring all afternoon, coatless, a pair of ornate braces looped over his pink silk shirt, a crooked cane depending from an elbow. In time I learned his history. He once had what today would be called a "piece" of Ned Hanlan, the great professional sculler, and he had briefly managed a pair of professional foot racers, Harry Bethune and H. M. Johnson. Still later, he had a five-chair barber shop in Detroit which he bet the wrong way the day in Carson City, Nevada, Robert Fitzsimmons knocked out James J. Corbett to gain "the proud diadem of Fistiana," as the sportswriters defined the world's heavyweight championship. After that, he joined a bookmaking firm until he opened the Hofbrau, one of Detroit's better restaurants.

Usually, during his stay in town, Cousin Fred stopped one night for supper at our house before proceeding to the Whitcomb House, which, during race week, was said to be so "horsy" that straw supplanted the rugs on the lobby floor. The Whitcomb House and the Hotel Eggleston, a little farther west on Main Street, were the sporting hotels of the town, and the stud games that were played in the upper rooms of both hostelries during the week of the race meeting and in early autumn when the big apple buyers came to town were high, wide, and handsome. When Cousin Fred, coming to our house for supper, passed over the front door threshold a delicious fragrance emanated from his person and seemed to rise as high as the second story. I suspect it was Jockey Club perfume.

Each day I made a tour of Crittenden Park that took me from the grandstand to the edge of the betting ring, to the rail of the tawny half-mile race track, and to the stables. The stables were a fascinating montage. I never wearied of studying the techniques of the swipes who bandaged, rubbed, and ministered in other ways to horses that were being prepared to race or had just returned from the course, hard-blown, sweat glistening on their coats, still hitched to their skeletal little race rigs. The soft summer air was touched pungently with the odor of wood fires burning under huge water kettles. Black men, with tattered caps caught any way on their heads and with towels hanging from the rear pockets of their ragged trousers, bantered good-humoredly with one another, or sang snatches of deep South melodies, or whistled a bar of a popular air, as they led blanketed horses in the walking rings. Cards were played on a bale of hay; dice thrown on a horse blanket. Small dogs played under the canvas awnings that shaded the stalls, and lead ponies and an occasional goat were tethered nearby. Life around the stables, it seemed to me, was remote from anything on the outside—a sort of gypsy microcosm, of which I often wished I were a part. One afternoon, leaving this backstage area, I came to a large shiny buckboard which struck me, at first glance, as being burdened with the fairest flowers of femininity my eyes had ever beheld.

The rig was drawn close to the fence at the turn into the backstretch, almost at the eighth pole. The horses had been detached from the shaft and were tied to a nearby tree. On the cross seats behind the driver's seat were six or eight young women done up in colorful summer finery, each of whom seemed as beautiful as Aphrodite. My eyes swept over them admiringly. Then I saw in the front seat, sitting sideways, with her legs crossed, a stoutish older woman with a bosom so shelflike it might have held an ornamental row of Copenhagen porcelains, who wore a brilliant red dress and a great overshadowing red hat, and who—to my utter wonder, as I watched—drew from a reticule at her side a large black cigar, which she lighted, and blew forth billows of smoke.

Galvanized by this phenomenon to a spot twenty feet from the buckboard, my eyes must have bugged out far enough to hold a derby hat. As I continued in this fixed position, I saw two or three of the younger women light cigarettes and puff on them as nonchalantly as a youth in a poolroom. This was quite the most unusual sight I had seen all week at the race track, and that night, which was the night Cousin Fred came to supper, I was full of the subject of the woman in red with her cigar and the tender buds with their cigarettes in the seats behind her. My mother embarrassedly shushed me down, and I saw that my father was chillily unamused. When my mother rose to take the dessert dishes into the kitchen my father ordered me to help her. As I started for the pantry door, I saw a grin cross Cousin Fred's tightly shaved face. He winked, and I heard him say, *sotto voce*, "That was Jen Russell, the kid saw. She's got a place down the line."

My father told me next day that the race track was a good place to keep away from. But he never mentioned why I shouldn't sneak through a loose board in the Crittenden Park fence. I learned later about Jennie Russell. Her place was well down the line, at 56 Hill Street. She was there for years, apparently with a highly satisfied clientele. Alfy Valentine, a little man of great good humor, who stands only a little higher than a fireplug, knew Jennie Russell well. As a youth, he played piano in her place and in a great many other places in a sixty-year career as a Rochester musician. He thought Jennie Russell a kindly sort of madam who, on a pleasant summer afternoon, would hire a shiny buckboard from Higgins' Livery, and call out to her youthful compeers, "Come on, girls. We're going racing."

Alfy said Jennie was partial to Orange Blossom cigars.

Chapter 15

In the autumn and in the early spring, the Reverend Algernon Sidney Crapsey wore over his canonicals a loose-fitting garment, a little like an opera cape. The cape imparted to his small figure a slightly theatrical aspect of which, I am sure, he was not unaware. He was a man of unusual eloquence, and a remarkable reader. He had what I have been told is the Greek knack of rendering poignant emotions with complete simplicity.

At the Sunday-school Christmas parties of St. Andrew's Protestant Episcopal Church he read an abridged version of Dickens' *Christmas Carol* that held dozens of his youthful audience enthralled. I remember even now how vividly he represented the "squeezing, wrenching, grasping, clutching, covetous, old sinner" Scrooge; how we sat in breathless awe as he evoked the filmy image of Marley's ghost, and how we struggled to suppress the impulse to shout in triumph when the wicked old man was miraculously transformed into Bob Cratchit's and Tiny Tim's benefactor.

". . . Here's the turkey. Hallo! Whoop! How are you! Merry Christmas!"

Rochester has known a number of eminent divines. They have led Jewish congregations in the synagogues, they have taught in the seminaries, they have occupied the pulpits of the larger churches, and they have filled the bishoprics of the Roman Catholic and the Protestant Episcopal dioceses. Several of these men gained national renown; none knew the world-wide attention that for a time was fixed on Algernon Crapsey.

Dr. Crapsey was rather a man of destiny. His early education was sketchy. At the age of fifteen, he quit his job in a Cincinnati hardware factory when one of his bosses castigated him as a "lazy good for nothing," and ran away to enlist in an Ohio infantry regiment that campaigned early in the Civil War in Kentucky and Tennessee. The boy's tender years and undeveloped stature unsuited him for the rigorous part of a wartime infantryman. Crapsey himself has said that his sixty-pound pack weighed almost as much as he did. Forced marches, exposure, and bad food broke his health, and he was confined to a field hospital. The army medicos diagnosed his disorder as a hypertrophied heart and invalided him home to die. The lad defied the prognosis; he lived. After the war, he moved to New York City and tried clerking in a commercial house. He soon abandoned his place to study for the ministry. He was first a deacon, then he was ordained a priest and served as a staff member of the enormously wealthy Trinity parish in New York. The young clergyman was high church, and precise in liturgical function. He was an admirer of the Roman Catholic Mass. He subscribed very earnestly to the doctrine that faith, without good works, was not enough. In the Trinity parish he worked backbreaking hours among the poor of the district and virtually lived among tenement dwellers. His salary was substantially raised. New York seemed to offer a promising future. But Crapsey wanted to preach, and a parish staff worker had few opportunities to do so. He also very much wanted the autonomy of his own church. In 1879, he left Trinity parish to come to Rochester with his wife and the first of the couple's nine children to assume the rectorship of St. Andrew's Episcopal Church.

The call he accepted offered a formidable challenge. Situated at Averill Avenue and Ashland Street, St. Andrew's was considered a back-street parish. The church was small, impecunious, down-at-heel, and at the time of the young clergyman's arrival the communicants could almost be counted on the fingers of his hands. The status quo was quickly altered. Crapsey was a frail man. He scarcely weighed 120 pounds, and when I knew him there was a stoop to his shoulders that made his stature seem even smaller than his straight-up height of five feet six inches. He was not a prophet of muscular Christianity. But day and night, in all sorts of weather, he moved about the parish with the short quick steps that characterized his peregrinations, comforting the sick, consoling the bereaved, bringing sustenance to the needy, and cheer to the forlorn. He had the kinetic energy of a six-day bicycle rider, complete dedication, a compelling personality, and a sincerity as transparent as glass.

His wife, Adelaide Trowbridge Crapsey, was a woman of noble character and high intelligence who complemented her husband's devotion to the church itself and to the parishioners, who were drawn to it in increasing numbers in part because, as someone re-marked, St. Andrew's was "a clearing house for good impulses."

In his early ministry, Crapsey was a formalist. He preached the doctrine of the fall of man, redemption by grace, and the miracu-lous birth. If his sermons were often inspiring, they did not violate the orthodoxy of his church. He was later to become a great advo-cate of the Christian social gospel, and denounce the expensive trappings of great cathedrals and elaborate bishoprics in areas where men and women lived in the degradation of poverty, filth, and vice. He would ask what all this pride and pomp had to do with the religion of Jesus of Nazareth. But the social gospel he was later to preach was first expressed in the scope of his pastoral services. The variety and number of these services seemed almost to add a new dimension to the clergyman's function.

Dr. Crapsey and his wife started one of the first kindergartens in the city of Rochester, to which was added a course for training kindergarten teachers. A women's guild that met each week to sew clothing for needy families was inspired and directed by Mrs. Crapsey. In the parish house across Averill Avenue from the church, the Crapseys founded a night school with classes in domes-tic science and the mechanical arts that were taught by paid teachers. Crapsey organized what was called St. Andrew's Brother-hood, an ever-growing non-sectarian order devoted to sociability, discussion, mutual aid, and efforts to advance the hard-pressed cause of community decency.

St. Andrew's, when I first joined its Sunday school and some-times accompanied my mother to church, had a populous congrega-tion. The little rector had attracted communicants not only from the slightly submiddle-class neighborhood in which the church was located but also from remote parts of the city, and among those outside the parish boundaries who gravitated to St. Andrew's were members of several of the wealthiest and most socially prominent families in Rochester.

The personality of the rector, his rock-bottom genuineness, and his eloquence were responsible for the assemblage in St. Andrew's of a strata of society that were a little incongruous in a small neighborhood church that before had been narrowly parochial. The members of this heterogeneous congregation were led in the wor-ship of God by a man whom they themselves revered almost to the point of worship.

Crapsey's reading was extensive; his thinking advanced. He denounced the church for giving lip service to Christ's teaching while failing to apply the great social lessons Christ had promulgated. His studies had brought him conclusions that opposed the convictions of his earlier preisthood. Still deeply believing in Jesus, he was convinced that the infancy stories were not historical. St. Andrew's morning services were fully attended; at evening prayers, the choir sometimes outnumbered the occupants of the pews. To correct this condition, the rector decided on a series of lectures that would deal with the relations of the church to the state. His parishioners quickly took notice and returned to St. Andrew's Sunday evening; outsiders came; the press fully reported the lectures. Crapsey ordinarily spoke without manuscript or notes. He departed from this practice for the series of lectures. He wrote the twelfth lecture without, as he himself related, taking pen from paper except to dip it in the inkpot, and delivered what he wrote without alteration on a February Sunday in 1905. In part, he said:

> In the light of scientific research the founder of Christianity, Jesus, the son of God, no longer stands apart from the common destiny of man, in life and death, but he is in all things physical like as we are, born as we are born . . . Scientific history proves to us that the fact of his miraculous birth was unknown to himself, unknown to his mother, and unknown to the whole Christian community of the first generation.

At once, the fat was in the fire. This sort of higher criticism had been tolerated, in the light of historical investigation and scientific hypothesis, when applied to Genesis and other chapters of the Old Testament; Crapsey's expressed doubt of the biblical story of Christ's birth rudely impinged against a very vital area of the Christian organism. The press services voraciously gobbled up his words and the story of his startling dissent went winging round the world. Overnight, the little back-street parish priest had become a figure of world prominence.

The Right Reverend William David Walker, bishop of the western New York diocese, called upon Crapsey to recant the statements in his twelfth address that already had excited fulminations from a multitude of pulpits and inspired wide editorial comment. The rector refused. It was not long after this that he was indicted for heresy by a special committee of the diocese, and the next year he was tried before an ecclesiastical court in the nearby city of Batavia.

The court found the defendant guilty, as charged. In earlier days of the church, medieval judges sometimes earnestly asked that heretics sentenced to be burned at the stake be treated with all possible tenderness. The Batavia court, unable to hand over its heretic to an executioner, felt no need to recommend tenderness. "All that we have heard of this defendant is most lovely and Christlike," said one of his accusers, laying a hand on Crapsey's head, "but that makes his crime all the greater."

The Crapseys had lived for more than a quarter of a century in the red brick rectory that adjoined the church. The small plot upon which it stood had been ornamented with trees and hedges and gardens planted by their own hands. It was a pleasant habitation. It had something of the character of an English vicarage, and it had known a great deal of living. Crapsey children had been born in the rectory, and two had died there. It was virtually the only home the family had ever known. Now they were to be dislodged.

Bishop Walker himself visited St. Andrew's rectory to attempt to present Mrs. Crapsey with a paper that was tantamount to an eviction notice. The paper was not accepted, but the eviction was achieved. The Crapseys were not, however, put into the street. A wealthy admirer of the defrocked clergyman, who was not a member of St. Andrew's, gave them a house in Averill Avenue, a short distance east of the rector's beloved church.

Crapsey's postministerial life was not idled away in laments or in jeremiads against his fate. He became a leading advocate of the social gospel. He continued his lecture series, now speaking from the stage of the Lyceum Theater. He was active in civic affairs and in labor movements. When he discovered that retail clerks worked inhumanly long hours on Saturday, he led demonstrations that brought about the closing of downtown stores at 6 P.M.

A few days before Dr. Crapsey's death, December 31, 1927, a prominent Episcopal clergyman broadcast from New York a radio talk that discussed the Second Person of the Trinity very much as Crapsey had dealt with this subject in his famous pulpit lecture. But this time, hardly a hackle was raised in the speaker's denominational community. Algernon Crapsey apparently was ahead of his time.

When the St. Andrew's rector faced the ecclesiastical court in

Batavia, a daughter, Miss Adelaide, was at his side. She predeceased Dr. Crapsey by several years. A teacher and a brilliant scholar, she achieved through a slim posthumous volume of verse a fame that has outlasted the world-wide notoriety that came to her father when he impugned the validity of the Apostles' Creed. How strange—how passing strange—that the supposedly dull, smug, uninspired city of Rochester should have produced *The Last of the Heretics* and a daughter whose place among the women poets of this country is thought by some to be second only to Emily Dickinson.

*　*　*

Thirty-odd years ago, the Reverend David Rhys Williams, minister of the First Unitarian Church, and the Reverend Willard L. Johnson, minister of the First Church of Christ Disciples, named a number of deceased Rochesterians whom they designated as the city's "immortals" (the quote marks are mine) of the past century. Williams nominated eleven candidates; Johnson, fourteen. The two men were in accord on the following eight choices, and here they seemed particularly judicious:

Susan B. Anthony, Professor Walter Rauschenbusch, George Eastman, Frederick Douglass, Dr. William C. Gannett, Dr. Algernon S. Crapsey, Lewis H. Morgan, and Nathaniel Rochester.

Williams' list included another Crapsey, Miss Adelaide, whose poetry, he said, "has been favorably compared to that of Swinburne"; the Right Reverend John Francis O'Hern, bishop of the Roman Catholic diocese, a man of urbanity, wisdom, and tolerance, whose good offices as a churchman and as a citizen did so much to enhance the rapport between his own people and their non-Catholic townsfolk; and Rabbi Max Landsberg, distinguished leader of Jewish culture, who worked hand and glove with liberal churchmen in the promotion of what is known as social Christianity.

Johnson's added nominees were Martin B. Anderson, first president of the University of Rochester; Dr. Edward Mott Moore, often called the father of the Rochester Park system; John J. Bausch and Captain Henry Lomb, founders of Bausch & Lomb, Inc., and two more divines, Dr. Augustus H. Strong, president of the Rochester Theological Seminary, and the Reverend Paul Moore Strayer, who, in the years of his charge of East Avenue's Third Presbyterian Church, outraged some of his staid, wealthy, orthodox parishioners by participating in strike rallies, by marching in Labor Day parades, and by contributing a weekly column to the *Labor Journal*.

Dr. Gannett, minister of the First Unitarian Church, Strayer, Crapsey, and Rauschenbusch, who held a professorship at the Rochester Theological Seminary, were for a time the leading Rochester prophets of the social gospel. The preaching and the social, civic, and welfare activities of the first two gave them wide local renown; Crapsey, of course, was a world figure after the publication of his heresy, and Rauschenbusch was noted far beyond the confines of his native city (he was born, and he died in Rochester) as a speaker on religious and social subjects, and celebrated in wide areas of America and in countries abroad as a writer.

With the exception of the brilliant, present-day Rabbi Philip S. Bernstein of Temple B'rith Kodesh, whose *What the Jews Believe* has sold an astronomical number of copies, no Rochester writer on religion has produced a book that has had the circulation of Rauschenbusch's major works which, in the opinion of some critics, have had an influence on the thought of the American Protestant Church similar to that exerted in an earlier day by Jonathan Edwards and Horace Bushnell.

Heredity and environment had a good deal to do with Walter Rauschenbusch's choice of a career. A number of his German forebears were brothers of the cloth, and his German-born father was a professor of the Rochester Theological Seminary, from which institution the son was graduated after first obtaining a degree at the University of Rochester. He heard the call of God very early. He was a Baptist, and his prime design was to enter the field of foreign missions. However, authorities on Baptist Foreign Missions denied him an appointment. They had heard that he had expressed liberal views on the Old Testament, and they were finicky as to what the heathen Chinese should be taught about the first chapter of Genesis and of Jonah's three-day repose in the belly of a whale. Instead of sailing to foreign lands, the young clergyman took the pastorate of a small, hard-pressed little church in the Hell's Kitchen district of New York City.

He had been an alert and observant youth. There is a story that on the day the tragic news of Lincoln's assassination was disseminated to the world, the four-year-old Rauschenbusch boy was seen draping crepe on the door of his Rochester home. At his birth, his pious father had prayed, "Lord, hover over this child . . ." As a seminarian, young Rauschenbusch resolved to live literally *by the teachings of Jesus Christ;* he wanted, as he said, "to do hard work for God." He did it for more than ten years in a tenement district of New York.

During his growing years and during the pastorate of his early manhood, he had seen the dazzling post-Civil War upsurge of industrial inventiveness, the astonishing growth of industrial power, and the concentration of vast wealth in the hands of a limited number of Americans who often seemed to lack all social consciousness and who frequently appeared to have little more use for their riches than to employ them in gross and vulgar displays.

The contrast he observed during his time in New York between the luxury and profligacy of the very rich and the disease, the vice, the insecurity, the rickety undernourished children, and the indigent aged—the whole prospect of sodden poverty in the slums —convinced Rauschenbusch that Christ's social principles were being ignored, and from then on he strove unceasingly to have them put in force in order that "the world as it is" might be changed to "the world as it should be."

Very late in the last century, Rauschenbusch, who was proficient in the German language, returned home to teach the New Testament and other subjects in the German department of the Rochester Theological Seminary. Later, he was given a chair in church history in the English department of the seminary, and he became the most vibrant and vital teacher in the institution. An illness suffered in New York had destroyed his hearing, but this in no wise lessened his efficiency as a teacher or detracted from his effectiveness as a speaker. He had lucidity, wit, and a lively sense of imagery. He was continually in demand as a platform speaker, both inside and outside of Rochester.

He frequently spoke at Sunday forums at the Rochester YMCA, and this writer, then a young newspaper reporter, was occasionally assigned to cover his lectures. Although sex in those days was rarely discussed in public meeting, Rauschenbusch chose for one of his Sunday talks the subject of social diseases. He indulged in no rant or tawdry sensationalism, but his description of prostitution as a dreadful form of slavery, and his lucid explanation of the contamination that was frequently the corollary of sexual impurity aroused compassionate thoughts for the tragic sisters of whoredom and engendered among his youthful audience resolutions to hold to the straight and narrow no matter what libidinous lures might be dangled before them. Rauschenbusch was an enormously compelling speaker.

But his books were the great tokens of his influence. He wrote four in German, seven in English. Some were translated into French, Finnish, Norwegian, Chinese, Russian, Japanese, and German. His greatest work, *Christianity and the Social Crisis*, sold well over fifty thousand copies. Henry Emerson Fosdick said that this book alone made Rauschenbusch "one of the most renowned and influential personalities in the American churches." It was followed by others, several of which were also widely circulated.

Many of the reforms that Rauschenbusch would surely have included in his own program for the melioration of humankind were put in force by legislative acts after his death. He died in 1918, long before Social Security, Unemployment Insurance, Medicare, slum clearance, racial desegregation, and housing developments for the underprivileged had become the concern, not only of the churches, whose social conscience had been piqued by his writings, but of federal, state, and municipal governments.

Rauschenbusch knew that perfection was not possible in man, and that Utopia could not be achieved on this earth. But he believed that one should unceasingly strive for the ideal, even if it were not to be realized. The ideal that animated his own efforts and that he continually reiterated was first expressed by the Lord Himself, "Thy Kingdom Come; Thy will be done on earth . . ."

He was a great and good man, if hardly—any more than the others on the joint list of Rochester notables—an immortal. The closing years of his life were saddened by World War I, which continued four months after his death. Loyal though he was to his native land, he was warmly attached to the peoples of the land of his ancestry, and he was an admirer of their culture. He hated war; he opposed American intervention in the terrible struggle in Europe. His opposition, his heritage, and his German name made him suspect. He was maligned and even threatened. And brilliant though he was, he was not above silly utterances. Early in the war, and after the Kaiser's hordes had violated Belgium and were devastating the northeastern cantons of France and thousands of Poilus had died on the "field of honor," Walter Rauschenbusch ingenuously remarked, "I believe the Germans are fighting France without anger this time; only with pity, as a matter of necessity."

But time of war is never a time for judicious thinking or for philosophical detachment. Reason goes haywire. An army private (of no military distinction whatsoever), I was one of a captive audience of soldiers in the Rochester Armory who, shortly before we sailed to join the AEF, was addressed by a ranting local clergyman. He was livid with war fever. His phillipic against the "unspeakable Hun" ended with a screamed exhortation, "Strike the most terrible blow you can—but strike it *fairly!*"

A squad fellow at my shoulder emitted a short, mocking laugh. "The sonofabitch must think this fight is under the rules of the Marquis of Queensberry," he said irreverently. "No shooting below the belt."

Chapter 16

A recent newspaper report that a fifteen-year-old girl student had slapped the principal of West High School in the face sent me scrabbling through a file of newspaper cuttings and other printed memorabilia that pertained to the early history of that institution and to the inchoate period of its slightly older sister, East High. I was curious to compare the attitude of the students presently enrolled in these schools with the attitude of their earliest predecessors.

West High first opened its doors to students at the beginning of the autumn semester, September 1905. Soon these boys and girls, gathering in the school's assembly hall, raised their lusty young voices in chorused tribute to the splendid new building in which they were being taught and to the members of the dedicated faculty who were teaching them.

> Sweet be thy memory, High School of ours,
> Fair be thy destiny, fadeless thy flowers.
> Hearts that have loved thee have won in life's fight
> Names that we honor, thy standards hold bright.
>
> Our Alma Mater dear, to thee we sing,
> May all thy future years new honors bring,
> May friends thy banners raise, thy foes grow less,
> All love and praise to our old R.H.S.

Since the Board of Education had provided no decorations for classrooms and corridors, the students organized a committee to raise funds for the purchase of statues and pictures. Sororities and fraternities contributed *objets d'art*. A member of the first graduating class built with his own hands a handsome case for athletic trophies. The second graduating class presented the school with a heroic statue, *The Wrestlers*. Free public school though it was, the caliber of its teaching staff, the distinguished principal who

208

administered it, and the spirit and cohesion of its student body gave West High very much the aspect of one of the better private secondary schools in the east.

Today Rochester has an impressive number of high schools, when once it had only East and West High. All have suffered the disruption of teaching programs and the violence that seems pandemic in American educational institutions. There have been fights, stabbings, robberies, and even rape in these buildings. Fires have been set by students, windows broken, equipment destroyed, and teachers assaulted. Vigilance committees have been organized by parents to protect their affrighted children. Recently the premises of one of the finest high schools was invaded by forty city policemen with loaded riot guns.

Years ago, *The Occident*, West High's student magazine, earnestly admonished its youthful readers against the use of slang, fearing that this habit might cause adult listeners to believe that something less than pure English was being taught in its beloved alma mater.

East High began its teaching courses April 15, 1903, which allowed its senior class only two months to enjoy the beautiful new building, said to have the largest floor space, per student, of any public high school in the United States. In 1904, the second graduating class issued an elaborate Senior Annual. It was dedicated to Albert Henry Wilcox, the school's principal, "In token of our esteem and affection."

Persistently the assertion is made that modern youth compose the most alert, intelligent, competent, and forward-looking "younger generation" the world has ever known, and it would be ungracious, impolitic, and perhaps unsafe for this antediluvian party to raise a piping, aged voice in disagreement.

In the early days of the century, the Establishment was deeply entrenched, and perhaps out of habit we deferred to it. It controlled the schools. It did not allow permissiveness to run rampant. Teachers in East and West High, oddly (as it may seem today) not only enjoyed the respect of their students, but often knew their very genuine affection. The students were immensely proud of the new buildings. They did not carve their initials in the wooden desk tops, allow papers to clutter floors of the corridors, mar the walls, or desecrate the grounds. They participated in an

Arbor Day planting. Their junior prom was as ceremonial as a coronation. Their support of the football team was impassioned.

There is a daguerreotype character to these curious-looking boys and girls as they appear in class pictures in the schools' yearbooks and magazines. The girls with their pompadours, high-collared shirtwaists, lockets, brooch watches, sorority pins, and skirts that reach not gropingly for the ankle, but beyond—to the instep. The boys with their neatly pressed trousers and jackets, high shoes (sometimes high-buttoned shoes!), stiff linen collars and carefully bowed foulard ties.

The curriculum imposed upon them, I suppose, was partisan; it was designed to fit those who were subjected to it to a social system that the Establishment had decreed. But there were innovators and iconoclasts among these youth. There were boys and girls of brilliance, of character, of high merit. They were not retarded by what present-day judgment might consider an obfuscating environment and many distinguished themselves in various realms of human endeavor.

For all the sharp chiding to which members of the older generation are now exposed, all were not fusty and unenlightened. Although their ranks are woefully decimated, there are still in our city men and women of noble achievements whose characters were formed and whose careers received their first impetus in the earliest years of East and West High Schools.

* * *

Until the opening of East High in the third year of the new century, the Rochester school system provided secondary education in a building on South Fitzhugh Street known as the Rochester Free Academy.

The four-story brick structure, which is now called the Education Building, rests on a site that has a historic heritage. It was on this plot of land in 1813 that the hardy pioneers who were founding a village at Genesee Falls threw up a crude one-room schoolhouse perhaps with the noble notion of offering a place of "light and reason" to their progeny.

Other schoolhouses of better size and impoved facilities succeeded on this location the tiny frontier hall of learning; and in 1874, over the persistent opposition of a group of mossbacks who believed that advanced education was not a public responsibility, a high school curriculum was established in what at that time was considered the handsome French-Gothic building of the Free Academy.

The Free Academy Building is now used exclusively for the offices of the Bureau of Education. During much of its long career as a teaching institution, it was, as were all other public schools in Rochester, the pawn of a school board that often seemed more interested in politics than in providing proficient instruction for youth.

Indeed, there were times during the most flagrant period of Rochester bossism when political patronage rather than public service appeared to be the *raison d'être* for the school system, the police force, and all other departments of municipal government. This was not entirely unnatural. All over America, in the years that intervened between the close of the Civil War and the time when such muckrakers as Lincoln Steffens, Ida M. Tarbell, and Samuel Hopkins Adams began their exposés in *McClure's Magazine* and *Collier's*, and Teddy Roosevelt began to lay about with his Big Stick, graft and corruption in politics and big business were so common as to achieve almost the status of legitimacy. It was hardly to be expected that the members of the Rochester School Board and the politicians who manipulated them should be beyond their age in virtue.

The School Board was composed of a representative from each ward in the city. It was outsized and unwieldy, and so susceptible to political influence that the nod of a politician was often more important to an applicant for a teaching post than pedagogic competence. There was a feeling that monies that should have gone into teachers' salaries were being diverted into other channels; there were shameful instances where women teachers were paid the subliving wage of $450 a year. Complaints that the school system was being grossly mismanaged failed to disturb the imperious quiescence of Boss Aldridge until they were fired off like booming salvos by a group of prominent citizens who organized what was known as the Good Government Party.

Joseph T. Alling was the leader of the Good Government movement. His confreres were men of good spirit and various talents who hoped to impose their practical idealism upon the city of Rochester. Alling himself was not a professional reformer or a rabble rouser. He was a partner in the large and successful paper company, Alling & Cory. He was an earnest churchman, head of one of the largest Bible classes in western New York, and president of the Young Men's Christian Association. Clergymen, businessmen, and lawyers, including Walter S. Hubbell, George Eastman's legal counsel and close friend, were part of the nucleus of the Good Government Party.

The opposition ridiculed the Good Government people as Goo Goos, and disparaged Alling as a "Christer." The epithet was not applicable to his business partner, Harvey E. Cory. Cory was briefly enlisted in a fund drive for the YMCA. Encountering difficulty with a wealthy prospective contributor, he insisted, "You've got to give something. You ought to give a hundred, at least. I'm telling you," he emphasized, pounding a fist on the prospect's desk, "this YMCA's making goddamn good Christians out of a hell of a lot of young fellows who'd be no good without it."

The first objective of the Goo Goos' agenda for municipal reform was to free the School Board from political control. They wanted a small elective board; they got it when Aldridge realized that the peripheral pressure they were exerting on his domain might develop into a centripetal force.

The School Board was reduced to five commissioners, and very early in the century its president, who continued in office for six years, was Andrew J. Townson of the Sibley store. A new high school, which was needed to relieve the congestion of the Free Academy, was in prospect. When the question of its location arose, Townson acted with his usual forthrightness. Procuring a street map upon which all city lots were shown, he thrust a pin into every lot from which a child went to high school. When he placed a finger in the geometric center of the thicket of pins, he discovered that the place on the map his finger touched represented a plot of land on Alexander Street not far from the corner of Main Street East. In the spring of 1903, East High School, which had risen on this site, opened its doors to 1502 students.

Besides having a good deal to do with the selection of the site of the new high school, Townson and a fellow commissioner, Professor George M. Forbes, of the University of Rochester, were in large measure responsible for replacing the not-quite-up-to-standard principal of the Free Academy with a young educator from the University School in Chicago.

Albert H. Wilcox did not seek the principalship; the commissioners sought him. He was chosen only after a number of other prospects had been considered and rejected. His importation provoked criticism of the Board of Education. The *Post Express* asked snippishly if our city was culturally so barren that a Rochester educator could not be found who was capable of administering the Rochester high school. Townson and Forbes were unfretted by the newspaper's printed stricture or by the oral censure of other critics. They believed they had found the best available man for the job, and time proved the wisdom of their choice.

Wilcox was thirty-two years old when he was appointed principal of the Free Academy. That was in 1900. Three years later, with the opening of East High, he took over the principalship of that institution and continued in office until he retired in 1938. His career as a Rochester educator was a triumph. He was the town's great schoolmaster and probably the most beloved Rochesterian of his time.

Actually, Wilcox was not so much of an importation as those who criticized his appointment implied. Although born in Massachusetts, he had moved to Rochester as an adolescent, had attended the Free Academy, and been graduated from the University of Rochester, Phi Beta Kappa, and top man of his class. When he left the university, he also left Rochester. For the next decade he taught in two or three secondary schools, and advanced his scholarship with graduate studies at the University of Chicago.

The opening of East High, and two and a half years later, the opening of its counterpart on the west side of the river, stimulated interest in secondary education in Rochester. In the spring of 1901, the Free Academy had an enrollment of 920 students; by the autumn of 1905, with classes being held in the two new schools, the public high school population had increased to 1981. High school dropouts had been common in the Free Academy, especially among male students. One year, during the Gay Nineties, only thirty-three boys in a graduating class of 131, stayed the course. This three-to-one ratio was sharply reduced when the new schools came into being. Indeed, five years after West High had risen in Cyclopean splendor on lands that only a short time before had been plowed and sown by farmers "out Genesee Street way," the girls who received diplomas on Commencement Day outnumbered by only a count of one their classmates of the opposite sex.

Herbert S. Weet, West High's first principal, continued in that post only half a dozen years. He had come to the high school from an east side elementary school, which he had also served as principal. He had more of an air of command than his friend and gentle colleague Mr. Wilcox at East High, but nothing of the Draconian attitude of the old-fashioned cudgeling schoolmaster. He was kind, approachable, understanding. He was esteemed by faculty and students. He was removed from West High in 1911 to become superintendent of all Rochester schools and gained, during the twenty-odd years that he remained in that office, a national reputation as a public school administrator.

Because of his limited tenure as a high school principal, Mr. Weet was known personally to fewer high school alumni than Mr. Wilcox. The latter seemed to have the homage of the whole town. Walking a single block in a downtown street he would be enthusiastically greeted by half a dozen former students. His courtesy was all embracing. An alert man, of medium height, his bright blue eyes would seek out passersby who appeared to belong in the age group of East High alumni and upon them he would bend his kindly smile. Fearful that he might fail to recognize some former student, he sometimes bowed or tipped his hat to a new arrival from Sacramento, California, or Richmond, Virginia, or Joplin, Missouri, who wondered if this salute from a perfect stranger was typical of Rochester's friendliness to visitors.

In 1923, Mr. Wilcox became the defendant in a trial in the school assembly hall that was presided over by Superintendent Weet. The indictment was that he had worked twenty years without a vacation. He was found guilty and presented with a check for $6,500, raised by East High alumni, two thousand of whom were witnesses of the "legal" proceedings. The Board of Education added $1,000 to the alumni fund, and Mr. Wilcox and his wife were "sentenced" to a year's sabbatical, which they passed in European travel.

Compared to the turbulence of the current educational climate, Mr. Wilcox's principalship at East High and the school superintendence of Herbert Weet and that of his extremely able, hand-picked successor, James M. Spinning (who, like Dr. Weet, was nationally renowned as a public school administrator) were relatively serene. Spinning, who had previously served as principal of West High, was twenty-one years superintendent of schools. He was followed by a succession of three incumbents, only one of whom served as much as a third of Spinning's tenure. The most durable of the three was Herman R. Goldberg, who executed a difficult assignment with courage, skill, and integrity until, a few months before this was written, he resigned to become Associate Commissioner for Elementary and Secondary Education in the United States Office of Education in Washington, D.C.

Recently, Dr. John M. Franco, who served as acting superintendent after Goldberg's resignation, was confirmed in the office. His term will continue six years. The job will be beset with more vexing problems than ever before, and the incumbent will need —besides high adminstrative skill—tact, patience, and a good deal of intestinal fortitude.

Chapter 17

Following the lead of the University of Rochester, which in 1889 made football an organized sport, the Free Academy put a team in the field that staged some hairy contests early in this century, and passed the game on to the two new high schools where it became, a few years later, such an obsessive extracurricular activity that the authorities were constrained to cause its abolishment. Principals Wilcox and West and the Board of Education decided that the game had gotten so far out of hand that the football tail was beginning to wag the academic dog, and the prohibition they enforced after the 1909 season continued for thirty years.

As it was played in 1902, the last year the Free Academy fielded a team, football was a different game from today's elaborately devised spectacle, with its geometric patterns of play, its offensive and defensive platoons, its passing and kicking specialists, its motion picture analysis of opponents' techniques, its skin-tight uniforms, and its multiple coaching staffs. It was a lusty, hard-scrabbled, not very carefully ordered game that belonged primarily to the boys who played it, though the Free Academy eleven did have a paid coach. He was Jack Hayden, a member of Rochester's professional baseball club, who remained in town after the close of the baseball season to take the job. The team manager was a senior, John D. Pike, today one of Rochester's leading contractors. Professor John E. Glen, who for more than a quarter of a century taught Latin and other subjects at the academy, helped, as president of the Students' Athletic Association, to direct the destinies of the team; its star was a universally idolized youth, H. Acton Langslow.

During his three years as principal of the Free Academy, Mr. Wilcox was heartily in favor of football. He felt that the game provided a safety valve for exuberant youthful spirits and that pride in their school was excited among the students by a winning team. He discovered evils in the sport only after he transferred to

East High. John Pike's father, who had a carpenter shop in Minerva Place, in downtown Rochester, complained bitterly to the principal that he hadn't sent his son to high school to become a social fop as a member of Alpha Zeta fraternity or to waste time as manager of the football team. He wanted the boy to acquire an education. Gently, Mr. Wilcox explained to the irate father that his son's managerial duties were providing him with experience in practical affairs that couldn't be acquired in the classroom, and the elder Pike deferred to the principal's judgment. One of the lessons in practical affairs young Pike learned was how to save a Latin professor from a mob.

One of the Free Academy's opponents that year was Genesee Wesleyan Seminary, and the contest was staged on the seminary's gridiron in the nearby village of Lima. Professor Glen's devotion to the Rochester eleven had the passion of an eleventh-century crusader. Football with him was not a Saturday afternoon pastime for youth; it was a conflict of Armageddon violence and import. Every game saw him prowling the sidelines, a heavy furled umbrella in hand, his piercing eyes searching for any microscopic infraction of the rule that might disadvantage his beloved gladiators. Early in the game in Lima he discovered a monstrous transgression: An out-sized fellow, who seemed old enough to have fathered his teammates, and who had neither Wesleyan leanings nor academic affiliations, was masquerading in a seminary uniform. With a scream of protest, the professor bounded onto the playing field and started whacking every Lima head he could reach with his umbrella. Outraged partisans scrambled down from the stands and spewed out on the field. A full-blown riot was developing, and Glen might have suffered mayhem or worse, except for the daring and ingenuity of young Pike, who spirited the professor under the grandstand, got him out on the road, and bribed a peddler in a horse-drawn rig to rush him out of town before the pursuing mob could lay its collective hands upon him.

Later that same year, in the big game, the Thanksgiving-Day match with Cascadilla Prep of Ithaca, at Culver Field, Professor Glen failed to raise a pipe of protest when Jack Hayden, the Free Academy coach, put on a uniform, disguised his features with an oversized nose guard, and went in as quarterback for a lad named "Butch" Kurtz, who had overeaten at the Thanksgiving board and was too ill to suit up for the fray. Hayden was doing well until his nose guard was knocked askew and his identity disclosed.

Anguished cries of protest arose, threats were exchanged by the opposing players, and Professor Glen, who felt that in this dire emergency Hayden's deception was in no wise improper, stood menacingly over the visitors with his cudgel-like umbrella at the ready. Demands of forfeiture were made, polemics fizzed and sparkled like a Catharine wheel, but when Hayden withdrew and a second substitute relieved him, the game was resumed. It was won by the Rochester team when Langslow, the fullback, made a last-minute touchdown plunge, which bulged out his stature (in the eyes of his idolators) to All-American dimensions.

When Rochester was a much smaller and more closely knit city than it is today, and its personages were more sharply sculpt in bas-relief against the conglomerate of its general population, Acton Langslow was frequently a conspicuous figure on the Main Street scene. On pleasant evenings he would often be seen lounging close to the facade of the store of the B. M. Hyde Drug Company ("Your Health" read the store's motto, "Is Our Business") on the north side of Main Street a few rods west of the Clinton Avenue corner. He stood usually with a handful of courtiers and satellites, perhaps deliberately on display; certainly not insensible of admiring glances of adult passersby, of the worshipful eyes of high school youth, who haunted Hyde's because it was the rendezvous of high school heroes; of the ogling of little shop girls, who pulled out their gum and snapped it back, and made their whispered homage, "Gee, ain't he grand!"

When Langslow died in the back yard of his Irondequoit home in 1956 of a self-inflicted gunshot wound, I learned of the tragedy from his younger brother, Dick. There was a pause after the broken-voiced announcement "Lang is dead!" and thick choking sobs quavered over the newspaper office telephone wire. "He could have done anything," my informant went on convulsively, after a moment. "Lang could have done anything in the world he set his mind to do. *Anything.* . . ." the voice trailed off tragically; and I recalled that there had once been a time when Dick Langslow's statement would not have seemed unsound or the least exaggerated.

The annals of local historians contain no mention of Langslow, and the omission is understandable. He was not a historic figure, and his contribution to the city's life, in the light of the considerable impress he made upon the city, is negligible. His certifications of potential greatness are skimpy, but the aura of glamour that seemed to envelop him gave to a great many young people in Rochester the impression that he was God-like, omnipotent, and that any achievement (as Dick Langslow had compassionately remarked) was within the compass of his talents.

Sports writers mixed metaphors and ran out of adjectives recounting his exploits as a high school football player and telling of his Frank Merriwell performances during the single season he played for the University of Rochester. But Langslow's athletic prowess alone does not account for the legend he became or explain the mystique that enshrined him in the memory of youthful contemporaries whose accomplishments in adult life were often far more substantial than his own.

He played football superlatively well for those days and in the sort of competition in which he engaged. He played baseball, basketball, and was a member of the track team. He was a "heavy" in high school theatricals, and here he may have been more fittingly cast than as a hero on the athletic field. He was large of stature, with sloping, bearlike shoulders. His broad, rugged handsomeness, which persisted late in life, should have made his fortune in Western movies. He had a voice like a barrel organ. When he made the imperious inquiry in *Macbeth:*

> How now, you secret, black, and midnight hags!
> What is't you do?

one felt that even the witches trembled on their broomsticks.

At the time of Langslow's death, Colonel William M. Emerson, corporation counsel for the city of Rochester, told the *Democrat and Chronicle* of seeing him play the title role in a high school production of *Strongheart* at the Lyceum Theater.

"Lang dominated the stage," said Colonel Emerson. "He was an immensely arresting figure. I can't think of another person who had a part in the drama, but Langslow's performance is as vivid to me today as it was fifty years ago. I was so carried away by it that if he had called, 'Emerson, jump out of that gallery,' I think I would have jumped. It was amazing the magnetism the man had, the youthful worship he was able to command."

When Langslow left high school he became the object of a campaign of proselytism on the part of eastern colleges and universities that was not unlike the missionary zeal of the followers of Ignatius Loyola. They wanted him not for his academic accomplishments, which were not notable, but for his football talents. Langslow was indigenous to Rochester; his propensities were oddly provincial. In 1904, he matriculated at the University of Rochester, starred on the football team (singlehandedly he scored against Cornell, no mean feat in the era of close, gouging mass plays that often moved the ball only inches; in a day when the light U of R eleven was contemptuously used as an early season trial horse for the Big Red), and left college in six months.

Langslow coached the West High football team for three or four years, had a brief fling in vaudeville with an act he formed called The Three Collegiates, served with distinction for twenty-two months with an AEF engineering outfit in World War I. In a sudden, intense, patchy program of reading he came upon *Rights of Man* and other works of Tom Paine, and became an oracle on Paine in downtown speakeasies. Paine was his idol; he expounded on him eloquently, impressively, if not too profoundly, for gape-mouthed barflies who were as susceptible to his magnetic appeal as the youth of his high school days. He developed the feeling that he had a message and a mission; he tried politics and became the Democratic candidate for a seat in the state assembly. His opponent was the multimillionaire Republican, Pritchard H. Strong, whose grandfather had been president of the Eastman Kodak Company. During his campaign, the press spoke of Langslow as once having been "the most glamorous figure in the city of Rochester." The reference related to the very early 1900s, when he might have run for mayor, and won; now he was deep in midlife, the shine of youthful brilliance had worn away, and Mr. Strong, campaigning in an entrenched Republican district, won handily.

The day the news of Langslow's death was printed in the newspapers, a man who refused to divulge his name called on my telephone in the *Democrat and Chronicle* office. "I knew Acton Langslow, man and boy," he said. "I am older than he was, but we were in high school together. I can tell you this. He had the greatest potential of anyone in town who was anywhere near his age. His potential was ruined by youthful adulation."

And that may have been true. Only those who knew him or knew of him sixty-odd years ago are able to appreciate the extent of his potential. Walker S. Lee, who played on Langslow's high school football teams, may have been a better all-around athlete. But when Lee and such paladins as Theodore (Punk) Hageman, Orlo Waugh, Archie White, John Finucane, and Francis (Midge) Carroll gathered with Langslow in front of Hyde's Drug Store, it was the last named who was the cynosure of all passersby. The clothes he wore, and even his walk were imitated; the most popular iced confection at the drugstore's soda counter was the "Langslow Special." If youthful success had not come so easily and youthful fame so quickly; if his resolution had been as fibrous and sinewy as the muscles of his powerful body, Langslow might have gone far, far in any one of half a dozen pursuits, to fulfill the enormous promise of his early manhood.

* * *

Until the opening of East and West High Schools, Rochester youth who were destined to matriculate at the more fashionable of what today would be called Ivy League colleges, often received their secondary training at such schools as The Hill, Phillips Exeter Academy, Hotchkiss, Lawrenceville, Andover, and now and then St. Paul's and Groton. Now parents of means, who formerly might have agreed with Anthony Trollope that the best education, like the best broadcloth, was to be had only at a price, impressed by the splendid accommodations of the two new school buildings and familiar with the fine teaching staffs assembled by Principals Wilcox and Weet, frequently exposed their sons to a couple of years of public school education before packing them off to an eastern preparatory school.

The two Rochester high schools were not, in a true sense, unique. Nevertheless, there was something rather special about them. They excited in the young a sense of glamour. There was distinction in being known as an East or West High student, especially in the first decade of the century when a minted freshness still glowed on these institutions and the gloss of novelty had not yet been dulled. The schools bubbled with enthusiasm. Many of the teachers were young, and a number of them were great favorites with the students, in whose extracurricular activities they often participated; they delighted in the eager receptivity of the boys and girls who were under their instruction. Of her own volition, Miss Winifred Ball, who had taught the classical languages at Vassar, transferred to a lower academic level to teach at West High, and reveled in the experience. She had found an all-women's college too cloistered; the college women were so enthralled by men that she said they would run to a window to watch a man collect the garbage. Youth of both sexes sat in juxtaposition in her West High classes and she admired the honesty and lack of hypocrisy in their relations.

West High, where this writer registered as a second-term freshman the day the school first opened, was quickly permeated with a familial spirit which gave cohesion and unity to the student body. There was dignity and orderliness in the class rooms; outside of class there was sometimes a rapport between the students and the younger teachers not unlike the comradely relations between the students themselves. Boys were known to have "crushes" on the still maturing feminine members of the faculty. There was a pert, pretty, lively little woman—*girl*, really, since she had come directly to West High from Vassar—who seemed to me to have something of the grace and charm of the musical comedy ladies Miss Adele Ritchie, Miss Edna May, and Miss Bessie McCoy, whom I had loved, vicariously, from the top balcony of the Lyceum Theater. But I disliked school, I rejected the fine opportunities West High offered, I was shy, and I never talked with Miss Ruth Crippen except in the English class over which she presided. Joe B., a handsome, stylish, alert youth, who participated in many school activities, was quietly enamored of an English and elocution teacher who is here identified as Miss X.

Joe wrote to her, he met her after class, he called upon her at her home. He kept a diary during the school year which is more than vaguely reminiscent of Holden Caulfield. Miss X was a frequent entry. Joe was a great beau; he was "By Love Possessed." Girls were his obsession, although at times he tried manfully to put them out of mind.

"Did not have breakfast until eleven today and the day has passed quickly," he wrote on July 23, while vacationing at Conesus Lake. "Saw Lois on the boat tonight. She is the goods. I honestly have a crush on her and I am going to renew my acquaintance in town. Oh! no, damn it all, I have resolved to cut the social stunt next year. It's my only hope. I simply have to make good. God grant me the sense and grit to keep at study. It's going to be hard as hell to cut girls but I'm going to do it. It's a beautiful night. . . ."

"Fussing" was the term used in high school for cuddling and kissing back of the vines on the front porch, in a bosky covert at the class picnic, under the robes on a sleigh ride, on the living-room sofa after a girl's parents had gone upstairs or out to the theater. Joe was frequently reproachful about the practice. To "Dear Diary," he wrote: "I wonder if it is really wrong to fuss with a girl"; then, on second thought, "I must have one good session with Gladys."

He paid tribute to Miss X: "She is one fine woman. Lord, if you could only put her brains in some young girl's head."

When he called upon her, at a later date, he suffered conflicting emotions:

"Went to see Miss X tonight. Expected to have a good talk, but didn't have such a devil of a good one. I wasn't feeling right, to tell the truth, and she didn't seem to be in good form herself. I am somewhat afraid of her at times. There have been times when I actually thought she wanted to fuss. I suppose it is all imagination but she certainly does act queer in that way. She is the goods, though. She can have my friendship as long as she wants it."

There was a very lively social life in the two high schools in the years immediately following their opening and a variety of non-athletic extracurricular activities that today would likely provoke disgruntlement and dissent and possibly physical violence. Following the pattern of well-known colleges, the high schools made a good deal of the Junior Prom. For weeks boys, who ordinarily were content to subsist on an allowance from their parents, worked Saturdays delivering meat for the neighborhood butcher, doing garden work, running cash in the basements of departments stores, sawing wood, cleaning cellars—anything to obtain enough money to rent formal attire (not a dinner jacket, not a tux, mind you! but tails and white tie) for the Prom.

The Junior Prom was a programed dance, as were all high school dances that had any pretense of formality. The male escort received a folded card with a fragile lead pencil attached when he passed into the hall. The card listed the number and types of dances, and it was the duty of the male escort to fill the card for his companion. If he were fortunate enough to have a current charmer—a girl who was in great vogue—his task was simple; if his companion lighted balefires in his own eyes, but failed to kindle desire in the eyes of the general male population, he might dance many dances with the lady of his choice and dull his primordial ardor in the process. There was no "cutting in"; that came later, in the F. Scott Fitzgerald era. There was no looseness in the dance hall deportment; everything was precise, very *de rigueur*. From chairs pressed flush against the wall, lynx-eyed chaperones maintained an unremitting surveillance of the dance floor. Femininity was resplendent at the Prom; girls, as well as boys, planned for weeks for the occasion. All were eager to spring their elegent raiment on the *monde*.

Fraternities and sororities had a large part in the social life of the high schools until, not long after football was abolished as an interscholastic sport, the authorities decreed the disbandment of these secret *soi-disant* literary societies with such Greek-lettered appellations as Gamma Sigma, Kappa Epsilon, Pi Phi, Alpha Zeta. Several of these organizations had had a relatively long history at the Free Academy and both undergraduate and alumni members protested that their abolishment would destroy something precious in youthful fellowship, but Dr. Weet, as superintendent of schools, and the Board of Education held firm. The sororities and fraternities were deprived of sanction.

The reproach of the authorities was chiefly directed toward the fraternities, each of which maintained downtown rooms. There had been rumors that women had been spirited into these chambers and that "booze parties" had been held in them. There may have been some truth to the rumors, but these were not common practices. The rented quarters were used as club rooms, initiations were performed in them, and there on meeting nights the slight cabalistic rites of the order were carried out. Each fraternity had a faculty counselor at whose instigation the members at times engaged in formal debate, practiced dramatics, and held literary discussions.

My oldest sister was an Arethusa, which was supposed to be the nonpareil of sororities. She seemed to achieve a kind of sublimity when she spoke of the sisterhood and its members. She was deeply impregnated with its spirit and I, as a younger high school student, was bored by her repetition of the oracular pronouncements of the Arethusa girls; of her asseverations concerning their beauty, their wisdom, and their charms. Nevertheless, her devotion gave support to the protest that something of value would be lost with the extirpation of the fraternities and sororities, since the "girls of Arethusa" who had formed the nucleus of her girlhood friendships continued in adult life as her cherished intimates.

Bancroft Carson, who, for a time, was a beau of my oldest sister, rushed me for Alpha Zata. I was pledged, but I had no spirit for the honor. On the night of the initiation I escaped my tormentors and ran home. They came for me. They inducted me into the order without subjecting me to further indignities, but my participation in fraternal activities was limited to my being present on meeting nights (a fine of ten cents was imposed on absentees) and my attendance at "rushes" at private homes, where the fellowship was pleasant and the food plentiful.

Alpha Zeta was one of the oldest of the "frats." It was conservative and fairly social. It was not as social as Gamma Sigma, many of whose members bore a striking resemblance to the latter-day Arrow Collar boy. The Gamma Sigs were favored by the popular high school girls. They were sharp; they were conversant with the forms and punctilios of social deportment. They went afield in their courting and squired young ladies from such private schools as Miss Hakes, Livingston Park Seminary, and the Columbia School for Girls. Pi Phi enrolled the leading athletes; they were the rough and ready boys. And they accepted Roman Catholics.

The fraternities and sororities occasionally sponsored dances. The AZ's gave a very large one in the ballroom of a downtown hotel at the time the state convention of the fraternity was held in Rochester. It was called a ball and the elaborate preparations made for it warranted the designation. My sister very much wanted to attend, but Carson, who was still her beau, was in Ithaca preparing to enter Cornell University, and my father asked me to take her. I rebelled; I had never attended a high school dance, and I had no training or practice in the terpsichorean art. My father insisted. Seething with anger and resentment, I started forth on the night of the ball in a red shirt, which my father descried before I descended the front porch steps. He ordered me to change to a white shirt. The whole affair was a horrible ordeal, and I am sure my sister regretted the impressment of a surly, stupid, ungainly young brother as an escort.

As I look back from the coign of vantage formed by the piled-up years, I am struck with the notion that there must have been something pathological in my perverse and persistent rejection of the opportunities provided for me in adolescence. With the exception of my closest friend, Charlie Maloy, the boys I knew best were AZ's. For the most part they were alert, eager youth who took a lively interest in scholastic affairs and admirably fulfilled their obligations as citizens of the high school community. When I was initiated into the fraternity its president was Max P. Shoop, an East High senior, who was a standout among the youth of that institution. His was the fattest entry in the "Who's Who" of the school's Senior Annual. He was president of the class, president of the debating society, editor in chief of the *Clarion*, manager of the football team, chairman of the commencement committee, captain of the basketball team, secretary of the school's executive council, a performer in class plays, and praetor of the Roman Forum. He was a straight A student. He was immorally handsome; he dressed like a boulevardier. It was said that any girl in East High to whom he beckoned came mewing to his knees like a kitten.

Max went to Amherst where his high school successes were repeated in the amplified dimensions of collegiate life; to Harvard Law; to China, and then to Paris for the famous law firm of Sullivan & Cromwell. In Paris he was president of the American Club, and a friend of the Prince of Wales. Leaving Sullivan & Cromwell, he joined the international law firm of Condert Brothers. When the Germans invaded France in 1940, Shoop repaired to Switzerland where, during the remainder of the war, he gave important aid to the French resistance movement. After the war, he was the first American to receive the Legion of Honor. His first marriage to a wealthy divorcee ended in a divorce; his second, to a French woman half his age, ended in his death from a stroke at the American Hospital in Paris.

Shoop was the internationalist in our group, and we saw nothing of him in his postcollegiate days, almost all of which were spent abroad; he had grown completely out of our ken. But the AZ's had another prize barrister, T. Carl Nixon, who remained all his long and useful life in his native habitat. His excellencies were many: He was the senior partner of Nixon, Hargrave, Devans & Doyle, the largest law firm in town; he was brilliant, witty, approachable, and loyal to a fault; he was a director of several corporations and active in the promotion of many worthy civic

226

causes; he was a powerful behind-the-scene force in the Republican Party. He was intransigently of the Establishment and proud of it; never a fumbling apologist. If a count was wanted, Nick stood straight up to be counted; there was neither uncertainty in his bearing nor ambiguity in his speech. He was one of Rochester's very good citizens.

And the AZ's had Howard T. Cumming, of West High, recipient of the first Yale scholarship given in Rochester. To everything he attempted, and he attempted a great deal, Cumming gave what the ball players call the old college try. It was his nature; it was congenital with him. He was business manager of the school paper, leading man in school plays, active in intramural councils, a fine student, a capable orator, and a quick thinking scrambling little towheaded quarterback on the football team, who, knocked about by outsized burlies, managed, because of his smartness and resolution, to be effective.

Leaving Yale, he soon went into business with a Yale classmate, Douglas C. Townson. They took over a slumping old-line Rochester canning company, Curtice Brothers Company (noted far and wide for Blue Label Ketchup) and made it a very going concern. Eventually, Cumming retired as chairman of the board.

But long before the close of his business career, he was actively concerned with a number of agencies and organizations whose purpose was the advancement of the public weal. Mr. Cumming did not join committees merely to *join* committees; he did not sit in conference *merely* to confer. He was up and doing, and he was enormously effective. There is no cant and so little showiness about Howard Cumming that it took the city some time to realize just what this earnest, dedicated man was up to, and to know that the dossier of his good works would press out the side of a dispatch case. Then the unbidden honors began to fall upon him. They ranged from the Silver Beaver, the highest award in Scouting, to the Civic Medal from the Rochester Museum and Science Center for "service to the community and to humanity." He won medals like a champion skeet shooter. From the Chamber of Commerce for "Meritorious Leadership in the Field of Civic Development," from the Real Estate Board for his contribution to civic improvement, from the Rotary Club (of which he was not a member) for being—as the citation read—"the Rochester citizen who made the greatest contribution to the community during

227

the year." Howard Cumming represents what Rochester delights to believe is typical of its citizenship.

Unlike most of my brother AZ's, who at the very least made credible showings in high school I was a harrowing failure. I studied desultorily; I took no part in extracurricular activities. I was obsessed only with the idea of running a mile three seconds faster than the long standing world record of 4 minutes 12¾ seconds, and when I should have been attempting to identify the ablative absolute or conjugating a Latin verb I would be figuring on the flyleaf of my Latin grammar the quarter mile times one would need to run to bring the feat into being. I hurried home from school to run, and run, and run, mostly alone, but sometimes with Charlie Maloy riding the bike at my side. I never "went out" for the West High track team; that was schoolboy stuff. I was shooting for the stars. There was no great pulse of haste. Immortality wasn't achieved overnight. George was thirty years old when he performed his epic; I had a dozen years to prepare for mine. I was puerile beyond belief; the extremist case of arrested development.

In time I dropped Latin, then German, which I had substituted for Latin. I remember Mr. Weet scribbling a note for the German prof, saying that I was to be permanently dismissed from his class.

"Henry," he said, handing me the note, "you haven't the hankering after linguistics that characterizes a philosopher." I was impressed by the aptness and spontaneity of the line, and hurried to the study hall to write it in the front of my German book.

I managed to reduce my daily stay in the school building to three hours. I was home each afternoon by one o'clock, lugging a packet of books which I scarcely opened. My failure was complete at the end of the spring semester. I told my father I was sure I would succeed in another school and quickly matriculate at college.

He enrolled me in Phillips Academy at Andover, where I shamefully abused the high privilege he had granted me, failed as miserably as I had failed in high school, and broke my father's heart. He suggested at the end of the school year that I hire out to a man he knew who operated a large fruit farm. Instead, I applied to

228

Morris Adams, city editor for the *Democrat and Chronicle*, who allowed that I might have a probationary period, not as a cub reporter who would be paid for his efforts, but as a "sub," who would be rewarded with streetcar tokens if he were sent to obtain a three or four-paragraph item on a strawberry festival at an outlying church, or a bit about a clambake at Birds and Worms, or something on a lodge picnic at Point Pleasant or the Newport House down along the bay.

That was the inauspicious beginning of a newspaper career that continued nearly sixty years in my native city with only a couple of brief sorties into other journalistic fields. In an earlier day, when cynics and sophisticates put down Rochester as a "hick town," a man with whom I was walking on New York's Broadway accosted George S. Kaufman, one of the wits of the Algonquin Round Table, once a drama critic for the New York *Times*, then a well-known playwright.

Mr. Kaufman had been married in Rochester to a Rochester girl, the former Miss Beatrice Bakrow, and I had written an account of the wedding for the newspaper. I was now in New York at Frank Gannett's direction to cover the great dinner in the Waldorf-Astoria of the Society of the Genesee, which each year attracted a trainload of prominent Rochesterians. Presenting me to Kaufman, my friend remarked that "*everybody* from Rochester was in New York for the Genesee dinner."

"What a wonderful time to be in Rochester," Kaufman said wryly.

But *I* believed any time was a wonderful time to be in Rochester. I suffered no divine discontent. The deeper verdure of the distant fields failed to allure; faraway places gave to me no promise of greater rewards. The world was not my oyster, but Rochester was my microcosm. I loved it. As a newspaper reporter I was privileged to peep back of the curtains, to plumb the crypts of the city's secrets, to tinker through the woodwork and make microscopic observations in the chinks. I was conversant with Rochester's traditions, I knew of its follies, its vanities, and its virtues. Its people I knew by the hundreds. I knew them from all strata of society. Walking through Main Street, which for many years was my beat, I delighted in being waved at by my fellow citizens, in being stopped and spoken to. I felt as indigenous to the street as the lampposts at the curb. And each day I wrote a little of Rochester's living history for the newspaper and told about its people. I immensely liked doing that; my job made a very satisfactory life.

BOOK II

Chapter 18

As I waited in Normandy, in the spring of 1919, to be shipped back to the United States, a cable came to me from Lewis B. Jones, of the Eastman Kodak Company, asking that I call on him when I returned to Rochester. Two weeks later, out of the military—which I despised, although it hadn't treated me badly—I knocked at his office door.

Long before my day in the newspaper business, Mr. Jones had been a reporter for the *Democrat and Chronicle*. He must have had a conspicuous talent, for George Eastman heard about him, sent for him, and hired him after a single interview. Mr. Eastman had been in quest of a "live young man . . . who can do some writing and would have the ability after a time to take entire charge of the advertising department," and Jones handsomely qualified. The live young newspaperman became in time not only head of advertising but vice-president in charge of sales. His promotions by the printed word of Eastman products were often classical examples of the advertising art, and Jones was one of the art's foremost practitioners.

He was a friendly, urbane man, who liked people. He delighted in sports and sociability. He was a prominent member of the Rochester Yacht Club. He lived on a handsome country estate in Pittsford (now the property of another eminent publicist, Paul Miller, head of Gannett newspapers), where he raised blooded cattle and hackney ponies. He was one of a five-man committee that administered Rochester's great outdoor Horse Show, which opened Labor Day afternoon and continued throughout the week, and he exhibited his own champion hackney, Clover Clockwork, on the horse-show circuit.

I had become acquainted with Mr. Jones when I was assigned during the prewar years to write about the Horse Show for the newspaper, and our friendly relations continued after the United States joined the Allies in World War I, and Jones was recruited by George Creel, chairman of President Wilson's committee on Public Information. He served the committee as a dollar-a-year man. His working week was equally divided: He gave three days to the Eastman Company and three days to the Creel committee, and the latter service often took him to Washington and New York.

For a short time before I went overseas I was stationed at Fort Dix, New Jersey, and during that period Mr. Jones was a guest in the Hotel Biltmore. Two or three times he had me over to New York for dinner, and once took me to the theater. He was a gracious, kindly man. One evening I spoke to him about one of the first models ever hired by the Eastman Company, a beautiful girl named Mary Sandway, who had been a student at West High School. She had left Rochester to try a stage career and I asked Mr. Jones if he knew anything of her whereabouts. He gave me a quick, quizzical glance. We were waiting for Mrs. Jones under the Biltmore clock. "Henry," he said, whispering back of his hand, "I'm ninety-five per cent good. She's playing with a stock company up in White Plains."

When I reported at his office in the State Street building of the Eastman Company, he greeted me warmly.

"I've got a job for you," he said directly, and delight at being able to render a kindly service for a young friend shone in his twinkling eyes. He rated himself 95 per cent good; I made him better than that. "I want you to come to work for me."

I was not surprised. I was sure Mr. Jones's cable had not summoned me to a social call. But I was just free of the regimentation of army life, although, come to think of it, my army life had not been rigidly regimented. My contribution to winning the "war to end war" had been coaching an army track team, serving as interlocutor for an army minstrel show, and working for the *Stars and Stripes,* with a car of my own and extra money to eke out my pay as a private, first class. I was unmarried; I had no sentimental attachments. I asked Mr. Jones if I might have a couple of days to consider his offer.

"Why, of course," he said. "Take your time. You need a few days to orient yourself to civilian life. To reaffirm your sense of values."

Two days later I returned to his office and embarrassedly, stammeringly explained that I did not want at that time to tie myself down to an office job. He looked across the desk at me with eyes whose frank astonishment quickly kindled to anger.

"I'll tell you something," he said. "Before I got this job, it was offered to an older newspaperman. Fellow named Woodruff. He turned it down." There was a portentous pause; when he resumed his words were devastating. "Woodruff was buried in a potter's grave. That'll be your fate."

The interview was over.

I do not know, of course, whether my future with the Eastman Company would have been brilliant. Probably not. But it would have been solid and secure, and the retirement pension would have been very acceptable. And likely, in time, I would have had a broad desk with a button on it to summon from the anteroom a secretary with a notebook, and a secretary has always seemed to me a luxury not dissimilar to a court suite at the Paris Ritz, or a sunken black-marble bathtub with solid gold spigots, or a chauffeur-driven Rolls. I remained, however, in the newspaper business. And when I contemplate the radical changes that would have been wrought in my life had I accepted Mr. Jones's offer (for one thing, I inevitably would have married the wrong woman), I am glad I declined. I never achieved the status of having a secretary. But once, after I went back to work, I had an "office" of my very own in a broom closet, and another time, seeking solitude for my lucubrations, I was granted desk space among the lumber and litter of the attic of the newspaper plant.

Before the war, I had worked seven years at newspapering (as it is called today), and during that time I had become deeply imbued with the spirit of the craft; I was no longer repressed by the nagging indictment of my catastrophic early failures, and I had attained a decent competence.

Beginning in the summer of 1910 as the lowliest subreporter on the *Democrat and Chronicle* I was subjected to all the grubbiness of that humble office. If I was not assigned to cover a picnic or dispatched to obtain a photograph of a citizen of some prominence who had died that day or one of two persons who were celebrating their golden wedding anniversary I was kept in the office to transpose on a battered typewriter "Notes of the Pedro Clubs." All of the women in Rochester seemed to play pedro. The notices of their tournaments began fluttering into the newsroom by mid-week, and they were prominently displayed under a two-column head in the Sunday edition. The various clubs strove with limited success for distinctive names. There were the Evening Stars, the Firesides, the Happy Belles, the Eager Dealers, the Come Early Pedro Club. The scrawled notices were sometimes as difficult to decipher as Vedic Sanskrit, but if names of the pedro players were included in them, Mr. Adams, the city editor, insisted that they be correctly spelled, and this meant a tedious checking of the city directory.

Struggle though I did to master the craft of news writing, I was so dreadfully inept that after months of working without pay, I was called aside by Mr. Adams, who not unkindly, but matter-of-factly, told me I was unsuited for what I was trying to do, and suggested that I try something else. I pleaded for extended probation; he granted it. In April, ten months after I had begun my menial vassalage, he again called me to his desk, and told me that he had altered his opinion of me, that he was going to make me a regular member of the staff and that on Saturday I would have an envelope from the cashier. I had arrived. The $8 stipend in the envelope made the first real triumph of my life.

Two years later, increasingly pleased with what I was doing—liking the little sketches I brought in off the street, counterpoint to my regular assignments—Mr. Adams aksed me to do a column, "Seen and Heard." The continuity of the column was broken by my enlistment in the Army and by my employment by other newspapers, but fifty-six years after the first "Seen and Heard" was printed I submitted the last one, and began a sort of fragmentary retirement from the newspaper business that required almost a year to consummate.

* * *

A few days after Morris Adams died of a heart attack in his home following his daily visit to Jerome Keough's billiard hall, I had a note from Mrs. Adams asking me to call. I went at once. Mr. Adams had not married until he was well into his seventies. I had met Mrs. Adams only once before, on the day of her husband's funeral. She was a woman of imposing personality and keen intelligence who had been a teacher at the state Industrial and Agricultural School in Industry. To my astonishment, a moment after she greeted me, she handed over a handsome gold pocket watch.

"The men in the *Democrat and Chronicle* newsroom gave the watch to Morris when he went to the *Journal*," Mrs. Adams said. "I am sure he would have wanted you to have it."

I was sensible of a very real compliment. I was not working for the *Democrat and Chronicle* at the time the fund for the watch was raised, and I had no knowledge of the gift.

I accepted the watch. It became one of my cherished possessions. I was young, naive, and impressionable when I went to work for Mr. Adams and my mature judgment of the man may still be influenced by a youthful assay of his quality. But of all the fine people I have known in a long career in the newspaper business, he alone excited a sense of veneration.

In 1910, when I began as an apprentice newspaper reporter to learn something about life in areas of my native city that lay beyond the parochial confines of Linden Street and the Fourteenth Ward, Rochester's population was fixed by the federal census at 218,149.

The city was fleshing out, but its growth was not tumorous or unwholesome. It was slowly taking on weight as a well-nourished, eupeptic burgher gains girth as he advances into middle life. We were no longer the Flower City. George Eastman's giant industry had given Rochester a far-flung fame and a new by-name. It was now the Kodak City.

It was still very much a city of homes. In the blooming months of spring and summer the foliage of the fine trees that ornamented even Rochester's lesser streets gave to an observer atop the Pinnacle Hills the illusion of a community ingeniously arranged in a forest. There were small residential enclaves in industrial areas that had the aspect of rural villages. Gardens were made in back yards that were not yet consumed by asphalt drives and two-car garages. Although no longer a rarity in the streets, the motorcar was outnumbered by horse-drawn vehicles.

Orderly and attentive crowds gathered in city parks for concerts by the park band, directed by Theodore Dossenbach. The summer's greatest public spectacle was the annual water carnival on the upper Genesee, with twenty or thirty thousand spectators lining both banks of the stream and huddling against the rails of Elmwood Avenue bridge for a view of the elaborately decorated floats and canoes. Eight theaters in Rochester offered theatrical attractions and more than a dozen nickelodeons and ten-cent cinemas were scattered about town. Main Street on Saturday night teemed with shoppers, window shoppers, diners out, theatergoers, and persons who came downtown merely to watch the passing show. Owl cars ran all night on certain lines; there were numerous all-night lunch rooms ("I opened the door, then threw the key away," said Al Fineberg, proprietor of an excellent one at 5 Clinton Avenue North. "We never close").

Mules still hauled canal boats through the heart of the city to countervail our proud declamations of municipal "progress." As they made their slogging approach to the Exchange Street bridge, or the one a few blocks beyond on West Main, bells clanged, street barriers dropped, the bridge rose, and pedestrians, trolley cars, and horse-drawn and motor-driven vehicles stood immobilized on each side of the narrow ditch until the "hoggee," maddeningly indifferent to exhortations of haste, guided his mule and its floating burden beyond the structure of the bridge.

Eagerly striving to establish itself as a convention city, Rochester had two new hotels, the Rochester and the Seneca. It had a myriad of saloons, and one of these, Rattlesnake Pete Gruber's famous museum, bar, and display of reptiles in Mill Street, helped not a little to promote the universal fame of the city. Smack on the Four Corners was Adolph Faucher's noted watering hole for lawyers, bankers, brokers, and unclassified two-fisted drinkers, which took its appropriate name, Mighty Dollar, from the silver dollars mosaicked in the walls, ceiling, and marble floor. In South Water Street was Lafayette Heidell's Byzantine rendezvous for show folk.

There were saloons in factory districts that had the character of workingmen's clubs; and dives that caught up the dregs and driftage of humankind, winos, pickers who had come into town to booze away their apple harvest money, and the unregenerate, off-the-beach beachcomber. These places, during the cold months, flaunted FREE HOT SOUP signs in their windows; other resorts had as a come-on a LADIES' ENTRANCE with rattan curtains to protect the tender buds from the grossness of the barroom. Rochester's piety was sometimes tartuffian. It tolerated a short, concentrated Red Light District which lay in forbidding juxtaposition to the City Morgue, and made a girl bathing barelegged on a public beach liable to arrest.

We had six daily newspapers including the German language *Abendpost*, and the *Democrat and Chronicle* substantially led the other five in circulation and advertising lineage. The *Democrat and Chronicle* was colloquially referred to as the *Democrat*, which the misinformed supposed represented the newspaper's adherence to the Democratic Party. It was Republican to the core. Founded in 1833 as the *Morning Advertiser*, it became *The Morning Democrat* the next year, the year Rochester received a city charter, and thirty-six years later, combining with *The Chronicle*, it assumed the name by which it is presently known. When I began there it was published by the Rochester Printing Company, whose officers were W. Henry Matthews, president; Colonel Nathan C. Pond, secretary and treasurer.

Mr. Matthews was an elderly, bewhiskered, scrupulously groomed little man in elegant raiment, who sat in his office in the rear of the counting room as remote and inaccessible, it seemed to the rank and file of his employees, as the peak of the Matterhorn.

The colonel was long and lank and bony. He was a Civil War veteran. Tradition had it that he had been a roistering fellow in his salad days, but his salad days were far behind him. His wife, who was a large lady of formidable demeanor, met him at the close of each business day in an electric brougham. I doubt if there was any latent rakehell in the colonel, but if there was I feel sure that Mrs. Pond would have competently dealt with it. One might very well imagine her stopping him, if he were bent on some clandestine hanky-panky with a firm patting of a foot on the floor, and an ineluctable declaration: "Nathan, you go out of this house tonight, and you go out over my dead body!"

I never recall seeing Mr. Matthews in the newsroom. His presence there would have required a five-story ascent in a shabby little rope-pulled elevator which creaked protestingly every sluggish inch of its up and down movement. I half believe Mr. Matthews looked upon the people who wrote the news for his newspaper as necessary evils.

Despite any fancy-formed notions to the contrary, precisely in the manner of a dairy route, a department store, a neighborhood bakery, or a hotel, a newspaper succeeds only as it shows black figures on its ledger. This the *Democrat and Chronicle* did conspicuously. But Matthews and Pond, unlike some of their fellow publishers, made no overt professions of journalistic idealism. If they carried a torch for reform, it was hardly higher than a pilot light. Outside of gaining a handsome profit, their single purpose was to perpetuate the Monroe County oligarchy of George W. Aldridge, the Republican boss.

Colonel Pond was slightly less remote from the workers in the city room than his partner. During the heat of a political campaign he occasionally disembarked from the elevator at the fifth floor, lowered over the reporters at their desks, and with a stamp of his congress gaiters shouted out, "Riddle the damn Democrats! Riddle 'em, *I say!*" No one accepted the exhortation in quite the spirit of Napoleon's "Soldiers, from the summit of yonder pyramids forty centuries look down upon you."

The younger members of the reportorial staff were jealous of their craft. We were *newspapermen.* If we thought of them at all, we thought disdainfully of Matthews and Pond, whose connection with our high calling was limited to the prosaic affairs of the business office. We considered them out of our realm, a couple of old fogies who didn't know which end was up when it came to the news content of the newspaper. In truth, they were a couple of very astute "old fogies." Reluctant though they were to pay a decent wage to reporters, they knew very well that without the full coverage the *Democrat and Chronicle* gave, particularly to local and vicinity news, circulation would fall off and advertising revenues would suffer as a consequence. Matthews and Pond kept a keen and critical eye on the news and editorial columns and their newspaper wisdom was further displayed by their employment of Morris Adams who, to us and to many persons who had personal contact with the editorial department, *was* the *Democrat and Chronicle.*

Reporters reported for work at two o'clock in the afternoon, and Mr. Adams was always at his post half an hour before our arrival. He was a tall, well-conditioned man, with fine masculine features and coal-black hair, who sat erect as a grenadier on a straight-backed kitchen chair in the darkest corner of the newsroom. This was a long gloomy alleylike room divided longitudinally by two facing rows of small desks.

A typewriter, usually of a vintage sometime before the Flood, rested in a slot in each reporter's desk, and on a spindle back of this was a thick roll of copy paper. The loftlike fifth (and top) floor of the newspaper building also had a couple of cubicles for editorial writers; a larger room for the managing editor O. S. Adams, the city editor's father; a room in which vicinity news was handled; and, paralleling a third of the length of the newsroom, a flimsily partitioned corridor where the telegraph editor sat in command of four or five telegraphers, including the man whose "bug" was the Associated Press wire. The sports editor had a roll-top desk back of a partition between the entrance to the elevator and the entrance to a large bindery, which was part of the Rochester Printing Company's profitable job printing plant.

With the exception of a four months' break to test my nascent skills on Frank A. Munsey's New York *Press*, and a fling as a European correspondent, during the war winter of 1915-16, when my experience was greater and my skills more sharply honed, my journalistic milieu was the *Democrat and Chronicle* from 1910 until I left seven years later for the Army. It was a period of learning, dedication, excitement, occasional discouragement, great fun, minor triumphs, and small pay. Will Richards, one of the talented younger men in the newsroom, advised me at the beginning, "On a morning newspaper, you'll have no time for a social life."

Richards was right, but since my propensities were not social, and I had no talent to lead a cotillion, my sense of denial was not acute. When in time I became an accredited member of the staff, and showily wore a large tin badge on an upper tip of my vest which allowed me to pass through fire lines, I was often impatient on my day off for the working routine of the morrow, for if each working day did not truly produce a shining adventure, its beginning excited a tingling sense of anticipation that something momentous might occur before the day ended. Wilson Mizner, the well-known wit and roué, once remarked that no civilized person gets up and goes to bed the same day. If the aphorism has meaning, the reporters on the *Democrat and Chronicle* qualified as civilized persons.

Beginning our working day at two o'clock in the afternoon, few of us ever left the newsroom until well after midnight and then only when individually we received Mr. Adams' nod of dismissal. He himself put in brutal hours. He began the compilation of the assignment book half an hour before the staff assembled and he was invariably at his desk at one-thirty next morning. For the first year that I worked for him he read and edited every stick of local copy that went into the newspaper.

The *Democrat and Chronicle* was his mistress, his single devotion, his absorbing concern. He took one day off a week, Friday. Occasionally, in midafternoon, when the early news was light, he would leave his desk for three quarters of an hour to play a match at three cushion billiards in Johnson's Billiard Room, around the corner from the Four Corners; in the evening, he took an hour for dinner. The rest of the time he was at his desk, and never slumped at it; he sat straight up, authoritatively. He spoke firmly but briefly, and never profanely. He was remote from the bravura and wantonness of *The Front Page*, and other picturesque newspaper dramas. He was, quite definitely, a gentleman.

Crerar (Harold) Harris, who succeeded Mr. Adams as city editor, later worked for William Randolph Hearst on the West Coast, and retired from the newspaper business after nearly thirty years with the New York *Times*, both in New York and London, called Mr. Adams "a classic character, a masterful craftsman, and for many of us an inspiring father figure.

"He could well have had national stature if he had operated in a metropolitan environment," Mr. Harris continued, writing to me after Mr. Adams' death. "I am often amused to recognize in myself many of his mannerisms and viewpoints, and I have often wished that some youngsters in the business now had had the benefit of the lessons in news sense, good usage, taste, and tact that he transmitted to us almost by osmosis."

Chapter 19

The seven years in which I was employed in the newspaper business before the United States joined the Allies in World War I were part of the last decade in which newspapermen to a marked degree *were* the communications industry. The newsboy calling "Extra!" symbolized not only the papers' monolopy on tidings but the peoples' isolation. If the people wanted news, they had to have our product. They couldn't get the news by pressing a button and cocking an ear; or by twisting a dial and directing their gaze to a screen upon which a news event was being enacted.

It may be that in the decade that ended in 1920 newspapermen achieved the summit of their influence. After that, the first tinny cacklings of radio newscasters brought an end to our sovereignty. Newspapermen were no longer *the* news medium, but *part* of the news media. We lost a little of our jauntiness, something of our cockiness. Once, though we might have been down at heel, shabby of raiment, short in pocket, we were consoled by the knowledge that we were the collectors and dispensers of the news of the world. This was a vital function. We tenderly nurtured the notion of our high estate; we exulted in a sense of our prestige and of our importance.

"I'm from the *Democrat and Chronicle*." In Rochester and its environs, that was open-sesame! The other newspapers, the stanchly Democratic *Union & Advertiser;* the *Evening Times,* a penny shocker which would run a screaming banner line if a prominent figure sprained a toe, the *Post Express,* a rich man's play thing, and the enterprising, well-edited *Morning Herald,* had their following. We had canonical authority. In our part of western New York, the *Democrat and Chronicle* was next to the Bible.

The five English-language newspapers in Rochester competed for the news with athletic intensity. To be beaten on an important news story, "scooped," as the saying goes, was a serious matter in the city room. This exciting element in newspapering in

Rochester is gone. There are only two newspapers, both under the same ownership, and the news that goes into both is supervised by a central office news director to whom both managing editors are subordinate. If the *Democrat and Chronicle* misses an important news story, it is picked up by the *Times Union*, and vice versa. But of course today, the news "beat" is often achieved by radio and television.

In my early years on the *Democrat and Chronicle*, each of the younger members of the newspaper staff was required once each week to hold the "dog," or long watch. You began your working day at 2 P.M. as usual, and quit the next morning at four. It was a lonely vigil after two o'clock, when everyone else in the editorial department had left except perhaps an operator taking late dispatches in the telegraph room. The rats came out from the bindery, where they feasted on glue, and up by tortuous ways from the bowels of the old building to indulge in nocturnal festivals which sometimes, from their squeals and mad scamperings, became extravagant and Corybantic.

They were river rats by breed, for the foundations of the building were fixed in the left bank of the Genesee. They were large and formidable. In the late stages of his ordeal, the man on watch rested his feet on the bottom of a chair or on a desk top as a precaution against bubonic plague. One giant rat was known to all of us as Old King Cole. Visiting the newsroom late one night, Moss Mosely, a great friend of newspapermen and a prolific news source, who was superintendent of railway mail at the New York Central Station, whistled sharply as he stepped from the elevator. We all looked up. King Cole was scampering across the floor.

"Oh," Moss said, "I thought that was an airedale."

The purpose of the long watch was to have a reporter available if an important news event broke after the basement presses had started throwing off the city edition. It was then the reporter's job to get the story any way he could, write it, and have the skeleton crew in the composing room make over the front page to fit it in. If the news was big enough, the reporter was empowered to issue an extra.

One morning, twenty minutes after the watchman had left, fire broke out in a Main Street store and a report of it was widely displayed in an extra issued by the *Herald*. We then learned that the "old fogies" downstairs knew a thing or two about our side of the newspaper business. Matthews and Pond were outraged that the lordly *Democrat and Chronicle* had been beaten by its less statuesque morning rival, and an order came from their sanctum that henceforth the watch would be extended to six o'clock in the morning. We groaned and moaned and made feeble protests. The decree was not revoked. Our publishers had compassion, however. After his sixteen-hour stint, the man who held the watch was not required to report that afternoon with his fellow workers. He could come in at two-thirty instead of two o'clock.

Women's Lib was unknown in the second decade of the century, and some newspapers, notably the highly regarded Springfield (Massachusetts) *Republican,* flatly refused to hire women reporters. Others took them on reluctantly. The newsroom of the *Democrat and Chronicle* during those years was almost exclusively a male domain. It was stark and barrackslike and destitute of any refinements; its furnishings were old, hard used, and purely utilitarian. Men chewed tobacco. There were large brass water-filled spittoons at every other desk. For years there was only one woman in the editorial department. She was Augusta Anderson, a tall, angular, genteel, kindly, competent, soft-spoken, painfully conscientious spinster, who wore floor-sweeping skirts and carried a reticule half the size of a Gladstone bag, the contents of which frequently excited our speculation.

"What t'hell you suppose Augie carries in that big satchel she lugs around?" Will Richards wondered one day, in the presence of Jim Fraser, the youngest, nerviest, most impudent member of the staff, whose enterprise and brilliance soon transferred him from our ranks to a starring role on the New York *Evening Journal.*

"Aw, I know, I pawed through it," Fraser answered. "Tonight's dinner, a bird in a cage, a folding pool cue, a new corset, a Victor talking machine, and a pair of ice skates."

For several years, Miss Anderson was the only woman on the staff. If she was accepted by her male colleagues with some condescension, and sometimes made the butt of gentle japes, she was well liked. We had no quarrel with her; she amused us. And outside of the office, she had considerable status. She was the pet of the clergy, and the clergy at that time may have wielded a greater influence in Rochester than they do today. She was beloved by club women, by feminine members of fraternal auxiliaries, by amateur theatrical groups, whose histrionic enterprises she helped promote. She covered cat shows and was in close touch with the Society for the Prevention of Cruelty to Animals. Educators thought highly of her. Reformers sought her aid; she was friendly with G.A.R. veterans. She was voluminous, but her column and a half screeds were read by her peculiar followers; in a way of speaking, Augie was a Rochester institution.

Miss Anderson's devotion to her job was perhaps second only to the dedication of Morris Adams. I am sure she had no interests outside of her vocation. Her working hours may not have been as arbitrarily regulated as ours, and they may have been longer, for she made herself available any hour of the day or night. She sat at the end of one of two facing rows of city room desks in a deep pool of concentration that was unruffled by the bustle, the disorder, and the sometimes disorderly behavior of male workers in her immediate vicinity.

There were only three or four extension telephones in the *Democrat and Chronicle* newsroom and the reporter who was nearest to the phone that rang was expected to answer it if the copy boy was not at hand. This was a baleful inconvenience for all of us. In the feverish hours of midevening a reporter might snap a receiver to his ear and hear a dulcet feminine voice say, "Would you please put me on with dear Augusta, it's about the cat club . . ."

"Augie! Augie!" the reporter would shout angrily. "For Gawd's sake, snap into it. The champion siamese is at it again. She's in a delicate condition."

She was famous for her absent-mindedness. She moved about the city room with the indirection of a sleepwalker. She was forever stumbling over spittoons, sometimes with disastrous consequences. One blizzardy, subzero midnight she left the office carrying her huge handbag, but sans gloves, sans rubbers, and without hat or coat, and had hailed a streetcar at the Four Corners before she realized how bereft of protection she was against the bitter elements.

* * *

Two or three years before I left the *Democrat and Chronicle* to enlist in the Army, a second woman worker was inducted into the editorial department. She did not come as a reporter, and I doubt if she came at Morris Adams' solicitation. I am sure that Mr. Adams realized that Miss Anderson was not a negligible member of his reportorial staff, and I am equally sure that he felt that one feminine staff member was enough. His relations with Miss Anderson were as reserved, as brief, and as businesslike as were his relations with the rest of us, but he made one distinction. When giving out the day's assignments, he separately called each male reporter to his desk. Invariably he left his own desk to go to Miss Anderson's when it was her turn to be advised of the day's routine. The discrimination further testified to Mr. Adams' quality.

The new lady in our midst was put on to assist in the handling of what was known as "Vicinity News." We'll call her Miss Pauline. She was not under the supervision of Morris Adams, but under that of his father, "O.S.," the managing editor, who presumably had hired her. She was a flittery, pixylike little creature, with a laugh so incessantly gay that it jangled. She was immensely pleased to be in such a predominantly male environment: to be "where the boys were." Absorbed in her own affairs, Miss Anderson seemed almost unaware of the presence of her male compeers and never participated in our non-professional activities. Miss Pauline never wanted to be excluded from them, if pushing would get her in.

"Jesus, that Pauline'll follow you right into the can, if you don't slam the door on her," Jim Fraser remarked annoyedly. "She's predatory. Never saw a dame so hot pants for a man."

Miss Pauline left after a year, and Miss Anderson for a considerable period was again the only woman in the editorial department. The former had not been dismissed for cause or because of incompetence. She left of her own volition, suffering a wound of the heart. In the witching hour mists of the upper room of John H. Callahan's South Water Street saloon she had become betrothed to the sports editor and discovered in the brassy light of high noon that his protestations of love and abiding devotion were brummagem rhetoric; the meaningless effluence of the overserved.

The sports editor was Charlie Kinney. He was an authentic caricature, a figure that would have delighted George Cruikshank or been agreeable to the genre of Hogarth. His huge stooped torso was supported by incredibly thin legs, encased in rain-pipe trousers. His tailoring was not poor; but his waistcoat, with its upper pockets stuffed with cigars and sharpened lead pencils, resembled a bandolier; his jacket, which hunched up around his deeply sloped shoulders, was not unlike a tightly drawn sack.

He wore highly polished street shoes, with stilettolike toes, which he replaced with carpet slippers when he reached the office.

Kinney was a prodigy of excesses. Someone remarked, over-crediting his agility if not his capacity, that he could drink a quart of whiskey and walk a tightrope. He was a tremendous worker, an awesome trencherman, a guzzler of unbelievable intake, and so enduring that he could eschew sleep, except for forty winks in a barber's chair or a cat nap on a pool table, and function for twenty-four hours aided only by such restoratives as a shave and massage by a barber, a shoeshine, and a liberal dose of cologne.

He was already a legend in the newspaper business when I first met him, and I was awed by him, as a novitiate would be in the presence of one whose exploits reputedly were extraordinary, if not indeed in the realm of the miraculous. There was, for instance, as it was known, "The Great Kinney Plunge."

One early evening the ancient who operated the office elevator discovered that he could not close the fifth-floor door and he lowered the car to the basement to seek help from a maintenance man. The elevator was still at the bottom of the shaft when Kinney, who earlier had been wassailing with the manager of a prizefighter, left his desk and stepped through the opening.

As his gross body floundered in the air, a shriek like that of a horse in a burning stable shrilled out of the shaft and vibrated through the newsroom. He must have been as grotesque in his tragic flight as an overstuffed scarecrow caught in the eye of a cyclone. As his arms flung out in mad parabolic gestures, one hand and then the other grasped the elevator cable. Clinging with a death grip to this, and blessed with the luck of the inebriate, he slid five floors down the cable, to land on top of the elevator, and suffered no more than a couple of hard knocks about the legs and two badly burned palms.

In the after-midnight hours, after Kinney had marked "30—" on the last piece of sports copy, if he didn't hire a hack to carry him three or four hundred yards to the Hotel Eggleston, where he might indulge in a couple of boiled lobsters and two dozen clams, he often returned to Callahan's, where he usually dined, to enjoy a combination supper and breakfast, and imbibe such potions as were necessary to pique his appetite and aid digestive processes. He particularly favored Callahan's after work. It was cozy there, and he sometimes remained until noon. Then to the barber's for a nap, for the barber's ministrations, for a shoeshine. Then to work.

At six o'clock one morning, in the days before the long watch at the *Democrat and Chronicle* was extended to that hour, Charlie Kinney, filled with Callahan's supper and many a distempering draught, was snoozing at a table when John Diprose prodded him in the ribs.

"Wass-a-matter? Wass-er-idear?" Charlie asked sourly, coming half awake.

Diprose, who was one of the bosses in the composing room, told him.

On his way home from work, he saw detectives and uniformed police entering the Chamber of Commerce Building, at the southwest corner of Main Street East and South Avenue, and learned, on inquiry, that the two night watchmen had been bound in the basement by yeggs who had then broken into the jewelry store of Philip Present, on an upper floor of the building, blown a safe with a nitroglycerine charge, and escaped with thousands of dollars' worth of jewels.

Knowing that there was a good chance that Kinney would still be in Callahan's, Diprose hurried into Water Street, gave the after-hour rap, and found his man.

"It's a hell of a story, Charlie," Diprose said excitedly. "You write it, and I'll get back to the shop and have it set."

Kinney was a trouper; a newspaperman to the marrow of his bones. He shook himself a couple of times, rubbed the cobwebs from his eyes and struggled to his feet. Holding him by the arm, Diprose guided him into Water Street and across Main to the Chamber of Commerce Building, where a considerable crowd of the curious had now gathered.

"Kinney, of the *Democrat!*" Charlie pronounced commandingly. Freeing himself from Diprose's guiding hand and bringing what military erectness he could to his permanently stooped shoulders, he hedged through the crowd, obtained the facts of the robbery in ten minutes, wrote a two-column story in little more than half an hour, and the "Extra" that the *Democrat and Chronicle* soon had on the street was hailed as a triumph of newspaper enterprise.

Kinney had been a husband on occasions, but his conjugal relations were sketchy, his marriages were not perdurable, and he wore no miniature portrait of a spouse on his lapel. He herded with members of his own sex, and his haunts such as the Hotel Eggleston, which accepted only male guests, were generally free of feminine influences and refinements. He zealously guarded his sports section from womanly intrusion—it took microscopic searching to discover a woman's name on his pages, and to my recollection a woman's picture appeared there only once. And this concession required something tantamount to a summit conference.

Kid McCoy, the great middleweight boxer and inventor of the corkscrew punch, who had married four or five times, shot one of his wives *dead!* Kinney was an admirer of the Kid, who had been in Rochester with a racing car that he had driven in a time trial on the Kenilworth race track in Buffalo. He had entertained Kinney and me. He was a fascinating figure. He had a card-sharper's craftiness, a sinister handsomeness, and great *savoir-faire*. He had talked to me eruditely at dinner in the Hotel Seneca on the subject of theosophy, of which I knew nothing. For the time being, theosophy, rather than women, was McCoy's *thing*.

"The poor Kid. Aw, the poor Kid," Charlie lamented, when the news of McCoy's arrest came over the wire. "A great fellow. A great pal. A *very* great middleweight."

He got out a picture of the boxer to go with the sensational story of the shooting.

"But what about his wife, the woman he shot," suigested Will Richards, who was helping out on the sports desk. "Ought to run a cut of her, too."

"A woman's mug on my pages!" Kinney bellowed. "On my *sports* pages! Never!"

Richards argued the issue persistently. He appealed to Kinney's sound sense of news values; finally broke his resistance.

"Well, just this once, maybe it's all right," he said, relenting, "since the dame's dead. It ain't as though she's one of those damn women golfers. Or some frail trying to break into the Giants' infield."

So the slain woman's picture was juxtaposed with the picture of the husband who had shot her, but Kinney was queasy and uncomfortable about it. He felt that his consent might have established a dangerous precedent.

The sports editor's brief romantic fling with Miss Pauline came about in this way. Parkhurst Whitney, a handsome, stylish, talented member of the staff, had obtained a job on the New York

Tribune, and his newspaper friends arranged a party in his honor the night before he departed for New York. It was to be held in Callahan's upstairs room after midnight. It was to be all male, of course, but Miss Pauline pleaded, "I want so much to say good-by to dear, dear Parkhurst," and reluctantly her pleas were acceded to.

By inadvertence rather than by design Miss Pauline and Kinney were seated next to each other. There was good food, and a plenitude of liquor, and because it was a festive occasion, or because of Kinney's inherent propensity, he drank a good deal. He had large pale eyes which protruded like the eyes of a huge crab and their tendency was to grow larger and more protuberant as he increased his liquid intake.

He listened quietly to the customary tributes to the guest of honor, quaffed, quaffed, and quaffed again, and now and then leaned to whisper into Miss Pauline's ear. After each of these confidences an angelic smile formed on Miss Pauline's lips, and those of us who were heedful of this unusual intimacy seemed to detect a poetic, a Byronic glint in Charlie's eyes: *He* [had] *sighed to many, though he loved but one.*

The festivities were nearly over when Kinney, supporting himself with one hand on the table top and the other on Miss Pauline's frail shoulder, rose in a fragmentary motion, wobbled precariously, recovered himself, and announced, "Issanhonor for me to tell you, the lil'l lady an' me, we're going t'walk the flowery path of matrimony. We-we're engaged ta-ta . . ." His words died off, and Kinney seemed to die with them. He fell clumsily back in his chair, his mouth agape, and was asleep on the instant.

We crowded round Miss Pauline to extend our felicitations, which she accepted with modest blushes and confusions, while Kinney slept, now noisily (he snored!). The party ended, and Charlie was removed in a hack.

When he arrived in the office, in the full light of day, shaved to the blood, powdered, brushed, smelling heavily of cologne, and his shoes highly polished, he hadn't even a palimpsestic remembrance of the troth he had pledged only a few hours before. It took some doing to talk himself out of a situation that for a time portended litigation, a breach of promise suit. The matter, however, did not reach that pass; soon the disenchanted, heart-hurt assistant on the vicinity desk packed up and left. Kinney was not at the station to wave her a fond good-by.

Chapter 20

Although his appearance, his no-nonsense manner, and his brief, directly-to-the-point talk should have discredited the notion that there was anything arcane or mysterious in the make-up of Morris Adams, some of us who worked for him had the feeling that he was clairvoyant.

When I first knew him, Mr. Adams lived in the Davenport Apartments at the corner of East Avenue and Broadway, but whether he walked to and from the apartments and the newspaper or rode in a cab or on a streetcar I never knew. I rarely saw him on the street, and when I did, he was always about to enter the newspaper building. His long office routine seemed to absorb his life. He was not a theatergoer. He never attended political rallies, social gatherings, sporting events, concerts, Chamber of Commerce luncheons, or art exhibits. Yet his knowledge of Rochester and its people was more precise and detailed than that of the reporters whom he assigned to write about various aspects of the city and to report on the activities of its citizens. Occasionally a reporter, diverted during the evening hours from the true course of duty, would fake a story rather than return to the office empty-handed, but the fiction never escaped the perspicacious eye of the city editor. If the contrived piece was sufficiently entertaining, he might tolerate its being printed, but he never failed to let the author know that he had not been taken in by it. His omniscience astonished us, and we credited it to a preternatural gift.

He encouraged colorful writing. He liked humorous and human-interest pieces. But these were the embroidery, the ornaments of his pages. Hard-core news—not the sob story, not a recipe for mocha cake or apple strudel, or a pediatrician's suggestion about little Willie's bed wetting—was the soul and essence of the newspaper, and Mr. Adams insisted that the facts represented in a news story be checked and checked again against error. I recall hearing him summon to his desk a reporter who had handed in a piece of copy stating that ever since the beginning of the century George Eastman had employed more workers than any other Rochester industrialist.

"Better do some research on this," Mr. Adams said, returning the copy to the reporter. "A few years ago it wasn't Eastman, but his next-door neighbor, who was the town's largest employer."

"His next-door neighbor? Who's he?" the reporter asked wonderingly.

"Lucius W. Robinson. Around 1902-3, and possibly later, he had about twelve thousand workers on his payroll. Eastman, at that time, had about two thousand."

The reporter's ignorance was not surprising. Mr. Robinson was unknown to a great many people in Rochester. His name rarely appeared in the local newspapers. He engaged in no civic enterprises. Here, by his own design, his lights were pretty well hidden under a bushel, and he may have been better known in moneyed circles in Palm Beach and New York than in the city in which he lived.

Robinson was the head man of possibly the most important nexus of bituminous mine operations in America, which he directed from the offices of the Rochester & Pittsburgh Coal & Iron Company (a unit in a multifarious combine) in the building of the Buffalo, Rochester & Pittsburgh Railroad, in Main Street West. He was also president of the Adrian Furnace Company, the Reynoldsville & Falls Creek Railroad, the Rural Valley Railroad, and the National Bank of Punxsutawney, Pennsylvania.

In one sense, of course, he was not a Rochester employer. The payrolls of some of the various companies he served as president were made up here, and part of the money came from Rochester banks. But his contribution to the local economy was negligible. Here he maintained only an executive cadre. The operating offices of most of his companies, and the employees of these companies were located in the bituminous region of western Pennsylvania, which Robinson frequently visited, traveling over the roadbed of the Buffalo, Rochester & Pittsburgh in his private railroad car, as became an industrial nabob of his stature.

The Robinson dwelling in East Avenue, which stood immediately to the north of Mr. Eastman's residence, was a replica of a famous house in Florence, Italy. It was constructed of yellow brick, which was trimmed with carved stone of a color lighter than the brick. Reputedly the only wholly fireproof house in town, its walls were so dense that an electric drill was needed to bore a hole for a picture hook. It was not as large as the showy Eastman mansion, but its interior and its gardens were more elaborate. It was three stories high, and a ballroom extended across the front of the upper floor. The house was fronted by an eight- or ten-foot iron fence, with an iron gate, which gave it a fortresslike security and more exclusiveness than any other dwelling on the Avenue.

Mr. Robinson was a handsome, beautifully tailored man, who on occasion carried a gold-headed walking stick. He was a Yale Sheffield graduate. His industrial life was extremely active; his private life in Rochester luxurious but so quiet that his name was only lightly impressed upon the proud lexicon of the city's ultra-affluent. Yet Mr. Eastman once remarked during a Community Chest drive, "Someone go see my neighbor Robinson. He has more money than I have." When Robinson died, at the age of seventy-nine, three years after his lonely and despairing little neighbor had taken his own life among the rich trappings of his museumlike pile, the obituaries in the newspapers told that he was considered one of the most successful mine operators in America and "rated among the richest if not actually the wealthiest citizen in Rochester."

He indulged his two attractive daughters and his son, equally dividing among them—according to rumor that had the earmark of validity—three million dollars, as each issue reached the age of twenty-one. When Florence, the older daughter, married the popular Fred H. Gordon, of Brockport, the pair left Rochester for New York on the first leg of a European honeymoon aboard Mr. Robinson's private railroad car, the Ruth deMoss, named after his wife.

Later, during the 1910–11 holiday season, the Robinsons' younger daughter, Ruth, "came out" at a party in the Genesee Valley Club (then located at East Avenue and Gibbs Street), which was a bench mark in social entertainment until, possibly taking a cue from his next-door neighbors, George Eastman staged a New Year's ball that had the dazzle, the pomp, and the magnitude of a Versailles soiree at the height of the Sun King's glory.

But the earlier affair, which caused a few reasonably well-informed Rochesterians to wonder where this bounteous host and hostess had been hiding, was superbly arranged. The Robinsons were sophisticated people, and their party for Miss Ruth was a striking departure from the clubby, pleasant but rather provincial entertainments that had been given in the past by persons whose names were apotheosized in Miss Emily Munn's Saturday column in the *Post Express*. The Robinsons had no sense of trying to keep up with the (Rochester) Joneses. Indifferent to this sort of competition, without striving, they ran beyond them.

A decorative scheme that involved lighting, floral, and stage effects, and that included a raised fountain at one end of the ballroom, so completely transformed the appearance of the Genesee Valley Club that members avowed that all that remained to give identification to their own building were the stalls, the washbasins, and the towel racks of the lavatories. The spectacle was continually exclaimed over; nothing quite like it had ever been seen in town before.

Dinner was served at the beginning of the evening, and the exquisiteness of the food complemented the beauty of the decorations. Dancing continued until five o'clock the next morning, with Herman Dossenbach's orchestra, the presence of which was *de rigueur* at a function of this character, alternating with a Negro band which Mr. Robinson had fetched, for the night, from the Hotel Poinciana at Palm Beach.

At dawn, with tables set for breakfast and a fresh copy of the *Democrat and Chronicle* laid at each place, the guests enjoyed eggs, bacon, pancakes, and other breakfast viands as gaily attired black performers pranced about the tables, belting out popular songs. This was a party to outdo all other Rochester parties; and so it was considered by those who attended until Mr. Eastman's gargantuan "do" gave festive welcome to the new year of 1914, which was to end in the cataclysm of world war and bring an end to a way of life whose vestigial traces remain only in the memories of an extinguishing race whose members were born in another century.

I was a guest at the Robinson party; I was not asked to Mr. Eastman's grand fete. Neither were the thoroughly eligible W. Peck Farleys, whose omission from the list must have been owing to a prejudice on the part of the gray-haired dynasty (a junto of eager ladies who had arrogated to themselves Eastman's social mentorship) who had helped compile it. Peck Farley was one of the gayest, wittiest, and most attractive young men in town.

"I'm sorry we weren't asked to Mr. Eastman's," Farley said, when he learned that the invitations were out, "I was thinking of buying the house."

Somehow the remark reached the host, and Mr. and Mrs. Farley belatedly received an engraved card soliciting their presence at the ball.

Though the invitation had come secondhand, the occasion was not one to slight. The Farleys appeared for this Arabian Night's entertainment, duly passed through a *cordon sanitaire* formed by a detail of Rochester police, found a place in the line of twelve hundred guests who were received by Mr. Eastman and a small group of beautifully attired feminine coadjutors, who now and then pronounced the name of some guest which the industrialist may never have heard before. As the Farleys came to Mr. Eastman, the cold eyes of the host, behind their steel-rimmed spectacles, gave the faintest indication of a twinkle, and his tight lips relaxed. But his voice was firm.

"I want you to take a very, v-e-r-y good look around, Farley," he said. "I want you to see everything. We'll discuss price later."

Usually deft in repartee, Peck Farley, in this instance, was reduced to an incoherent mumbling, and he was happy to escape from the line.

Winfred J. Smith, who for years had been entrusted with the arrangements of fashionable weddings, debutante parties, and other large social affairs, was the major domo at Mr. Eastman's party, and Isaac Teale, the town's top caterer, prepared the food. Smith was to be paid $1,000. The host, pleased with Smith's management, added a bonus to his set fee. His check read $1,200. Teale was less fortunate. Eastman's microscopic attention to detail was the bane of all under his authority who attempted to scrimp, short-cut, or make do with so-so efforts when his perennial quest was for perfection. Probably inadvertently, for the caterer was a man of high repute in the community, Teale failed to provide the musicians with the supper that had been contracted for. When Eastman discovered the delinquency, he required Teale to make an allowance of $1 per meal, and the money was given to the underfed musicians.

Large as the great Georgian house at 900 East Avenue was, it was inadequate for the accommodation of such a concourse of guests, and two large temporary buildings, one a dance pavilion, the other a refectory, had been erected in the space between the house and the garage. All four buildings were connected by passageways, and the garage, as well as the other three, was a unit in the festive compound. Here, in the delightful setting of a wisteria garden, steamfitters, carpenters, plumbers, painters, florists, all who had contributed their skills and energies to the success of the ball, and their wives were entertained as sumptuously as the other guests and invited to mingle among them.

Thousands of dollars had been spent on the floral scheme. Daffodils, pink roses, smilax, wisteria, and hundreds of American Beauties were arranged about the buildings. Bottled champagne was the drink of the evening. On a platform raised about the dance floor seventy musicians were ensconced in a bower of cut flowers. In later years programs of chamber music were to become a twice-weekly custom in Eastman's home and something of an ordeal for unmusical guests who dared not decline what was tantamount to a command invitation. On the night of the ball for the first and second last time (a party for youth was given before the decorations were dismantled and the temporary buildngs razed) the corridors and chaste chambers of Eastman House resounded with such rackety dance tunes as "Ramshackle Rag," "Snooky Ookums," "Hitchy-Koo," and "When the Midnight Choo-Choo Leaves for Alabam'."

There was criticism of the Eastman party, but it did not come from hair-shirted social reformers or in loud salvos from the working classes who, a few years before, might have inveighed bitterly against the staggering prodigality of the affair. George Eastman was hardly a candidate for a popularity contest. He was secretly envied and whisperingly deprecated by rigid formalists in Rochester's tight little social hierarchy as *nouveau riche*. There were those in town who seriously believed they had gained through the transmission of chromosomes a more noble spirit than their fellow men and that the wealth they had inherited set them apart from those who had struggled and toiled to achieve affluence. Eastman with his new wealth was a parvenu; they forgot that the founders of the wealth they themselves enjoyed must once have been parvenus.

Labor leaders hated Eastman because of their failure to invade his plant; the rank and file of labor had no love for him. But the antipathy once held for him by many of his thousands of employees had been softened by evidence of a change in their employer's attitude toward themselves.

From the start, Eastman had never worked with any other than sovereign aims. His early career had been ruthlessly dedicated to the advancement of his company and there was widespread belief that the workers who were necessary to the furtherance of his ambition to control the photographic industry of the world were no more to him than the cogs and wheels and belts and ratchets of his factories. Now he had paused in his relentless pursuit of success; he had raised his head and glanced about. "It is only recently," he wrote to a Chicago industrialist, inquiring about a pension plan, "that I have waked to the realization that men are growing old in the company's service."

The essence of decency was deep in Eastman, and the observation had disturbed his conscience. Tentatively, at first; then studiously and carefully, he had in the recent past inaugurated a program of employee benefits which would expand under his direction and under the direction of such splendid and humane company officers as Frank J. Lovejoy and Marion B. Folsom until Eastman employees would be put in the happy condition of being the most cosseted and paternally protected wage earners in America.

In 1914, the year of Mr. Eastman's ball, many Rochester businesses were booming. The shoe and clothing industries, which had once been dominant in towns, beset though they were by labor troubles, were still important to the Rochester economy; there was the fine old German firm of Bausch & Lomb, which had begun the manufacture of optical goods before the Civil War and which had now added a diversified line of scientific instruments; there was the Gleason Works, never intensely publicized, but known the world over for its gear-making machinery; there were companies which produced furniture, typewriter supplies, beer vats, dental equipment, pharmaceutical dosages, fancy road vehicles—the list of light industries was extensive—and there was Haloid, a little photographic paper business hidden away on a back street which, under the new name of Xerox, would in coming years be hailed with glad high cries by astute investors as the Second Coming of Eastman.

Rochester was not wanting in industrial successes, but now it was acknowledged that the Eastman Company was the caryatid that gave chief support to the city's economy, and the wag spoke only partly in jest, who said:

"Take Eastman out of town, and they can put a sign on the New York Central Station, 'This *was* Rochester.'"

George Eastman had not yet become the Maecenas who would lend patronage to long-haired musicians, barefoot dancing girls, and opera divas in embryo. He was sixty years old. He would be four years older before he would consent to take leadership in a campaign to raise millions for Rochester's war chest. Other years would pass before he would build the most beautiful theater in America for the delight of the local public, contribute vast millions to the advancement of higher education and the promotion of medical science, and exert a political influence, fortified with coin of the realm, to bring about a radical alteration in the city's system of government.

At the beginning of 1914 the Kodak magnate was generally recognized as the big man of town, and Eastman haters to the contrary, not a few of his fellow townsmen were proud to know that one of their own was capable of throwing a party of the Promethean magnificence of Eastman's ball, and on the night of the festival a gallery assembled on the far sidewalk opposite 900 East Avenue to enjoy a vicarious sense of participation and to observe the arrival of the brilliantly attired guests.

A fresh fall of snow lay over the broad estate and the immaculateness of the soft white covering was emphasized by the beams of an artificial moon that was fixed in the upper branches of an elm tree and by numerous floodlights that were spotted about the grounds. Hundreds of small colored incandescent bulbs twinkled among the green vines which interlaced the façade of the house. Guests reached the massive front door through a marquee hedged inside with boxwood.

For Eastman himself, the grand ball may have been short of a rewarding experience. He was never happy at public appearances, and his place in the receiving line was a little like the platform position of a candidate at a political rally. He was reserved among strangers, and many of his guests were strangers. His role was that of the gracious host, and he made the effort to master it; but there were times as the evening advanced when his smile was a painted thing and his gestures of cordiality had the geometric jerkiness of a clockwork doll.

The New Year revelers swarmed over Eastman's house like Cook trippers. They admired with "o-o-o-oh's and a-a-a-ah's" of wonder its vastness and the perfection of its arrangements. They were awed by the prodigality of bathrooms. Even those who had come, as some members of the snootier older families had come, with an attitude of condescension toward this newly risen Midas, were impressed. It would have been difficult not to have been. Eastman had no instinct for the showy or the ostentatious; but this night he had stepped out of character to show the town what he could do in the grand style when he really put his back into it.

Indifferent to the punctilios of Rochester society, Eastman had created a schism in the ranks of the hierarchy by opposing his own New Year's Eve ball to the traditional one that for years had been given in the ballroom of the huge house of Mr. and Mrs. Warham Whitney, on South Goodman Street.

The Whitney ball bore no resemblance to a fireman's carnival. Hundreds of persons did not come to it, but those who did come were very well known to the host and hostess. It had a *fin de siècle* elegance. Mrs. Whitney led Rochester society. It was an institution of Edwardian forms and rigid dimensions, and these would be preserved until the joint effort of all Americans to win the First World War would bring about an interfusion of the classes and lower the barriers that seperated them. But now we were at peace and the old forms and dimensions prevailed. Mr. Whitney was old Rochester. He was world traveled. He had been a big game hunter. He had a grace and worldliness which he wore like a natural integument. Warham Whitney was a familiar in fashionable places in the East where Eastman was known only as a factory.

There were names on Eastman's guest list that only by the art of forgery could have gotten on the Whitneys'. But most of the people invited by the Whitneys also had received Eastman's card. Since the invitations had crossed in the mail, a choice was necessary. Some felt that if this new glamour boy (as some were fancying the sixty-year old industrialist) had decided to take over the social leadership of the town his great wealth would allow him to bring off the coup, and those who were not above expediency thought it better to align themselves with his camp rather than with that of the traditionalists. Others were not so sure. There was the risk that if they declined the Whitney card in favor of Eastman's the vengeance of Mrs. Whitney might render them social pariahs.

Some wriggled free of the impaling horns of a dilemma, regretted both invitations, and fled town.

Those who truly wore the cordon had no qualms of indecision. They were indomitably committed to the Whitneys. If this was a challenge from an insolent pretender, there would be no division of loyalty, no retreat. The Old Guard would meet the attack on the barricades. The coterie rallied round Warham and Fanny Whitney. The ball went on in a much smaller ballroom than Eastman's and the Whitney guests danced to an orchestra of far fewer pieces than the one that played for the swarming throng at 900 East Avenue. There was a belief that Eastman had actually taken over and some of his guests who had never succeeded in "crashing" the Whitney parties exulted is what they believed was the rout of the old regime.

But one grand ball was enough for Eastman, who had no aspirations to pose as a cotillion leader, and many who had attended his New Year party were never again asked to his house. And some of his guests who had defected from the Whitneys and had failed to impress their multimillionaire host found themselves in a sort of social no man's land.

Arnold Bennett's remark about Proust that he was not self-conscious, but rather "well aware of himself," might in part have been applied to George Eastman. In its extremity, his self-awareness sometimes led him into arrogance. When he installed an organ in his house, the first musician engaged to play the instrument while Eastman bathed, shaved, and ate his breakfast was George Fisher, a local church organist and piano teacher. Fisher had been on the job several months and presumably was giving satisfactory service when one morning Eastman left the breakfast table to enter the room where the musician sat at the console. Fisher stopped playing and turned on the organ bench.

"Good morning, Mr. Eastman," he said genially.

There was no cordiality in Eastman's cold eyes.

"It is customary," he said flatly, "for my servants to stand when they talk to me."

Fisher was a man of spirit. He rose from the bench, not in deference but in anger. "I am not your servant," he said stoutly. "I don't consider myself a servant. I'm a musician. An artist."

Eastman turned, without another word, and left the room.

"I sat down on the bench, trembling with anger, and some

fear," Fisher told me. "I expected Mr. Eastman would return with his butlers and his barn men and have me pitched out of a window. He came back in about fifteen minutes. He gave me some instructions about what he wanted played the next day, when he was having guests for breakfast, and again abruptly left. I continued to play for him for several months, but our relations, when we occasionally met, were the least strained. He could be difficult—arrogant, at times."

The Brahmins of the town considered that Eastman had been gross, ill-mannered, and arrogant in flouting the traditions by offering his party in competition with *the* New Year's ball, and there were some who never forgave him. But there was no open quarrel at first, only a hairline split in the social order. The crack widened to an unbridgeable chasm later on. The story is that during a war or a Community Chest campaign, which Eastman headed, Mrs. Whitney, who had not yet been solicited for a contribution, sent a check for several thousand dollars, which Eastman returned with a curt announcement that the amount of the check was insufficient. Mrs. Whitney may have torn up the check and stomped upon it, as it is said that she did. In any event, Eastman became for her and her intimates an anathema. She had a considerable talent for invective and she exercised it fully. One evening when hundreds of men and women in full fig were on their way to a performance in the Eastman Theater of the Metropolitan Opera Company, at which it was expected that Mr. Eastman, faultlessly attired and perhaps wearing the skull cap he had recently affected as a protection against drafts, would attend, I encountered Mrs. Whitney (then Mrs. Clarence R. Smith, for she had remarried after her first husband's death) in the lobby of the Sheraton Hotel. The hotel is a block from the theater.

"Well, I suppose you're going to the Met," I said.

"I am *not*," she said, emphatically. "I'll never set foot in that theater so long as that damn old man's alive."

That was a long time ago, and Rochester was not so hard-pressed as it is at present by the problems of crime, municipal financing, housing, traffic, drugs, racial dissent, welfare, and school disturbances, and a small bloodless vendetta such as the Whitney (Smith)-Eastman quarrel made amusing gossip and gave a fillip to urban life. Today it would be an issue of no meaning or interest.

Rochester has become complex, its close-knittedness is gone, its days of innocence are passed, and it has lost the provincial ambiance that once made it such a very pleasant place in which to live.

Chapter 21

Try though I have to temper the fancy, by attributing it to sentiment and nostalgia, the impression persists that the finest time to have been alive in the city of Rochester was during the ten- or twelve-year period that immediately preceded our entrance into World War I. The big change came after President Wilson renounced his earlier thesis that we were "too proud to fight" and committed us on that fateful April day in 1917 to the conflagration that raged over Europe. The ethos of the entire nation was changed by the war; in Rochester it violated our innocence and destroyed the snug provincialism we had so long enjoyed.

Rochester hadn't become in the approximate eighty years that it had had a city charter precisely a paragon among municipalities, but its unhurried growth, its mellowed maturity, and its grace made it for a great many of us a very comfortable place in which to live. We were envied by outsiders, who strove to anatomize our civic character. They knew that we lived under a sort of benevolent autocracy: the one-man rule of George W. Aldridge. But those who studied our political situation discovered that while ours was one of the most completely bossed cities in the United States, its people were among the most contented of city dwellers.

A Bridgeport, Connecticut, newspaper said of us: "Next to Detroit [this in an era before that city experienced the megalopolitan influences of the motor industry], Rochester is reputed to be the most beautiful city in the country. Its park systems, clean streets, police and fire departments are all magnificently efficient and the credit for this construction properly belongs to Mr. Aldridge."

Our city in those days was indeed a pretty blooming little place, and while it had its sink holes and mephitic swales, its brutalities and its areas of soddenness; and though we lightly tolerated the employment of children in the shops of subcontractors in the garment district, where they toiled long hours under deplorable conditions for an unholy weekly wage, there was brightness, cheer, and amiability over the greater part of town.

Our population was approaching a quarter of a million.

Capital invested, $95,708,000.

Tax levy (1915), $4,457,946.16

Tax rate (1914), 14.3.

We had more than fifty hotels (of sorts), nine hospitals, eight theaters (excluding motion picture houses). We were served by seven steam railroads. We produced more high-class ivory buttons, more thermometers, and more typewriter ribbons and carbon paper than any other city in the country. Our Chamber of Commerce, not yet established in the million-dollar headquarters Mr. Eastman would build for it, was a booming agency. It was directed by its secretary Roland B. Woodward, who could charm the birdies off the trees. Mr. Woodward was a plenipotentiary extraordinary for Rochester business and industry; he was so smooth, it was said, that a fly lighting on him would slip and break its leg. He and other high-pressure boosters were striving with no small success to make Rochester a convention city.

Our mayor was Uncle Hi.

He had mustachios and an imperial beard, a big round comfortable belly, a wardrobe that complemented his avuncular character, and a deftness at fondling little children whose daddies were needed in the Republican rolls at election time. He was Hiram H. Edgerton. He skittered all over town in a one-lung Cadillac roadster, red as a fire cart, and prodigal of burnished brass. It was the best-known vehicle in Rochester. "Here comes Uncle Hi!" the constituency would cry, when he chug-chugged into a neighborhood, and they'd run to the curb to pay their homage. He was homely and familiar. The constituency considered Mayor Edgerton one of their own. He went to ribbon cuttings, clambakes, grand openings, testimonial dinners, beauty pageants, water carnivals, and political barn-raisings. He was in the center of the reviewing stand on parade days. He opened Rochester's famous Horse Show, and threw out the ball at the opening of the baseball season. In his little red car, brakes taut, Uncle Hi descended the tortuous way from the plateau above the Newport House on Irondequoit Bay on the day of the supervisors' picnic, when George Aldridge, taking his traditional stance under the bayside willows, shook hands with thousands of the faithful and imperatorially designated his candidates for the coming election.

Uncle Hi adored the Big Fellow, the epithet commonly applied to Aldridge. Perhaps "worshiped" is the word. They had been firm friends for many years. When Aldridge died on a Westchester County golf course, and his body was removed to Rochester to lie in state in the foyer of the Monroe County Court House, the critically ill Edgerton left his bed to gaze for the last time on the face of his beloved chieftain. "Good-by—good-by, old pal, my heart is broken," he sobbed. He was led from the bier, and returned to his bed. He died four days later. "Pals to the End," is the caption of a photograph of the two men that makes the most conspicuous adornment in Republican headquarters.

Today Rochesterians talk little about George Aldridge. When he is mentioned at all, he is lightly passed off as a political anachronism. But people on the outside, who are concerned with the political history of the country, particularly as it pertains to municipal government, attest a continuing interest in the Big Fellow, and the feeling among some of these students is that a close review of his career has increased rather than lessened his stature as a political leader.

He was shrewd and wise, and while politics always came first with him (and though in an earlier day he had been singularly callous in his exploitation of the school system), Aldridge managed astonishingly well to keep his complex organization in line, the city on an even keel, and its people happier than the residents of many other communities of comparable size. We knew that we were bossed, but the knowledge of this was not oppressive; we felt that we were competently bossed, and thus relieved of a good deal of civic responsibility. We had an affection for our mayor, Uncle Hi. We applauded him; we thought that he did us well.

Aldridge had tried other mayors. To satisfy a clique of persistent and prominent men who were genuinely interested in good government, he had put James G. Cutler into office. Cutler was a man of wealth, of social position, of culture. He possessed inventive (he had invented, and he manufactured the Cutler mail chute which was used throughout the country) and business talents. His achievements in two terms of office may have surpassed those of any other mayor the city has known. But he thought for himself. His administrative actions were performed without consultation with the Big Fellow, and at the expiration of his second term, Cutler was out of the job. Hiram Edgerton succeeded him.

Uncle Hi would stand without hitching. His "Yes, George," was a reflex.

* * *

Hiram Edgerton was the town's pet; George Aldridge was its hero image.

As the epithet implied, Aldridge was a Big Fellow. He had huge shoulders and a large head and a prominent well-formed nose—the nose of a conqueror. His hands and feet were large. His legs, in their careful tailoring, were as solid as concrete snubbing posts. Always a formidable figure, he was particularly so in anger. Then his lips curved down like the inverted blade of a scimitar. And the laser beam intensity of his blue eyes, said men who had encountered his anger, would melt steel welds.

Aldridge was a man of moods and some of his moods were less pleasant than others. He was troubled by a weakness for drink, and once he succumbed, his carousels often developed into episodes of wantonness and violence. In his visits to New York, he sometimes tore apart the barroom of the hotel in which he made his headquarters. The bills for his depredations were forwarded to moneyed friends in Rochester who paid without demur and who granted full grace to the Big Fellow upon his return to town. In Rochester, if he became inordinately fractious, he was taken into protective custody by Captain William H. Whaley, of the Detective Bureau, or by two detectives Whaley trusted to act with patience, tact, and discretion. Until his tantrum quieted, he would be held incommunicado in a suite in Powers Hotel or cached in a comfortable cell in the Monroe County Jail.

Wenching occasionally was a corollary of his drinking. On his trips "down the line," he went only to one house, Maud Gordon's at 52 Hill Street. Madame Gordon was the *grande dame* of the red light district. Her custom included many men from prominent Rochester families, including one gay blade (closely allied with old-line banking interests) whose conceit was to "pay his dues," not with folding money, but with silver coins, which he dropped through a slit in a large metal drum which was kept especially for his use and brought out only on the occasions of his visits.

There was a ritual to Aldridge's amorous excursions. One of his friends and stanch supporters was E. M. Higgins, whose North Fitzhugh Street livery stable was the largest in town. But no hack from Higgins' ever carried the Big Fellow into Hill Street. The equipage for this purpose came only from Frank Payne's Jefferson Avenue livery and the hackman was either Timothy Foran or John Murphy, each of whom was noted, as were Captain Whaley's men, for discretion.

Aldridge now and then made a shambles of one of Maud Gordon's rooms, but the mistress of the establishment was tolerant and forgiving. The damage he caused was always mysteriously paid for. His favorite was Little Annie, and his power and prestige, and his prodigality—before surfeit soured and brutalized his temper—made him a desirable patron. When the segregated district was closed, following a rash of conventions during the summer of 1911—a summer, as someone remarked, notorious for the prevalence of loose women and boozy convention delegates—the story was that Aldridge had ordered the "line" shut down to avenge the loss of a cherished heirloom in Madame Gordon's. It was an absurd canard. Maud Gordon would never have remained at the same stand so long as she had, had her practice been to "roll" patrons. And none of her guests would have been more carefully tended than the Big Fellow. Aldridge did not order the closing of Hill Street, but he did not oppose it. It had become the fashion at that period to stamp out red light districts, and Rochester went along with the mode. The leading ladies of Hill Street, several of whom had become citizens of substance (one had educated a nephew who subsequently filled an important post in the Board of Education) retired; the starlets of the houses left Rochester or, in some instances, moved across the river to the Fourth Ward, which was very firmly controlled by a liege lord who, paradoxically, granted wide permissiveness to his subjects.

Rochester and, indeed, the county of Monroe was pretty solidly Republican. The small states, or wards, of the city, even when represented by Democratic aldermen were generally sympathetic to the Big Fellow. One of Aldridge's political skills was proselytism. When he appointed a Democrat to the first or police department he made sure that the appointee was replete with male kinsmen of voting age. The relatives shared with the appointee a sense of gratitude. They frequently became known as Aldridge Democrats. There were hundreds, possibly thousands, of these tacit converts in Rochester. They helped suture the lesions of party differences; they strengthened the sinews and gave new blood to Aldridge's political organism.

There were large wards that made great waves of Republican votes on election day. One of these was the Nineteenth, in the southwest section of the city, which was led by Joseph C. Wilson, a downtown pawnbroker, whose family got hold of the little Haloid Company, the chrysalis from which Xerox emerged, and whose grandson and namesake became board chairman of that mighty enterprise; another was the upper middle-class Tenth Ward, in a northwest section of town, which was managed with high skill by an alert, bristling little lawyer named Charles E. (Clip) Bostwick.

Wilson was a man of noted integrity, unshowy, quiet, and able, who kept his ward in line seemingly without effort. The city's general trust in him resulted later in his being elected comptroller and then mayor of Rochester.

Bostwick was a politician of a different stamp. He had played football on one of the earliest teams to represent the University of Rochester and he brought his gridiron combativeness into the courts of law and into the arena of municipal politics. He was studiously picturesque. He appeared to dress as carelessly as a cowherd. He wore a disreputable fedora with a loose brim that flapped over his eyes. He was amusing, witty, sharp. Some of his constituency held him in contempt but continued to lend him their support because of his unquestioned talent for leadership. His law practice was closely related to his politics. What he failed to achieve for a client in court he sometimes managed to accomplish by extralegal proceedings. With Clip Bostwick the saying was "The fix is in."

He was an irritant, a burr in the flesh of George W. Aldridge, whom he heartily disliked. He was jealous of the Big Fellow's pomp, prominence, and power. Bostwick believed that he himself could manage better the Grand Old Party of Monroe County. He fought the boss hard and often. He once attempted to wrest the county chairmanship form Aldridge, failed—failed at the time conspicuously—but years later, after Aldridge's death, he gained the post that earlier had been denied him.

Bostwick and Joseph Wilson were two of the most successful precinct bosses in Rochester, but they—and all other Republican and Democratic ward leaders—compared to the suzerainty exercised in the old Fourth by James T. O.'Grady, were virtually in their political nonage.

The Fourth was O'Grady's fief, indisputably, once he inherited it from William C. Craig, a former leader, who moved up South Avenue hill to become superintendent of the Monroe County penitentiary, and batten richly off this political preferment.

I recall, as an ingenuous young reporter, bringing into the *Democrat and Chronicle* newsroom a story that cited the considerable police record O'Grady had acquired as a member of a tough canal crowd known as the Weighlock Gang. The history of his malefactions had been dredged up by a citizen who scoffed at Rochester's "best governed city" boast when the city tolerated a ward leader who had often fallen into the toils of the law and who reputedly bought up votes and voted floaters all over the district under his control. The O'Grady story had come to me on Morris Adams' day off. The assistant city editor Curtis W. Barker read it and shook his head wryly.

"This is all true," he admitted. "But the colonel and Mr. Matthews wouldn't like it."

I question very much if Colonel Pond or Mr. Matthews had ever met O'Grady. I doubt, indeed, if the finicky Mr. Matthews would have consented even to have touched him with the tip of his umbrella. But O'Grady was becoming an important factor in Republican politics and a valued aid to Boss Aldridge; because of this he had become, by the criterion of the newspaper publishers, an "untouchable."

Jimmy O'Grady was a native of the Fourth Ward; there he lived all his life, and there he died. His aspirations did not transcend the narrow compass of the Fourth, which reached through the heart of town to Main Street East and took in the busiest stretch of Clinton Avenue South. He lived on Chestnut Street. There was a quip about Chestnut Street as it related to members of the gentler sex who resided in that thoroughfare. "Is she a lady? Or does she live on Chestnut Street?" In old city directories, O'Grady's occupation is listed as "inspector." The term is not qualified.

268

He was an inspector extraordinary. He had a microscopic familiarity with every square foot of the ward and he knew its people as if they were members of his family. He knew their weaknesses and their strengths, and he was conversant with their needs. Baskets of food would be laid on doorsteps Christmas morning for families that without these donations would be wanting in holiday cheer. Fuel was supplied for those with empty coal bins; a doctor would be aroused in the night to attend a child who seemed dying of pneumonia. At the time of O'Grady's death, Joseph Malone, the most astute political reporter in Rochester, wrote, ". . . he had a power out of all proportion to the geographic size and population of his field. Republicans, Socialists, Democrats, all partisans, became alike to O'Grady. Other ward leaders, hiding envy with an assumption of contempt, attempted to imitate his measures. But they had neither his conditions to deal with nor his skill and insight."

Albert (Barney) Levine, who served as a deputy in the civil branch of the Monroe County sheriff's office for more than thirty years, started his political career under O'Grady. He was a precocious politician.

"I met O'Grady the first year I voted," Levine said. "When I was twelve. I was selling papers and knocking around downtown.

"Jake Carey, and O'Grady and some other fellows had the fight club, the Flower City A.C. The bouts were held Monday nights in the old Genesee Hall, on South Avenue. That was the roller rink. Joe Chipp was going to fight Mike Gibbons. I wanted the checkroom privilege.

"'Go see Jim O'Grady,'" they told me.

"'Where?'" I asked.

"They told me he'd be in Jim Readeron's saloon in State Street. I saw him there. I told him my name and what I wanted. He brushed me off. As I was leaving, he put two fingers between his lips and whistled. 'Come back, Barney,' he said, speaking what was not my name (he called me Barney ever after), 'you can have it.'

"Naturally, after that," Levine continued, "I voted just as Jimmy told me. That first election day, he put a hard hat on my head and wrapped me up in one of Bill Craig's old overcoats and told me to go to the Stone Street firehouse and vote. Republican! Bill Craig was a very big man. I must have looked like a fellow going to run in a sack race. I voted when I was twelve, thirteen, fourteen, fifteen in the Stone Street firehouse. I used any name Jim gave me. There were inspectors in the firehouse wearing Democratic badges. Hell, the badges didn't mean a thing. They were all O'Grady's boys.

O'Grady and Albert H. (Al) Skinner, who had a patent on the sheriff's office, returning to it year after year after year, always with the largest vote given any candidate on the Republican ticket, are the heroes in Albert Levine's pantheon. Skinner, Levine said, was so rigidly ethical that he wouldn't take even a free ticket to the ball park; O'Grady, for his part, seemed to feel that neither government nor any other institution should coerce his private conscience.

Al Levine recalled Bill Lawson's proprietorship of the Home Plate, the most conspicuous resort in a line of dives in South Avenue that continued with a few interruptions from Main Street East to Court Street. The Home Plate derived its name from an imposing display of baseball memorabilia, some of which went back to the era when the first bounce was out. The place had another claim to distinction. At the tag end of his tempestuous career, the great Grover Cleveland Alexander, who pitched 374 winning games in the National League, briefly served there as a bartender. Lawson alternated barmen with barmaids. He put the latter in expansive decollete and set the draught beer spigots well below the surface of the bar.

Politically, Bill Lawson was one of O'Grady's handymen. He had seven rooms upstairs. One election day, thirty or thirty-five residents voted out of the Home Plate.

An election inspector came to inquire how so many lodgers were accommodated in so few rooms.

"Why, apple pickers live here," Lawson blandly explained. "They don't like beds. They curl up and sleep on the stairs."

In the mellowing, twilight years of his career, O'Grady decided that he'd like the dignity of elective office, and proposed himself as a candidate for supervisor. His acceptance was automatic: Republicans, Democrats, Socialists, and even members of the Law Enforcement Party warmly supported him in the primaries. He met only token opposition on election day, and cakewalked to victory.

He defected a couple of times from the Grand Old Party. A few years after Rochester had adopted a city manager charter, C. Arthur Poole, the current incumbent, snootily remarked that he didn't need support from the Fourth Ward. Poole was soon relieved by Theodore C. Briggs, who was lent to public service by the Lawyers Cooperative Publishing Company, of which he was one of the able heads. Briggs was old Rochester; he was a Princetonian. He had courage and ideals. But he knew very little about O'Grady's political pragmatism; he gave no heed to the latter's petition for patronage, and he too was soon out of office.

O'Grady was nettled by these rebuffs. One night, with Al Levine, his confidant, his fidus Achates and his chauffeur, he rode about town all night and came at dawn to a decision. He had searched his soul, and changed his politics. At the next election he threw the Fourth Ward over to the Democrats, which he could do standing on his head in a corner blind-folded, and the Democratic Party gained control of both the Board of Supervisors and the City Council. They also captured the Monroe County sheriffdom, a phenomenon not unlike the discovery in a county park of a whooping crane. O'Grady of course hadn't brought the coup off himself; but his loyal followers in the Fourth had substantially helped.

Chapter 22

Under the oligarchy of Bill Craig and his political satellites, and under the autocracy of his powerful successor Jim O'Grady, the Fourth Ward in certain areas was a lively mart of trade during the daytime hours and a place of fun and games at night. During these regimens, traveling salesmen, wanting to relax after a day of peddling, felt no need to hurry on to Buffalo or Syracuse to escape the Siberian bleakness which in later years supposedly settled over downtown Rochester after dark.

There were more than half a dozen theaters in the ward that exhibited living actors and paramount among them was the tinseled, tattered, grubby but wonderful old Lyceum through whose creaky stage door the greatest mimes and minstrels of this and the earlier century had passed.

The ward had the town's leading hotel, the Seneca, which was almost spanking new when I first went to work as a newspaper reporter. It had the Odenbach Hofbrauhaus, "undeniably the show place of Rochester," which was also Rochester's finest restaurant. The bar in the Hotel Eggleston, presided over by Harry (Spike) Wilson (who later shot at a fine young woman, and shot and killed himself when he missed) seemed as long as a city block. There were poolrooms with such an abundance of tables that they advertised "no waiting"; there were bowling alleys. Twice a week there was professional boxing in the Genesee Hall on South Avenue. There were ladies in the ward's hinterland who would come tripping to the Hotel Seneca, the Whitcomb House, or the Hayward to succor the lonely and lovelorn—provided the lonely and lovelorn were duly recommended by a bellman and given a number to call. Other ladies received at home. And if a man really wanted action of an evening . . .

There was a time when the "best governed city" was also the most wide-open gambling town in the state.

The "mob," which later insinuated itself into a submarginal

stratum of Rochester life, and which now and then abandons the dead body of an apostate, trussed-up like a fowl readied for market, on a lonely county road, was happily not in evidence early in the century. In that era members of the sporting gentry, if not fine upstanding citizens, often had the merit of being entertaining, and some were not unpicturesque. They gave a piquancy to downtown life. They were not violent to a homicidal degree, and several of them were well liked even by victims who may have suffered the introduction of a fifth ace in a poker deck.

The Fourth Ward was spotted with gambling hells, which also prevailed in numerous other sections of the city, particularly during the years that immediately preceded the adoption of the city manager charter, which the naive high-minded believed would be a panacea for all municipal ills. Operating or employed in these places were such characters as Stack-'em-up-Joe, Bearcat Beacher, Ox Connor, Montana Jack, Danny New Yorker, Potato Sacks, to name a few.

On Clinton Avenue South, between Main Street East and Court Street, were at least three resorts, the gaudiest of which dealt *chemin de fer*, roulette, and faro, along with such staples as twenty-one, poker, and crap dice. The place had an armed lookout in a steel cage. The police indignantly mandated the lookout out of the cage. In the event of a raid he might mistakenly shoot one of their own.

For years, and long before the "mob" moved in, the kingpin of Rochester's gambling industry was Luke, sometimes known as "Uncle Luke" or "Honest Luke" Smith. Employed as a youth in a Brockport shoe factory, he soon abandoned the confinement of honest toil to circulate about western and central New York with a floating dice game. He was quick with figures, a sort of Wizard of Odds. He learned in his chancy peregrinations about games other than crap dice. Eventually settling in Rochester, he operated a succession of gaming rooms and a commodious salon for the acceptance of horse bets that was as accessible to the public as Sibley's store.

Besides his Rochester commitments, Uncle Luke operated sporadically in Florida, in French Lick Springs, Indiana, and at other places where the goddess of chance was likely to be unmolested by the law. For years he was always at Saratoga Springs for the "season." He was a hardy soul, tough, unafraid, and as openhanded as the Welfare Department. The saying was "Luke'll hold still for it." If a man asked for five, ten, fifty, or a hundred, his hand would automatically reach into a pocket and he'd hand out bills as if they were Kleenex tissues. He was susceptible to all public charities. Luke Smith might have been one of the biggest non-Mafia operators in the country, not unlike James Carroll, of St. Louis, who computed the Winter Book on the Kentucky Derby, except for an incurable compulsion to bet horses himself. He was a bookmaker. His "office" in Clinton Avenue South, which also controlled the race wire leased out not by the Annenberg whom President Nixon sent to the Court of St. James but by the ambassador's father who was sent to jail, accepted hundreds of thousands of dollars in race bets monthly. If Smith had been satisfied merely to take a commission for handling these wagers he would have profited handsomely. His passion to bet himself would not permit him the passive role of middleman. He dissipated his profits betting horses with other bookmakers, and in death helped to certify the aphorism "All horse players die broke."

Smith's clients were widely diffused. They included a very high-playing Rochester meat packer who frequently bet as much as $10,000 and $15,000 a race and H. L. Hunt, the Texas oilman, who at the time reputedly had a larger income than any other person in America. For a considerable period Mr. Hunt called in every day shortly before post-time and immediately after the last race was run in the East.

"The old rascal's always trying to beat me on the price," Smith said sadly of Hunt. "You wouldn't think he'd be like that, him with all those oil wells."

Luke Smith was a man of complete detachment. He was indifferent to wealth, to position, and to fame. His concentration was not unlike that of the great Archimedes who was attempting to resolve an abstruse mathematical problem even as Syracuse tumbled about his ears and a blade ran through his tripes. He was in quest, if not one of the eternal verities, of the *beau ideal* of running horses —a sleeper, which one day would come awake and pay prodigious odds.

Uncle Luke had no gaudy or expensive tastes. He dressed like a man who might have come to repair a leak in the steam pipes or whitewash the cellar. He sought money, big money, ceaselessly, and it had no more meaning to him than the pegs on a cribbage board: He used it to keep the score of the game.

In the company of his friend and sometimes partner Cornelius (Red) Dwyer, proprietor of an elaborate restaurant and gambling casino in Geneva, forty miles southeast of Rochester, Smith collected $25,000 in cash from a Cleveland bookmaker, stuffed it into a brown paper grocer's sack, and the two men repaired to the Cleveland railroad station. The train that would take them to Rochester was not due for two hours. After they had breakfasted in the station restaurant, Dwyer rose with the announcement that he was going to the barber's for a shave.

Unlike his companion, Dwyer had a very warm feeling about money. He cherished it, nurtured it, and held it closely.

"Now remember, you Dutchman, the hard time we had getting all this money," he said severely. "While I'm gone, you keep it like it's your heartbeat. We'd oughta, like businessmen, had a briefcase to carry it in. But don't you let that sack get half an inch away. Understand?"

Smith looked up with round, incredulous eyes.

"Why, Reddo. Twenty-five gees! You think I ain't holding this like a loving mother with a child? You think not? Jesus!"

Dwyer went to the barber's leaving Smith with a racing paper, and the money bag held tightly under his arm. He returned half an hour later. The racing paper with a form chart torn from one of its pages lay on the table. Below, on the floor next to the wainscoting, Dwyer's horrified eyes descried the brown paper grocer's bag. So breathless with fright that the shriek of anguish that gulped up inside him escaped only as a faint squiblike hissing, he dived for the bag, closed his eyes, groped a hand inside it. The money was there. Clutching the bag with both hands, he dropped down on a chair. He was there, still atremble, when Smith came bustling back to the table. He was excited. His face beamed like the morning sun. He exuded cheer and hope.

"Hey, Reddo! I caught a real red hot one. He's going in the fifth this afternoon, at a hell of a price. At Monmouth Park. I just called Jersey City, and bet him through Acey Gordon's office."

"Wh—why you Dutch krauthead! You know what you done?" Dwyer held up the money bag. "You left this, to go running off to play tiddledewinks in Jersey City. This, all this swindle in here! Oh, you—"

Smith's face dropped. "Cripes, that's right. I—I did forget." He brightened quickly. "But, Reddo. I was only gone fifteen minutes!"

At one time, more than forty Rochester horse rooms received racing information from the race wire Luke Smith locally controlled. In Elm Street, unmolested by the police, Joe Santora, who had once racked balls in the billiard room of the Whitcomb House, had a blackjack—or twenty-one—parlor that was open all hours. In Aqueduct Street, at the other end of downtown, Thomas Leo O'Brien had a dice game, with the stick men uniform in short green aprons, that continued year after year, as legitimate—so far as the authorities were concerned—as an all-night drugstore. Santora who husbanded his winnings became wealthy; Tom O'Brien who seemed to feel, in the words of the late Gene Fowler, that money was something to throw off of moving trains died broke.

The reputation O'Brien had of being the town's most freehanded spender would be difficult to discredit. Hundreds of thousands of dollars passed through his hands; the profits from his dice game and a lucrative cafe, the Pillars, two doors from the Four Corners on Exchange Street. He was an easy mark for sycophants, hangers-on, and jugglers who clung to him like a lamprey to a sea bass.

He reveled in the role of bounteous host. He wanted people around him at all times, and he accepted even those whose purpose he knew was to attempt to fleece him out of large sums of money at a game of chance. When he drank, he wanted action—he wanted to play.

With the second or third drink, he would be afflicted with a shaking palsy which, if he was playing cards, would jerk his hands about and expose to an opponent every card that he held. The "peek," as the revelation was called, was said by gamblers to be better than two finesses. Frequently aware of the advantage being taken of him, O'Brien would blithely continue the play. Occasionally he won large sums at craps in the dice rooms of other gamblers. Sometimes he would lose five, ten, or twenty thousand dollars in his own café after the straight trade had been herded out at the legal closing hour and the place appropriated by his cronies and predators who, when word was about that Tom was skylarking, came out from under stones and emerged from the woodwork.

One of his true friends and devoted followers, calling him from a eucher game, pleaded, "Tom—Tom, that sonofabitch's got a ribbed deck. Don't you know? You're being robbed!"

"Yeah—yeah, I know," O'Brien said, nodding agreement. "But wh—what's the difference? I loaned him the money to play me."

O'Brien drank steadily when he was on a two- or three- or four-day spree, but he was not an alcoholic, and he paced himself so well that except for his palsied hands there was little in his physical behavior to indicate excessive indulgence. He was well mannered, quiet spoken, and never in temper. He abhorred filthy talk and would walk away from any group who were engaged in it. For a man whose illegitimate activities must have depended upon the corruption of the authorities, Tom O'Brien was not insensible of moral values. His rigid fidelity to and his unreserved adoration for his slim, pretty, golden-haired wife, Kit, was celebrated.

Well launched on one of his prodigal divertissements, which might cost him (outside of gambling losses) a couple of thousand dollars a night, O'Brien would carry his entourage from one resort to another until the legal curfew. Then the party would repair to the Pillars, often accompanied by a band and the floor show from a local nightclub. The women performers would receive $50 or $100, depending on the duration of their stay. O'Brien would pay them, but that would be his only contact with them. They were engaged to entertain his guests; he himself was indifferent to their charms and their talents. He was singly and abidingly devoted to Kit.

Unlike Luke Smith, O'Brien delighted in sartorial elegance. He was a difficult man to fit. His arms were unusually short, his shoulders sloped, and his paunch protruded; but his tailoring was the best to be had in town. He had a wide assortment of suits and numerous overcoats, several of which were appointed with velvet collars. His shirts were custom cut. He wore bench-made shoes. His appearance was studiously theatrical. He wanted to be known as the big-shot gambler and a mighty spender.

Luke Smith was well known in gambling circles all over America. Tom O'Brien's activities were limited to Rochester except during the Saratoga Springs racing season when, until the Kefauver investigation, he managed a gambling casino known as Newman's Lake House. He indulged in a bit of *hauteur* on these occasions. He established his wife and family in a large house on Union Avenue, eschewed drinking for the month of August, entertained with less flamboyance than was his custom in Rochester, and vicariously rubbed elbows with the Vanderbilts, the Du Ponts, the Whitneys, and others in the high echelon of racing society.

At a time when Rochester was more provincial and less sophisticated than it is today, the city gave attention to and enjoyed its eccentrics—its *characters*. Some of them, like Rattlesnake Pete Gruber, seemed part of our tradition. They were widely on display. Not so much because of his gambling, but because of the extravagance of his entertainment, Tom O'Brien was known to hundreds of persons. There were gamblers here who were much bigger than he, but they were less showy and little known to the general public.

There was Ox Connor, who might have passed for John Oakhurst, Bret Harte's gentleman gambler in *Poker Flat*. He was tall, slim, immaculately groomed, and always carefully dressed. He could be courtly on occasion. He prided himself on his delicate taste in wine, food, women, and race horses. He was a fascinating raconteur, and I delighted in his tales even when I knew that what he represented as fact was as improbable as Alice in Wonderland. He had wide connections outside of Rochester, and frequently traveled about the East and Middle West. Once, returning from a Chicago visit, he brought with him a professional gambler from that city and a Japanese reputedly worth millions. The Japanese was a compulsive wheel player, and Connor and his Chicago companion were at pains to satisfy his urge.

They rented a house near Wolcott, in the county of Wayne, which adjoins the eastern boundary of Monroe, stocked it with liquor and food, put a mug Connor knew in a white jacket to personate a butler, and invited the Japanese to be a weekend guest. He remained five days, lost $200,000 at roulette, paid $75,000, gave a marker—an IOU—for the rest, left town, and so far as the Ox and his Chicago conspirator ever knew, sank into limbo.

There were gamblers in Rochester who appeared to enjoy a sanction of comity. One of these was George Skinner, whose young relative Al later became an enormously popular Monroe County sheriff. Skinner was a large, mustachioed, good-natured man, who conducted a poker game sometimes in the Chapman House on South Avenue and sometimes in other quarters in the Fourth Ward. By report he was an honest dealer, but he occasionally had as a collaborator Pat Mangan, who never missed Mass of a morning, and never missed an opportunity to mark a card, load a dice, or fix a wheel, believing these practices were pragmatic and necessary to the success of his calling. Skinner was well liked by his patrons because of his custom of entertaining them with dinner sent in from Odenbach's Hofbrauhaus if the play was good in the evening, and with ham and eggs and coffee sent in from a nearby lunchroom if it was still lively next morning.

One night, an ambitious young police lieutenant from the Second Precinct on Franklin Street organized a raid on Skinner's game, but the "Cry Havoc" had hardly been raised when a thundering order came over the telephone, GET THOSE POLICE OUT OF THERE!

George Skinner was a pet of the Big Fellow, and George Aldridge took care of his friends.

Chapter 23

Living in the comfortable bourgeois community of Linden Street, I was blithely unaware, until I entered newspaper work, that conditions prevailed in certain areas of my beloved city that flouted its proud boast of orderliness, cleanliness, and exalted municipal government. Engrossed in youth in Horatio Alger fiction, my fancy had often eased the privations and hardships of one of Alger's New York waifs by transferring him from the heartless metropolis to our cheerful and friendly city; and it was not until later that I learned that some who moved to Rochester to improve their lot found it considerably short of the Elysian Fields.

Emma Goldman, the brilliant anarchist, was one of the disenchanted. She had come as a girl from her native Russia with dreams of the freedom and opportunity America offered the deprived and downtrodden and settled here with a married sister who had preceded her to this country. Her Utopian dream was quickly shattered and she found that the serflike oppression she had known in Russia persisted even in the New World. She took a job sewing ulsters in a men's clothing factory. Her daily stint was ten hours and a half; her weekly wage was $2.50. And not only, she later charged, did her employer "exact labor in his factory for nothing, but also insisted on the pleasures the young female wage slaves could give him. He had them or out they went."

In time, Emma left Rochester to pursue a career in radicalism that brought her world-wide notoriety. Her roots here were deep, and she often returned to visit Rochester relatives, one of whom was the late Saxe Commins, a dentist with literary aspirations, who, moving to New York, became a top editor for Random House and a close friend of Eugene O'Neill, the playwright.

On one of her visits to Rochester, Miss Goldman spoke before the Rochester City Club, which used to meet Saturday noon in the ballroom of Powers Hotel. Rochester abounds in lunch clubs which are addressed each week by a speaker, or entertained by a vocalist, or by an instrumentalist, or perhaps by a legerdemain. The City Club is different from the others. Someone has called it a club for "doubledomes," meaning the town's intelligentsia. Its speakers are not engaged to entertain the members, but to enlighten them on important public issues. Emma Goldman's appearance before the City Club came many years after she had offered herself as a street prostitute in the hope that by this means she might obtain money to purchase a revolver for her consort Alexander Berkman, who shot but failed in his purpose to kill the mighty steelmaster Henry Frick. It was also a long time after she had been sought by the nation's police as a possible accomplice of Leon Czolgosz, President McKinley's assassin, who confessed that his anarchism had been inflamed by hearing Emma lecture, but who stanchly denied that she had had any knowledge of his homicidal intent. She was deep into middle life when she came to the City Club, and while she had not, in the public's mind, achieved anything like respectability, her violent impulses seemed to have quieted, and the club members had no fear that she would fling a bomb among the luncheon tables.

Her talk was notable for one remark, and the conscience of the town may have been slightly pricked when she declared that the deprivations she had suffered in Rochester and her brutal experience as a garment worker were partly responsible for making her an anarchist.

Conditions in the clothing industry had improved since the time Miss Goldman had lived and worked in Rochester, but they were far from ideal in the second decade of the century and charges that women—and even children—worked inhumanly long hours for a piddling wage in unsanitary, ill-ventilated, and poorly lighted factories and sweatshops brought about an investigation by state officials, by a local committee of responsible citizens, and by the outside press.

The five local English-language dailies serenely exempted themselves from discussion of the issue. The town had a new catch phrase, "Do It for Rochester." One didn't "Do It for Rochester" damning the city's institutions. The uninhibited New York *World*, which sometimes made huge headlines out of half truths, clamorously indicted the clothing industry, saying in part: "In the model city of Rochester, where civic pride is eclipsed only by the pursuit of the almighty dollar, girls sit in unsanitary and unventilated rooms for ten hours a day stitching garments."

The Toledo *Blade* also got into the act. Its editor had studied a report of an investigating committee headed by the Sir Galahad of labor crusades, Robert F. Wagner, and concluded a stinging editorial with these words "Possibly it may not be denied that 'Rochester Made Means Quality.' But in the light of the factory report, 'Rochester Made' means disease, dirt, poor light and the exploitation of the flesh and blood of children."

The clothing industry was outraged at the "yellow journalism" (as it was stigmatized) of the New York *World*, which had injected not a little bathos into a rather loose-gaited report that cited incidents of sweatshop exploitation of women and children without identifying by name or address the victims of the alleged abuses. Harry Michaels, a prominent manufacturer, declared "There are no sweatshops in Rochester." Miss Emma W. Lee, secretary of the United Charities of Rochester, pleaded with the *World* and the Toledo *Blade* for the names and addresses of the anonymous "cases" of industrial cruelty mentioned in their columns. The *Blade* failed to reply; the *World* explained that the notes of the reporter who had written the story had been destroyed.

Despite the *World*'s categorical condemnation, all was not evil in the clothing industry. There were factory proprietors of humane instincts who had gone to considerable expense to provide decent working conditions. There was one who contributed $50,000 from his own fortune to establish a pension fund for deserving employees. But Henry Michaels' emphatic denial, ". . . no sweatshops in Rochester" had not spirited them away; there *were* sweatshops, and various other abuses that could not be glossed over. There were thousands of garment workers in the city, and the lives of many were warped and disadvantaged by a subhuman economy. Women, who outnumbered the men in the clothing factories, suffered disabilities induced by confinement and overwork. After a nine- or ten-hour stint in a factory or subcontractor's shop, they often took piece work to their homes to eke out their factory pittance. Mothers were frequently aided in these evening labors by children below the age of adolescence.

Common Good, a local "Independent Magazine for Civic and Social Reform," which vividly described the sad plight of Rochester factory women (and suffered, because of its frankness, a mortal hurt when "Do It for Rochester" merchants withdrew their advertising), spoke also of child labor.

"As we write . . . word is brought to us of a little Rochester girl, ten years of age, who had been found after school and after supper sewing on coats in the dim light of her home. She has only the little play she can snatch as she comes from school. Asked why her older sister of fifteen years did not help her, she replied, 'Her eyes is bad, she cannot see to sew now.'"

Generally, Rochesterians knew no more about the conditions under which their ready-to-wear garments were made than they knew about the conditions under which their table meat was slaughtered. We didn't deliberately peep into abattoirs or voluntarily penetrate the district east of the river and north of the New York Central Railroad tracks where Poles, Russian Jews, and Italians who executed the hundreds of operations required to fashion a single suit of men's clothing huddled in wretched houses often with outhouses out back and midden heaps at kitchen doors.

The New York *World* exposé was published in the summer of 1912. A little more than half a year later, and almost synchronous with the release of the issue of *Common Good* that told the despairing story of women garment workers, the touchy, uneasy peace that had held for some time between the clothing manufacturers and their workers was shattered by a bitter strike. Outside labor leaders, who spoke the several languages of the workers, were brought in to organize and give moral support to the men and women on strike; there were demonstrations, there were parades, presently there was rioting, and, finally, tragedy.

In late afternoon of a dreary, cold, early February day, I stood in the city's charnel house—the morgue on Elizabeth Street—as morgue attendants transferred the dead body of a not unpretty Russian girl from their macabre vehicle to a zinc slab with the professional nonchalance of a butcher depositing a side of beef in a refrigerated closet.

I was in the company of Albert H. Longbotham, whom we called "Tom" because of the similarity of his surname with the surname of Tom Longboat, the Indian marathon runner, who had once been prominent in the news. Longbotham was the labor reporter for the *Democrat and Chronicle*. I did mostly general assignments. But this day I had been told to collaborate with Longbotham on the story of an ugly fracas in the northeastern section of the city.

On the prowl in the garment district, a crowd of men and women strikers, which gathered recruits at every street corner, learning that women were working in the homeshop of Valentine Sauter, on Clifford Avenue, converged upon the small building, crying for the workers to come out and shouting obscene epithets at the proprietor. The strikers banged on the doors of the shop. The doors were locked. When some zealot flung a flowerpot through a window, the act inflamed the Jacobinic temper of the mob and excited imitation. Stones and other hard objects bashed in the glass of other windows. The panicky workers hid under benches and huddled in closets, pleading with Sauter to save them—to do anything to appease the assailants and divert the assault.

When the proprietor shouted from a window for the crowd to disperse, a stone was aimed at his head. He ducked, to reappear a few seconds later with a sporting gun, which he fired into the mob. The spray of shot brought screams of pain from several strikers, and a girl fell to the ground. Cries of "Kill him! Lynch him!" rose from the strikers, and the threats might have been executed except for the arrival of the police. A doctor bent over the fallen girl, but he did not let it be known that she had been mortally hit until the crowd was dispersed. She was seventeen-year-old Ida Braiman, a striker from the Adler plant, who had come to Rochester from Russia only a few months before.

I was never able to cultivate the blasé attitude that by some is supposed to be the hallmark of the experienced newspaper reporter. The sob story rendered me a bleeding heart. I was forever sentimentally involving myself with people about whom I wrote. I was touched as I gazed at the dead body of the Russian girl, who only a short time before had been alive, and vital and hopeful. There was a tragico-romantic aspect to this bad business. Ida Braiman had been engaged to be married, and plans for the wedding were going forward. I felt a bubble in my eye, and shamefully brushed at it.

Longbotham was lowly whistling a popular tune, the words of which, if memory serves, were, "Way up the river we will row, row, row . . ."

He looked at me. "What t'hell," he said. "You didn't pay to come in. This isn't *East Lynne*. You're working here."

"But that poor kid was going to be married. She was planning on it."

"Yeah," Tom said. He lit a cigar.

Tom Longbotham had the air of a man who had been everywhere and seen everything. But he had not been at Shepheard's Hotel in Cairo or at the Café de la Paix in Paris or at Raffles in Singapore where (it used to be said) one might see the world pass in review. He had worked for newspapers in Buffalo and Pittsburgh before coming to Rochester. He was a year my senior. He was tall, straight, with regular features. He had great brown eyes that looked straight into yours even as he told the greatest whopper. I never saw him ruffled or out of countenance. I was devoted to him. Many were. He was what was known as a "man's man"; women, whom he could take or leave—and he left many dangling—adored him.

During the garment workers' strike, I was occasionally with Longbotham when he interviewed labor leaders. The interviews were usually in the Hotel Eggleston, where the agitators who had come from out of town were quartered. They were burly fellows. They struck me as dour and unpleasant men. They were bitter, dedicated, impassioned. Tom would peremptorily enter a hotel room where a labor conference was under way, his soft hat slightly canted to the left, a long cigar in a corner of his mouth, and taunt the conferees.

The manufacturers had an organization known as the Clothiers' Exchange, whose secretary and legal representative was Sol Wile. Wile was associated with Percival D. Oviatt, Rochester's most brilliant trial lawyer, and he himself had many of Oviatt's skills. He had the aplomb and something of the appearance of a matinee idol. Longbotham would impudently tell the labor leaders that Wile would tie them up in knots, that they didn't have a living chance to win the strike, that they were licked before they started.

Had I made such a statement, they would have chucked me out of a third-story window. They heard Tom, started angrily, half grinned, then looked sheepishly down at their feet. He had an insinuating charm.

On the day the Braiman girl was shot, Longbotham and I went from the morgue to police headquarters, hoping to talk to the man who had killed her. Sauter already had been transferred from the police station to the county jail, diagonally across Exchange Street. We did not see him at that time. He had been charged with murder, first degree, and a hearing was scheduled fifteen days hence. He never appeared; the Grand Jury failed to indict him. Apparently in those days a man could defend his property with impunity against the assault of a mob. Released from jail, Sauter slipped out of town by the dark of the moon and hid himself in New York.

The strike dragged on for weeks. Mobs formed now and then, but there was no repetition of the tragedy on Clifford Avenue. Once mounted policemen charged a concourse of strikers who were blocking St. Paul Street. A handful of arrests were made. After long, labyrinthian negotiations a settlement was achieved and work was resumed in the factories.

Besides quarreling with their employers, the workers sometimes quarreled among themselves. Affiliations with different unions had caused union rivalry. This sort of contention ended a few years after World War I. At that time, the stitchers, the cutters, the buttonhole makers, and all others in Rochester engaged in the fashioning of men's ready-to-wear clothing were consolidated under the banner of the Amalgamated Garment Workers of America. They were headed then, as now, by Abraham D. Chapman. Chapman is an extraordinary organizer, and a man who knows all the blows and feints of labor-management negotiations. The advantages he has won for his union cohorts have put them into a condition of industrial life a light year in advance of the illegal sweatshop slavery from which Emma Goldman escaped to flaunt the red torch of anarchy.

* * *

If history, as Edward Gibbon has said, is "little more than the register of the crimes, follies, and misfortunes of mankind" the city of Rochester was blessed during the pre-World War I years of Uncle Hi Edgerton's mayoralty by furnishing few materials for history.

It was generally a halcyon period in the city's life though, to be sure, the newspapers were not without stories of tragedy, crime, and corruption. In the early stages of Mayor Edgerton's long tenure in office, Rochester was first agitated by an epidemic of fires, several of which were believed to have been set by an arsonist (261 alarms were rung in a period of three months), and then by a series of fatal street accidents, half of which were caused by speeding or carelessly operated automobiles. The traffic situation was particularly deplorable in downtown streets, and loosely enforced traffic ordinances caused the "best governed city's" Main Street to be tagged the "Alley of Death." Trolley cars slam-banged down Main Street hill and motorcars raced the trolleys. Frightened horses racketed dangerously through congested areas. I recall a piece I wrote that the city desk thought warranted a two-column headline of a man who leaped from a curb to stop a runaway horse and suffered a fractured skull for his valor.

I wrote stories about pickpockets, shoplifters, and now and then about a housebreaker or a professional yegg who had blown a safe. I told about men who were arrested in drunken brawls and about huge black women whom we identified as "alley workers" who lured inebriates into covert places and robbed them during the moment of embrace.

But we almost never heard of a mugging; forced rape was uncommon; and murder, which today is so commonplace that the Rochester newspapers often report it in a couple of sticks of copy on an inside page, was so rare as to make it always the story of the day. And the follow-up would continue day after day with the printing of every minute detail that had a bearing on the case which the unflagging zeal of a reporter could uncover.

Sixty years ago, however, even as today, there was concern in Rochester about drug addiction and Police Chief Joseph M. Quigley was striving to educate his subordinates to look upon the unfortunate addict as a person who was ill rather than criminal.

Quigley had been transferred from his former post as Commissioner of Welfare and Corrections to head the police force and veteran members of the force were displeased with the appointment. The new chief wasn't a copper but a social worker and old-timers disparaged him as "Holy Joe." They were prejudiced against the somewhat advanced police methods he attempted to introduce. Babying a hophead by treating him in a clinic rather than removing him from temptation by penal incarceration was like trying to dry up a habitual drunk like Chicken Murray without sentencing him to a stiff dip in the county penitentiary.

Some of us who frequented the big billiard room in the Whitcomb House in quest of a story or to play rotation or Kelly pool were familiar with at least one hophead, or junker. He was Boston Tommy, who was usually slouched in one of the high-legged chairs in a corner of the room, seemingly asleep. His shoulders were frail and stooped and his face was very pinched and his skin was the color of unbaked bread dough. He was a pool hustler.

The Whitcomb House billiard room was a popular rendezvous during the daylight and nighttime hours that it was open to the public. The entrance was on Clinton Avenue South, a few steps south of the Main Street corner and a few steps north of the alley that led to the stage door of the Temple Theater. If there was a male headliner on the Temple vaudeville bill he might repair to the billiard room immediately after the matinee, followed perhaps by a youthful claque who had applauded his afternoon's performance. The handsome Reginald Denny (later a movie star) who costarred with Miss Olive Tell in the stock company at the Lyceum Theater, diagonally across the street, shot a deft cue in the Whitcomb House. It was a good place for an actor to be seen and whispered about. The swingers among the traveling salesmen came in to shoot fifty or a hundred balls. You could pretty well tell one of these fellows by the sharp cut and careful press of his tailoring, by his buff-colored spats, and by the hothouse flower in his buttonhole.

Gamblers, who played no pool but hoped to find in the billiard room a "sucker who couldn't wait" to play *their* game, sat watchfully in the high-legged chairs against the wall. Dapper Dan McElligott, a cherubic little man, dressed to the nines, who wore diamond studs in his white-on-white shirts, and played high cards on crack New York Central Pullman trains, upstairs in the Whitcomb House, and in the Eggleston and Seneca hotels, was often there.

And so was Danny (the Greek) Stappas, whose vision was so extraordinarily sharp that some believed he could see through the backs of playing cards. Danny took great pride in his Greek beginnings, and loved to dissertate on Hellenic lore. He crammed on the subject in the public library. In one pocket he sometimes carried a pint of whiskey and a deck of playing cards; in another, a copy of Euripides. He was reputedly the best whist player in western New York. Once, with Johnson (Whitey) Horn, of Rochester, he was engaged by a Buffalo gambler known as Ruthie to play two crack whist players from Montreal for $200,000. The agreement was that Stappas and Horn would risk nothing, and nothing would be paid them unless they won. They did win, after playing seventeen days in the Hippodrome poolroom in Buffalo. Danny the Greek took his 10 per cent—$20,000—and went around the world with a lady of whom he was enamored, and hoped to marry. When the journey ended, he sadly discovered the lady had gone only for the ride.

Charlie McInerney was the attendant in the billiard room. He was a tall, willowy youth, with large soulful eyes, a finely chiseled nose, and a sensitive mouth. He had poetic inclinations. He professed to worship the memory of Lord Byron, and he had learned passages from "She Walks in Beauty," and other poems. McInerney hated what he was doing, and the need to be servile and obedient at the cry "Hey, Charlie, rack 'em up over here." He was frustrated. He felt that he was imprisoned and he expressed this feeling by quoting from the Seventh Canto of *The Prisoner of Chillon*,

> Since man first pent his fellow-men,
> Like brutes within an iron pen.

He had an odd affection for Boston Tommy, the pool hustler. "Poor Tommy, he's sick," he would say. "He's consumptive. You can see that."

And when someone would come in, some "mark," who might want to play fifty points for fifty cents a point, Charlie would slink over to Tommy's chair and gently shake him out of his somnolence.

"There's a game, Tommy," he'd whisper.

The hustler would rouse himself from his slouched position and shake the cobwebs from his head. Then he would bring from a pocket a small envelope and sprinkle a powdery substance on the back of his hand. He would sniff the powder, his dull eyes would become glittery, and he would leap up, whistling, strut across the room, pick up a cue, and perhaps run the table without allowing his opponent a shot.

I had witnessed this transformation on two or three occasions without at first knowing what the catalyst was that caused it. What Boston Tommy sniffed was cocaine. I was amused by Tommy—he seemed a harmless oddity. It was not until some time after he had left town and I had an intimate experience with another addict that I came to realize that the use of drugs was not a matter to be lightly passed off but a habit of extreme viciousness.

On days that I was assigned to the police beat it was my practice to visit police headquarters on Exchange Street a couple of times each night. I had fine friends there among both the uniformed men and the detectives on the second floor. One of the former was Lieutenant William McDonald, who was in charge of the uniformed men who worked nights out of headquarters. McDonald was a huge, slow-moving, slow-talking, unflappable, kindly man, of great muscular strength, whose favor I fully enjoyed.

It is difficult in this crime-ridden age to realize that once Rochester was so free of serious crime that often during long periods of the night police headquarters on Exchange Street was as void of tumult and almost as serene and quiet as an empty cathedral. In the detectives' room upstairs, Mike Doyle, seated at one of the small roll-top desks that were ranked through the center of the rectangular room, might be struggling with a quatrain. Mike was the Detective Bureau's minstrel and poet laureate. Sometimes he caught a criminal, but his great hope was to write a song—an Irish song!— that would catch the popular ear, and bring him wealth to allow him to visit the green isle of his forebears.

Except for Mike Doyle, I have known times when the only other midevening occupant of the detectives' room was Sergeant William McGuire, the nighttime boss of the Detective Bureau. McGuire was a man of courtesy, wisdom, and courage, whom I greatly admired and cherished as a friend and wise counselor. He was noted as the only independent Democrat on the police force, in contradistinction to a handful of Aldridge Democrats, and celebrated for a three-round boxing exhibition in the police gym with James J. Corbett during which, for a moment, the former world's heavyweight champion lay ignominiously on his back.

"No matter what they say, he tripped, I never knocked him down," McGuire steadfastly insisted. "But I didn't know, when he got up, how he'd take it. I thought he'd feel demeaned, and mean, and really come at me. If he had, I wouldn't have stood there and taken it like a sucker. I'd have kicked him in the belly. But he was Gentleman Jim, all right. He laughed, and kidded about it, and we shook hands."

The big room to the right of the entrance to police headquarters that was occupied at night by Lieutenant Bill McDonald was the daytime office of the police captain in command of the First Precinct. It had a couple of desks, files, and other office appurtenances, and it was separated from a short ante room leading from the corridor of the building by a high counter. McDonald was fingering through a file one dead quiet October night when I popped into the anteroom with the usual inquiry, "Anything doing, Lieutenant?"

"Oh, nothing that amounts to anything," he said, turning and reaching for the arrest cards. He laughed. "They brought in Chicken Murray early tonight. He's overdue. It's getting too cold to sleep in doorways and under bridges. In the morning the judge'll give him six months and that'll be about right. Chicken always says he likes to come out when he sees the first bluebird through the barred windows." He handed me the cards. "And there's another drunk, but he's just in to sleep it off. And a fellow for petty larceny."

Frank (Chicken) Murray was a well-known Front Street character who virtually petitioned the judge to send him away once the chill of the autumn winds penetrated his tattered raiment. In lieu of Palm Beach, he'd settle for the steam-heated penitentiary. His job there was tending the chicken run. He was a police-beat stereotype, but I could make a couple of paragraphs out of his arrest. The other rummy wasn't worth a line. I glanced at the third card. A man named Freeman Guyer was accused of snatching seven dollars from a lunchroom cash drawer while the cashier's back was turned.

"Why, Lieutenant," I cried, "I know this fellow, this Guyer you've got for larceny. He was in grade school with me. Last I saw him, he was a messenger for Western Union."

"Hum. Well, they caught him red-handed. If he's a pal of yours" —the lieutenant chuckled—"why don't you go see him?"

I wanted to see him, and McDonald led me back to the cell block, and the old turnkey, who sat in a rickety armchair reading a newspaper, pointed to the second cell in the row. The cell block smelled of urine, disinfectant, and unwashed human flesh. I knew it for many years. Its stench was immemorial and unvarying.

Freeman Guyer was pacing back and forth across the cell like a caged animal in a circus menagerie. I had seen him inside of a year when he occasionally brought a message into the *Democrat and*

Chronicle newsroom and we had talked briefly about our youthful acquaintance in No. 13 School. In the murky gloom of the cell block he did not at once recognize me but he stopped his pacing and grasped the cell bars with shaking hands and peered through the bars with galvanic intensity.

"Hank," he cried suddenly, "Hank Clune!"

"Wh—what got you into this, Freeman?"

His voice rose to a wild, womanish shriek that seemed to pierce through the entire building. "For God's sake, Hank, get me something. I'm dying—dying, I tell you." He released the bars and beat his temples with closed fists. He was theatrical, but I knew he was suffering, and didn't know why until he explained. "Get me something," he repeated, his plea shrilling higher. "You can do it. I gotta have a fix."

He resumed his mad pacing of the cell, but stopped once to tell me, in a hysterical voice, how early that night, needing a shot of heroin—anything to quiet the desperate tumult of his nerves—he had flung his infant daughter at his wife during a domestic quarrel, escaped the house, and pillaged the lunchroom cash drawer for money for drugs. It was a harrowing tale. I left Guyer, and went out to Lieutenant McDonald.

"That man's dying," I pleaded. "Can't you do something for him?"

"He won't die tonight," the lieutenant said calmly. "He's a junker. He's been in before. He won't die of *it*—yet."

"But if you could get him a shot of something. He's an old friend of mine."

"I thought you reporters were supposed to be so hard-boiled, so cynical. And now you're all broke up over a hophead. Well, I'll see. . . ."

It was necessary that I return to the office. I was there ten minutes when the lieutenant called me on the telephone. He had gotten hold of Dr. John A. Stapleton, the police surgeon, who would give Guyer an injection. Big Bill McDonald was that kind of a copper.

Guyer was given six months for petty larceny. He was fat and sleek and healthy when he came out, vowing that he was through with drugs for life. Two months later he was back on them and back also in police court. I never knew what happened to him in the end for I never saw him but once or twice after his six months in "stir." And I never again saw Boston Tommy after he left town. His leaving almost coincided with the sudden and unannounced departure of the attendant in the Whitcomb House billiard room, Charlie McInerney, but there was no compact between him and Tommy. Each went his separate way.

I was fond of Charlie McInerney and was sorry that he had been unhappy in Rochester. He left, never to return in the flesh, but many of us saw him on the silent screen, first in a bit part in *Broken Blossoms*, which starred Lillian Gish, and then in a more conspicuous role in another David Wark Griffith picture. Press releases mentioned him as a potential star and some of us were boasting that "we knew him when"—when a news dispatch told of his tragic death in Hollywood. A car in which he was riding skidded off the road and tumbled down a steep ravine.

Chapter 24

During my salad days in the newspaper business the younger men in the newsroom of the *Democrat and Chronicle* were often broke but very seldom bored. Rochester was relatively a small city, but the compact area of downtown was lively, populous, and often exciting, and we, in a way, were the Downtown Boys. We were in the know; we were part of the action. We considered ourselves very wise and worldly.

Besides Will Richards and Tom Longbotham and myself, the younger coterie included Harry Roff and Jesse Humelbaugh. Harry Roff must have stood six feet and a half in his stocking feet and Humelbaugh was so small that the top of his head scarcely reached past Roff's elbow. The pair were close friends and inseparable companions except when divided by their newspaper assignments. They were referred to as the comic-strip characters Mutt and Jeff. Roff had cultivated a slight stoop, some thought from continually leaning over to talk to his tiny pal. Longbotham attributed the stoop to another cause.

Harry Thaw, the defendant in New York's most spectacular early-century murder case (he shot and killed the famous architect Stanford White), visited Rochester on his release from an institution for the criminally insane. He had come here professedly on a lecture tour that was to take him to several cities in the East. Roff was assigned to interview Thaw. His story was sympathetic; Thaw liked it, and during his stay here he attempted to cultivate Roff's friendship.

Rumor had it that Thaw was a flagellant. Longbotham made the most of this. He stopped at downtown resorts frequented by Roff and Jesse Humelbaugh and lamented about "poor Harry's back." The dialogue I heard went very much like this:

"What's the matter with his back?" the bartender asked.

"Why, you've seen the way he stoops."

"Yeah. Maybe he's got the rheumatism."

"Rheumatism. Huh. You know he's been hanging out with that Harry Thaw. You know Thaw likes to have someone lash him with a whip."

"I know he's in the crazy house. I dunno he's that crazy. Why's he want anyone lashing him with a whip?"

"He gets his sex kicks that way."

"Hell of a way to get sex kicks. I'll have mine in bed."

"Well, you ask Roff when he comes in. Ask him about his welts. Maybe he'll tell you his back's out of shape from Thaw whipping him."

Not quite believing and still not fully disbelieving, for it was difficult categorically to discredit what Longbotham said when his great brown eyes stared unwaveringly into yours, the bartender might touch upon the subject of Thaw's supposed flagellation when Roff and Humelbaugh next entered his resort and cautiously question the former about his own devotion to this form of masochism.

Harry Roff was the kindest and gentlest young man I knew. He would grin and half embarrassedly explain that what the bartender had heard was "just some of Tom's foolishness." He was more amused than angry at Longbotham's jape. It would have been impossible for him to have borne a grudge. His small companion was outraged at what he called a "damn vicious attempt to slander my pal" and for a time ceased speaking to Longbotham. He called him a "calloused monster."

Humelbaugh had recently written a news story about a young woman, whose name I do not recall, who had stopped in Rochester to help promote a novel which had previously been serialized in *Redbook*. He had introduced the young novelist to Longbotham, who first found Tom "fascinating" and then "adorable." She postponed commitments in other cities to remain in Rochester for a week, staying with a friend whom she had known in college. Tom squired her about for two or three days; then found the attachment oppressive.

Longbotham's off-hour haunt and his hide-out during the hours he stole from his working day was the bar of the Eggleston Hotel whose only concession to femininity was a painting of a naked nymph. There, reveling in masculine companionship, he might forget a date he had made with the young woman or, if he belatedly remembered, appear an hour late for the tryst. His tardiness invariably provoked tears and bitter accusations, demonstrations which Tom thought tiresome and unwarranted. Pshaw, he said, everyone now and then had a lapse of memory. Before the novelist left town she tearfully reported Tom's boorishness and neglect to Jesse Humelbaugh, who had a keen sense of gallantry about women. Jesse was still angry with Tom because of the scandalous stories he had told about Harry Roff and he reviled him as a low-lived deceiver of women. The rest of us were amused. It wasn't Long-botham's deliberate intent to bring women under his spell; he charmed them by reflex action.

I remember a statuesque, rather glamorous middle-aged woman with a marked foreign accent who was in Rochester in the interest of a new line of cosmetics. She was vaguely identified as a countess and she looked as we supposed a countess should look. She was not tearfully submissive as was the young novelist but her interest in "dear, dear Toom" may have been as perfervid. She was not long gone when Tom received a set of platinum shirt studs. A small diamond was set in each stud.

"Now what the hell am I supposed to do with these?" he asked, with a disgust that was perhaps not wholly genuine. "If she'd only sent the money . . ."

A young woman, a show-business character, wrote Tom a note from Chicago which he allowed me to see. It was an ardent *billet-doux*. "Darling," the note read at one point, "my jaw's still sore."

"What's she mean by that?" I asked.

"Oh," Tom said, "we were fooling around, and I happened to pass her one."

When she wrote again, she promised that if Tom would only join her in Milwaukee she'd deed him a part interest in the 101 Ranch Show.

Tom Longbotham left the *Democrat and Chronicle* to serve with the Army overseas and left the Army to employ his considerable talents as a publicist in the interests of the Statler Hotel chain, Canadian race tracks, and other enterprises; Will Richards left for Detroit to become star man for the *Free Press* and ultimately to write a best-selling biography of Henry Ford, *The Last Billionaire;* Harry Roff and Jesse Humelbaugh slithered into limbo, and I know nothing of their endings. No one is alive who shared with me those lively, happy, hopeful years on the newspaper when the world seemed, in youthful fancy, our communal oyster.

*   *   *

Half of Rochester's history was wiped out by a better than 100-million-dollar building spree which, beginning in 1962, transformed the city's downtown into an area of great, high-shouldered buildings (not always of aesthetic delight), that obliterated several secondary streets, and that converted old familiar alleyways into parterres and ornamental terraces.

Cortland Street is gone. Part of it forms the entrance to Midtown Plaza, that bold and imaginative enterprise that marked the beginning of Rochester's tectonic renaissance. To many who knew it only at its northern extremity, Cortland Street was thought to be a blind alley, but it had, besides a Main Street opening, a more obscure outlet at Monroe Avenue, and it was intersected by Court Street. It was a narrow, generally shabby street, except for the handsome parish house of the First Unitarian Church, but giving on it was the stage door of the Lyceum Theater, and when the Lyceum was in its bloom the young Corinthians of the town clustered around its stage door like cows around a corn bushel.

I remember a boy swathed in an ankle-length coonskin coat, who had a topdown Locomobile parked at the Cortland Street curb and who was waiting for the show girls to emerge after a performance of a Jeff De Angelis musical.

"Jeez," he exclaimed ecstatically, gazing up at the night sky, his hands folded as if in prayer, "I got the tall blonde, second from the right of the chorus line, and she treats me just like a mother!"

The opening of the stage door expelled into the alley an odoriferous melange of musk, of attic staleness, and of grease paint. It was a heady odor. It excited in the youth who inhaled it a sense of romance and adventure. Most of us were stage struck at one time or another and the Lyceum encouraged our theatrical fancies. We might have stood aside in awe as E. H. Sothern passed along the narrow sidewalk on his way to the Hotel Seneca, almost as heroic in street attire—a long tight-fitting great coat with an astrakhan collar, a flat-topped derby, a walking stick hooked on an elbow— as in the buskined habiliments of *If I Were King;* or followed with

297

adoring eyes the tiny cameo-cut figure of Miss Anna Held, Florenz Ziegfeld's French import, whose large come-hither eyes, by her own vocalized confession, she could not make behave.

Like most young men I was in love with the lovely dark-haired mimic Miss Elsie Janis whose appearance at the Lyceum in such musicals as *The Vanderbilt Cup* and *The Slim Princess* automatically raised the SRO sign in the lobby. Miss Janis was a toast everywhere she went and everyone seemed to want to entertain her. There was a firm ritual about this. She never went anywhere except in the custody of her lynx-eyed mother whose surveillance was like that of a man with a gun guarding the Kohinoor. I knew Miss Janis slightly; once she sent me a small autographed photograph for my birthday. But my relations with her were extremely sketchy and I was envious of those who were asked to the big party given for her by E. Franklin Brewster in his South Fitzhugh Street home.

Frank Brewster was a rich, handsome, genial fat man who stuttered. He loved life and the fleshpots. At the annual waitresses' ball one might see him with the prettiest waitress in the room perched on his knee; at a Genesee Valley Club cotillion he would be gallantly attentive to the debs. He was facile and adaptable. The night of his party for Miss Janis (and her mother) the curtain for the show was held nearly half an hour as the guests lingered over the delicious food and imported bottled goods, and Will Corris, manager of the Lyceum, was put in a frenzy by the tardiness of his star.

Brewster had plied the young actress with small, not inexpensive gifts. As the guests were departing, Miss Janis espied a valuable fur coat on the halltree, slipped it on, and struck an alluring pose. "Ta-ta—take . . ." Frank started, but a friend nudged him and whispered a caveat, "For God's sake, Frank, don't give her that coat—or the house and lot!" and the host's intended offer was aborted.

The Lyceum was the greatest playhouse I have ever known and the most exquisite moments I have had in the theater were experienced there. It was built in 1888 by A. E. Wollf, who died early in the new century. Shortly after the founder's death his brother, Martin E. Wollf, succeeded to the control of the Lyceum, which, during most of its distinguished career, was the supreme temple for the performing arts in a city that was devoted to theatrical entertainment.

Its stage was huge, one of the largest in the country. Because this commodious platform allowed room to experiment with stage business and scenic and property arrangements and because Rochester was an easy sleeper jump from New York, producers liked to try out their new productions at the Lyceum. There was a feeling among some playgoers that the early season display of these sometimes rudimentary dramas and musicals stamped Rochester as a "dog town." Others protested that producers recognized our keen connoisseurship and knew that if we approved a play it was certain to succeed on Broadway.

This second thesis was given support by the critiques of George F. Warren, the sovereign quality of which caused them to be frequently quoted and carefully heeded by theatrical promoters. Warren was the drama critic for the *Democrat and Chronicle*. He had come from New York. There was a veiled story that the name he used was assumed, that he was the scion of a prominent New York family, and that he had escaped to Rochester to avoid a scandal. The mystery that cloaked his background, if indeed there was a mystery, was known only to the O. S. Adams' family with whom he lived. His career with the *Democrat and Chronicle* ended about the time I joined the newspaper's staff.

Warren was succeeded by Andrew Jackson Warner, known as "Jack" Warner, a socially prominent bachelor whose father and grandfather were distinguished Rochester architects, and whose mother, Jack's frequent companion at first nights, wore button shoes as high as buskins and remotely resembled the late Queen Victoria.

Mr. Warner was really not of the newspaper business. He was a pet seal who appeared in the newsroom only on nights that he did his theatrical and musical reviews. In time he transferred from the *Democrat and Chronicle* to the *Times-Union*, and thenceforth composed his essays in a room he rented in Powers Hotel. He was a friend and ardent partisan of King Edward VIII of England after that attractive young man abdicated in favor of Mrs. Wallis Warfield Simpson.

At a jet-set gathering in a great English country house, Warner received from the Duke of Windsor a cigarette lighter that became his most prized possession. Upon his return to Rochester he displayed it to his dear friend, Miss Helen Rochester Rogers, whose poodle grabbed it during Miss Rogers' examination of the gift, and chewed it to matchwood. Jack was heartsick at the loss of the royal memento; Miss Rogers was terribly, terribly chagrined. She searched high and wide for an exact duplicate of the destroyed lighter and presently found one in a Woolworth dimestore. She bought it for sixty-five cents.

Jack Warner was well learned in the arts of music and the drama, although he was not very original. His critical statements strongly reflected the judgments of a prominent New York critic whom he greatly admired. He wrote with some grace and his long tenure as a reviewer gave him a status of authority and considerable readership. He was rather prissy, aloof, and intuitively—but harmlessly—a snob.

I was sometimes assigned to review a piece at the Lyceum, and I was there one night for the opening of a raffish musical comedy that the theater's discriminate patrons had sedulously avoided and that had brought out the groundlings in droves. I sat directly behind Warner and his mother. The house was filled to the Plimsoll mark even before the pit orchestra began to tune their instruments. With a little flourish, Jack Warner stepped into the middle of the aisle, cast an eye over the jam-packed theater, and remarked, as he resumed his seat, "Mother, *really*, there is no one here tonight."

The Lyceum came upon lean days a few years before 1934 when a wrecking crew began to knock the grand old playhouse to pieces. The theatrical "road" had deteriorated and the plays that were being sent on tour were shoddy imitations of Broadway hits. There was competition for the entertainment dollar from the new Eastman Theater and from large new picture houses in the heart of the city. The Lyceum had run its course after having for nearly four decades provided Rochester with a great deal that was top drawer in theatrical entertainment.

* * *

Martin Wollf was the Lyceum's nominal manager, but the operation of the theater was left largely to Will R. Corris, Jr., a dapper, bustling little man who wore pince-nez and affected polka-dot bow ties, and who once aspired to wear the Roman collar of an Episcopal clergyman.

Corris started as an usher at the Lyceum during his student days at the University of Rochester. He had at first only a passing interest in the theater and had taken the job merely to provide himself with pocket money. He saw many notable players during the Lyceum season. He was enchanted by the imagery of Joseph Jefferson and Richard Mansfield. He gloried in the beauty of Maxine Elliott; he was deeply moved by the tragic roles of Modjeska and Ellen Terry. The world of fantasy and make-believe insinuatingly drew him into its orbit. At the close of his college course, young Corris renounced his churchly designs to work full time in the Lyceum box office and, inadvertently, to commit himself to a lifetime career in the theater.

He was the town's great showman. On opening nights, Will Corris, in a faultlessly tailored dinner jacket, greeted the theater's prominent patrons in the manner of a gracious host receiving in his home. The regulars of the carriage trade were his friends. He delighted in their elegance and in the glitter and ceremony of their arrival. The most spanking equipages in the city stopped at the curb in front of the Lyceum's marquee to discharge men with gleaming shirt fronts and brilliantly attired women, some with jeweled lorgnettes. A Lyceum opening put social Rochester on parade. There was a great hallooing in the foyer, a waving of gloved hands, a tacit vying in the matter of feminine finery, and a restrained striving for attention. The swank of these occasions had its duplication later on when the intermission promenade at an Eastman Theater concert was more important than the music to not a few concertgoers.

The Lyceum had a commodious balcony and a second balcony—a gallery, or "peanut gallery," as it was called. From this barren loft, which was reached after an Alpine ascent of iron stairs upon which the footfalls of the racing galleryites—for there was always a contest for down-front seats—rang like struck anvils, I saw a very early American performance of *The Merry Widow* and one of the first versions of Ziegfeld's *Follies*. There I heard the lovely, lilting plea of Miss Fritzie Scheff, "Kiss Me Again." In the Lyceum gallery I became so infatuated with that dainty darling of the musical stage, Julia Sanderson, that I shamefully deprecated my earlier love for Miss Janis as puppish and adolescent.

But my most memorable experience in the theater as a youth was the night I was shunted by an overwhelming crowd into the very last row of the gallery for Sir Henry Irving's performance of *The Merchant of Venice*. I was familiar with the play. I had read it and recited some of its lines in Miss Blair's grade in No. 3 School. Now in high school I was reading it again. Familiar as I was with the courtroom scene, my blood was congealed by the realism of Irving's portrayal of Shylock, and later on, in sleep, I could hear Shylock's ghoulish chortle:

> Ay, his breast:
> So says the bond: doth it not, noble judge?

and as he honed his knife on the sole of his boot I had the nightmarish conviction that Portia's ruse would fail and that the Jew would cut his pound of flesh from the region of Antonio's heart.

I discovered the wonders of the Lyceum in my early teens when Charlie Maloy and I would run up the long gallery stairs on Saturday night holding tightly our twenty-five-cent admission tickets; I became more intimately acquainted with the theater when, as a newspaper reporter, I occasionally reviewed its shows and frequently interviewed the men and women who starred in them.

Rochester no longer supports the living drama. Once it had theater the year round. The Lyceum, the Baker, the Temple, and even old Cook's Opera House, each, at one time or another, presented a stock company that played during the summer months. These were repertory companies that offered a new bill each week. Over the considerable number of years that local theatergoers willingly abandoned the evening cool of back yards and front porches to incarcerate themselves in stuffy, un-air-conditioned theaters they saw an array of young actors and actresses who later on became celebrated on the Broadway boards and in motion pictures.

With a long memory, one could go back to Francis X. Bushman, Margaret Wycherly, Jessie Bonstelle, and that perennial idol Bert Lytell, whom adoring women swarmed about as he left the Baker's stage door on matinee days. Florence Eldridge played a stock lead at the Lyceum and lived during the summer engagement on the shore of Conesus Lake with her husband, Howard Rumsey (Fredric March came later).

Bette Davis, an aspiring young actress, came to town with her mother to play bits for the Cukor-Kondolf Company, directed by George Cukor, who later won an Oscar for his direction of *My Fair Lady*. The pair found living quarters in a flat on Monroe Avenue, discovered the flat littered with call girls, and moved out.

The stock company people more or less settled down as Rochester residents. They related to the town. Local theater buffs gathered round them, members of the audience entertained them, stage-struck young men beaued the young women of the company. One of these stage-struck young men was Charles Ansley, who had played in local amateur theatricals. He was tall, dark, and handsome. His grandfather had deeded him a small business manufacturing apple-paring machinery. He met Miss Davis, and almost at once the ratchets, the blades, and the whirring intricacies of the apple-paring machines seemed horribly banal. The pair soon became engaged. Ansley took Miss Davis to Salamanca, New York, to meet his austere, banker-lawyer father. The meeting was not unpleasant, but the elder Ansley's dictum was stern: *Young man, you are not going to marry an actress.*

Bette Davis was soon dropped from the company by George Cukor, and she has never permitted him to forget what may have been one of Cukor's less inspired directorial judgments. She left town, and left young Ansley pining, disconsolate, and convinced that acting was the métier to which his life should be dedicated. Deputizing employees to manage his business, he went to New York, was cast in *Idiot's Delight* in which Alfred Lunt and Lynn Fontanne costarred and continued with these notable players through the long run of *There Shall Be No Night*, Robert Sherwood's second Pulitzer Prize play. In New York, Ansley repudiated his father's dictum. He married Miss Patricia Palmer, a pretty blond actress who was the *girl* in *Boy Meets Girl*, and who closed her stage career to settle in Rochester with her husband (who returned to the manufacture of apple-paring machines) after costarring with Canada Lee in *Native Son*.

In the mid-1920s, the Lyceum summer-stock company had as its leading man the immensely popular, roistering, romantic, hard-drinking, highly talented Louis Calhern. He was the hero of a small group of Rochester young men who were continually in the company of Calhern and the young actresses of the troupe. One of this group shared in some degree Calhern's rakehell tendencies. He was G. Curtis Gerling.

Gerling was a member of a fairly well-to-do family, long in Rochester, some of whose members were active in Democratic politics. There was nothing sauerkraut Dutch about Curt. He had the air and look of the man about town. In time he engaged in various enterprises, including the operation of a milk route, and appeared to profit from each of them. Women thought him "terribly sexy," and Gerling didn't mind that at all. He was sophisticated, witty, apt with words, and bawdy. Very early he realized that his bawdiness had a shock effect. After that, he made it his eye patch.

Several years after the Cukor-Kondolf Company disbanded, and Calhern and the pretty young actresses had quitted the town, Gerling organized a chain of country weeklies, and wrote a lively little book about Rochester, which he printed on his own presses in Webster. He called the book *Smugtown U.S.A.* In it he trod lightly on the kibes of several of our sacred cows, and told what a dull, stuffy, smug town was the city in which he had lived apparently with keen satisfaction all his life.

The satire and prose style of *Smugtown U.S.A.* were hardly reminiscent of Jonathan Swift but the book excited the indignation of those who had been the targets of Gerling's barbs and was sniggeringly acclaimed by Rochesterians who had perhaps a scunner on the town because they believed it had frustrated their business, or professional, or social aspirations. Gerling with some wit anatomized what he professed were the formulae for success in Rochester; he computed our millionaires; he put names chuck-a-block on every printed page and everyone whose name appeared in *Smugtown* got a copy of the book, even though some immediately afterward carried it with fire tongs to an open hearth.

In *Smugtown*, Gerling told nothing of his own earlier escapades or of his goggle-eyed devotion to Calhern. At one time he tried valiantly to match the style and manner of his hero, but Calhern was something special and apart. In full career, he left his imitators spent and panting in his wake. On stage he often represented an enchanting swashbuckler, and his off-stage performances were not lacking in dash and bravura.

At two o'clock one June morning, during the 1926 stock season at the Lyceum, Calhern, suddenly conceiving himself in love, took Miss Ilka Chase, who was playing with him in *Seventh Heaven*, down to the town of Irondequoit, where he knocked loudly on the door of Peace Justice Isaac Buyck. The justice was a terror to speeding motorists who were brought before him, and who denigrated him as a rock-hard old curmudgeon who would wave his own mother to jail if he caught her exceeding twenty miles an hour on Titus Avenue. But his carapace had porous spots; Ike was a romantic at heart. Stuffing his nightshirt into hastily drawn-on trousers, he admitted the about-to-be betrothed couple, and though they had failed to provide themselves with either a ring or a marriage license, Buyck arranged with the town clerk for the second item, and performed the ceremony without the first.

The couple set up "housekeeping" in the Sagamore Hotel. Calhern was a gallant, handsome, loving bridegroom, and a husband with no more talent for domesticity than a satyr. Although it was a time when the sale of hard liquor was prohibited by law, hard liquor was so commonly sold in downtown Rochester that a charge of grapeshot fired from the entrance of the Sagamore would likely have hit three or four blind pigs. Miss Chase had a little poodle dog which Calhern insisted on walking every night after the show and brought back sometimes not until nine o'clock in the morning.

"That dog of yours," he once explained to his pretty bride, with a wry shake of his head, "led me into some of the damnedest places."

Calhern continued as a stock lead in Rochester for several summers. In time he and Miss Chase were divorced, and he married Mrs. Lydig Hoyt, a New York society woman with stage aspirations. The new Mrs. Calhern did not play with her husband in Rochester, but attempted nonetheless to keep him under her surveillance. I knew Calhern well, and once had him for dinner at Scottsville. We were at the dessert course when the telephone rang. I answered it, and called into the dining room.

"Lou, it's for you. New York's calling."

I returned to the table. Calhern went out to the wall phone in the hall. In a moment we heard his very earnest protest.

"But darling—*darling*, this is not a saloon. This is Clune's house, in Scottsville."

Chapter 25

A great deal that was distinguished in the theater was exhibited in the Lyceum during the years of its glory, but it was not the universal playhouse of the town nor necessarily the one that brought the most loyal patrons into the parquet circle and the cheaper seats higher up. The Temple Theater, which succeeded Cook's Opera House as the home of big-time vaudeville, depended to some extent on devotees of this form of entertainment who reserved the same seats week after week throughout the season. And the Baker Theater, on North Fitzhugh Street, which came into being largely through the energies of the Shubert Brothers, those scrounging, hard-boiled, brilliant showmen from Syracuse, had audiences not only during the stock season of Bert Lytell but during periods when the house played 10, 20, 30 (cent) melodramas that would hardly have left the Baker for the Lyceum if given free tickets for John Barrymore in *Hamlet*.

The melodramas at the Baker, which later on played at the National Theater on Main Street West, were heart-rending efforts that were charged with gunshot, intrigue, and love. Purists, who approved of the drama only when it was very broad "a," and pious souls who disapproved of it in any form, protested that these thrillers incited boys to crime and induced waywardness in girls. I think myself the critics mistook excitement for perniciousness. The heroes of the pieces were always manly, upright, and valorous; the heroines, sweet and pure. In the closing scene the hero and the heroine invariably personified a triumph of righteousness.

I visited a theater for the first time in the winter of 1899 when my father took me to Cook's Opera House, where that week the feature of a seven-act variety bill was a bicycle race on home trainers between Harry Elks, a famous cyclist, and Mile-A-Minute Murphy, who earlier that year had ridden a mile in 57⅘ seconds back of a train on the Long Island Railroad. Some time later, unknown to my parents, I saw from a gallery seat in the Baker a matinee performance of *For Fame and Fortune*, starring the ex-featherweight champion of the world, Terrible Terry McGovern. The gallery was filled with youthful idolators, not a few of whom had come from downtown streets with bundles of unsold newspapers. Large signs were stenciled on the gallery walls, NO WHISTLING OR STAMPING.

In the final episode of the drama, Terrible Terry leaped through a window of an old mill to find Grace, his sweetheart, in the hands of Silk Hat Harry, the arch villain. Harry had Grace by the throat and was muttering death threats between clenched teeth. A trap door gaped over a mill race. Skipping swiftly across the floor, McGovern clipped the villain on the jaw. Silk Hat toppled over, and lay writhing on the floor. For a moment, the gallant suitor held Grace in a loving embrace. Freeing her, he raised his eyes to the gallery, and apropos of nothing in the script, issued a stentorian enjoinder.

"Boys," he called up to the galleryites, "boys, be good to your mothers!"

At such a moment, who would heed the gallery signs? Who, indeed? The curtain fell amid pandemonium.

* * *

Today, downtown Rochester has several movie houses. It has large new hotels whose elaborate lobbies are frequently populated by badge-wearing delegates to conventions. There are musical acts nightly in a restaurant atop Midtown Plaza. The towering Xerox Building has a large restaurant and a ground-level plaza that in winter becomes a skating rink. There is a go-go girl place on Court Street, and a hardy perennial of a strip joint at East Avenue and Broadway, catercorner from the Protestant Episcopal Cathedral and a few steps from the University Club. Years ago, when her disciples responded to her art as the faithful come forth at the muezzin cry, the insinuating Miss Rose LaRose filled the resort for seven nights, but since then the stripping, grinding, and bumping have been routine, old hat, and about as exciting as watching your Uncle Charlie whitewash a cellar wall.

West, across the river, the large and suitably designed War Memorial books a variety of attractions that include roller derbies, home exhibits, ice hockey, rock concerts, auto shows, and conclaves of Jehovah's Witnesses. The sparse theater we have is represented now in the auditorium of the Masonic Temple, well out Main Street East, which would do nicely for a competition of brass bands but is as inappropriate for intimate drama as a riding hall. The concerts of the Eastman Theater are consistently well attended, and Rochester prides itself on its devotion to good music.

People still go downtown in Rochester after dark, but not with the same rather festive spirit as years ago, in the last years of the pre-Prohibition era, when there were several excellent restaurants in the center of the city and when the hotels catered to people who were on the town for an evening and wanted perhaps a cold bottle, a hot bird, and a dance orchestra after leaving one of the six or eight theaters that were showing living actors.

Main Street was hardly Broadway, but Rochesterians enjoyed strolling its sidewalks in the evening hours, particularly toward the end of the week. It was the traditional artery of commerce, the place where one went in the daytime for one's material needs and for entertainment after dark. The character of the street changed after nightfall. It became at times even a little festive. There was a not unpleasant bustle at certain street corners. Lighted store windows offered glittering displays. There was a medley of sounds: the sharp, angry clang of trolley bells, the honk of motor horns, the mixed choir of the Salvation Army accompanied by the boom of the big drum and the high notes of brasses; the shrill denunciatory voice of a street curb orator ranting against the American system; the smoother tones of a pitchman at the Main and South Water street corner, where pitchmen had made their stand for years, bemusing his audience with an oral explanation and a manual demonstration of a patent knife sharpener, a new-fangled can opener, a spot remover guaranteed to remove the most persistent stain with no harm to the fabric, a gyroscopic top—"not a toy, but a fascinating scientific instrument . . ."

There were numerous all-night lunchrooms, the most notable of which was Hall's, fifteen or twenty steps into Front Street from the east corner of Main Street East. For fifteen cents one might have one of Hall's famous chicken pies, with its tasty brown crust beneath which vegetables and honest chicken slices were mixed in a thick glutinous gravy that would stick to a man's ribs and sustain him a full working day. The soups were rich and full bodied, not synthetic pourings from a can; the stews had honest chunks of meat like the chicken pies, and the coffee, served in mugs as thick as battleship plating, had a bristling, hair-raising strength.

Hall's brought in Front Street derelicts, of course. But its clientele was not limited; it had a cosmopolitan cast. At night it attracted printers, pressmen, and reporters from the morning newspapers; high school boys downtown for a romp; policemen, streetcar workers, liverymen and taxicab drivers, night watchmen, musicians, and fellows, sometimes with a skinful, who came in late—or very early in the morning—after the last licensed place on the line had closed. Socialites in tail coats and tall hats occasionally stopped for a midnight snack after a formal party. There were no tables. You ate off the spatulate arm of a chair. The busboy was a squat, hairy, taciturn, muscular young man named Livadas, whom many knew only as Jerry the Greek. He left. The next time I saw him was years later at a boxing show in Syracuse. Jack Dempsey, the world's heavyweight champion, was summoned from a spectator's chair to be introduced from the ring. With him was a squat, muscular man in varnished pumps, trousers with a knife-edge crease, a purple cummerbund, a well-tailored dinner jacket—and a checked cap! Jerry the Greek, who had become Dempsey's trainer and fidus Achates, proudly took a bow at the side of his beloved "chomp."

A. B. Sanderl, who later became manager of the Hotel Seneca, had a distinguished restaurant on the south side of Main Street East, not far from the Four Corners. Fred London had a fine eating place at Main and South Water streets that advertised Ransomville roast duck and kraut as the *pièce de résistance* of a menu that was largely composed of German dishes. Harry Bullock, the sportingest restaurateur in town, had Bullock's Cafe directly north of the Hotel Seneca. His steaks were choice cuts; his chops thick and succulent. Bullock's was a man's place, there was no Ladies' Sitting Room, although Harry was a great beau of the ladies. Show people were his friends. His gallery of autographed photographs of men and women of the stage was almost as large as Lafe Heidel's, on Water Street.

I was in Bullock's late one Saturday afternoon with a good friend, Edward J. O'Brien, from the Detective Bureau. Detectives were personages in those days; everyone downtown knew them and they were warmly received in downtown resorts. O'Brien was a genial and popular Irishman. In late afternoon, the bar in front of Bullock's cash register was always pyramided with delicious ham sandwiches, which were free.

We ate three or four ham sandwiches while Eddie had a beer and I consumed a ginger ale. We then went next door to the Seneca, where the bar was in the rear of the lobby. There were no printed menus for the free lunch, as there were in the Hotel Knickerbocker in New York, but there was a long table of free viands and a man in a spotless white coat to serve them. We had lobster salad and pickled beets. We crossed Clinton Avenue to the Hayward and had hard-boiled eggs and fried clams. At the Whitcomb House, there was spiced ham and potato salad. We went to two or three lesser places, for Herkimer County cheese, country sausage, a slice of cold turkey, salted nuts, and ripe olives. In one resort there was hot soup and pretzels.

O'Brien had a habit of snapping a forefinger against the under brim of his brown derby. He gave the brim a finger snap now.

"I'll tell you what, Mose," he said (they called me "Mose Christmas" around police headquarters, since that was my most violent expletive), "I'll sell you the rest of the route for $5."

The Ernest-Noeth Dairy Lunch Company had a restaurant in State Street called the White Kitchen and another on Main Street East, in Reynolds Arcade. These places had waitresses and bare marble-topped tables and a man in the front window tossing flapjacks from a hot griddle. They operated twenty-four hours a day, the waitresses working twelve-hour shifts. Noeth left the combine in time. Alfred C. Ernest continued with one restaurant, which he moved to the east side of the river. It became the Manhattan. It is now located in East Avenue a short distance from the Main Street corner, and it is managed by the sons and grandsons of the founder.

Years ago, Child's came into town, opened a huge restaurant on upper Main Street, presumably with the idea of winning over the Manhattan's patronage. Child's was a novelty, a big-city operation, and some of the Manhattan's patrons left the old stand for the new one. They were soon back. And it wasn't long before Child's began to cut its table space. In time, they cut it very fine, and then quit entirely. They had discovered such syndicates as Huyler's and Page & Shaw had discovered when they attempted to compete against the locally owned Whittle's candy store that Rochestarians of that era were peculiarly prejudiced in favor of local purveyors of goods and services and that interpolators were often suspect.

The Manhattan was widely known for the excellence of its food and service. Its prices were moderate. It was a commercial eating place. Wines and liquors were not served (they are today, at tables; there is no bar). People went to the Manhattan for breakfast, lunch, dinner, or for a midnight snack, but except in the late hours of the night rarely lingered for social intercourse.

Outstanding among the city's restaurants that lent themselves to what might be called "gracious dining" was the Hofbrauhaus on South Avenue. Its proprietor was Fred J. Odenbach, who had grown up in the restaurant business. His father had had an eating place and saloon. Fred was expert in all matters that pertained to the preparation and serving of food; he managed the Hofbrauhaus with Germanic attention to detail, and his personality and charm made him the most popular professional host in town.

There was earnest competition in those days among the larger hotels and restaurants for late business. Powers Hotel petitioned theatergoers to visit its rathskeller after the show and the Whitcomb House advertised that Joe Monk, locally famous as leader of the Temple Theater orchestra, would direct a dance band in the rathskeller of that hostelry from 10:30 P.M. until closing. The Seneca had dancing in its elegant Palm Room and the Eggleston made a specialty of after-theater suppers. Odenbach's Hofbrauhaus frequently added acts to its musical entertainment. A few years before Sonja Henie's ice shows zoomed into popularity, Fred Odenbach installed a rink that seemed no larger than a spread tablecloth and engaged Miss Katie Schmidt, one of the first professional women figure skaters, to perform on the tiny ice sheet. The act was a great novelty.

Odenbach advertised his musical and variety entertainment in the newspapers and theater programs. He made no public mention of a lithe, pretty little blond girl who circulated among his patrons handing buns and hot breads from a tray that hung from her shoulders and who in time was to become a toast of London, the dancing partner of Fred Astaire, and, briefly, the fiancée of the great Sir Winston's son, Randolph Churchill.

Claire Luce had fibbed about her age, which was fifteen, in order to work in the restaurant. When she had saved a small sum of money she summarily quit the Hofbrauhaus and fled to New York to answer a chorus call at the New Amsterdam Theater. She had run away from home before to join a third-class ballet troupe and had been fetched back, upon her parents' complaint, by the police. She was determined this time that her escape from home would be permanent, and it was. She had studied dancing under Mrs. Florence Colebrook Powers, a noted local instructress, and her training, her lovely figure, and her blond prettiness got her a place in the chorus line of *Little Jessie James*.

In my time in the newspaper business Miss Luce and Philip Barry, the playwright, who grew up on Amherst Street and was graduated from East High, were Rochester's most notable theatrical figures. Both were friends of mine. Claire has said that I gave her the first publicity she had ever had. During the height of her dancing career I saw very little of her. She was very much in vogue. She was the top dancer in half a dozen musicals, she married a youthful millionaire (from whom she was soon divorced), and lived in high style on upper Park Avenue.

She went to Paris, replaced the famous Mistinguett in the Casino de Paris, and became the pet of the boulevardiers. Upon her return to New York, Ziegfeld put her name up in lights in the last *Follies* he personally directed. Later, when Adele Astaire left her brother, Fred, to marry Lord Cavendish, Claire Luce became Astaire's dancing partner in *Gay Divorce*, which repeated its New York success with a long stand in London.

Miss Luce in time turned from dancing to the legitimate theater, played Curley's wife in the production of John Steinbeck's *Of Mice and Men*, and had other notable roles in New York and London. She was in England during part of the war, and remained there through the terrible, soul-searing ordeal of the London blitz. Beneath her flowerlike fragility—her ethereality—there was strength and courage and sinewy determination. "I can't go home," she wrote, from the United Hunts Club, where she was living after being bombed out of the Ritz. "These people have been too wonderful to me. I've got to stay and try to help."

After the war, I saw quite a little of Miss Luce. I arranged for her appearance with an East Rochester stock company, where she costarred with Francis Sullivan, the English actor. I occasionally beaued her around New York. When people turned to look at Claire, I enjoyed a reflective bid at fame. One evening, as we crossed the threshold to a large and fashionable party on West 57th

Street, a woman cried, "Claire—Claire, dah'ling!" and threw her arms around my companion. It was the first Mrs. Anthony Eden.

I took her to dinner with Claude Bragdon, who had abandoned the most distinguished architectural practice in Rochester after a series of disagreements with Mr. Eastman, for New York and a new career as stage designer. The intellectual Mr. Bragdon and the ex-bun girl hit it off at once. Miss Luce was studying French and painting and Shakespeare (*Time* once trumpeted her as the first American-born actress to play a leading role at the festival at Stratford-on-Avon). Bragdon was extremely knowledgeable on the subject of painting and Shakespeare and Miss Luce heeded his counsel. The pair played chess together. There was a hope that the converted stage designer might one day set a show in which Miss Luce would star. The hope died aborning.

I was to call for Claire at six o'clock one evening at Delmonico's, where she was then living. We were to dine together. When I arrived at the appointed hour, the desk clerk told me Miss Luce had left the hotel late in the afternoon and had not returned. I left word that I would wait for her on the top floor of the hotel, which had been assigned for the exclusive use of Leo Dewey Welch, with whom I had lunched that noon at a bankers' club.

It is an undignified epithet, and perhaps a little irreverent, but I always think of Leo Welch and Harry Hagerty as the Rochester Whiz Kids; the Whiz Kids who *came* from Rochester! Welch, a native of what was formerly Charlotte, left the University of Rochester to go into banking in South America. Hagerty left old Cathedral High to take a job as timekeeper for the street railway company and then to work in New York for the Metropolitan Life Insurance Company.

After representing the National City Bank in the Argentine for twenty years, Welch moved to New York presumably to continue his banking career in that city. Instead, he went over to Standard Oil of New Jersey where, in what seemed to me a surprisingly short time, he rose to chairman of the Board. He left Standard Oil to become chairman of the Board (and, incidentally, the subject of a *Newsweek* cover story) of the inchoate Communications Satellite Corporation, which was about to launch a stock issue of something like $220,000,000.

Harry Hagerty, Welch's senior by half a dozen years, remained with Metropolitan Life in New York and zoomed, as Welch did, into the golden ionosphere. As financial vice-president of that cyclopean corporation, he managed perhaps the largest investment portfolio in the country.

"The kind of money Harry Hagerty handles," a Wall Street investment counselor once told me, "would make J. P. Morgan, the first, seem like a fellow buying mining and railroad stocks from a street peddler."

When Aristotle Socrates Onassis needed two million for his first oil tanker he went to Hagerty for the money and the old Cathedral High boy later on let him have other millions.

A group of brass from a great English oil syndicate, assembled in a board of directors' room in New York, were trying to ask Mr. Hagerty for something, but he couldn't understand what. Their English accents were too thick. A man rose from a chair in the rear of the room.

"Mr. Hagerty," he said, "I guess you and I are the only people in this room who have the same ancestry. My name's Boyle. What we'd like from you are one hundred twenty-five million."

Mr. Hagerty took the request under advisement. He didn't go all out: he let the oil people have ninety million and they got the rest elsewhere. I knew something about the man in the British delegation who had enunciated the request for the loan, and it was because of this that Hagerty told me the story. He was Joseph W. Boyle, Jr., of London, a director of and counsel for Shell Oil, and my wife's brother.

*　　*　　*

The day I lunched with Leo Welch in the bankers' club and later ascended to his apartment on the top floor of Delmonico's was shortly after he had arrived from the Argentine with the idea of settling in New York. His wife and daughter had not yet joined him. Claire Luce came in time to the apartment and she and Mr. Welch quickly discovered that they had mutual friends in Buenos Aires, London, and Paris. Welch wore beautifully tailored clothes. He was slim, handsome, with a Continental mustache and a cosmopolitan sheen. His role was that of an international financier; he looked it in every aspect, and filled it brilliantly. Although the blond charmer had come to the apartment under my auspices I soon found myself in a corner listening to catches of French songs which the Luce-Welch duo accompanied with a four-handed performance on a piano. Claire returned to my escort only when Welch decided that a previous commitment prevented him from joining us at dinner. I rather regretted this. Miss Luce and I went to the Plaza. It would have been nice, when the check came, to outfumble a man who was on the way to becoming Board chairman of Standard Oil.

Chapter 26

On rare occasions during my early years in the newspaper business I suffered an acute sense of denial. I resented the nocturnal bondage that was the lot of the morning newspaper reporter. I felt that as a night worker I was missing many pleasures that were enjoyed by young men of my own age who were engaged in conventional daytime pursuits. The feeling was most taunting in the spring: "In the spring" when, as the poet sang, "a young man's fancy lightly turns to thoughts of love."

Returning to the *Democrat and Chronicle* on a pleasant spring evening with two or three news stories that would keep me cooped up in the newsroom until after midnight I might linger at the curb a few minutes before entering the newspaper building. Main Street was then a cavalcade of automobiles, as it is today. But in those days motoring was still something of a novelty and many motorists came downtown in the evening "merely for the ride." If one were bent on a pleasure spin it was better to hold to the pavements of prominent city streets than chance a blowout, or a stalled engine, or the failure of a squinting headlight on one of the narrow, un-paved, unlighted roads of the adjacent countryside. It was a vogue-ish thing to drive through East Avenue and into Main Street and out as far as Bull's Head, at West Avenue and Genesee Street, and back on the south side of Main Street.

In many of its aspects Rochester at that time was still "small town." There was a homogeneity and neighborliness about the city that regrettably has now disappeared. We Rochesterians knew one another. We met in restaurants, in the theater, in the waiting room of the New York Central Station, in movie houses, on public dance floors, in stores, at park band concerts, in the ball park, on the ice rink of the Widewaters, and called one another by name. It seemed to me, if I lingered at the curb in front of the newspaper building, that half a dozen motorists would wave or call to me in not many more than that number of minutes. And if these salutes came from gay blades of the town I might be assailed by the torment of envy for, invariably, Ted Yates, or Lambert Dunn, or Dick Finucane, or Kenneth Likley would each have a pretty girl at his side and the tonneau of the car might also be occupied by another young couple. They were joy bound and carefree. They might parade Main Street a couple of times and then go on to Simm's Inn, far out East Avenue or proceed to one of the dance places down along the lake. Turning from the bright kaleidoscopic spectacle of Main Street to the drudgery of the newsroom I'd feel martyred for an unworthy cause. These black moods never persisted long. If my work-a-night routine restrained me from the pleasant goings-on of my young contemporaries my job had its compensations. With a rap on the door I would be admitted backstage to the Temple Theater, a privilege my friends would have cherished, and none enjoyed.

I dined with Barney Oldfield, whose euphonious sounding name was considered a synonym for unearthly speed; I swaggered through fire lines with a tin reporter's badge fixed to my lapel; interviewed notorious criminals; visited with the nation's huge, amiable Chief Executive William Howard Taft; consorted with the spectacular evangelist Billy Sunday; took May Yohe, the raven-haired, fog-horned contralto, one-time possessor of the Hope Diamond (named after her former husband) to tea, which, for Miss Yohe, consisted of pony after pony of brandy; sat enthralled part of an afternoon with Bessie McCoy, the wonderful Yama-Yama Girl, who married the idol of all youthful newspapermen, Richard Harding Davis.

There were boxing shows every Monday night during the winter in the old Armory on Clinton Avenue South, which was then called Convention Hall. In the summer the bouts were held under the auspices of the Airdrome Athletic Club in an open-air arena next to the Masonic Temple on Clinton Avenue North. Jake Carey was the matchmaker and one of the promoters of the clubs. His other occupation was booking running horses. In World War I the Knights of Columbus sent him overseas to manage the extensive boxing program sponsored by that organization. In this capacity Carey introduced the Marine Gene Tunney, who won the AEF championship, and after a span of years, the heavyweight championship of the world.

On fight nights I usually managed my assignments so that I could be passed into Convention Hall or into the Airdrome shortly before the main event. Prizefighting was prohibited by state law at the time and professional matches were announced as exhibitions. And there was a liturgy about the introduction of the boxers. "Both boys," the announcer was at pains to proclaim, "are members of our club." No decisions were made from the ring and the gamblers bet on the decisions of the boxing writers of the five newspapers, best three out of five. Charlie Kinney covered the bouts for the *Democrat and Chronicle*, and it was Charlie's practice—for fight nights were always occasions of festival—to stop on his way to the arena for a long hour at the Eggleston bar.

One night, after witnessing a rather important heavyweight contest from the rear of the arena, I went on to a late assignment before returning to the office. It was close to midnight when I left the elevator. I stopped before going on to the newsroom at Kinney's roll-top desk. The sports editor was stutteringly poking two fingers at the keys of his typewriter.

"That was quite a thing, that main go," I said. Kinney half straightened from his slouched position and looked up with bloodshot eyes. I knew at once he had overindulged.

"You she-e it, kid?"

"Yes. Every round."

"Hum. Schumfight." His hunched torso sagged. He looked down at the copy paper in his typewriter and my eyes followed his gaze. He had been writing for half an hour but had not once shifted the carriage of the machine. All that he had for a fight story was a single smudged line of type. He struck a key with a faltering forefinger and offered me a one-sided grin.

"You she-e it, kid, you go on. You write it."

My late assignment amounted to very little. I disposed of it in less than ten minutes and wrote the fight story Kinney had flubbed. His gratitude was deep and abiding. Two weeks later he came to whisper in my ear that a dear pal of his, the manager of Fred Irwin's *Majestics*, a burlesque show playing at the Corinthian, had a girl in the cast named Roxana who the manager would lend me any night on half a day's notice. "Bennie tells me she's a real honey," Charlie said. "Bennie's getting old, he can't hold Roxana's clip, and he don't want her getting restless and out on the town. I told him what a nice clean kid you were . . ." He gave me Roxana's room number at the Bristol Hotel on Central Avenue.

I never met Roxana and my disinterest was so extreme that I never bothered even to watch her performance from the audience side of the Corinthian footlights. A few weeks before, I had met a titian-haired prom trotter from Amsterdam, New York, who seemed to me to embody in total the beauty, the charm, and the graces of womankind. She was visiting Bessie Clum during Horse Show Week. Bessie Clum was a very nice girl, whose family had originated on Jefferson Avenue and whose father had at one time been a molder in a brass foundry. He had progressed. With growing affluence Philip Clum moved into the Tenth Ward, and growing still more affluent, with a brass foundry of his own, he built a fine house on East Avenue a couple of doors west of Culver Road. There Bessie gave a party for Ruth McN——, her Amsterdam guest, and displayed her all week in the Tea Tent and at a box at the Horse Show.

I was enamored of Ruth McN——. My devotion continued unabated from Horse Show Week in early September to deep into the winter. I am sure of this because of an incident one near-zero February night on the sidewalk at the Four Corners. I met there a friend of Bessie Clum's, Colin Brown, who had been at the party at which Bessie had introduced her Amsterdam friend. Colin was familiar with my ecstasy and sympathetic about my suit. He listened attentively in the biting February cold while I rhapsodized about the titian-haired beauty from the Mohawk Valley. Then, gingerly touching his ears with gloved fingers, he said apologetically:

"Sorry, Heinie. But I guess I better be going. I guess my ears are frozen." And they were!

I ardently pressed my suit, but this was a unilateral courtship. A girl who had been swinging over the circuit—Yale, Princeton, Williams, and Cornell—sorting out suitors as she might sort out swatches of fabric at a couturier's had no more interest in an $18-a-week night worker than in a Zulu chieftain. Soon she married a wealthy stockbroker from New Orleans. I was not invited to the wedding. The invitations, I learned, were engraved by Tiffany.

* * *

The Horse Show, to which Bessie Clum had taken her house guest, was the most notable social-sporting event Rochester has ever known. It was an offshoot of the Rochester Industrial Exposition, which had originated in Convention Hall as a display of industrial products. Restricted to a single building, the Exposition was soon a cluttered, spatchcocked sort of show, and in 1911 it was transferred to the forty-acre site formerly occupied by the State Industrial School. That institution for delinquent youth had left its gray-walled, Bastille-like city compound for an ample acreage of unwalled farm lands in the upper Genesee Valley and added agricultural studies to its academic and industrial curriculum.

In its new location, which was called Exposition Park (later changed to Edgerton Park to honor the memory of our self-perpetuating mayor, Uncle Hi), the Exposition had room to expand and develop. There were several buildings on the grounds that were suitable for industrial, home, educational, and other displays that needed the protection of a roof and walls. Livestock and farm machinery were exhibited under canvas. A midway with rides, fun houses, whirligigs, mild girly shows, and a tent where fake wrestling matches were staged was introduced over the stenciled protests of niggling do-gooders who seem always to strive to make virtue a bore. A nationally known band gave matinee and evening concerts.

But the management realized after the first year that a new and novel attraction was needed, and the next year (1912) a man in a red coat and a tall hat blew a flourish on a horn and the "equine aristocrats," as the advertisements called them, pranced into a white-fenced, flower-banked oval of putting green turf at Exposition Park and Rochester's famous Horse Show was under way.

At its inception the Horse Show was supposed to be merely an adjunct to the Exposition. Instead, it was soon the dominant attraction and without it the Exposition would not have survived. It caught on at once with the general public and it became a rite and an article of faith with that limited element of the community known as Society. Starting rather tentatively as a three-day show, it was extended in succeeding years to six days, with the opening on Labor Day, with scores of classes, with entries from the greatest stables in this country and Canada, and with crowds that totaled more than 100,000 during the week. As a social function there has never been anything like it in town; as a sporting event it has been rivaled only by the National Open Golf Championship, twice played over the course of the Oak Hill Country Club.

The Rochester Horse Show was an afternoon exhibition, but the fun and excitement did not end with the judging of the last class of the day and the departure of the grandstand spectators and those who occupied a tier of boxes that was separated from the show ring by an esplanade known as Peacock Walk. You couldn't bring carloads of some of the wealthiest and most prominent people in the land into town for an afternoon competition and neglect them during the evening hours, and they were not neglected. The opportunity to fraternize with Vanderbilts, Wanamakers, du Ponts, Gimbels, Rockefellers, Stotesburys, and others of that stripe was unique, and the eager beavers of our social hierarchy made the most of it. It was a gala week. There was a stupendous Horse Show Ball, there were elaborate dinners and dances in private homes, in social clubs, in the ballroom of the Seneca and, after that hostelry was built, in the Hotel Sagamore's roof-top Wisteria Garden.

The term Horse Show has a snooty connotation. Hearing it, one is inclined to think of Piping Rock, or Locust Valley, or the Olympia in London, or Devon, Pennsylvania, or the great full-figged coronationlike National in Madison Square Garden. Oddly, in our town, large numbers of run-of-the-mill folk, who had no social aspirations and didn't know the withers from the fetlock of a horse, delighted in the performances of saddle horses, jumpers, hackneys, and others, and it was their patronage that kept the Rochester Horse Show a going enterprise for nearly twenty years. They clamored for tickets for the grandstand, overcrowded it, and the management was soon constrained to flank it with smaller seating structures. They were warmly partisan about the competitors in the ring. For years Miss Loula Long (later Mrs. Combes) of Kansas City, Missouri, enjoyed the sort of popularity ordinarily reserved for the leading player on the Rochester Baseball Club. A fashionably dressed lady, of great good nature, who drove harness horses, Miss Long had that nameless something called *je ne sais quoi*. The grandstanders loved her. "Loula! Loula!" they called to her gleefully. And often when the judges fixed the blue on one of her champions and the stands rose en masse in tribute she would embrace them with a gesture and smile upon them, and their thumping applause would follow her shiny little rig as it wheeled through the gate into the paddock.

The guiding spirit of the Rochester Horse Show, and the man who made it, next to the Madison Square Garden show, the finest competition of its kind on the continent, was Norman VanVoorhis. A large, witty, gregarious bachelor, Mr. VanVoorhis had a talent for management and a wide acquaintance among leading exhibitors of show horses. As chairman of the Horse Show Committee he organized and directed the autumn spectacle without charge to the Exposition, and at considerable personal expense. In the early days, some exhibitors admitted that they came here "only because of Norman"; and some no longer came after VanVoorhis, following a quarrel with Edgar F. Edwards, the well-paid over-all head of the Exposition, renounced his labor of love and quit his chairmanship.

One of the eagerly anticipated events of Horse Show Week was a stag clambake at the VanVoorhis home on Ridgeway Avenue. Men who rode, drove, owned, or judged horses found greater delight in this hearty, masculine, uninhibited entertainment than in any other social function arranged for their pleasure, and no one eligible for an invitation wanted to miss it. Here there was a great leavening of fellowship and no deference to position or titles, and Sir Adam Beck and Sir Clifton Sifton were there, along with guests with names that represented great American fortunes. The house itself seemed designed for whacking affairs of this sort, and when Norman VanVoorhis left it and moved to Rome, New York, it lent itself readily to public entertainment. Under the title of Terrace Gardens it became the best-known night club in town and memorable for a display of gallantry by brave men who, one midnight, risked their necks diving to the rescue of Miss Jean Harlow who had tumbled into a lily pond back of the bar and was floundering desperately in two feet of water.

The Horse Show was more than an equine carnival and there were times when the spectacle along Peacock Walk and in an ornate Tea Tent that was situated at one end of the esplanade vied with the fancy quadrupeds in the ring for public attention. The Tea Tent was presided over by Mrs. Warham Whitney with grace, style, and the indubitable authority the town's social matriarch was able to exert. Mrs. Whitney believed that ladies did not smoke and women who did were rigorously precluded from this indulgence in the Tea Tent.

Each afternoon there was a continual promenade along Peacock Walk and at one time or another the prettiest ladies on the grounds visited the Tea Tent to display their chic and be tested in the lists of fashion. For years it was my pleasant task as a newspaper reporter to cover the human interest and social aspects of the Horse Show. At times I shared this assignment with William P. Costello, a fellow reporter who was one of the best-dressed, most handsome, and attractive young men in Rochester, and together we kept score on the debutantes. If a girl appeared twice during Horse Show Week in the same costume we declared her out of contention, and if it was necessary to mention her at all we did so slightingly and at the bottom of our space.

One summer, during the interim between his graduation from Yale and his matriculation at George Pierce Baker's Drama Workshop (then at Harvard), young Philip Barry worked as a reporter for the *Post Express* and covered the social side of the Horse Show for that socially conscious newspaper. On one occasion he did an amusing satire in which he described Miss Bonnie Beattie, who appeared in an orange sweater and hat as a "double Bronx"; remarked how Miss Blanche Dumont moved about the Tea Tent "with chin high, as is her custom, and an occasional smile for the fortunate"; and with these, and other sallies, aroused the ire of certain members of the hierarchy who appealed to Francis B. Mitchell, proprietor of the newspaper, to fire "the impertinent and irreverent young upstart." Phil needed no pink slip from Mitchell. He was going on to Harvard the next week, his trial run as a newspaper reporter over; and no one had any expectation that in coming years the bright young man from Amherst Street would bring forth such perceptive and stylish comedies of manners as *Paris Bound, Holiday*, and *The Philadelphia Story*—to name a few —and be assessed by Professor Baker as a greater playwright than the Nobel Prize winner Eugene O'Neill.

The Tea Tent was not, of course, the exclusive domain of local fashionables, some of whom took turns during the week handing about chocolate cookies and pouring tea from great silver urns. There one would frequently see Miss Jeane Browne Scott, of Cynwyd, Pennsylvania, whose harness horses occasionally defeated Loula Long Combes's entries but who failed to match Mrs. Combes's popularity with the gallery. Miss Scott was very lovely to look upon. But there was a chill, chaste cast to her beauty and an aloftness of mien that put her at a remove from the grandstand crowds.

Men came to the Tea Tent as well as women, some accompanied

by pretty ladies, and others to look about and perhaps find a pretty lady to escort. I have seen there Commodore Aemlius Jarvis, whose hunt team was a sensation in the ring; William J. (Wild Bill) Donovan; Governor Charles S. Whitman, a house guest of Mr. and Mrs. Warham Whitney; Walter H. Hanley, the rich Providence brewer, who displayed a twelve-horse hitch in downtown streets in the morning and saddle horses ridden by his wife in the show ring in the afternoon. William H. Wanamaker, who owned the big store in Philadelphia, would come in for tea with his stunning daughter, Miss Isabella.

And one pleasant afternoon, a well-larded man with an imposing mustache, who wore a handsome double-breasted blue suit, and carried in hand a hard straw hat, came in with a tiny blond girl, and upon this pair all eyes were quickly bent.

"It—it's Mr. Vanderbilt—and the Candy Kid!" a deb in a corner gasped in whispered awe.

"It's the *Bessie* one," her companion confirmed. "W-e-l-l!"

It was indeed the Bessie of the Candy Kids, who was the butt of Eddie Cantor's canard when she danced in the pony line of *Ziegfeld's Follies*.

"We've got a very loving and conscientious girl in this show," Cantor would tell the audience. "Little Bessie Fuller. The management pays her fifty dollars a week, and every week she sends her mother a hundred."

Whittle's famous Rochester candy store had moved from Main and North Water streets, where I had known it as a boy, to a large, glass-fronted emporium at East Avenue and Main Street which had, besides such decorative effects as gold-framed mirrors, period furniture, great gilded chandeliers, and an open hearth, the ornamental Candy Kids—Bessie Fuller and her tall, stately, dark-haired fellow clerk, Peggy McGill, and the pair, reputedly, had more beaux than any other two girls in town.

Whittle's was the trysting place of the affluent young. Girls would roll down the Avenue in their humming little electric automobiles, park at the East Avenue curb, and hold hands with boy friends under the little tables and exchange long level stares of utter devotion over a fudge nut sundae or a liquid drink concocted of Whittle's delicious ice cream and rich syrups. The youthful patrons knew Bessie and Peggy, knew them as the Candy Kids, and the girls who came in the humming little electrics were sometimes envious of their popularity, for once the store closed, Bessie and Peggy were definitely on the town.

Bessie Fuller came from a large Nineteenth Ward family, and Peggy McGill lived over the stables back of a residence that was built in the early 1880s at a cost of hundreds of thousands of dollars by William S. Kimball, who made a fortune manufacturing cigarettes and won medals for the excellence of his chewing tobacco.

The Kimball mansion, as it was often called, was during the early years of the Kimball's occupancy of it the most elaborate private dwelling in Rochester. It stood on a rise at the southeast corner of Clarissa and Troup streets, a lavish, sprawling, three-and-a-half story building that had been designed by Louis Tiffany. Kimball lived only a dozen years after the completion of the house, but during that time he went all out to make it the show place of the town and, inadvertently, an incongruity in the Third Ward, where the natives made a fetish of "elegant simplicity," and cast their eyes down their noses at pretense and ostentation.

In time the thirty-room house, with its fifteen-foot ceilings, its exquisitely carved woodwork, its great pipe organ, its ankle-deep oriental rugs, its well-filled art gallery, its score of servants, its adjoining greenhouses for the cultivation of rare plants and flowers, and its stables, out back, with an elevator that raised and lowered beautifully groomed horses and an assortment of fashionable horse-drawn vehicles, was abandoned. The city took the property for taxes a short time after John Hill Kitchen, popular broker and socialite, and his East Avenue friends staged a cocking main in the ballroom of the house which the state police interrupted.

But this was some time after the death of Mrs. Kimball who had continued during more than twenty years of widowhood to maintain the prideful Kimball demesne in the high style that had graced it during her husband's life. It was she who hired the expert coachman Pat McGill, Peggy's father, and put him and his family in quarters over the stables. Peggy was proud of the Kimball connection. She felt that it gave her status. Requesting some unknowledgeable young man to take her home after the theater, or after some other entertainment, she would direct him to the corner of Clarissa and Troup streets, and wave him adieu from the steps of the great house. She would wait until the young man was out of range, then dart around back and ascend to the stable apartment.

But Peggy had quit Whittle's candy store and left town and Bessie Fuller had had the experience of two shows, the *Follies*, which she left after a few weeks to join the cast of *The Midnight Whirl*, which was playing on the roof of the Century Theater when she met Reginald C. Vanderbilt. The meeting occurred on the Century Roof at a time when *The Midnight Whirl* was about to close, and Bessie informed her new acquaintance that the next week she was going to visit her home in Rochester. Vanderbilt seemed delighted at this intelligence. He explained that he himself would be in Rochester the next week, judging harness classes at the Rochester Horse Show. He told Bessie that he would see that she had a box seat for the show and proposed that they renew their acquaintance when he got to town. Vanderbilt was in a sort of no woman's land at that time. He was divorced from his first wife and not yet engaged to Gloria, one of the glamorous Morgan twins.

In *Double Exposure*, the book written by Gloria Morgan Vanderbilt and her twin, the Duchess of Furness, Mrs. Reginald Vanderbilt tells that her husband hated to dance. Bessie Fuller, now the widow of Clarence Mooney, feels that Gloria didn't take him to the right places.

"I thought he was a very good dancer," she said. "We danced at the Little Club, Montmarte, the Waldorf, the Palais Royale, and other places. We had fine times together."

During his week in Rochester Vanderbilt was disinclined to become involved in the entertainment provided by our local hosts and hostesses and passed much of his time in the evening hours with Bessie Fuller. He not only brought her to the Tea Tent, but took her to dinner at the Seneca and other places. One late afternoon after the Horse Show, the pair were seen cavorting on the midway of the Exposition, and sharing a bottle of brandy by the use of two straws.

The friendship that developed in Rochester between the scion of the great Vanderbilt family and the former Candy Kid continued for three or four years. During this time Bessie Fuller was frequently entertained by Vanderbilt in New York and occasionally at Newport, Rhode Island, and on an insular spot of Vanderbilt land in Block Island Sound known as Sandy Point.

"I was at Sandy Point for parties, but never large ones," she said. "I met a number of Reggie's friends, Biddles, Whitneys, and others. And I met his daughter by his first marriage, Cathleen Nielson. He was a grand person. He drank, sure. Sometimes like crazy. But he was always kind and considerate."

I knew and liked Bessie Fuller when she worked in Whittle's; I remembered her relations with Vanderbilt, and shortly before these words were written, not having seen her in many years, I inquired of a man in New York if she was still alive. To my surprise, he gave me her address: An apartment building on University Avenue, across from the Memorial Art Gallery, and I called there to talk with her.

Bessie was always noted for her good nature and, contrary to her former companion, Peggy McGill, for her lack of pretense and a disposition to false display. She had come, a good-natured little old lady, the widow of the son of a Rochester undertaker, not precisely upon lean days but certainly not upon very prosperous ones. It was a warm late summer afternoon. The building lacked air-conditioning. Bessie's single room was cooled by a large electric fan.

We collaborated in the revival of amusing incidents and spoke of interesting Rochester personalities of nearly fifty years ago, and Bessie told me that one night in a New York night club she had met Walter Hagen with a lady who was not his wife and introduced him to Vanderbilt. Bessie and I had a pleasant visit. She told me that she was trying to move into one of the modern apartment buildings that accept only elderly persons but that she was discouragingly far down on the waiting list. "You've got to have influence to get in." She sighed, and for the first time since I had been with her she was the least pensive.

"You know, Heinie," she said, after a moment, "If I'd played my cards right, maybe I could have married Reggie Vanderbilt. We were that close once. He told me that he had spent all his money, and all he was living on was a trust fund of several million. But my God, I could have got along. . . ."

I said good-by and left, and thought, how nice it would have been for Bessie.

Chapter 27

For a time during my longest hitch on the *Democrat and Chronicle* the city editor was Wilbur G. Lewis, who hated the name Wilbur and liked to be called Bill. He was an intelligent and sensitive man who strove to obfuscate his kind and sensitive feelings by bellowing into the telephone and at workers in the newsroom and by explosions of blasphemy. It was the sort of thing you see in movies.

Bill called to me one afternoon to meet Yehudi Menuhin at the New York Central Station and added a brief staccato line as to how I would know him and precisely where in the station I would find him. On my way to the meeting I realized that he hadn't identified Yehudi Menuhin or told me what I was to talk to him about, but once in the waiting room I knew I had found my man—or boy. Yehudi wore short velveteen pants, such as a small boy in a very fancy elementary school might wear; but he seemed too big for the pants. He was no subteen-ager; he was a big boy, with fat legs under his black stockings—legs, it seemed to me, as fat as California hams.

He was with a man whom he introduced as his manager. For a moment I thought Yehudi must be a youthful billiard prodigy, a new Willie Hoppe or a Young Jake Shaefer. But when we got into a cab to ride to the Sagamore Hotel the talk was remote from anything one would hear in a pool hall. I took a shot in the dark.

"How long, Master Menuhin," I asked, "have you been playing the piano?"

And the pair of 'em, with a concerted cry of anguish, tried to throw me into the street.

There might have been an excuse for my not knowing the virtuosity of a young concert violinist who at that stage of his career was hardly as well known as Fritz Kreisler, whom I had previously interviewed, knowing perfectly well what instrument *he* played. In any event, my error caused me no embarrassment. Nor was I embarrassed two years later when, as I crossed the threshold of young Mr. Menuhin's suite in the Sagamore, he leaped from a settee, fixed me with an accusing finger, and cried out angrily in front of a group of idolators, "Oh, there's that awful man who called me a piano player!"

As a newspaper writer, I committed my share of blunders, some the result of ignorance and others the result of carelessness. But the keenest embarrassments I suffered were caused by the discovery that someone on the outside had turned up a story about a Rochester personality that I had known nothing about. I hated to be scooped on my own beat, and for many years stories about Rochester personalities were my stock in trade.

I had done most of the stereotypes over and over again. There were set pieces in Rochester newspaper offices that were dragged out and refurbished for new display on days when the news was light. Sunday on the *Democrat and Chronicle* was such a day, and Sunday I occasionally wrote a piece for Monday's paper about my old friend Pete Gruber—Rattlesnake Pete—who, ever since his arrival in town from his native Oil City, Pennsylvania, had been a catalyst for newspaper copy.

But Pete was better than the ordinary newspaper stereotype. He was a colorful old fellow with a flair for showmanship and the fusty gimcrack museum, which was the motif of his big Mill Street saloon, was a magnate for yokels who came into town on Saturday excursions and a place of curiosity for more sophisticated visitors who had heard of Gruber's "cures" and his deft handling of poisonous reptiles.

Pete's museum was a clutter of trivia. But visitors who were stimulated by potions at the saloon's long bar before beginning their round of inspection o-o-oh'd and a-a-ah'd in wonder at such virtu as a jar of pickled brains, the Meerschaum pipe said to have been smoked by John Wilkes Booth, Lincoln's murderer; a crude contraption represented as the first electric chair ever used for an execution. There were weapons and fright masks on the walls and the stub of a cigar a famous murderer was supposed to have cast aside a moment before he was hanged. There was a strength-testing device that spouted water up a man's pant's leg when he tugged at the handles; another mechanical japery that promised a peephole view of a naked woman and rewarded the eager voyeur with a blow from a boxing glove.

The climactic attraction of Pete's museum was a large glass case that held half a dozen rattlesnakes. They had not been altered in any way. They were vicious-looking and as poisonous as in their natural state. When they were disturbed the buzzing of the horned segments of their tails fascinated both the occasional visitor and the day-to-day habitué of the resort. Pete had been bitten by his own snakes. His treatment was to stab the wound with the blade of a large horn-cased pocketknife and suck out the poison with his lips. His gnarled hands were a mosaic of cicatrices. He was celebrated for having saved the life of a man in the Bostwick animal show in New York who had been poisoned by a rattler. He was sought by sufferers from goiter who submitted to having harmless black snakes laced about their bare throats. The contraction of the snake's body massaged the protuberant goiter and gave temporary relief, but effected no cure.

Now and then I went with Pete on a snake hunt that would be motivated by an informant in the adjacent countryside who believed he had seen a rattler. I never knew him to return with the quarry, but the expedition was always ceremonial. He would carefully accouter himself in his snake-hunt costume, which included a waistcoat and gloves made of rattlesnake skins. His automobile, with other gaudy accessories, had a long curved brass horn fashioned to resemble a boa constrictor which had a peculiar, an individual toot. Tooling through the city streets he would toot the horn and the citizenry would gather at the curb very much as they did when Uncle Hi Edgerton appeared in his one-lunger. In the country he was a scary driver, for his joviality and his desire to draw everyone into his fellowship caused him to raise both hands from the steering wheel to wave at farmers in the fields, children in farmyards, and farm wives on doorsteps. Everyone knew him, and he seemed able to call an extraordinary number of people by name. Rattlesnake Pete was probably Rochester's most conspicuous citizen. He was not inherently a charlatan or a quack. He believed in his goiter and other cures and offered them as a kindly service to his fellowmen.

*   *   *

Peter Gruber was never prosecuted by the law for his cures nor bothered by the medical societies, which would not have been the exemption of some of the out-and-out charlatans who practiced their trade in Rochester in the days before the medical profession was as challenging of quackery as it is today and in an era before the passage of the Pure Food and Drug Act.

We had here at different times a beehive of medical fakers. Some of them were well accepted in the community, several amassed fortunes, and one proposed with magnanimity and public spirit to endow the struggling little University of Rochester with $100,000 provided it be renamed after his pet nostrum. It would have become then the University of Hop Bitters.

Asa T. Soule was the creator of Hop Bitters, which he advertised as the "Invalid's Friend and Hope." It did have an analgesic quality. The liquid concoction was generously laced with alcohol, and a good swig of the "medicine" did a man as well—or as badly —as a shot of hard liquor at a bar.

Soule explained his proposal to retitle the university to Ernest L. Willard, one-time editor of the *Democrat and Chronicle*. "Good God, no!" Willard cried in protest. "They'd bestow on you the degree of Bachelor of Booze."

We had in Rochester Duffy's Pure Malt Whiskey for which all sorts of curative claims were made, and which now and then turned up in second-class saloons as an inferior intoxicant; we had K. Leo Minges, a tall handsome man who operated a highly profitable mail-order business that sold a system for making short men tall; we had H. H. Warner, who erected a monument in the form of an observatory on East Avenue to Warner's Safe Kidney and Liver Cure and put Lewis Swift, a Rochester astronomer who had been honored here and abroad for the discovery of intra-mercurial planets, in charge. I knew about these quackeries and their promoters. To my deep chagrin I never heard of E. Virgil Neal until his name popped up in an article in *The New Yorker* that dealt with the career of Émile Coué, an ex-pharmacist from Troyes, France, who, back in the 1920s, had millions of people in this country and Europe chanting the hopeful precept "Day by day, in every way, I am getting better and better."

Coué, who advocated hypnotism and autosuggestion as cures for physical and mental ills, on his first visit to this country was lionized by the public and hailed by the press as a new messiah. One of his sponsors was Mrs. William K. Vanderbilt. Henry Ford entertained him in Detroit and told the newspapers that Coué's method of autosuggestion was practiced in his household. Mary

Garden, the Metropolitan diva, attested that his formula had made it possible for her to reach the top note of an aria from *Tosca*. Such antithetical personalities as John Barrymore and Mrs. Andrew Carnegie were the master's disciples. His book, *Self Mastery*, was on the best-selling lists. When he lectured, police reserves were needed to restrain the crowds. His triumph in Europe preceded his arrival in this country. There, as here, everyone was declaiming with profound hope, "Day by day, in every way, I am getting better and better." King Albert of Belgium, and Lady Beatty, wife of the hero of Jutland, believed Coué had discovered a panacea.

And the inspiration and provenance of this messianic sweep of two continents, *The New Yorker* believed, was a Rochester company—an Institute of Science—of which E. Virgil Neal was president, which sold a mail-order course in hypnotism.

A resourceful fellow, who sometimes exchanged his baptismal name for the fancier one of Xenophone La Motte Sage, Neal found numerous ways of turning a quick dollar. He appears first in our city directories in the last years of the old century as a partner in the Neal-Clark Manufacturing Company (office specialties) at 24 Church Street. Charles S. Clark and Thomas F. Adkin were other members of the firm.

Directories issued early in the new century indicate that Neal was active in numerous and varied enterprises. He was an editor of what was known as the New York State Publishing Company and coauthor of a book called *Modern Illustrative Bookkeeping*. He had once been a stage hypnotist. This experience led him into the business of selling hypnotism by mail, and one of his European customers was Émile Coué, an obscure French pharmacist. Coué may also have found inspiration for his role of universal healer from a book published and edited by Neal, *Hypnotic Suggestion: a scientific treatise on the uses and possibilities of hypnosis, suggestion, and allied phenomena*. To this work he contributed a chapter on "The Power of Fascination." Clark wrote one on "Personal Magnetism," and Adkin a third, "Suggestive Therapeutics." As editor, Neal modestly affixed an A.M. and Ph.D. to his name. When he used the nom de plume Xenophone La Motte Sage, he retained the two foregoing degrees and added a third, LL.D.

After Neal acquired considerable wealth from the mail-order business he moved to New York and sold his interest in the company. Clark and Adkin remained for a time in Rochester and the mail-order business continued until 1914 when it was stopped by the postal authorities. Clark apparently had also made money selling the course in hypnotism. He lived for a time in a fine house on East Avenue. After World War I, he settled in Paris. Adkin tried the cosmetic business for a time, then he too left Rochester.

If Neal, as *The New Yorker* suggested, devised the line "Day by day, in every way, I am getting better and better," which was intoned like a prayer by millions and called "doing one's Coué," he made no fuss about Coué's adoption of it, although he was alive when the ex-pharmacist made the first of two visits to this country. The magazine speculated that it was "possible that Neal did not try to cash in on Coué's fame because by the 1920s he had become too rich to care much about it, as a result of having taken a flyer in the patent medicine business."

* * *

Of course, the great Rochester story since the middle of the century is the story of how Xerox exploded off the launching pad and rose into the stratosphere before most Rochesterians knew what was happening. I remember hearing an investment counselor earnestly admonishing a client in the late '50s to keep away from Xerox: It was too chancy. Newspaper people generally were no more perceptive than the investment counselor. My recollection is that we were slow to realize that one of the miracles of modern American business was being performed in our own bailiwick.

Some of us knew vaguely about the little Haloid firm that manufactured photographic paper (of all things, in the province of the great Eastman Company!) over on Haloid Street, and I myself had known the three Wilsons who at different times were active in the company's management: old Joseph R. Wilson, Republican boss of the Nineteenth Ward, downtown pawnbroker, and successively comptroller and mayor of the city, who was one of the founders of Haloid; Joseph R., Jr., better known as Dick Wilson, one of twelve employees at the time of the firm's inception in 1906; and Joseph C. Wilson, Dick's brilliant son who had so much to do with the development of a company that in three decades increased its revenues more than 4000 per cent and advanced them in the early days of its tremendous boom by more than $22,000,000 in a single year.

333

Familiarity, in this instance, did not breed contempt. But my acquaintance with all three Wilsons, and with one of Dick Wilson's fine sisters, who had given me a cordial letter of introduction to the wife of a sculptor in Paris, who was kind to me during a stay in that sad and frightened city in the winter of 1915–16, made it hard for me to conceive that any one of these fellow Rochesterians might have a hand in the accomplishment of a prodigy. They seemed very much like other men I knew casually around town. You might meet Joseph C. Wilson on the street, or in a restaurant, or at a party, and say, "Hello, Joe," and think not at all that he was a figure to glamorize. He was accessible, friendly; there was no *side* to him. This slight incident, which took place after I had come fully to comprehend how far he had gone and how prodigious was the enterprise he headed, may help to illustrate my point.

One evening, at a time when I was in desperate quest of a plumber to repair a leak in our sink drain in Scottsville, I passed the new Xerox Building on Xerox Square. Already risen to full height, the building made the salient peak on the Rochester skyline, but it was not yet occupied and work was still being done on its interior. It was brightly illuminated, and as I ran my eyes over its many stories I thought enviously of how this huge corporation was able to install myriad washbasins, water coolers, toilets, and, for all I knew, shower baths, and I couldn't engage a plumber for love or money. I was sure Xerox had all the plumbers in the county on hire and the next day I gave a brief, plaintive expression to this thought in my newspaper space. Two days later I had the following note:

Dear Henry: I wish I could help you get a plumber, but we're not yet finished with our building. I hope for you. Sincerely, Joe Wilson.

When Sol M. Linowitz, an exceptionally talented young lawyer, with an eye fixed sharply on the main chance, moved into town and began to cut a figure in legal, civic, and business circles, he sent me three or four philosophical essays to which at different times I devoted the full linage of "Seen and Heard." Later he sent me a few typed sheets of verse. These effusions I did not publish and now regret my failure to do so. It was not long after this that Mr. Linowitz became closely associated with Joe Wilson and Xerox or a great while before he rose to the chairmanship of that colossus with stock holdings that probably run into millions.

I should like to think that it was I who motivated any poetical aspirations he may cherish.

I never met Sol Linowitz until he was about to leave Rochester to become ambassador of the Organization of American States under President Johnson and, ultimately, a partner of the international law firm of Coudert Brothers. I was introduced to him in a large concourse of people in a hotel lobby; we exchanged pleasantries and parted in less than a minute. Brief as our meeting was, I derived from it the impression that Linowitz was a friendly man, approachable and unstuffy.

The great leaders of Rochester's great industries are no longer ivory tower boys. They are alert to civic needs and sensible of human problems. They have a shoulder-to-shoulder contact with the people. It has ceased to be fashionable to disparage our town as Smugtown. If the epithet was ever applicable, it lost all meaning after the shocking experience of the black riots of '64. It would be absurd to charge smugness to such Bausch & Lomb leaders as Carl S. Hallauer or Herbert Eisenhart; to think of such humanists as the late Frank J. Lovejoy, one-time head of Eastman, or Marion B. Folsom, former treasurer of that company, who left to become Secretary (under President Eisenhower) of the Department of Health, Education, and Welfare, as stuffy.

Late one afternoon I was standing at the bar of Earl's Grill, a small spaghetti house and saloon at the edge of the Negro district on Exchange Street with a man named George whose job was sweeping out offices in the *Democrat and Chronicle* Building when Thomas J. Hargrave, whose job was directing the Eastman Kodak Company, entered the resort.

Earl's was on the route Mr. Hargrave took from his office to his home, he was friendly with the proprietor, and he stopped two or three times a week for a beer. I introduced him to George. Mr. Hargrave bought three beers. We talked for several minutes. Mr. Hargrave finished his beer and started for the door. Then he turned and asked:

"Did our office call you today?"

"About a story?" I asked eagerly.

He hesitated, seemed reluctant to explain. I pressed him.

"Well," he said, "our advertising people ought to be the ones to tell you. We want you to be the voice on our radio program."

The program was to be broadcast every Friday evening from

Kilbourn Hall of the Eastman Theater. Hargrave told me the money they would pay. I was excited. Without a contract or a written word, I made a deal in a neighborhood saloon with the president of the Eastman Kodak Company, and a possessor of the Distinguished Service Cross. I lasted six months, when the program was taken off the air. The copy I wrote for my brief Friday address passed through perhaps a dozen hands and was meticulously edited. Minor changes were occasionally suggested. I couldn't imagine working for more pleasant or considerate employers.

*   *   *

Xerox millionaires are very much in fashion in Rochester these days, but it is not so easy to pinpoint them as it is to put a finger on large holders of Eastman Kodak stock. We know that Xerox has created a vast amount of new wealth but we are not always sure who outside of those professionally associated with the company have substantially profited from the increment. It is too early to fix the Xerox shareholders solidly into our Establishment. The Eastman millionaires have generally been around long enough to have achieved a sort of institutional status. Their life style is familiar to us. We know of their places of abode, of their philanthropies, of their virtues and foibles. Sometimes we know of their hobbies.

For example, the late Mrs. Margaret Woodbury Strong, whose Eastman holdings, according to her lawyer, had a value somewhere between fifty and one hundred million—the lawyer hinted that the latter figure is more nearly correct—went in, not for a seagoing yacht, or Sybaritic entertainment, or the Grail-like pursuit of a Kentucky Derby winner, but, almost impassionately, for the collection of dolls and doll houses.

The Sagamore Hotel, later renamed the Sheraton, now known as 111 East Avenue (a "prestige address," according to the advertisements) was once, and is still to a certain extent, the residence of numerous wealthy widows whose occupancy of the upper floors gave to this area of the hostelry—as mentioned in an early page in this book—the title of "golden aviary." The majority of these ladies subsisted off of the dividends of Kodak stock they had inherited from their husbands. Among them for a time lived Florence A. Dailey, a spinster, who enjoyed no inherited wealth.

She was odd—odd, as someone remarked, as two left shoes. She had no intercourse with her neighbors. She lived, as discovered by hotel attendants who were reluctantly admitted to her apartment, untidily and so meagerly that the management often wondered how she got up the rent money each month. No one visited her, she appeared to have neither friends nor relatives, and it was not until she died in her eighty-seventh year that these brief biographical facts came to light:

Very early in the century Miss Dailey left her home in Ludlow, Vermont, for Rochester where, after a brief course in the Rochester Business Institute, she became secretary for Albert O. Fenn, then vice-president and cashier of the Alliance Bank, predecessor to the Lincoln Rochester Trust Company.

Miss Dailey was always on time for work. She was quiet, efficient, and unobtrusive. She was a devout Roman Catholic. Fenn was a friend of George Eastman, whose hustling and growing Kodak Company had at that time net assets of $6.4 million. Fenn, who had infinite faith in the company, one day said to his secretary, "Florence, put your money in Kodak."

In 1911, Miss Dailey left the bank, retired permanently from gainful employment, and returned to Ludlow where her father had recently died. She remained there for several years and during this period buried her mother, brother, and sister. With no one left of her immediate family she came back to Rochester but retained the Ludlow house as a summer retreat. Here she resided first in the Normandy, an apartment hotel on Alexander Street, and later in the Sagamore.

Miss Dailey lived virtually as a recluse in the Sagamore, and as she grew older her behavior became increasingly strange. On occasions she visited New York. There one midwinter day she was seen chasing imaginary butterflies through midtown streets with a net. Her clothes were shabbily bizarre; her hats as grotesque as the headpieces of Halloween witches. Late in 1959 she was found unconscious in the filth and litter of her hotel apartment, and was transferred to St. Ann's (Catholic) Home. There her circumstances were considered so impecunious that no bill was submitted by the physician who attended her. Her death in St. Ann's on February 6, 1966, was recorded in a tiny paid paragraph in the obituary columns of the Rochester newspapers. Miss Dailey seemed destined to be utterly forgotten when the astonishing disclosure was made

337

that she had left a portfolio of Eastman Kodak stock valued at $19,000,000!

A native Vermonter, Miss Dailey was innately frugal. She knew very well the value of a dollar. She scrimped, saved, and heeded Albert Fenn's advice, "Florence, put your money in Kodak," and saw, over the years, the stock split, and split again and again and again, and her modest investments pyramid into an important fortune.

A litigation ensued. Miss Dailey had made two wills. One, a mutilated document that bore no date, which was found in a trunk in the Ludlow house, deeded the bulk of her estate to two nephews and a niece. The other will, dated 1933, made the Universities of Georgetown and Notre Dame chief beneficiaries. The contest to determine which will was valid might have gone on for years had not the interested parties agreed upon a settlement that gave the universities the greater part of the fortune but did not leave the niece and nephews out in the cold.

* * *

There was no secretiveness about the wealth of Mrs. Homer (Margaret Woodbury) Strong and her twenty-one page "Last Will and Testament" was drawn to eliminate all ambiguities and to do precisely what this stocky, individualistic, strong-willed hobbyist intended it to do.

She left $10,000,000 to the Episcopal Diocese of Rochester, $40,000 to St. Paul's Episcopal Church, $15,000 to one relative, and $5,000 to another, both cousins.

She was commendably liberal with the many people who worked on her grounds, and in the huge house on Allens Creek Road, Pittsford, which she had taken over from the late Alvah Griffith Strong, no relative, who himself had inherited Kodak millions but who had not very rigorously contained them.

Mrs. Strong died July 16, 1969, about a year after the death in the town of Perinton of Chester F. Carlson, inventor of the Xerox copying machine. Carlson's will distributed $45,000,000 to sixteen organizations. Mrs. Strong, whose fortune probably exceeded Carlson's (reputedly she owned more Eastman stock than any other individual), made bequests to various organizations, the largest of which, excluding her gift to the Episcopal Diocese, was

$60,000 to the Pierpont Morgan Library, in New York, "which sum I request, but do not direct the Library to expend in providing facilities for the better care and display of book plates."

She left $30,000 to Cornell University, in honor of her husband, who was graduated from the Cornell Law School; $30,000 to the University of Rochester, and $20,000 to the university's Strong Hospital; $20,000 to the Rochester Institute of Technology, and $20,000 to the Genesee Hospital. She was an enthusiastic gardener, and garden clubs benefited from her will. But the major share of her great estate will likely go to the founding in her Pittsford home of what she desired to be known as the Margaret Woodbury Strong Museum of Fascinations.

Mrs. Strong was a collector. Of eighty-four thousand book-plates, of inkstands, of doorknobs, of buttons, of paperweights, of china and glassware, of seashells, of coins, of toys, of barbershop tonic bottles—heaven knows what all!—and dolls, and doll houses. She had sixty miniature rooms, each packed with tiny pieces of furniture, and in one of the rooms, which represented an eighteenth-century house, she had installed a replica of a modern bathtub. Her collection of dolls, which she prized more than all of her other displays, numbered twenty-two thousand. Her acquisitive fancies sometimes took odd turns. Once she went in for the collection of full-sized bathtubs, which she filled with flowers, and some of the women who used to bowl with her said they wished she had saved out one for her personal use. She dressed as she pleased in the mode of general housework. She wore no girdle and flounced out beefily fore and aft, and no one on the bowling alley, on the golf course, in a garden, at an auction, or at meals in a restaurant, or in her home ever saw her without a hat.

Guiding an awed visitor through her multifarious collections she might wave a hand over her doll's village which included a great variety of Lilliputian buildings, constructed with exquisite skill—she called the layout "Rochester's Tiniest Suburb"—and suggest, with a little smirk, "Silly, isn't it? But it's fun."

She had something of the arrogance of wealth and no shrinking sense of modesty. Mrs. Joan Lynn Schild, who wrote authoritatively on antiques for the Rochester *Times-Union*, was one of nine women lunching at a local club when Mrs. Strong joined the party.

"Well," she said with hearty assurance as she sat down, "someone at this table is going to be named in my will."

The silence that followed was pregnant with suspense and the nine other women glanced furtively, hopefully, at the speaker. "I, *Margaret Strong*," Mrs. Strong proclaimed firmly, and followed the announcement with a loud, pleased chuckle.

Mrs. Strong delighted in telling that when she ordered her chauffeur to drive her into town she never knew which of her five automobiles would draw up at the door. She was shrewd in her transactions with dealers and was not easily put upon. She reveled in her ability to buy out, if the fancy struck her, an entire collection and in the deferential backing away of other dealers when she appeared at an auction. Entering an antique shop she might ask, "Do you know who I am?"

If the answer was "No, I'm sorry. I don't," she would turn curtly on her heel and walk away.

Her wealth had come from both sides of her family. Her mother was the daughter of the proprietor of a successful flour mill in Rochester in an era when Rochester was still the Flour City; her father, John C. Woodbury, made a fortune manufacturing buggy whips in partnership with Colonel Henry Alvah Strong.

Colonel Strong, while living in the boardinghouse conducted by George Eastman's mother, became interested in young George's photographic enterprise, backed it, and persuaded Woodbury to invest in the little Eastman company of which Strong eventually became president. The only child of middle-aged parents, Mrs. Strong inherited money from her mother, and all of her father's Eastman stock, which in subsequent years proliferated into an enormous fortune.

Margaret Strong's childhood, perhaps owing to a lack of rapport between herself and her middle-aged parents, was not particularly pleasant; her marriage to Homer Strong, a non-practicing lawyer who managed a State Street machine shop, was hardly brilliant; in adult life she suffered the tragedy of the death by suicide of the couple's only child, Barbara, after the young woman had experienced two unhappy marriages.

Following the death of her daughter and her husband, the passion of Mrs. Strong's life seemed to be collecting, and her great house, one of the two or three most elaborate residences in the Rochester area, which, when built by Alvah Griffith Strong was the scene of the town's largest and gayest parties, became a clutter of expensive virtue and henceforth will be the Museum of Fascinations.

Chapter 28

During the days of my newspaper apprenticeship I was occasionally assigned to cover polo matches at Genesee Valley Park between teams called the Freebooters and the Riding Academy. My accounts of these contests were printed in the local section of the newspaper rather than on the sports page. I suspect that Charlie Kinney, the sports editor, considered polo, if he deigned to give it any attention, a fribbling sort of pastime, perhaps like morris dancing, unworthy of space in a department of the newspaper that was devoted to such profundities as baseball, boxing, and horse racing. The polo matches attracted small galleries composed of casual park visitors who knew no more about the game than I did but who found entertainment in the swift flights and turnings of the ponies and in the mad flailing of mallets, and a small group of country-club people whose motorcars were ranked along the sidelines. Polo had been a sport at the Country Club of Rochester until the field upon which it was played was given over to the extension of the golf course and the country-club part of the gallery was properly demonstrative. "Oh, well hit! Well, hit, indeed!" they would shout. "What a corking goal!" They were friends of most of the players. They were sophisticated and esoteric. They knew what was meant by a chukker.

Jesse Lindsay, of the Sibley, Lindsay & Curr Lindsays; Walter Howard, John Weis, and James Sibley Watson, Jr., rode for the Freebooters, and one Saturday afternoon I asked Watson if John Cooney, who was playing with the Riding Academy four, wasn't his family's chauffeur and stableman. He said that my surmise was correct, and explained that he had lent Cooney, the best rider on the field, to the opposition to give it added strength. Our conversation was quickly over. I never went back for polo at the park after that day and it was more than fifty-five years before I again spoke to Watson, who then had a medical degree. On that occasion I called on his wife in the hope of learning something about a man of varied and very unusual talents whose self-willed anonymity seemed almost pathological. I had been in the house only a short time when Dr. Watson sidled noiselessly into the room to abort the purpose of my visit. It would have been futile to have questioned him about his multifaceted career. He was shy and self-effacing to the point of furtiveness. As I left the house I indulged the whimsey that Watson was a fugitive from the FBI.

His family is old Rochester and very wealthy old Rochester. His mother was a sister of Hiram W. Sibley. She married twice, was divorced from her first husband, by whom she had a son, James G. Averell, who studied architecture at Harvard and in Europe and who was practicing his profession in Boston at the time of his death in his twenty-eighth year. In his memory, Mrs. Watson gave to the University of Rochester the Art Gallery that stands on the old Prince Street campus. Later, she and her husband provided a sum for the enlargement of this handsome building, designed in the manner of the Italian Renaissance, the memorial character of which is indicated by a sculptured portrait of James G. Averell with these words engraved below it:

He Loved Life and Beauty and Honor.

Sibley Watson (the James is usually admitted from his name) was ten years old at the time of his half brother's death. It would have been natural if the loss of her older son should cause the mother to be pampering and overprotective of the younger. Young Watson had six years of excellent secondary education at Groton. In a bare-bones biography in Who's Who, no mention is made of Harvard, from which he was graduated, and one might infer that Watson's alma mater was New York University, from which he received a medical degree.

As the only living son of a family that possessed an ocean-going steam yacht, Sibley Watson was indulged. He was able to travel at will. He played polo. He won ribbons with saddle horses at the Rochester Horse Show. He flew an airplane of his own, and frightened the wits out of Alec Wilder, the witty, distinguished, and prolific Rochester composer, whom he flew from Rochester to Portland, Maine, in an era when Wilder (with poetic license) averred there was no landing field between the two cities.

"I really shouldn't have worried," Wilder said admiringly. "Sibley put that plane up perfectly, flew it perfectly, and put it down perfectly, with the kind of genius he has."

In the autumn of 1911, Miss Hildegarde Lasell, a beautiful brown-haired heiress from Whitinsville, Massachusetts, who was visiting in Rochester, was chosen to sing the lead in *Betsey Abroad*, an amateur musical comedy that was given in the Lyceum Theater for the benefit of the Rochester General Hospital.

The book for the piece was written by a local poet, Miss Elizabeth Granger Hollister, and the music by John Adams Warner, a fine Rochester musician and composer, who later married the daughter of Governor Alfred E. Smith and served for several years as superintendent of the New York State Police.

Scores of young Rochesterians were used in the cast; there were twenty-four musical numbers and a good deal of dancing. The show played four performances to packed houses. Such well-known amateur Thespians as Harry B. Crowley and Angelo Newman made important contributions to the production. Miss Roberta Beattie, who left Rochester to become leading lady for William Gillette, was prominent in the cast. A reviewer said that the dancing of Miss Charlotte Whitney, the lovely, spritelike daughter of Mr. and Mrs. Warham Whitney, was "one of the distinctive features of the performance"; remarked that Miss Clara Louise Werner, who, half a century later was to receive the Civic Medal from the Rochester Museum and Science Center, won encore after encore for her singing of "It Pays to Go Abroad"; and warmly attested that Miss Lasell as Betsey was "in every sense a star."

Sibley Watson was a teen-age student at the time *Betsey Abroad* was represented on the Lyceum stage, and I have no knowledge as to whether he witnessed it as a member of the audience. But very likely he knew the leading lady, and presumably was a guest at her parents' home, a famous "open house" for Harvard undergraduates. There was a courtship along the line. In October 1916, Sibley Watson and Miss Lasell were married in Whitinsville.

John Vollmer, who often "did" the big weddings in Rochester, took a crew of five or six men to help "do" the nuptials at Whitinsville. He and his men were there a couple of weeks. They were merely auxiliaries. The prime responsibility for the elaborate affair was a large corps of decorators, florists, caterers, etc., from nearby Worcester. Vollmer's eyes bugged when he spoke of the Whitinsville commission. "That wedding," he said awesomely, "must have cost $100,000!"

If it did, the Lasell family, who had made a fortune manufacturing milling machinery, could well afford it. And the wedding must have been some sort of a bench mark in the career of Sibley Watson, who ever after seemed no more given to large display and ostentation than a Carthusian monk.

The young Watsons for a time made their home in New York. During their residence in that city, Sibley Watson joined Scofield Thayer, a Harvard graduate, slightly his senior, in the revival of the literary magazine *The Dial*. The enterprise was called by someone "a gallant intellectual adventure." It was also an expensive one.

In the ten years of the magazine's phoenix rebirth it lost annually between $30,000 and $50,000. Thayer served it for several years as editor and Watson was continuously its publisher. They were wealthy young men, and they took their losses uncomplainingly. At its beginning, *The Dial* might have seemed to some the tinker toy of a couple of rich artistic *flâneurs*. It was far more than that, and its proprietors were anything but precious triflers. Both Watson and Thayer were men of extraordinary gifts. They were extremely sensitive to aesthetic values and their artistic and intellectual integrity was unquestioned. They wanted the best, or what they considered the best, and from 1920 until it succumbed with the July 1929 issue *The Dial* published the works of many of the finest artists and writers in this country and Europe. It brought T. S. Eliot, later winner of the Nobel Prize, to public attention with the publication of *The Waste Land*. It introduced E. E. Cummings and Marianne Moore. The list of its contributors is a formidable one and includes, as a sampler, George Santayana, William Butler Yeats, Wallace Stevens, D. H. Lawrence, Bertrand Russell, Picasso, Ezra Pound, Matisse, James Joyce, Sherwood Anderson, who won the $2,000 prize *The Dial* awarded annually, Claude Bragdon, the onetime Rochester architect, and Adelaide Crapsey, the Rochester poet.

"*The Dial* still remains the greatest American magazine of arts and letters of our century," Nicholas Joost wrote, in his full-blown history of the magazine, and many sound critics agree.

Always seeking anonymity, Watson wrote for the magazine under various pseudonyms, made brilliant translations of the decadent French poet Arthur Rimbaud, fulfilled his taxing duties as

344

publisher of *The Dial,* and managed, before he left New York to make his home in a fine old house at East Avenue and Sibley Place, to obtain a medical degree. In Rochester, he began experimenting with motion pictures and produced two films, using Hildegarde Lasell Watson and a cast of Rochester amateurs, which have been acclaimed in cinema circles around the world.

James Card, noted authority of motion pictures, who is director of the Department of Film at the George Eastman House, said of the first of these productions (the second was *Lot in Sodom*):

"The start of the 1970s has seen a renewed fascination with the avant-garde film made by Hildegarde and James Sibley Watson, *The Fall of the House of Usher.* The Museum of Modern Art which circulates the film is pressing Eastman House, custodian of the original negatives, to replace prints worn out by the predictable enthusiasm of the new generation of film students as they find it hard to believe a film so far advanced could possibly have been achieved in the 1920s and in the United States.

"In truth, the medium of film has never really outpaced the Watson production. Its influence on early beholders cannot be overstated. Seeing it for the first time in 1932 decided this former film society director to become an archivist and *Usher* was the first in a film collection which ultimately grew to become the George Eastman House Motion Picture Collection, second largest in the world.

"Technologically, *Usher* introduced the optical printer to motion picture production and synchronized the potentialities of prisms, mirrors and distorting lenses to visual poetry.

"Aesthetically, *Usher* stands as the sole example of a wholly expressionist film which successfully invades surrealism as it confronts the viewer.

"Emotionally, the film provides an experience of recurrent wonder and persistent images . . . it is a miracle of performance that Sibley Watson was able to give effective form to a conception so infinitely fragile and complex. . . ."

Dr. Watson is listed in Who's Who as "radiologist." An associate of his at the School of Medicine and Dentistry at the University of Rochester has suggested that after radiologist there should have been a parenthetical reference (Renaissance man).

"Sibley Watson isn't, of course, omniscient," this man said. "But his range of knowledge is wider than that of any other person I have ever met. And the things the man is able to do! Why, do you know he was once a great pistol shot? Here, in our field he is the man who made the Medical School the leader, in the 1940s, in the development of cinefluorography (X-ray motion pictures) which has become such an important tool for medical diagnosis, research, and teaching. He was top man in this speciality in the country."

Twenty years after he had obtained a medical degree in New York, Watson took a three-year resident course in radiology at the Rochester Medical School. He was particularly interested in the gastroscope, an instrument for the inspection of the stomach, and in time made modifications to the gastroscope which enabled him to take colored pictures. He collaborated in his experiments with Dr. Harry L. Segal and Sydney A. Weinberg, of the Medical School.

As the result of the pioneering work at the university's Medical School X-ray motion picture apparatus modeled on those developed by Dr. Watson and his associates are being used in medical schools and hospitals throughout the world, and equipment designed by Watson and Sydney Weinberg are now being produced commercially.

Dr. Watson is well into his seventies. He still continues his investigations and experiments at the Medical School, which he visits almost daily. He has been a consultant in medicine since 1947 and a research professor in charge of X-ray motion picture development for more than a dozen years. He has lectured on his medicial specialties and written voluminously about them. Writer, linguist, artist, inventor, medical man, expert in cinematics, he is, beyond this, a first-rate human being, according to the few intimates he appears to have, who venerate him as much for his benevolence and secret charities as for his multifarious talents.

* * *

My interest in Dr. Watson is excited by the fact that this native Rochesterian, who may be very close to genius, if known at all to the rank and file of his fellow townsmen, is known merely as the scion of a very wealthy Rochester family. At the time these paragraphs were being put together I was given lunch at the University Club by a friend who had been graduated from Yale, who had retired as board chairman of a successful industry, and whose profound devotion to numerous civic causes and agencies have won

346

him a portfolio of citations. I mentioned Sibley Watson as one of the town's truly remarkable men. My friend looked at me wonderingly. "Remarkable?" He had once met Watson but he had no knowledge whatever of his talents and achievements, and I could see that he had put him down as a rich social fop. I told him Watson had a medical degree and was doing research in radiology at the university's Medical Center. "But do they really take him seriously up there?" my friend asked, in all seriousness.

My friend, who knew almost nothing about Dr. Watson was, of course, aware of the eminence of Dr. George H. Whipple, who came to Rochester under the persuasion of Dr. Rush Rhees, president of the University of Rochester, to assume the deanship of the university's medical school. He took the post in 1921, when the school was founded, and held it nearly thirty-five years. One of the leading pathologists in the country, Dr. Whipple brought renown both to the university and to the city when he shared with two other medical men the Nobel Prize for Medicine for research in the use of liver in the treatment of pernicious anemia.

Dr. Whipple was covered so thoroughly by the local press that I never found very much to say about him in my column "Seen and Heard." I met him once, and never until now printed a cherished memento of that meeting.

One of this distinguished man's good friends was a good friend of mine, Dr. Howard Prince, who for years had been one of the town's leading surgeons. He was a large, bearish sort of man, blasphemous in an easy, natural, inoffensive manner; humane, kindly to a fault. His interests and intellectual speculations far transcended the parochial confines of his profession. Samuel Hopkins Adams, the writer, once remarked that "Howard Prince has the most interesting mind of anyone I know." He was bluntly honest and profoundly individualistic. His children inherited this last characteristic, and their parents encouraged them in free expression. When a couple of the youngsters decided to venture into merchandising, the father caused a wooden booth to be erected on the front lawn of the family's fashionable East Side residence. When the interest in selling pop, candy, and novelties waned, they established a pet shop and a large sign appeared on the front of the booth.

PUPPIES FOR SALE
BITCHES $4. SONS OF BITCHES $6.

347

Dr. Prince was the pet of the medical carriage trade. He cared for ward patients as scrupulously as he administered to the wealthy, but with the latter he was a cult. They felt that their lives depended upon him. "Get Howard Prince," they would say, if someone had the sniffles or an ingrowing toenail. "He's the only one. . . ." And if he disgruntedly told some wealthy dowager, who had summoned him from the club, "You haven't a burst appendix. It's just a little bellyache you've got," and left her a soda tablet, and walked out of the room, he would still be adored by the dowager. "Dear Howard is sometimes so whimsical."

He delighted in good food, good liquor, and good talk. He, like Dr. Whipple, was an ardent fisherman. Dr. Prince had rights on a stream near Osceola, New York, and he once pressed me to accompany him and two of his friends on a three-day trout fishing expedition. I protested that I had never been fishing in my life and that because of this I would be a drag on the party. He insisted; I presently acquiesced. When we met for the four-hour motor trip to Osceola I was surprised to find that Dr. Whipple was to be with us. The fourth member of the party was a well-known surgeon from the southern tier of the state. Dr. Whipple and I were assigned to the same room in the little fishing shack at Osceola but the great scientist, who is something of a hypochondriac, wanted fresh air and chose to sleep on the porch. In the company of a trio of doctors I thought at least I would learn something about the medical profession, but all I heard for the first two nights was a discussion of the comparative merits of the wet and dry fly.

It rained the third night. I sat in one corner of the room with *The Goncourt Journals*. The three medical men were clustered in another corner. And now, having exhausted the subject of angling, they had got on the subject of medicine. My eyes were on my book, but I had an ear cocked, and I heard Dr. Whipple, a taciturn, no-nonsense New Englander, say sharply, "But you very well know, Howard. No operation ever performed is worth more than $500."

Dr. Prince wasn't disconcerted or apologetic. He was merely explanative. "Well, you know, George. If you don't get anything from the poor, you have to get a *little* from the rich."

I looked up. Dr. Whipple was shaking his head vigorously. "Nevertheless, no operation is worth a penny more than $500."

I probably looked up too quickly. The medical discussion ended at once, and the next words I heard again concerned fly fishing. I am sure all three medical men felt that the lay ear should not have been exposed to Dr. Whipple's earnest declaration.

* * *

Rochester has never produced an All-American football player, but a native son was one of the founders of the professional game that on autumn Sunday afternoons and Monday evenings provides an opportunity for armchair linebackers, tight ends, fullbacks, etc. —all the millions of Walter Mittys who live inactive, sedentary lives—vicariously to slug someone in front of a television screen. "Hit him, hit him—HIT THE SONOFABITCH!" they shout in a voice as commanding as the voice of the late Vincent Lombardi. The game has been speeded up, jazzed up, made show business on a lavish scale, and the Walter Mittys, intent on their TV sets, who snarl and grit their teeth, and clench their fists, and imagine that hair grows on their chests like Australian prairie grass, revel in the violence of it.

It is a far cry from the big-business sport professional football has become to the time shortly before World War I when Leo V. Lyons, who never played football in college or even in high school (since he never enrolled in a high school), managed a semipro team called the Jeffs, which sometimes evoked sufficient tribute from the spectators—when the hat was passed at half time—to make a painful subsidy from the manager's pocket unnecessary.

Lyons' devotion to football was not unlike the fervor of a religious zealot. His labors in the promotion of the professional game hardly violated his amateur standing for he enjoyed no pecuniary rewards and almost lost his home, his paint store, and his wife, trying to make the Jeffs a going enterprise. He wanted name players, the glamour boys from college teams, to give cachet to his barnstormers. He was a resourceful recruiter, and sometimes had in his line-up performers whom Walter Camp had tapped for All-American. His out-of-town hands, some of whom might represent the Jeffs only once during the season, would arrive in Rochester Sunday morning, be introduced to their teammates at the Front Street playground, the unintegrated eleven would run a few play patterns in that narrow compound, the players would lunch hastily, and repair to Sheehan's field at Monroe and Elmwood avenues, or to the Bay Street baseball park for the Big Game.

In July 1919, Lyons became something of a historical figure when he and four other managers of semiprofessional football teams met in an automobile showroom in Canton, Ohio, and organized the country's first professional football league. The great Indian athlete Jim Thorpe was made president of the organization. The league expanded, and soon changed its name. It became the National Football League. With his team now playing a fixed schedule of league games, Lyons desired to transfer the Jeffs to the Polo Grounds, the home of the New York Giants baseball club. His proposal received this reply from John McGraw, manager of the Giants:

"Professional football will never be a success in New York and we are going to stop the college teams from using the Polo Grounds because the football cleats dig up the baseball field."

In the matter of professional football Lyons was prescient but profitless. He has in the basement of his Pittsford home a large display of football memorabilia, part of which he has exhibited at annual meetings of the National Football League. He is mentioned in the histories of the professional game. But the millionaires who control the league, of which he is a surviving founder, give him short shrift. Few of Rochester's TV football fans ever heard of Leo Lyons, and his waning claim to fame is rather wistfully self-proclaimed. The license plates of his automobile read:

NFL I

*   *   *

Chapter 29

When I was young, very new in the newspaper business, and rather naive, I sometimes passed my night off, which was Friday, bumbling around the polished floor of old Germania Hall, where they roller-skated to mechanical music. In midevening a sign would go up, "Ladies' Choice." I always sat that one out. On two or three occasions the center attraction was a blond stylist who was pursued like a rabbit at a dog track. She dressed way beyond any of the other girls and when she sped gracefully past me on the arm of some fortunate swain she exuded a fragrance that I am sure provoked aphrodisiac torments in all the young men on the floor. Her name I learned on inquiry was Mabel—Mabel Boll. She soon left town; returned, ceremoniously, some time later in a green Rolls Royce, with a chauffeur in livery, to bestow upon her father, George L. Boll, a downtown bartender, and her mother, Josephine, a largess in the way of a $50-a-week allowance.

Living it up at a gallop Miss Boll ran out her string at the age of fifty-four and died in a mental institution on Ward's Island. Born in Rochester, she was also buried here, in Mt. Hope Cemetery. Our town gave her no citation. But two continents knew her for her flamboyance, her beauty, and, most of all, for her jewels. She was heralded as America's "Diamond Queen," a title which irked her arch rival Peggy Hopkins Joyce who (according to Louis Sobol's *The Longest Street*) stepped across the floor of a night club one night, claws out, to commiserate with Miss Boll.

"Darling," said Miss Joyce, a moment before she tipped a glass of wine over Mabel's dress, "I heard you had such a time with your last face lift."

Miss Boll was married five times, and three of these ceremonies were performed in Paris. Among her husbands was a Polish count, an American businessman, and a South American named Hernando Rocha, who must have cared for her deeply. His wedding gift was $1,000,000. This was used by Miss Boll (as she was perennially known, despite her numerous marital ventures) to give added brilliance and solidity to her already imposing collection of diamonds, emeralds, pearls, and other precious trinkets.

Mabel Boll had a penchant for publicity and a talent for keeping in the headlines. Much of her time was spent in Paris, where she cut a wide swath in the café society of the time. A young French dancer, enamored of the then Countess De Porceri, shot himself—*slightly*—and left a note on the grounds of her chateau saying that life without Mabel was hopelessly barren, but the dancer was soon back working at his trade.

A year after Charles A. Lindbergh had become a world figure, Miss Boll announced that she wanted to supplant the title of "Diamond Queen" with the title of "Queen of the Air" and offered $50,000 to anyone who would fly her across the Atlantic. Bert Acosta and Charles A. Levine booked her for a flight from England to America but bad weather thwarted the take-off. With Levine she later made the first non-stop flight from New York to Cuba. Still later, she thought she had engaged Wilmer Stultz, a well-known pilot to fly her west to east across the sea. Stultz honored another commitment. He did fly the Atlantic, leaving from Trepassey, Newfoundland, but it was not until he was approaching Burry Port, Wales, that Miss Boll distressedly learned that he had as a passenger Miss Amelia Earhart, who thus became the first woman to make a trans-Atlantic crossing by air.

Edward Ross, now of Palm Beach, whose late father, Edward Rosenberg, was chairman of the board of Fashion Park, Inc., when that company manufactured men's clothing in Rochester, knew Miss Boll when Ross (then Edward Rosenberg) was a senior at Yale. He met her through a male relative, a New Yorker, who was quite a man about town.

"Take her to El Morocco," his relative advised young Rosenberg. "She'll be fun."

"I will if she doesn't wear those jewels when I meet her," Rosenberg said. "I don't want to get knocked off in a robbery."

Miss Boll agreed not to wear her jewels when the young man met her or, rather, when she met him, with her Rolls. In the ride to El Morocco, Rosenberg later reported, his companion, without the glint of a diamond, or of a carved emerald, or of a pearl seemed verily denuded. On the box with the chauffeur was a bulky man who seemed as wordless as a Trappist monk, who accompanied Miss Boll and Rosenberg into the night club and joined them at the table.

Once seated, Miss Boll deliberately opened a large jewel bag, coiled a rope of pearls about her throat, put rings on her fingers, and affixed a diamond sunburst to the bodice of her gown. "Now," she said, "we'll dance."

"But you promised—" Rosenberg protested.

"I promised not to wear them when I met you. And I didn't. Get up, please. I love that Cole Porter number."

As Rosenberg hesitated, the bulky man nudged him. He spoke for the first time.

"It's okay, Mac. No problem. Take her out on the floor."

The bulky man was Miss Boll's bodyguard.

* * *

Glittering though her jewels were and gaudy the displays her wealth allowed her to make, the career of Miss Boll, a prejet jet setter, paled into insipidity when compared with the bravura performances and Rabelaisian exploits of her fellow townsman, Walter Hagen.

A lad from the "wrong" side of the tracks, whose father was a millwright at the East Rochester car shops, Hagen began caddying at the Country Club of Rochester when he was ten years old. Three years later he quit school. He aspired to be a professional baseball player, but expected he would have to learn a trade. His aspiration failed, and he learned no mechanic art, though he tried successively working as a piano finisher, a taxidermist, and a garage mechanic. These were cold-weather occupations. In the summer he caddied at the Country Club, helped around the pro's shop, became, in time, assistant pro, under Andrew J. Christy. When Christy left to take a job in Vermont, Hagen was made the club's professional.

Hagen played in a few small tournaments when he was able to wangle a few days off from his teaching job, and in one prestigious one, the Canadian Open. Someone has said, "Only mediocrity can be trusted to be always at its best," and by this criterion it was soon very obvious that Walter Hagen was far from mediocre. He finished thirty-sixth in the Canadian Open. The next year, in the National Open at Brookline, Massachusetts, he was directly back of Harry Vardon and Ted Ray, the great English golfers, who lost in a play-off to the Brookline amateur Francis Ouimet.

That winter, Hagen spent a few weeks in Florida, where he was given a cursory tryout with the Phillies, the Philadelphia National League ball club. Golf was his job, but he didn't think much of it as a game and he wanted very much to become a member of the aristocracy of sport, the "400"—the four hundred major league ballplayers. Pat Moran, the Phillies' manager, let him throw against some hitters. Hagen had a strong arm, but no more control than a rudderless yacht in a typhoon. Moran told him to go home, forget golf, practice batting, and come back the next year prepared to try out as an outfielder. But that summer, under the urging of Ernest L. Willard, a Country Club golfer, Walter again tried the National Open, this time contested at Midlothian, outside of Chicago, won it, beating among others in a good field, Ouimet, the titleholder.

In 1914, the year of Hagen's triumph, golfers were not rated on their money earnings. Walter received $300 for his Open victory and returned to Rochester with little more panache than a factory hand punching a time clock in the morning. His brief vacation was over; he went back promptly to instructing club members in the niceties of a game in which he had won supreme honors. There was no dancing in the streets and streamers were not festooned between the lampposts with huge stenciled letters, "Welcome Home, Champ." The Country Club members were conservative souls; they liked their pro, they were pleased with his victory, but golf was a pastime with them, not a passion. Hagen had grown up around the course and learned his game there and overnight they couldn't canonize him merely because he had played a round in 292.

Walter Hagen remained in Rochester nearly four years after he won the National Open for the first time, but it was not until he left that an aura of glamour began to form around him, that he became a legend in his own time, and probably the most colorful figure the world of golf has ever known.

His new distinction began to work a change in his habits. Hagen was not a Tony Lumpkin, a yokel, for all his truncated schooling and the catch-as-catch-can manner of his bringing up. He had been for a long time associated with genteel people, many of them leaders in the community, and he had observed and cultivated their social graces. Now he discarded the bandana neck scarf he had worn and replaced it with colorful neckties. He began to dress "sharp." He had a white, sporty-looking car with a hood that looked six feet long and a motor underneath no larger than a shoe box. He liked to dance; he knew many girls. Then, for a time, he was with one girl, Margaret Johnson, whose father, George W. Johnson, managed a farmers' hotel—the Clinton, which had stables out back for farm rigs—at South Avenue and Court Street.

Margaret was a thin, graceful girl who dressed in the fashion of Mrs. Castle, in whose dance contest, when Irene and Vernon Castle came through Rochester on their whirlwind transcontinental tour, she and her brother George had competed with distinction. She was witty, ambitious, and at first more sophisticated than Hagen, whom she married in late January 1917. Walter was temperate in those days: he neither smoked nor drank.

I remember one night being with the Hagens and another couple at the old Windsor Hotel, which stood near the lake at Summerville. Our table was at the edge of the dance floor and back of the bar, and the bar faced the lake. Margaret left the table. Later, I was called away for some purpose. As I passed the bar, Mrs. Hagen was downing her second tom collins. When she returned, her husband looked up questioningly.

"Why, where you been, dearie?"

"I just went out to get a drink of water."

"Why, there's water right here on the table," and he indicated a filled tumbler at her place.

Hagen was still rather naive a few months later when he summoned me from the office late one Saturday night to tell me "something important." He and Margaret and a group of friends were dancing in the Pompeian Room in the Hotel Seneca.

"What d'you think," Walter said, when I reached his table. "They want me out in Detroit, at a new millionaires' club. The Oakland Hills."

"Well, you're going, aren't you?"

He had seemed eager and enthusiastic when he had made the announcement. Now his tone changed. He shrugged his shoulders and made a flourish with his always expressive hands.

"Jeez, I don't know. I was born around here. I've always lived here. You know how it is. When I walk along the street everyone knows me. Out there—"

"But you're a national figure," I protested. "My gosh, you won the Open. You've won other tournaments. Everyone in golf knows you. Detroit's a big city. You say it's a big new club. I should think you'd jump at the chance."

"Well, I don't know," he said. "I'm thinking it over."

And there the matter rested, so far as I knew, until the next Saturday night. Then I had another call from Hagen at the Seneca, and I again joined Margaret and him and a group of friends in the Pompeian Room.

Elatedly, he told me he had accepted the Detroit offer. Mrs. Hagen was even more elated. She enjoyed no club privileges at the Country Club of Rochester, although Hagen's admirers had put a small house on the club's grounds at the couple's disposal. "In Detroit," she said, "I'll be just like a member."

Margaret had always wanted Walter to be a Fancy Dan, a gentlemanly sporting man, and in Detroit her desire was fulfilled. The Hagens settled there immediately after the war, and Walter quickly adapted himself to the ways of the new millionaires at the Oakland Hills, who made him their pet. Golf was supposedly his vocation but it sometimes seemed as if his dedication was to the *joie de vivre*, and this and his light-o'-love peccadilloes hardly made for domestic felicity. Mrs. Hagen herself loved high life, but she had not bargained on her husband soaring into the stratosphere; and it wasn't long before the couple were separated, then divorced.

In 1919, playing out of the Oakland Hills Country Club, Walter Hagen again won the National Open, which was contested at Brae Burn, near Boston. He was not only the most brilliant golfer on the course but the most spectacularly attired. In the short time since he had left Rochester he had learned showmanship and become very aware of his status. He suffered no priggish modesty. He knew that it was possible for him to command the favor of the gods and to subjugate fortune. Already, in bearing, he was ready for the title of Sir Walter that the golfing world was soon to bestow upon him. It has been said that Hagen was the first athlete, provided one grants that golf is an athletic discipline, to earn $1,000,000. Whether he did or not he always managed to live like a millionaire, and that, with Walter, was the pragmatic test.

The year after his second win of the American title, Hagen went to England for the British Open with all the pride, pomp, and circumstance of a Roman conqueror on parade, and four trunks filled with clothing. I was working for the *Free Press,* in Detroit, and Walter tentatively suggested that I go along as a press agent. I had never played a round of golf and he knew my knowledge of the game was very limited.

"Hell, what's the difference," he said. "You can fake it."

Fortunately, I was not allowed to attempt "to fake it." Al Wallace, the "Millionaire Kid," who was backing the British expedition, vetoed any proposal concerning me Hagen may have made. Wallace had a young man who could do the publicity and also shoot a round in the high seventies and who could be used now and then in the series of exhibition matches that would be scheduled after Walter won the British championship.

Professional golfers in England had little more status than servants. At Deal, where the Open was played, they were herded under a tent at lunch, while the amateurs were entertained in a clubhouse. The not-yet knighted Sir Walter would have nothing to do with this. He hired an airplane and flew to a well-known inn where he had strawberries and other delicacies. It was a gesture of emancipation, and the British pros looked up and took notice. Walter then went on to finish fifty-fifth in the tournament, playing every shot to the end, and the British press howled with sardonic glee. So this was the great American champion! Rubbish! And there were no Hagen exhibitions.

Two years later he became the first American-born golfer to win the British Open, and in subsequent years he won it thrice. His cavalier attitude toward the game, which he never seemed to take seriously; the spectrum of his wardrobe; the conjunction of fact and apocrypha about his dissipations; the incident of his keeping the Prince of Wales waiting half an hour at the first tee; his success with women; his extravagances; his habit of winning; and the impressive record of his eleven national championships made Walter Hagen the Babe Ruth of golf, and the scores of tournaments in which he competed and the hundreds of exhibitions he played around the world helped enormously to make golf the universally popular sport it has become.

* * *

One Friday Hagen called up from Albany, said he would be in town the next day with a brand new Cadillac, "with $500 worth of extra accessories," which had been given him by John McEntee Bowman, president of the Hotel Biltmore and the Westchester Biltmore Country Club. "Get me a pretty girl, get your wife, and we'll have a party tomorrow night at the Sagamore."

I telephoned one of the prettiest girls in town, whom I scarcely knew. When I asked if she would care to be the dinner companion of the great golfer Walter Hagen, she was delighted. We were to dine in the Wisteria Garden on the roof of the Sagamore. When I met Hagen in his hotel room, he asked, "You get me a pretty girl?"

"A honey," I said, and told him her name.

He was bathed, shaved, and was fitting himself into splendiferous raiment. He made a knot of a colorful necktie and winked at me in the mirror.

"Don't say anything to the young lady," he said, "but I'm getting married again next week."

We had a pleasant and leisurely dinner on the Sagamore roof and I could see that Hagen and the pretty girl were getting on famously. In midevening he suggested that we go on to a roadhouse several miles in the country. In those days a new white Cadillac with an array of glittering gadgets was a status symbol. I am sure that the girl felt that the car complemented its owner. We started into the country. To my recollection, Walter never called his companion by name, which I fancy he had already forgotten. It was always "my dear," or "sweets," or "honey." He drove with one hand, his other arm lightly embracing "my dear." They were cuddling a little in transit. Quite obviously, my wife and I were *de trop*.

"Walter," I said, "we're just an old married couple. It's getting late for us. Why don't you take us home, and you two go on alone?"

He couldn't turn the car fast enough. In ten minutes, he dropped us at our doorstep.

A headline in Sunday's paper told that Walter Hagen was to be married that week, and the name of the bride-to-be was mentioned in the story below.

The pretty girl I had gotten for Walter never spoke to me again.

Chapter 30

Today Rochester has only two English-language daily newspapers, both of which are owned by the same corporation. This situation, duplicated in many cities in the country, isn't an ideal or a particularly healthy situation but who, so far as Rochester is concerned, is going to change it, or try to do so? Who would gamble with that kind of money? Years ago, when publishing costs were far less than they are today I asked Thomas J. Hargrave how much would be needed to found a third newspaper in Rochester. Mr. Hargrave was head of the Eastman Kodak Company and one of two top men in the largest law firm in town. He knew something about the newspaper business. He had drawn up several contracts for publisher Frank E. Gannett.

"Ten million dollars," was his answer. "And ten years' time. And there would be no certainty that the effort would succeed."

Gannett was bitterly inveighed against for monopolizing the news field in Rochester. His critics were myopic and unreasoning. It was not his fault that after the death of its guiding genius the *Morning Herald* lost its spark and vitality, or that Francis B. Mitchell, to save the Kimball tobacco fortune he had inherited, sold his play toy, the *Post Express* to William Randolph Hearst's *Rochester Evening Journal,* or that Hearst gave up the ghost after he learned, at a cost of millions, that his sort of journalism was incompatible with the conservative tastes of Rochester.

A forty-one-year-old hustler with a gleam of conquest in his eye and an irresistible air of purpose, Gannett arrived here early in 1918 from Elmira, where he had owned an interest in a newspaper since 1906. His plan, which he quickly put in force, was to merge the *Evening Times*, the function of which had been to apotheosize George W. Aldridge and give scriptural authority to Aldridge's political mouthings, with the more successful Democratic *Union & Advertiser.*

In the beginning, Gannett was suspect in Rochester. He had

been a Democrat, and he was supposed to be a liberal. His suggestion that the *Times-Union* would be an independent newspaper was not encouraging. The town was preponderantly Republican and it wanted a strong Republican and conservative press. Was this bouncy newcomer going to cut capers? Go in for "causes?" Attack time-honored institutions? And good God, the man was a Prohibitionist: a he Carrie Nation, some thought.

Eliminating one newspaper, reducing the number of English-language dailies to four, he had only papier-mâché opposition from the *Post Express*, some competition from the *Morning Herald*, and a great deal from the *Democrat and Chronicle* which, in spite of the enfeeblement of its former masterful proprietors, still enjoyed in its circulation area the status of a theocracy.

Frank Gannett had a combination of qualities that made him an excellent newspaper entrepreneur and that probably would have served him equally well had he chosen instead of the newspaper business any one of various other lines of endeavor that offered the promise of wealth and position. He had enormous energy, keen aptitudes, and an insatiable ambition. A poor boy from a western New York farm, he had entered Cornell University with $80, worked his way through, and come out with $1,000. He had a very sound notion of monetary values. He was the sort of fellow who would look through an areaway grating and see a nickel and get a string and a hook and fetch it up. Samuel T. Williamson, his biographer, speaks of Gannett's lack of egotism. Mr. Williamson, of course, was writing under his subject's editorship. Gannett's egotism, combined with a surprising naivete for one of his sharp insights and acumen, exposed him to subtle knaves who whispered meretricious flatteries in his ear and led him sometimes into grotesque indiscretions. The last person to stoke the fires of his vanity was the person who gained his ardent favor. With all of this, he was a very decent and worthy man, who became a leading figure in his adopted city, to which he made notable contributions.

I never knew Mr. Gannett until several years after his arrival in Rochester. I was in the Army when he came here, and after the war I worked for a short time for the *Free Press* in Detroit. There I shared an apartment with my old friend from the early *Democrat and Chronicle* days, Will Richards, who was the star man for the *Free Press*. We had good times together, but except for

Will Richards' stimulating companionship, the only thing I liked about Detroit was the great Tyrus Raymond Cobb, then approaching the close of his sensational career, but a baseball player whose act of spitting on his glove seemed to me more heroic than the performance of any other athlete on the field.

My congenital provincialism caused me to long for home, and late in 1919 I returned, but not to the *Democrat and Chronicle*. I caught on instead with the *Morning Herald*, published by Louis M. Antisdale, to whom all things Republican, except the Republican bankers who now and then lent him money, were anathema. Antisdale was brilliant, courageous, eccentric, inexorably prejudiced, and a man I came to respect more than any other person I then knew in the newspaper business with the exception of Morris Adams. It was fun working for the *Herald*. There were few taboos and we were as uninhibited as gypsies.

Antisdale wrote crackling editorials that continually attacked the Republican Party, its institutions, and, most of all, its local liege lord. His collaborator in these assaults was John Scott Clubb, a witty, quiet, kindly cartoonist of outstanding talent whose caricatures of Aldridge and his henchmen, never bitter but wonderfully expressive, amused stanch Republicans and caused even George Aldridge to chuckle.

The *Herald* covered the city spiritedly and well. The members of the small predominantly youthful staff were bright, enthusiastic, and devoted to "Uncle Louie," as Antisdale was secretly referred to by his employees. There was a fine *esprit de corps* in the newsroom. Antisdale was intolerant of any lowering of his own exacting standards of newspaper work. And while his discovery of careless or slipshod work did not agitate him into rant or blasphemous displays, for he was a man of propriety and cultivated manners, all were in dread of the ordeal of being "called on the carpet." We were loyal to Uncle Louie. We knew that he would print the news without fear or favor, and that he would stand stanchly behind a member of his staff in the face of complaints from the most influential people in town, including bankers who held his paper, if he was convinced that what the reporter had written was correct.

The city of Rochester took on a somewhat different character immediately after the war, and it seemed to me that the *Herald*, so long as it continued under Mr. Antisdale's editorship, quite accurately reflected the sea change we all experienced during the 1920s, the era, as it has been called, of Wonderful Nonsense. Suddenly we threw off the shackles of our traditional provincialism and acquired a rather ostentatious sophistication. We were even a little raffish.

Before the war we had been pleasantly small town despite the gradual increase in our population and the expansion and sensational success of some of our industries. In the winter, people skated on the Widewaters, had season tickets for the vaudeville at the Temple, joined bowling leagues, had sleigh-ride parties in the adjoining countryside, and went downtown Saturday night for dinner. There were dancing clubs all over town and some of the movie houses advertised "grand ballrooms." There were church bazaars. In the spring the hand-organ man and his monkey emerged from hibernation at the same time bock beer signs appeared in the windows of neighborhood saloons. During the summer months matinee ladies cried their eyes out at *East Lynne* at the Baker Theater, there were fireworks and other free displays at Ontario Beach Park, and young men took their best girls canoeing on the upper river, the girls ensconced among a clutter of fancy sofa pillows and protected from the sun by silk parasols.

We boasted about the magnolias on Oxford Street and the lilacs in Highland Park. The national pastime was played before enthusiastic throngs on the Bay Street diamond. At the big German outings at Schuetzen Park the band made heaving "oompha-oompha" sounds as the picnickers gorged themselves on sauerbraten and potato dumplings set out on rough wooden tables. The circus paraded through Main Street. There were tumult and disorder in certain areas. There were gangs: the Swillbergers, whose center of activity was Clinton Avenue South and Goodman Street; the Rapids Gang, far up Plymouth Avenue South. They were scrappy and mulliganish, but not homicidal. There was crime, of course. But our city streets weren't asphalt jungles, and a woman might walk from her doorstep to the corner mailbox in the evening without the need of a canister of mace.

Serene and innocent our town was in the years that immediately preceded the first Great War. It liked the status quo; it yearned for no great change. At that time, had William Randolph Hearst established one of his lurid newspapers in our midst the act would not have been unlike the presentation of a copy of *Lolita* to a Girl Scouts' reading class.

And even in the summer of 1922, when many of our better citizens were boastfully violating the Eighteenth Amendment and the New Freedom that was an aftermath of the war allowed women of repute to smoke in public and girls of good caste were rolling their stockings and leaving their stays in dance-hall cloakrooms, the launching of the Rochester *Sunday American* had the effect of a seismic tremor. If Frank Gannett's supposed liberalism had been mildly frightening in 1918 the threat four years later of Hearst's "scandalmongering" newspaper was considered in some circles catastrophic.

The anger and resentment excited among prominent Rochesterians by the introduction of the *Sunday American*, and the *Evening Journal* that was soon to follow, when reflected upon from the remove of half a century, seems absurd to the point of juvenility. One would have thought that the plague had descended on our fair city.

George Eastman was so intensely disturbed that he attempted to persuade Ernest A. Paviour, a confidant who had no connection with the Eastman Company, to let local merchants understand that it would be well for them not to advertise in the Hearst newspaper. Paviour had often done Eastman's bidding in the past. He was a highly respected citizen who had performed splendid services for the University of Rochester and the Community Chest, two of the magnate's pet interests, for the YMCA, and for other worthy institutions and agencies, at a cost of time, energy, and probably money; but this mission was one from which he subtly shied away. He himself had once been a newspaperman and he knew how impolitic and even dangerous the boycott at which Mr. Eastman had hinted might be.

But a tacit boycott apparently prevailed for a time, though what influence Eastman had in this is not known. It more or less relaxed when Arthur Brisbane, Hearst's famous editor (the one-man university), arrived in Rochester and called on the Kodak head. Brisbane was not unfamiliar with this part of the state. The late Jim Sam Wadsworth used to tell of Brisbane's roistering about the Big Tree Inn in Geneseo when, as a young man, the editor rode with the Genesee Valley Hunt and courted and married a daughter of the sporting Carey family of Buffalo.

The visit of Brisbane became known to the public, which indulged in loose speculation as to the nature of the dialogue carried on between the two men. The general assumption was that Brisbane advised Eastman that if he thought a *coup de grâce* might be effected against Hearst's local publications by cutting off advertising revenues he better get that nonsense out of his head. He left town, and shortly after his departure the Eastman Theater, which opened Labor Day, 1922, began advertising in the new newspapers.

Harry Gray, a highly talented newspaperman, and a former professional dancer, who was a protégé of Mrs. Hearst, brought the *Sunday American* into being. He wanted as a nucleus for his staff Morris Adams, the brilliant Bill Costello, and a bright and handsome young woman named Ruth Chamberlain, all from the *Democrat and Chronicle;* the telegraph editor of the *Post Express,* whose name I have forgotten, who was formerly a United Press correspondent; Cray Remington, sports editor, and myself from the *Herald.*

I was the only holdout. I had no scruple about working for Hearst, but I had a curious intuition that he would never succeed in Rochester. In time Gray, who had become a good friend of mine, raised the original offer he had made me by $20, a phenomenal wage in those days of scrimpy newspaper salaries. I still resisted. He then contracted to pay my wife $400 for three articles on swimming, which someone in the office wrote under her name. Harry thought the articles would have meaning because as Charlotte Boyle, my wife had been a member of the American Olympic swimming team, and because she and another young champion are credited in the Encyclopaedia Britannica with the development of the six-beat crawl, now the universal swimming stroke.

Payment for the articles was made in two installments, and Gray had given my wife the second installment of $200 the day we attended the wedding in Avon of Miss Jocelyn Macy, of that village, and William E. Sloan, Jr., of East Avenue, Rochester. The bride and bridegroom were both socially prominent and the wedding was attended, as a newspaper was to say next day, "by a large delegation of Rochester fashionables."

Among these was Mrs. Edward W. Mulligan, wife of a prominent surgeon, who for a long time had been George Eastman's social mentor as her husband for a considerable time had been the Kodak head's personal physician. Mrs. Mulligan was a woman of competence, charm, and vitality. She was noted for many good works. The high position in the community given her by her talents, the force of her personality, and by Dr. Mulligan's professional standing was enhanced by the close relations she and her husband enjoyed with the city's leading citizen. Mrs. Mulligan's lively awareness of her status at times caused her to assume an almost proprietary attitude toward the town.

My rejection of the Hearst offer was hardly a matter of moment, but oddly it had become a subject of considerable discussion and people from all over town had spoken to me about it. Now, at the Macy-Sloan wedding reception in the elaborate Macy home in Avon, Mrs. Mulligan hurried across the large room in which the bride and bridegroom were receiving and grasped my hand. "Oh, Mr. Clune," she cried in a voice that trembled with emotional warmth, "you don't know what people are saying about your wonderful citizenship, your loyalty to decent standards, in refusing the offer of that viperous Hearst newspaper. Oh, the viciousness of it!" She struck her hand against her upper breast. "I awake in the morning and feel a weight on my chest like an incubus. I come fully awake and realize that it is caused by the presence of that horrible yellow journal in our midst."

My wife, who had been in Rochester less than a year and knew very little about our folkways, stood at my side and I knew that Harry Gray's last payment of $200 was cached in her handbag. Someone touched Mrs. Mulligan's arm, spoke to her, and interrupted her philippic.

"Don't for God's sake," I whispered to my wife, "mention you got that money from Hearst."

"I was just going to," she said impishly, "if you hadn't reminded me."

Louis Antisdale, who abominated Hearst, also spoke of my "loyalty," though self-interest alone was the reason I chose to remain in his employment. I had always enjoyed Mr. Antisdale's good graces. Now I became a court favorite and he avowed—and he meant what he said—that so long as he published the *Herald* he would do everything possible to keep me happy in my job. But the year after the coming of Hearst, Antisdale died. He had related very closely to his newspaper, and its viability had depended upon his personality, his editorial expertise, and his vigorous leadership.

With its leader gone, the *Herald* was a stricken thing; it was apparent that its days were numbered, and I left it not to make another newspaper connection but to succumb to the petitions of two young men who wanted me to launch, with their money, a weekly—a society weekly, as it was initially designed, over my protests—which made an amusing experience for the period of its mayfly existence.

Morning after morning when I left police court where I daily put together some of the best newspaper copy I ever wrote for the *Herald*, I would find a young man, whom I had never known until he initiated these visits, waiting for me in the corridor. He was Philip Y. Hahn. He was bright, swift of speech, erratic, a "little nutty," I thought. Tenacious! During lunch he would expound his idea for a Rochester society weekly and attempt to override my protests that the town was too small for such an enterprise. His persistence became wearisome.

My wife and an infant son were my prime concern. "I'll tell you what," I said. "You put $500 in a savings bank in my name, which I'll use the first week you fail to pay me, and I'll go to work for you."

Hahn fell silent. He rose and left with scarcely another word. I had called his bluff, wanting a look at cold cash, and I was sure he would be a bother no longer.

To my surprise, three days later he was back in the police court corridor. He had with him a tall, lean, aesthete with nicotine-stained fingers, whom he introduced as Leon J. McNierney. Hahn had summoned McNierney from Harvard, where he was doing graduate work in literature. Solemnly the tall young man handed me $500 in cash and asked how soon I would be able to report for work. I put the money in a savings bank, and two weeks later transferred from the *Herald* newsroom to a makeshift office at the top of a Main Street loft, and Hahn, McNierney, and I were ready for business.

Hahn inspiredly gave the magazine the title of *five-O'Clock*, which hinted at the character he intended it to have. He was to be business manager, McNierney would be editor and write a literary essay under the heading *"Lucubrations,"* and I would do the donkey work as managing editor.

After a period of painful partribulation, *five O'Clock*, neatly printed on slick paper, made its appearance, April 22, 1924. The cover was appropriate. It was a portrait of the handsome former Miss Jessica McCullaugh, of Buffalo, who had recently married the handsome Yale graduate, Charles W. Weis, Jr., of Rochester. Jessica—or Judy, as she was better known—had become in the short time she had lived in Rochester the leader of the younger set. A lean, graceful, leggy young woman with a great deal of oomph and enterprise, Mrs. Weis had helped organize the Chatterbox Club, and had sung and danced in the lively *Chatterbox Revue*. In middle life she would renounce the falderal of the social whirl to head the National Federation of Republican Women's Clubs and represent the Thirty-Sixth Congressional District in the Lower House. Now her pretty head was unconcerned with political stratagems and ponderosities. She was very much a fun-and-games girl.

five O'Clock's appearance on the newsstands was hardly a sensation. It was filled with social chitchat and very little else; but there was nothing salacious about this persiflage and shop girls and factory hands didn't queue up for a copy hoping to learn something scandalous about the fancy folk on the other side of town. We sold it to the city's "400"; but I protested to Phil Hahn that we couldn't survive with such a limited audience, and presently he saw the light.

We continued as a class publication, but broadened our base. We went in for music, art, the theater, books, and gentlemanly sports. We had two or three lively pages immediately following McNierney's "Lucubrations" that bore some resemblance to *The New Yorker*'s "Talk of the Town." I persuaded Mrs. Jocelyn Macy Sloan, who later sold verse to *The Saturday Evening Post* to do a society column called "Jottings." I hired, at a shameful price, George S. Brooks and Marjorie Kinnan Rawlings. Brooks was a young reporter on the *Herald*, with whom I had occasionally collaborated on short fiction. We were close friends.

When the *Herald* collapsed, shortly after the passing of *five O'Clock*, Brooks went to New York where he wrote dozens of short stories for many of the leading magazines in the country and the play *Spread Eagle*. Mrs. Rawlings did not remain in Rochester, the home of her first husband, throughout the life of our magazine, and her contributions to it were less frequent than the page of excellent copy Brooks produced each week. Under the elegant pseudonym, Lady Alicia Thwaite, her delightful caricatures of

367

such institutions as the Corinthian Burlesque Theater and the wrestling hippodromes at Convention Hall gave some indication of the talents she was later to display as a novelist, and she and Brooks wrote the best material *five O'clock* published. When Mrs. Rawlings won the Pulitzer Prize in 1938 for *The Yearling*, I boasted immodestly, and probably extravagantly, that it was I who started her on a writing career.

five O'Clock improved, expanded, and gained in circulation. One week, instead of a pretty young woman, we decorated our cover with a photograph of George Eastman. Eugene Goossens, conductor of the Rochester Philharmonic Orchestra, was later chosen for this honor.

We lowered our sights. We tried using pictures of men of lesser distinction whose popularity we thought might bait newsstand customers. But the stigma of class consciousness adhered to our publication and it never became sufficiently unrefined to appeal to popular taste. I had served it eleven months when my pay check bounced, and I quit. My employers very quickly made good, but *five O'Clock* ended with the next week's issue. Somewhat lighter in pocket after his Rochester experience, McNierney retired to his home in a small city in Pennsylvania. I lost track of Hahn for several years. When our paths next crossed he was a glittering success, head of the Crossman Arms Company, Inc., and a millionaire several times over. He had a home here and another in the far West, a new wife, and, unhappily, emphysema.

Since *five O'Clock*, Rochester has had several weeklies, the most enduring of which is *WE*, defined by its first publisher-editor, John Corey, as a news magazine. Corey was an enterprising, hard-nosed reporter, with considerable courage, whose forte was presenting in detail news stories that the more conservative daily press either adumbrated or omitted. He died, and *WE* passed into other hands, but I hear much less about it than formerly. The *Catholic Courier-Journal*, an excellent sectarian publication, has a circulation close to eighty thousand.

In the broader field of metropolitan Rochester, the *Brighton-Pittsford Post* has been consistently judged the finest weekly in New York State and in 1970 was chosen as one of the finest in the nation.

Its goal, apart from fully reporting events in the community, has been perceptive, detailed reporting, more like that found in magazines than in the average metropolitan daily. It has run profiles which amounted to short biographies up to five thousand words. The publisher-editor of the *Brighton-Pittsford Post*, and four smaller sister weeklies, is Andrew D. Wolfe. A Harvard graduate, the husband of an heiress of the Sibley store fortune, and a former crack reporter for the *Times-Union*, Wolfe has won national recognition as an editorial writer since becoming the proprietor of what are known as the Genesee Valley newspapers.

* * *

Before Hahn and McNierney had a chance to indemnify the bouncy check they had given me, I walked down Main Street to the *Democrat and Chronicle* and applied for and was given a job by Alan Ross, a kindly little man, who had been moved up from editorial writer to editor. This was in 1925 and the place had changed since I had left it seven years before for the Army. Editors and reporters no longer worked in the scrubby alleylike little room in the back of the building. They had been moved forward to a commodious, well-lighted, airy, antiseptic "editorial department," which displayed in large letters on one of its walls the high-minded newspaper creed of the former Ohio journalist and late pilot of our great ship of state, whose remembrance was as yet unsullied by Teapot Dome, Nan Britton, or the scandal of the Veterans' Bureau.

The Warren Gabriel Harding creed had been ordered stenciled on the wall by Herbert J. Winn, who now served the newspaper as president and treasurer. His adjutant in the operation of the plant was Fred S. Todd. A bachelor and a highly respected industrialist, Mr. Winn's real job was directing the destinies of the Taylor Instruments Company. Mr. Todd had formerly been in the shoe business. Their joint knowledge of the newspaper business might vaguely be compared to the knowledge a rhesus monkey might have of the Montessori kindergarten disciplines.

Winn was a friend of George Eastman and Todd was a relative of George W. Todd who was a close friend and confidant of the Kodak magnate. I suspect that after the death of Colonel Pond and the retirement of Mr. Matthews that Eastman arranged to have the custody of the good gray mother of Rochester journalism given to Winn, who would make very sure that the old girl wouldn't get skittish, kick up her heels, or tip over apple carts. The coming of Hearst was a shuddering thing, and it was thought imperative that the *Democrat and Chronicle* not go to outside owners who might fail to give obeisance to the established order, including the Kodak Company, the Chamber of Commerce, whose building was Eastman's million-dollar gift, the University of Rochester, which the Eastman fortune was making mighty, and Eastman's scheme to have Rochester administered by a city manager.

Winn and Todd operated the newspaper precisely as they were expected to operate it and it wasn't long before it was about as spirited and colorful as blancmange. Their cardinal blunder as newspaper proprietors was in allowing the prestigious and dedicated Morris Adams to be lured from his city editorship by Hearst's pay boost. Had he remained with the *Democrat and Chronicle* he might have managed, by some feat of journalistic legerdemain, to print most of the news and still accede to the "interests." Instead, this fine newspaper became a broadsheet for Chamber of Commerce handouts, the effusions of pamphleteers who represented leading industries, bank reports, and similar releases, many of which were brought in by Hiram Marks, a crack reporter, who was also a successful businessman on the outside, and who, as the saying was, had Herbert Winn in his vest pocket.

Mark's copy often went to the city desk marked "must," and J. R. Cominsky, the second city editor to follow Mr. Adams, would shake his head dolefully but be sure that what was handed to him went into type, and perhaps a column and a half of type verbatim, were it no more newsy than a seed catalogue. Cominsky had succeeded Crerar (Harold) Harris, who had immediately succeeded Mr. Adams on the city desk. Both brilliant young men went in time to the New York *Times,* which Cominsky left to become publisher of the *Saturday Review.*

When, sometime after the death of Louis Antisdale, the *Herald* was about to founder and sink, the *Democrat and Chronicle* took it over in order to frustrate any design Hearst might have to buy it, restore it, and expand his Rochester operations into the morning field. The *Democrat and Chronicle* profited some from the elimination of its morning rival. But it was not the journal it would have been under the management of expert newspapermen, and in 1928, Winn, apparently tired of bucking another man's game, sold it to Frank Gannett. I remember the day the sale was consummated. I was in the office elevator, on my way to the news-room, when Mr. Gannett popped into the car. He was brisk, ebullient, smiling. It was easy to see he was vastly pleased to have this important newspaper added to his expanding group of news-papers.

"Well, Heinie," he said, in hearty greeting, "I always said I'd have you working for me, even if I had to buy the newspaper."

It was a pleasant piece of twaddle for a new employee to hear, and I knew right away I was going to like the boss.

Chapter 31

I was at the tag end of a long career in the newspaper business when Xerox became almost overnight a news story of the first magnitude and Rochester gained new fame as the scene of one of the miracles of modern American business. Xerox made a glittering epoch in the city's industrial life, but it was a matter that was out of my professional sphere. I never met Chester F. Carlson, the genius of the copying machine, and I had only sketchy, touch-and-go relations with Joseph C. Wilson, whose faith in Carlson, whose prescience, and whose talents as a business organizer had so much to do with the dramatic development of the corporation he served as board chairman.

But I knew Joe Wilson well enough to appreciate his outstanding citizenship and to be aware of his keen sense of responsibility. The business he directed is a prime example of the often maligned corporate colossus. Wilson, of course, needed at all times to be alert to meet competition, to persistently seek new power for his industry, to expand and ramify it by research and the creation of new products. At the same time, ambidextrously, he managed to exert the virtues of humanism. He was tolerant of the rights of others, sympathetic to the suffering of others, and he ceaselessly strove to improve the lot of his fellow men. He was indigenous to Rochester and devoted to the city of his birth and to the local university that had educated him. For safety and health a man is probably better off operating somewhat below maximum capacity but Wilson was unable to conform to this sort of pedestrianism; he burned out his reserves and died suddenly and unexpectedly in his sixty-second year when, as a moist-eyed admirerer remarked, "Joe should have died hereafter."

The Xerox story came late for me, but I grew up with the Eastman legend and first met George Eastman at the opening in November 1902 of the new building of the Rochester Athletic Club which stood on Clinton Avenue North two hundred yards from the Main Street corner. My father had raised the money for the building partly by selling life memberships. He was president of the club, and he stood with Mr. Eastman, Julius M. Wile, the banker, and two or three other men in a reception line in front of a heroic statue of a discus thrower. I shook hands with Mr. Eastman. He peered down at me with cold eyes. "Young man," he said severely, "do you know that your mother was on the first payroll I ever had?"

I was twelve years old. I had no knowledge of this intelligence. Recently, in my investigations for this book, I called at Eastman House and examined a small, dog-eared little notebook, bound in stiff brown paper, that Jim Card removed from a display case. The names of five women workers, including my mother's maiden name, Hattie Bruman, were inscribed on the first page of the book, with the amount of pay each had received. The payroll date was March 12, 1881. The names represented the first employees of the Eastman Dry Plate Company.

It was nearly thirty years later, and not many months before his death, that I met Mr. Eastman for the last time. Between these two meetings I had seen quite a little of him since, after I started to work for Mr. Gannett, my employer frequently sent me to talk with the Kodak head in his home, or in his office, or, on occasions, in New York where I interviewed him upon his return from one of his African safaris or some other excursion to foreign lands. He was unfailingly courteous in these meetings, which were completely devoid of any personal intercourse. He submitted correctly to the minor ordeal of an interview and was relieved when the interviewer reclaimed his hat and departed. "Good day," he would say, and turn at once to the activity that had engaged him at my entrance. There was a difference on the occasion of this last meeting. I had difficulty getting into his house. The female major domo, in charge of more than a score of household servants, who was finically protective of her master, often gave me a hard time, and she did this day. Mr. Eastman was unwell; he was not to be disturbed. I argued with her. She was obdurate.

"You know my coming here was arranged between Mr. Eastman and Mr. Gannett," I told her. "I can't break into your house. I'll go back and tell Mr. Gannett you won't let me in."

I had started away when she hailed me back to the door,

without asking me to enter. "You wait, I'll see." She returned to say, "You can see him for ten minutes. He's sick. Ten minutes, no longer."

I was shown into one of the smaller downstairs rooms. Mr. Eastman was lying on a settee in front of a wood fire. He did seem unwell. He was wan, tired, and his skin was yellow and unwholesome. His cold eyes were strangely soft. I had an odd feeling that there was something of yearning in them.

He raised himself on an elbow at my entrance. "Hello, Clune," he said, and smiled faintly. He motioned to a copy of the *Democrat and Chronicle*, which was open to "Seen and Heard."

In a comic vein I had told in the column of a new hat I had received the day before from William P. Barrows. Barrows was president of the McFarlin Clothing Company, which operated a men's store in Main Street. He was also the brother of Marie Barrows (then Mrs. Seton Porter) about whose shimmering beauty, which had brought the former Oxford Street girl international celebrity, one might rhapsodize at length.

Barrows' gift had come with a sharp note, which I had printed in the column, slanging me for the shapeless, battered, unclean fedora I had been wearing for months, and accusing me of disgracing Main Street. My hats, it was true, always seemed to lose dignity and style a short time after I had acquired them, and once each year Barrows would send me a new one, always with a covering note of abuse. It was a sort of ritual.

"I see by the paper," Mr. Eastman said, "Barrows had to give you a new hat."

"Yes," I said. I set to work immediately, submitting the questions I was supposed to ask. The interview was brief. I reached for my new hat.

"You interested in guns?"

I had no interest in guns, but I made the orthodox reply. "Yes, Mr. Eastman."

He rose slowly from the settee and left the room. I followed obediently. We ascended in an elevator. He opened the door of a small room on the second floor which had racks and cases of guns and fishing rods. There were elephant guns, guns for bird shooting, guns for this and that, and other animals, and fly rods, salmon rods, and rods that seemed stout enough to bring in a whale. He would take down a gun with shaking hands, break it if it was a shotgun, and offer an elaborate disquisition on its merits. He was similarly expository about the fishing gear. We were an hour in this examination. I thanked him, and again started to leave. He said abruptly, "Let's look at some motion pictures."

A few years earlier, in the summer of 1928, I had been present two days in Mr. Eastman's house when home movies in natural colors were introduced to a notable company that included Thomas A. Edison, Owen D. Young, Sir James Irvine, Harvey Firestone, Adolph S. Ochs, publisher of the New York *Times*, and General John J. Pershing. The camera at that time had been operated by an expert from the Eastman plant.

On the day that I was Mr. Eastman's only visitor he himself operated the projector, which was set up in a room adjacent to the one in which we had inspected the guns and fishing rods. The pictures were not particularly inspiring. They seemed predominately concerned with the antics of the very young whom I presumed were the grandchildren of Eastman's acquaintances. One stretch of film showed three small girls romping wildly across the Eastman lawn.

Half timorously I said, "It's strange you have so many pictures of children, you a bachelor."

"Huh," he grunted. "Those young girls are more graceful than some of the damn dancers we have down at the [Eastman] theater."

At the end of the exhibition, we returned to the main floor and I expected to leave at once. He beckoned me into the room with the settee and open fire. Our talk was hesitant and inconsequential. He became listless and silent. I rose. He extended his hand, "Well, good-by, Clune," he said. His eyes looked into mine and the yearning was unmistakable. I realized that he had no personal interest in me but I realized also as I thought on the matter that I had provided him with an interlude of companionship and I sensed how lonely this wifeless and childless old man had become. Lonely in a house filled with servants! And it struck me, when I recalled the look in his eyes, that Eastman was tired, very tired; weary of life. His great works were behind him; the future, a darkening cul-de-sac.

It was only a few months after my long visit with Mr. Eastman that William F. Butler, a friend of mine who was city editor of the *Times-Union*, received early in the afternoon of March 14,

375

1932, this excited telephone query, "Is it true George Eastman's dead?"

Butler was a hero in World War I and a reserve officer of many years' standing. He was as brusque on the city desk as on a parade ground.

"Not that I know," he said sharply; and shut off.

Soon boys were hawking in downtown streets Hearst's *Evening Journal* that told in a huge banner line that Mr. Eastman had killed himself. Immediately the Gannett press was accused of trying to suppress the news and it had inadvertently briefly held up the story of the Eastman tragedy.

When the Kodak magnate's body was found in his home with a lethal self-inflicted bullet in his chest, an effort was made by persons in the Eastman house to make a contact with Frank Gannett, publisher of the city's two largest newspapers. Gannett was out of town. Leroy E. Snyder, who had the post of assistant to the president in the Gannett organization took the Gannett call and hurried out to 900 East Avenue.

Mr. Snyder was a man who dressed meticulously. He looked freshly minted, antiseptic, and straight out of a bath. He wore spats. He was a gentleman in a very true sense of the word. His case history of civic activities was an impressive one. Successively, he had been Mr. Eastman's adviser on civic affairs, director of the Bureau of Municipal Research, manager of labor relations for the clothing industry, president of the high-brow City Club, and candidate for mayor. In another city he had had a brief newspaper experience.

In time Mr. Snyder advised the Gannett newspapers that Rochester's greatest citizen had died, but he did not reveal the shocking, uncodefied manner of death. Always the gentleman, he seemed to feel that the true fact of the tragedy was not a fact that should be promulgated; that the act of suicide for a man of Mr. Eastman's stature was not *de rigueur*. When the real news reached the *Times-Union*, Bill Butler's execrations could be heard from Times Square to the Four Corners.

*   *   *

Rejoining the *Democrat and Chronicle* after the collapse of *five O'Clock* in 1925 I continued with that newspaper into 1969 which (counting the six years I was there before the first World War) gave me a record of half a century of employment, but no gold watch. I was not miffed about this. I didn't retire cleanly and sharply; I sort of drifted away. Besides, the gold chronometers given retirees are wrist watches. I carry a pocket watch with a gold chain festooned across my waistcoat.

After Frank Gannett had rescued the *Democrat and Chronicle* from the morass of mismanagement into which its amateurish proprietors had allowed it to sink, I liked working there. Mr. Gannett was not noted for paying high salaries. A poor farm boy, he had managed to acquire $1,000, once considered the keystone of fortune, even while working his way through college. Now as the owner of several newspapers he was becoming wealthy and he seemed to assume that everyone around him also had money. The Newspaper Guild badgered him. I believed in the purposes of the Guild, but I had never been a "joiner" and the Rochester chapter had been in force for sometime before I became affiliated with it. And almost at the moment of my joining, a strike was threatened and some of the young militants in the two Gannett offices appeared on downtown streets and circulated among crowds at the Auditorium Theater bearing signs, "Gannett Unfair to Labor." I was secretly distressed about the placards. Only that week, the Gannett company had issued bonuses to its employees, and mine was sufficient to pay all expenses resulting from the recent birth of my youngest son.

I liked Mr. Gannett, I liked very much the sort of work I was doing for the *Democrat and Chronicle*, and at times I gratuitously attempted to defend him against the calumnies of readers who protested that he suppressed news or slanted it to conform with his own political philosophy which, as his wealth grew and his abomination of Franklin D. Roosevelt intensified, was— as one of his top-executives remarked—"firmly to the right of Louix XIV."

There was, it is true, some suppression of the news. Gannett was bone dry, and honest and consistent in his attitude. He lost hundreds of thousands of dollars by his refusal to accept beer or liquor advertising, and he may have lost some readers by the failure of the Gannett newspapers to admit that anyone in Rochester ever attended a cocktail party. He enforced a peculiar double standard in the matter of divorce. If a newsy divorce

377

story originated in, say, Hollywood, Buffalo, New York City, or even in Utica it might be used, properly expurgated. But when two Rochester couples of considerable social prominence were divorced in Reno and remarried, switching husbands and wives, the story was not thought suitable for Rochester readers. And the Gannett press never spoke of the harrowing aftermath of the great stock market crash of October 1929 as a "depression." The word was expunged from our newspaper lexicon, perhaps to confound poor fellows selling apples on street corners who surely knew that their wretchedness was not the concomitant of a boom.

Frank Gannett had his whims, his crotchets, his fetishes, but it did not seem to me that they very seriously detracted from the presentation of the news. And even in the maddest period of his dislike for President Roosevelt he never, as old Colonel Pond might have done, stormed into the newsroom crying, "Riddle the damn cripple! Riddle him, I say!" and with this order invested his editors and reporters with the license of hatchetmen.

Working for the *Democrat and Chronicle* during Mr. Gannett's active management of his newspaper properties was an interesting, happy, and sometimes exciting experience. I wasn't getting rich by any means. But in the heart of what we dared not (in print) define as the Depression I was given a substantial raise. I had wide latitude in what I wrote in "Seen and Heard," and although I am sure my employer sometimes disapproved of my effusions he was tolerant, patient, and kind.

One morning I had scarcely reached the office when the telephone rang and Mr. Gannett briskly inquired, "Heinie, what'd you think of it?"

"Think of what?" I asked.

"Why, haven't you read the paper? Look at the first page of the local section."

I did and was shocked to learn from a two-column headline that I was to be a speaker at the dinner of the Society of the Genesee in the Waldorf-Astoria two weeks hence. As a reporter, I had covered these dinners in the past. They were huge, stuffy affairs that each year packed the Waldorf ballroom with prominent Rochesterians and former Rochesterians of some distinction, all done up to the nines. I could think of no reason why I had been chosen as a speaker except that a few days before the newspapers had announced that a novel of mine had been purchased by Warner Brothers and that Edward G. Robinson and Miss Bette Davis had been cast in the leading roles. Perhaps this made me a Rochester curio. But I protested to Mr. Gannett that I had never made a speech in my life.

"Why, I thought you'd made hundreds of speeches."

"Never a one," I insisted.

"Well, you can't let me down now," he said and shut off. And, of course, since he was my boss, I couldn't.

I found, when I read the story under the headline, that I was cast in rather fast company. Three of us were to speak at the dinner. The other two were Thomas W. Watson, head of the International Business Machines Corporation, and Dr. Jacob Gould Schurman, president emeritus of Cornell University. I was to speak fifteen minutes. Mr. Watson and Dr. Schurman were given longer tenure.

For two weeks I tried speaking from notes on small cards I could secrete in the palm of my hand. I practiced Delsarte in front of a mirror. It seemed to me that I was fluent and very witty when I delivered my address before an audience composed of my small sons.

I went to New York the day before the dinner, rented tails and a white tie, got up on the speakers' platform the next night, looked out over the vast expanse of gleaming shirt fronts and feminine finery, and was so overwhelmed that my beautifully rehearsed speech fizzled out in two minutes and fifteen seconds. I am sure of the precise duration of my oratory. Mr. Watson sent me a phonograph record of what I had said. I heard the record once, timed it, and broke it. It was dreadful.

Those of us in the newsroom of the *Democrat and Chronicle* who were genuinely fond of Mr. Gannett suffered through his effort to gain the Republican presidential nomination in 1940, aided by a herd of elephants, very openhanded hospitality in smoke-filled Philadelphia hotel rooms, and a few sweet-talking soothsayers, one or two of whom, it was later learned, had dipped rather deeply into the campaign tambourine.

The whole business was a sorry misadventure, and sometimes a cause of shuddering embarrassment. A few years before Mr. Gannett publicly aspired to the presidency, he and his newspapers, in bitter attacks on James W. Wadsworth, helped to defeat Wadsworth's bid for re-election to the United States Senate. Gannett's antipathy toward the Geneseo senator was provoked by Wadsworth's opposition to Prohibition. Now, infected himself by the bacillus politico, the publisher petitioned Wadsworth, the most able and prominent Republican in the area, to introduce him as a candidate for the Republican nomination for President at a gigantic dinner in Powers Hotel that launched the Gannett campaign. It was a tactless, thoughtless thing to have done, but political expediency is often the effluvium of political passion.

Before what might be called Mr. Gannett's political contretemps, he had his employees wondering if they might lose their local boss and fall under the authority of a syndicate when discovery was made one morning that the Gannett newspapers were virtually in the hands of the International Paper Company. The *ignis fatuus* of Mr. Gannett's hopes at that time had not been the governorship of the state or the presidency of the United States, but a newspaper empire that would have units in the greatest cities in the land, and as a starter he had purchased the Brooklyn *Daily Eagle* with money lent him by the head of the paper company.

This, as Mr. Gannett later admitted, was one of his grave mistakes. Paper companies were getting into the business of supplying hydroelectric power, and Gannett—long a clamorous champion of the "free press"—was inveighed against as a pawn of the power trust.

It took some doing to extricate himself from a rather menacing situation, but aided by the company's financial wizard, Herbert W. Cruickshank, Gannett disposed of the the Brooklyn *Daily Eagle*, freed himself from all obligations to the paper company, borrowed large sums from banks, and to help pay off these loans sold Gannett preferred stock to his employees and any other customers that could be found. I remember a time when even reporters were asked to peddle stock along their beats. I was hoity-toity about this; I thought it infra dig, and tacitly declined. But I bought a little of the stock myself, as did other employees, and all who did—and held on—hug themselves today.

Mr. Gannett left the company in very good hands. Several years before his death, and some time before physical infirmities made necessary his withdrawal from the active management of his newspaper properties, he induced Paul Miller, the handsome, young, and extremely able chief of the Washington bureau of the Associated Press to come to Rochester. The move provoked jealousy among some old-timers in the higher reaches of the Gannett organization. Predictions were free that despite his fine record as an administrator of the press association Miller would soon be in transit. He was shunned. The hope was to cause him to feel forlorn enough to leave. On other occasions in the past the Chief, as Gannett was known to his subalterns, had brought in wonder boys from the outside, established them in posts close to the throne, and intramural observers had gleefully watched them flounder, fail, and disappear. But in this choice Mr. Gannett had been more intuitive than he had been in some of his other selections and it was soon obvious, as the gamblers say, that Paul Miller "had come to play."

Miller came to Rochester in 1947, and ten years later and even before Gannett's death on December 3, 1957, he was president of the continually growing Gannett organization. He, in his turn, brought in Allen H. Neuharth, a young ring-tailed snorter from the Knight newspapers. Together, this pair have expanded the Gannett Company until now, in the matter of numbers, it owns more newspapers than any other publishing company in the country, with units extending clean across the continent, and into the Pacific to the state of Hawaii and the isle of Guam. Fifty-two newspapers in all! This astonishing proliferation has resulted in a gratifying proliferation of Gannett stock, and old employees and retired employees who were lucky enough to buy it early have nest eggs grown to a size beyond their most hopeful fancies.

For my part, I feel beholden to Mr. Gannett and to Paul Miller. The latter, many times president of the Associated Press, chairman and chief executive of the Gannett Company, in spite of his multifarious duties and concerns, managed during the years I was in his employment to achieve a surprising rapport with the people on the Rochester papers. I cherish the green-paper notes he often sent to me. And his reiterated statement, extravagant though it may have been, that "Seen and Heard" had a following greater than that of any other local column in the country, like Mr. Gannett's remark in the office elevator, was a kind thing for an employer to say to one of his hired hands.

Epilogue

Rochester's English-language daily newspapers, two in number for the past thirty-five years, have changed markedly in the past few years. And the *Democrat and Chronicle*, still the greatest paper in the Gannett group, bears no resemblance to the journal it was when I started there four years after Paul Miller was born and fourteen years before the birth of Al Neuharth.

But the change in the format and character of the Rochester newspapers is as nothing compared with the changes that have taken place in the character of our society and in the physical appearance of the city's most conspicuous areas. If a native Rochesterian, returning after an absence of fifteen years, was set down at the corner of Main and Water or Broad and Stone or Court and Exchange streets he would hardly know his old home town. Front Street, which was so indigenous to the city's heritage, is no more. The buildings on Main Street Bridge, whose shabby and dilapidated back sides, overhanging the Genesee, were symbolic mementos of old Rochester, are gone. From the bridge there is a clear view of the river, north and south. There is a large new hotel on State Street, and another at the corner of Main and St. Paul streets which has an arcade of small shops and a picture theater, the entrance to which is only a few rods east of the site of the city's early nickelodeon, the Bijou Dream.

The city's banks must be rich and getting richer. The Lincoln Rochester Trust Company is building a twenty-seven-story tower, the first unit in a project to be known as Clinton Square, which will transform beyond all recognition the block that extends south from Main Street between Stone Street and Clinton Avenue South. The Security Trust Company has a gracefully designed tower at East Avenue and Main Street East, and another glittering banking high rise, a good iron shot from the Xerox Building—still, for size, the bully boy of the city's skyline—has gone up on what is known as Marine Midland Plaza. The Seneca Hotel is being replaced by an office building. The old brick jail on Exchange Street, the scene of the last hanging in Rochester, has been razed. We have, as part of our Civic Center, what is called the Hall of Justice. All of this is quite recent.

When the ribbon was cut in 1962 that marked the opening of Midtown Plaza and its lofty tower, an enterprise of bravura if ever the town knew one, Rochester exulted in the first notable contribution to its skyline since a jig-step clergyman with a carnival barker's come-on raised $3,000,000 and a fourteen-story office building and house of worship at Franklin Street and Main. That was nearly thirty years before. The clergyman was the Reverend Clinton Wunder, D.D. He named the structure the Baptist Temple Building, and it became the Cheops to his memory. It opened four years before the market crash of '29. After that debacle, Dr. Wunder left his spiritual flock in the ground-floor Temple, and the beauticians, insurance salesmen, dental technicians, accountants, dentists, chiropodists, and experts in the removal of surplus hair, who occupied the floors above, for a new town, a new wife, and to serve such unchurchly agencies as the Academy of Motion Picture Arts & Sciences, the Dale Carnegie Institute, and the National Live Stock Exchange.

The erection of the Baptist Temple Building and the dedication a few years earlier of the beautiful Eastman Theater effected no great change in the configuration of downtown Rochester. No one expected that the city would experience a building renaissance in the foreseeable future and few felt that there was any need of one. At times we had heard weighty gabble about plans to improve the convenience and appearance of our downtown area, but generally the public seemed satisfied with the status quo. We felt comfortable with old landmarks and familiar institutions.

Midtown was the most exciting event that the center of the city had known in years, and its novelty as the first major urban shopping center in the country brought national recognition to Rochester and considerable applause from merchants, architects, city planners, and others interested in dispelling the stasis that was making the mercantile areas of many cities as lifeless as a herbarium. It stimulated the great building boom that followed and that will continue for years to effect dramatic alterations in the heart of Rochester.

Building big downtown buildings and preserving, as the Landmark Society is so nobly doing, some of the fine relics of our antiquity will not alone make Rochester the sort of community the idealists dream of its becoming. Improving the physical aspects of certain sections of the city we will need also *pari passu* to improve the social and economic condition of many of its inhabitants. It is no longer the small, friendly, neighborly place it was fifty or sixty years ago, when one seemed to have kissing cousins all over town. We have become heterogeneous. City Hall says we have fifty thousand blacks who, for all the efforts made by fine members of their own race and by good men and true of another color, have not yet been assimilated into our civic organism. They are suspicious, sensitive, and often hostile. Houses of decency are needed for these people, and more education.

Here, as in other cities in the land, "Violence is risen up into a road of wickedness," and our newspapers, reflecting the tenor and temper of the town, fill their columns with distressing reports of homicides, armed robbery, rape, bombings, muggings, racial disturbances in the schools, and the arrest of youthful dope addicts.

Manners which, in earlier years of the century, encouraged community amenity, seem extinct; religion is frequently denied by the very young. Youth in our town swaggers about with a chip on its shoulder, scornful of the notion that the experience of an older generation might in any way aid the solution of the vexatious problems with which Rochester and most other cities in the land are confronted. The general feeling among youth is that one of my age should be taken out back of the barn and shot.

There are times when I briefly succumb to the philosophy of my friend Cliff Carpenter, brilliant "think" columnist on the editorial page of the *Democrat and Chronicle* who, like Jonathan Swift, seems to have little hope for mankind; but in Rochester there are fine, intelligent, earnest men and women, among them Mr. Carpenter, who persistently seek ways and means to make our city a better place in which to live and, I believe, in the end, they may succeed.